AF412221

Narrative, Perception, Language, and Faith

Narrative, Perception, Language, and Faith

Edmond Wright

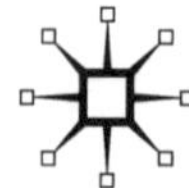

First published 2005 by
PALGRAVE MACMILLAN
Houndmills, Basingstoke, Hampshire RG21 6XS and
175 Fifth Avenue, New York, N.Y. 10010
Companies and representatives throughout the world

PALGRAVE MACMILLAN is the global academic imprint of the Palgrave Macmillan division of St. Martin's Press, LLC and of Palgrave Macmillan Ltd. Macmillan® is a registered trademark in the United States, United Kingdom and other countries. Palgrave is a registered trademark in the European Union and other countries.

ISBN-13: 978–1–4039–9067–9 hardback
ISBN-10: 1–4039–9067–0 hardback

This book is printed on paper suitable for recycling and made from fully managed and sustained forest sources.

A catalogue record for this book is available from the British Library.

Library of Congress Cataloging-in-Publication Data
Wright, Edmond Leo, 1927–
    Narrative, perception, language, and faith / Edmond Wright.
       p.   cm.
    Includes bibliographical references and index.
    ISBN 1–4039–9067–0 (cloth)
    1. Narration (Rhetoric)   2. Wit and humor—Philosophy.   3. Plots (Drama, novel, etc.)   I. Title.
    PN212.W75 2005
    808—dc22   2005047612

10   9   8   7   6   5   4   3   2   1
14   13   12   11   10   09   08   07   06   05

Printed and bound in Great Britain by
Antony Rowe Ltd, Chippenham and Eastbourne

*To
Ella, Maya and Louis*

Contents

List of Figures

Preface

For philosophical stimulation in conversations and editorial and other encouragement relevant to my work my thanks are due to Roy Bhaskar, Rainer Born, Harold Brown, the late Richard Brown, Mark Crooks, James Giles, Ernst von Glasersfeld, Peter Hare, Jonathan Harrison, Kazimierz Jodkowski, Michael Levine, Jonathan Lowe, Graham Dunstan Martin, Barry Maund, Matjaz Potrč, Kenneth Reinhard, Shlomith Rimmon-Kenan, Bede Rundle, Barry Smith, Philip Smith, John Smythies, Leslie Steffe, Patrick Thompson, Richard Woodfield, and Slavoj Žižek; also to Bjorn Wittrock for arranging visits to the Swedish Collegium for the Advanced Study of the Social Sciences and to Professors Teruhiko Nagao and Takafusa Tanaka at the University of Hokkaido. For setting me on my way long ago, the late Fredric Coplestone, Brian Loar, the late Gareth Evans, the late Harold Osborne, and the late J. O. Urmson.

I owe a debt to my children, Anna and Oliver, for their just being who they are, and a particular one to my late wife Elizabeth, whose (continuing) support has helped me write this book.

Acknowledgements

To Gilbert Adair for the passage from *Alice through the Needle's Eye* (London: Macmillan, 1984).

To Peter Brookes (for permission to use the 'Cat/Mouse' and 'The Return of the Native' drawings).

To Stephen Gibian (for permission to use the short story 'An optical illusion' by Daniil Kharms, from *Russia's Lost Literature of the Absurd: Selected Works of Daniil Kharms and Alexander Vvedensky*, translated and edited by George Gibian, W. W. Noton & Co., 1971).

To Kieron Griffin (for permission to use W. H. Davies's poem 'The Fog').

To Genevieve Hirsch (for permission to use the drawing 'Five Faces' by Joseph Hirsch) and to Jocelyn Doden, the owner of the picture.

To Eric Staub, Président-Directeur, Imagerie d'Épinal (for the two devinettes).

To the Japan Society Inc. (for permission to use the story 'The Crows and the Archers').

To the Royal Institute of Philosophy for matter in Chapters 4 and 5, derived from articles in *Philosophy*.

To Robert Vine of the NatWest Brand Strategy Department, NatWest Bank plc (for permission to use the 'Get your business off the ground' advertisement).

To Oliver Wright for the picture of the Japanese ducks.

For the reproduction of 'A promontory of land like a mans head', by W. Hollar, p. 44 of *Graphice: the Use of the Pen and Pensil, Or, The Most Excellent Art of Painting in Two Parts*, by William Sanderson (London: Robert Crofts), which appears on p. 35, permission has been given by the Syndics of Cambridge University Library.

Every effort has been made to trace all copyright holders, but if any have been inadvertently overlooked, the publisher will be pleased to make the necessary arrangements at the first opportunity.

Tsuyu-no-yo wa
Tsuyu-no-yo
Nagara sari nagara

A world of dew
Is but a world of dew –
And yet, and yet . . .

Kobayashi Issa

1
The Joke

> This same folly creates societies and maintains empires.
>   (Erasmus)
>
> Do we know one another? what need of ceremony between friends. We all have a touch of *that same* – you understand me – a touch of the motley.
>   (Charles Lamb)

1.   How to analyse a joke

So many philosophers have thought it best to begin with Logic: it is much better to begin with the Joke. This is from the opening of Leigh Hunt's essay 'Wit Made Easy or a Hint to Word-Catchers':

A: . . . Well, B., my dear boy, I hope I see you well.
B: I hope you do, My dear A., otherwise you have lost your eyesight.
A: Good. Well, how do you do?
B: How? Why, as other people do. You would not have me eccentric, would you?
A: Nonsense. I mean, how do you find yourself?
B: Find myself? Where's the necessity of finding myself? I have not been lost.
A: Incorrigible dog! come now; be serious.
B: [*comes closer to A., and looks very serious*].
A: Well, what now?
B: I am come, to be serious.
    (Leigh Hunt, 1929: 317–18)

So we are come to be serious, and about 'doing as other people do', and about 'finding oneself' when one has been 'lost'. Plutarch tells us that Homer died because he could not think of an answer to a riddle. If we are to try to avoid it, for it is not an uncommon mode of dying, we could start with a riddle – our aim being to find out what a riddle is. Philosophy always comes round to riddles in the end. It is not just in titles like *The New Riddle of Induction* – the topic of riddles is always coming up, but, riddlingly enough, that is not how the actual speakers see it. One, talking of Wittgenstein's Private Language Argument, called it 'a notorious logical conundrum'; yet another, C. I. Lewis, referring to the problems of metaphysics, called them 'cosmic riddles' (Lewis, 1929 [1916]: 4). There are examples all over the academic literature. But none of the thinkers takes a step back and asks what a conundrum or a riddle is.

You would think it might be some help to find out what is common to all these dilemmas. The serious mind when faced with a logical puzzle assumes that it is a puzzle to be worked out *within* logic, but the word 'logical' can be shifted in meaning. Aristotle noticed long ago that the word 'healthy' can slide from meaning *safeguarding health*, as in 'healthy diet', to *indicating health*, as in 'healthy complexion' (Aristotle, *Metaphysics*, Book Γ, ch. 2). In the same way 'logical' can shift. Take 'logical puzzle' when it is being used of philosophical problems (like the relation of the 'particular' to the 'universal' or 'appearance' to 'reality'), not as meaning a puzzle to be worked out *within* logic, but as a puzzle 'arising out of the nature of logic', being something to do with what logic is.

So what is the structure of a joke or a riddle or a conundrum? We shall start with a very simple one from a child's joke book:

A: Knock knock!
B: Who's there?
A: Cook.
B: Cook who?
A: That's the first one I've heard this year.
    (Ahlberg and Ahlberg, 1982: 8)

The first point to notice is that a joke, riddle or conundrum always works with something the meaning of which is multiple, ambiguous, equivocal. So the first thing to look for is that ambiguous element, wherever it may be. Here, as you quickly discerned, it is 'Cook who?'

There is one strange thing to notice about it. The joke is typically *told*, not written or printed as here, so the ambiguous element is really the sequence of *sound* that 'Cook who?' indicates.

There is a passage in Gilbert Adair's *Alice through the Needle's Eye*, that *tromp l'oeil* pastiche of Lewis Carroll, which brings this home (a character called the Grampus is speaking to Alice):

'...the best meanings ca'n't ever be written down, that's how precious they are.'

'I think I should hear an example,' Alice cautiously replied.

'And so you shall!' it exclaimed, and it suddenly began to recite the following:

> *In spring the farmer sows his field:*
> *What crops in autumn will it yield?*
> *In spring the farmer's wife sews too:*
> *A baby's mittens – pink or blue?*
> *From early morn, with cock a-crowing,*
> *They both set busily to –*

The Grampus left off to address Alice. 'And what do you think the next word ought to be?'

'I'm pretty certain it's "sewing",' replied Alice.

'Quite right. And how would you write it down, may I ask?'

Alice didn't even bother to reflect before answering. 'Why, that's easy: s-e-w-i-n – I mean –' she broke off thoughtfully, 'no, it ca'n't be that for it would only apply to one sort of sewing. So it should be: s-o-w-i –' she broke off again. 'Except that now it only applies to the *other* kind! I know – it should be spelt: s- . . .' More confused than ever, Alice fell silent for a moment. 'Now I understand,' she said, brightening up: 'the word ca'n't be spelt at all, because – '

'That's what I call a meaning!' the Grampus interrupted her in triumph. 'And I trust you'll remember this lesson in years to come . . . '
    (Adair, 1984: 80–1)

So (sew? sow?) the core of a joke cannot really be spelt at all: the Grampus is right (Adair has made him as much of a philosopher as Carroll's Humpty Dumpty). We could not even get away with it by printing the core of the joke we started out with in the International Phonetic Alphabet, thus / **kuk hu:** or **kuku:**/, for that would be to suggest that we already knew that this particular sequence of sound was human speech made up of what the linguists call individual 'phonemes' like /**k**/, /**h**/ and /**u:**/, and a glance at the joke – for you have got the point that one of the meanings involved *is not human speech at all* – even though we have a way of spelling it! There's glory for you, in the form of a first philosophical crumb: in a joke, and in much else, we are dealing with something that lies outside words.

What is going on can be most easily demonstrated by using a visual illustration of the structure, one provided by the professor of aesthetics, Sir Ernst Gombrich. The diagram that he uses was produced to show the effect of existing memory expectations upon features of the distribution of a visual field. He took the familiar Rubin Vase (Figure 1), which we can subject to a switch of gestalts between two profiles or a vase. He added clues which strengthened our expectations, first a pair of ears, which encouraged the

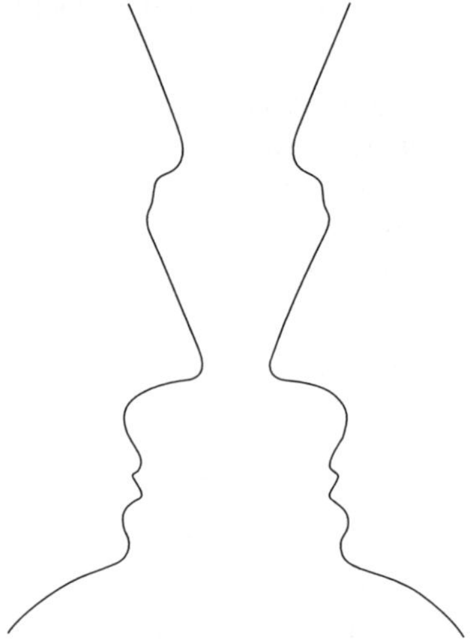

Figure 1

Figure 2

Profile interpretation (Figure 2), or a few flowers at the top, which strengthened the Vase interpretation (Figure 3). His significant move was to include
both sets of contextual clues, as in Figure 4. He points out that if you mask
either set of clues 'the reading becomes assured' (Gombrich, 1973: 239). The
interesting aspect of this demonstration is that the rival gestalt-figures play
over what is a contestable visual ground which cannot be described in the

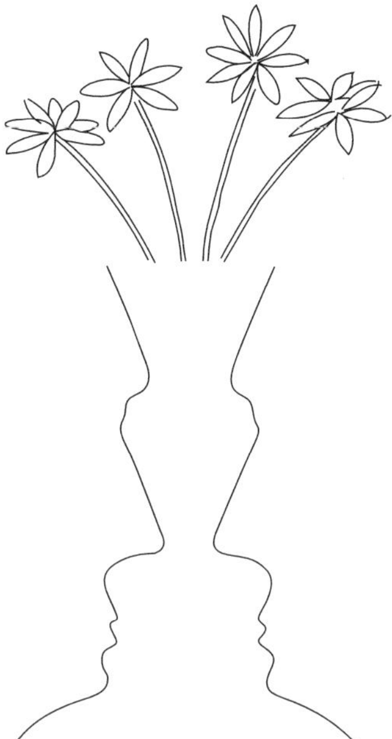

Figure 3

Figure 4

terms that are used of the gestalts *per se*. It is not the case that the distribution of lines has only two ways of being described: there is a neutral ground from which the two percepts, vase and faces, are being *selected*. It is noteworthy also that the two gestalts *do not share the same portion of that ground, only a boundary*. It is not the case that one entity (the vase) changed wholly into another two entities (the faces). Compare the version of the Rubin Vase in Figure 5, in which one 'vase' can change into two faces or one face (the actual drawing of the faces provides one set of clues, the candle works for the 'Vase' interpretation).

Let us produce a diagram of this structure that can apply to a joke and such drawings as these indifferently. It can be begun by placing the Ambiguous Element in the middle of a page (Figure 6). We shall have to compromise here and put either one of the spellings or the phonetic spelling to pass for the actual sound. Strictly speaking, we should have a cassette player in the middle producing the sound sequence itself.

Figure 5

Ambiguous Element
/kuku:/

Figure 6

Next we shall look for the first meaning that comes to mind as one progresses through the joke. Again you will have no difficulty in deciding that it is 'Cook who?', where 'Cook' is taken as an unusual forename and B, in saying 'Cook who?' is asking for the surname, which is the ritual performance in all these 'Knock knock' jokes. Again there is a significant but at the moment small problem – if it is a 'meaning' it is clearly something being *thought*, so the printed words 'Cook who?' are only a proxy for what is really happening. However, we shall make do with them. We shall place them below the Ambiguous Element in the lower right-hand corner of our diagram, and label them 'Meaning I', using the Roman numeral (Figure 7).

Next we look for what it is that is making us interpret the Ambiguous Element as someone asking for someone's surname in this way. Well, it is the ritual of the 'Knock knock' joke that we are expected to ask this, but, if we are going to be pedantic and thorough, we must say in addition that, if one hears a knock at the door and one has asked 'Who's there?' and one hears a forename, then it is extremely likely that, if one is still puzzled who it is, then, if they have said 'Sigmund', one asks 'Sigmund who?' With all that run-up, the memory is not given a very difficult task in interpreting the sounds that follow. All these, therefore, constitute a set of memory-clues by which we can guide our interpretation. We do it so spontaneously that you could say it was second-nature to respond with this meaning. We now know what preparations for action, *what set of intentions*, we need to bring to the sound we are hearing. These we shall label 'Clue(s) to Intentional Perspective I' and place them in the top left-hand part of our diagram, drawing an arrow through to Meaning I to show that it was the clues that encouraged the interpretation (Figure 8). (We have written 'Clue(s)' because in some jokes there is only one such clue, but in others there are more.)

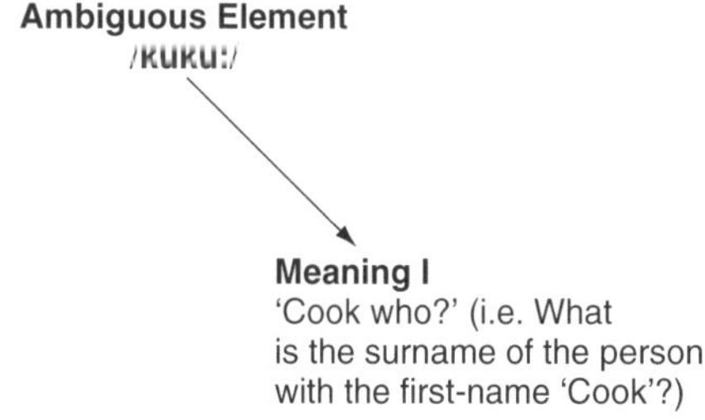

Figure 7

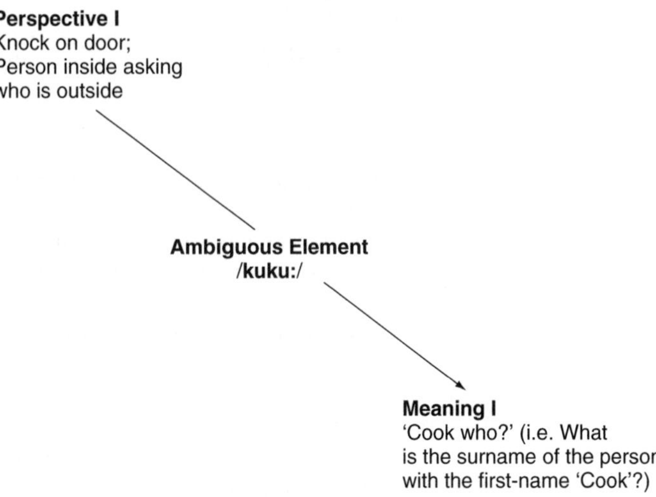

Figure 8

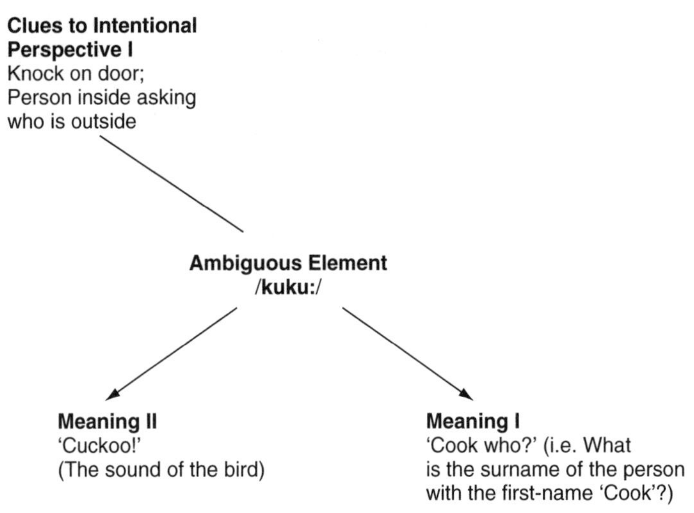

Figure 9

Now we look for the second meaning, which you have no problem in identifying as 'Cuckoo!' and we shall place this in the lower left-hand corner, marking it as 'Meaning II' (Figure 9). Again the caveat must be borne in mind that this spelling only stands for what happens in the minds of the teller of the joke and his or her hearer.

Finally we look for the contextual clue or clues that excite this second meaning, and it is obvious that the last line performs this task in the joke. In a way one hardly needs this last line, for the laughter of the joker would be sufficient clue. One doesn't need to be acquainted with Delius's 'On Hearing the First Cuckoo in Spring' or be a regular reader of *The Times* to associate the call of the cuckoo with something being heard for the first time in spring. So we can place this clue from the joke in the top right-hand corner of the diagram and label it 'Clue(s) to Intentional Perspective II' and drawing the arrow through to Meaning II to show what reminder to settle our expectations is working to create the meaning out of the sound (Figure 10).

This now completes the initial analysis of the joke. What triggered the laugh in this case was the provision of the Second Clue, although, as has just been noted, the Second Clue could arise out of memory by itself, aided no doubt by the clue of the laughter of the joker. Many jokes, however, do need a clear Second Clue; otherwise Meaning I remains unchallenged and then there is nothing funny to laugh at.

This, for example, is a joke with its Second Clue removed: 'What do babies wear in the rain?' – 'Gumboots.' With the Second Clue missing the core of the would-be joke, here 'gum' retains only one meaning, that is, *rubber*. Insert the Second Clue and the joke is activated: 'What do jelly

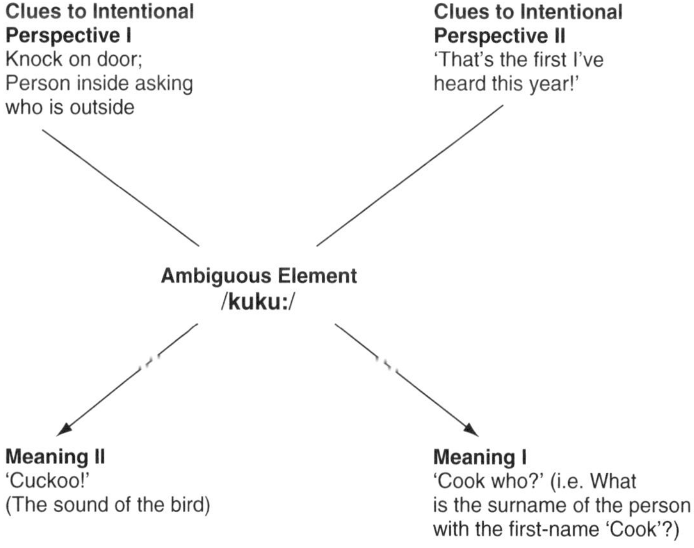

Figure 10

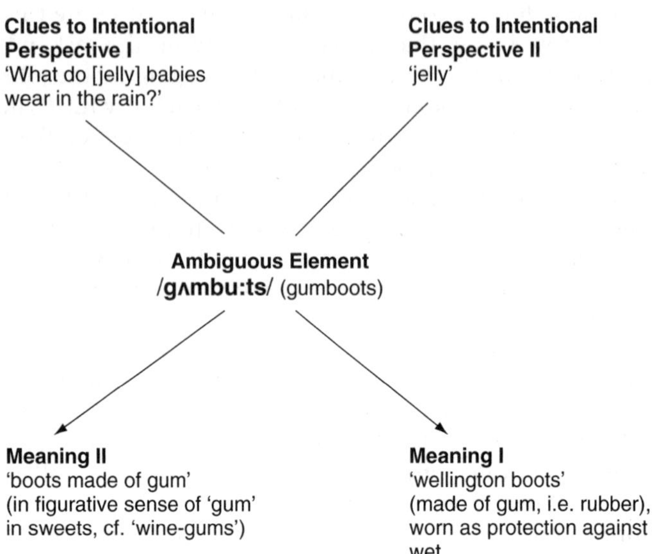

Figure 11

babies wear in the rain? – Gumboots' (Ahlberg and Ahlberg, 1982: 88). The five-part analysis can now be performed as in Figure 11.

Jerry Suls, a psychologist interested in jokes, insists that there has to be the 'resolution' of an 'incongruity' in order for the joke to function. He gives as proof the effect of certain substitutions in the following joke:

> DISTRAUGHT PARENT: 'Doctor, come at once! Our baby has swallowed /(a) a fountain-pen (b) a rubber-band/.
> DOCTOR: I'll come right over. What are you doing in the meantime?
> DISTRAUGHT PARENT: /(c) Using a pencil (d) We don't know what to do/.
>   (Suls, 1983: 45)

(a) and (c) together produce the joke because they contain both the incongruity and the resolution; (b) and (c) produce an incongruity but no resolution; (b) and (d) have no incongruity to be resolved. By the analysis here, only (a) and (c) produce the joke because the Ambiguous Element ('What are you doing in the meantime?') is only given two intentionally contrasting interpretations by the First Clue 'swallowing a fountain-pen' (which gives the serious and troubling interpretation 'What medical measures have you begun?', and the Second Clue 'Using a pencil' which gives the absurd black-comedy interpretation 'How are you managing now that you have lost your writing implement?', which carries the horrifying implication that the writing task was more important than the state of the baby. What the Suls example brings out is that the joke will have greater power the more incongruous the intentions are in the joke, and that draws in the emotions associated with the two meanings.

A further point about the Joke's structure. Sometimes it is the Second Clue that comes last and triggers the Joke, as in the Cuckoo joke, and sometimes it is the Ambiguous Element itself which is the trigger, as in the Gumboots joke.

In this passage from Dickens's *Great Expectations* Orlick uses a series of Second Clues against Pip in exactly the same way as Leigh Hunt's interlocutor. Can you pick out the two Second Clues and what Orlick renders ambiguous thereby? Pip asks the first question.

'How did you get here?'
'I come here,' he retorted, 'on my legs. I had my box brought alongside me in a barrow.'
'Are you here for good?'
'I ain't here for harm, young master, I suppose.'
(Charles Dickens, *Great Expectations*: Ch. 29)

2.   More than one joke in the joke

Jokes, as Freud well knew, contain far more than appears on the surface. The joke about the Cuckoo, for example, had more than one ambiguous element drawn into it. The Joker made the Hearer say 'Cuckoo!' without his realizing it, making the Hearer into a fool, since the sound 'Cuckoo!', because of the history of its metaphorical association with cuckolding (the strange fledgling left in the 'nest'), has always been a source of mocking fun. To quote Shakespeare: 'Oh word of fear, / Unpleasing to a married ear!' So the Hearer of the joke is made into an Ambiguous Element in the context: on the one hand an innocent listener to a joke whose fun he was invited to share (Meaning I); on the other the very butt of the joke itself (Meaning II). So one clue was the apparent welcoming well-known set-up of the 'Knock knock' joke (First Clue), the other arose out of this familiarity for it induced him to utter the key phrase 'Cuckoo!' (Second Clue) (Figure 12). And isn't this second interpretation of the joke actually where the real fun of it lies?

There are therefore two diagrams to draw for this joke, and two for the Jelly Babies one, which encourages us to visualize the ambiguous image of jelly babies stomping along in gumboots, which is open to an indefinite

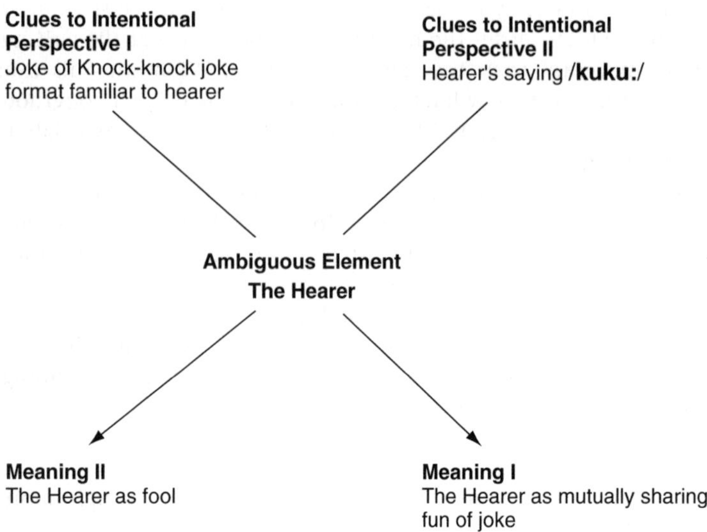

Figure 12

series of interpretations, allowing us to see adults as foolish (equivalent to curiously vulnerable babies in their thinking that some apparently impressive protection will guarantee them security); children as bold and admirable in taking up what adult life can offer in education and instruction (trying out in playful performance something belonging to adult life – which was Wordsworth's thought in the 'Immortality Ode': 'As if his whole vocation / Were endless imitation'); and, if the similarity of each of a large number of those jelly babies struck the fancy, a less amusing, uncanny interpretation, that of faceless and expendable citizens in a totalitarian dystopia under the illusion that they are protected as they march together (but then, I have recently seen a science-fiction film about such a dystopia). Jokes, it is plain, are not limited to humorous readings, for it depends who is reading them, what intentional perspectives those persons bring along – a second philosophical crumb.

But to take one step at a time. If some jokes, then, have multiple Ambiguous Elements that present themselves for rival intentional perspectives, let us start with those with fairly obvious ones. Here is a familiar one from childhood:

Why did the coal scuttle?
Because it saw the kitchen sink.

There are two Ambiguous Elements, 'scuttle' and 'sink'. Both of them have *three* interpretations, because for each of them three sets of clues can be discerned.

'Sink' can mean (i) an item of kitchen equipment used for washing dishes; (ii) to move downwards – in a general sense; (iii) to move downwards specifically in water. The diagram (Figure 13) can most readily display the clues to these.

'Scuttle' similarly has three meanings: (i) a metal container for coal; (ii) to run away in haste; (iii) deliberately to sink one's own ship (Figure 14).

Notice that what occurs as Ambiguous Element in the first structure works as a clue to intentional perspective in the other.

Various absurd but unconsciously powerful scenarios hover around this complex of meanings. To take one: we see a coal scuttle running away as a whole kitchen suddenly sinks downwards – this could be someone giving up hope and 'running away' (*scuttle*) from a responsibility when he sees another do the same (*sink*), as a coward in a situation demanding courage; or, according to old pre-feminist prejudices, someone associated with coal may be a man and the one associated with a kitchen may be a woman, so that sketches a picture in the background suggestive of marital failure. Another, just of a spouse giving up on a marriage altogether, 'kitchen' here being a metonym for the home (a metonym, you recall, is an image that works by one thing being found with another in some kind of associative context, the 'Crown' standing for *the monarch*,

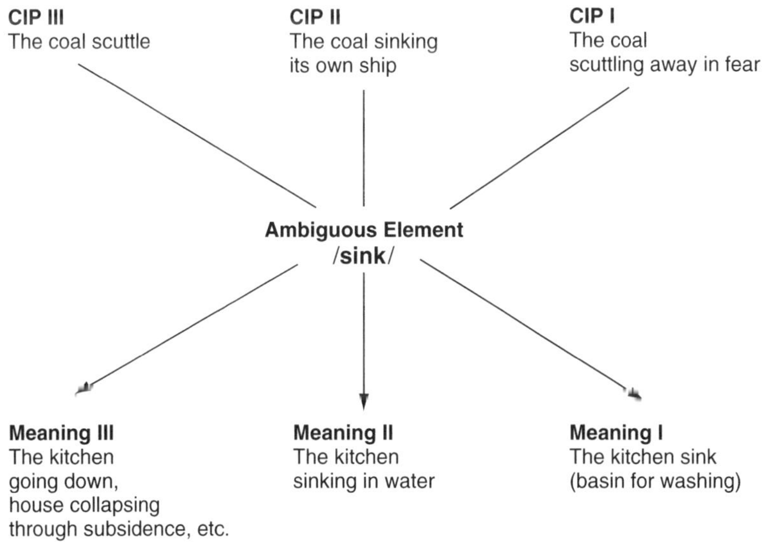

Figure 13

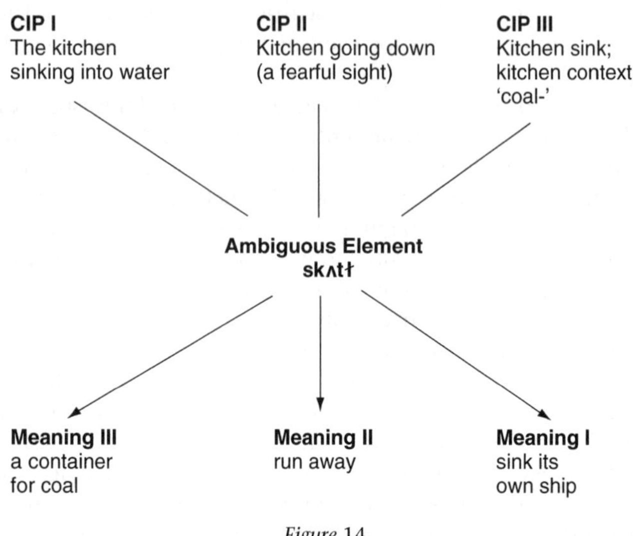

Figure 14

or a 'nine-to-fiver' being one who keeps their work to those set hours). In each case of these possibles – and there are many more – the kitchen equipment brings in the harmless context and the other the emotionally threatening one.

Strictly there is no limit on the number of meanings that can be involved in a joke. In this joke from the Fool in Shakespeare's *King Lear*, one can manage to discern six meanings since adequate clueing can be found in the text, both immediately and from wider implications of the story before and after. One allows the Ambiguous Element to be pronounceable as hovering between /**æsiz**/ (asses) and /**aːsiz**/ (arses), for whoever acts the Fool can fudge between them:

LEAR: . . . Be my horses ready?
FOOL: Thy asses are gone about them.

One can detect and justify all the following meanings for 'asses' in the context of the play: *donkeys*, *fools*, *servants*, *bottoms* (and hence, by metaphor, *disregarded persons*), and *animals* (from connotations of the human/animal imagery and its special significance throughout the play, bringing in the nature/culture antithesis which plays so central a part in the background implications of the tragedy; see Spurgeon, 1935 and Danby, 1949) (see Figure 15).

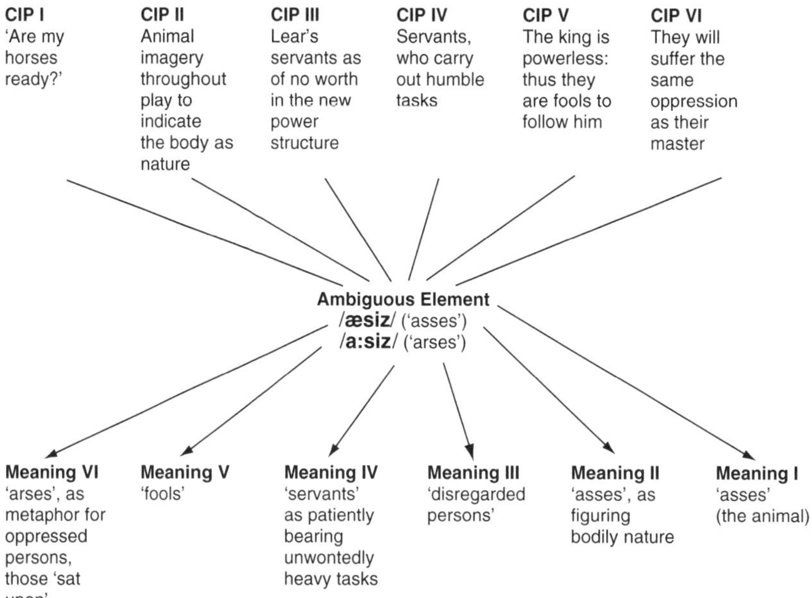

Figure 15

3.   Changing boundaries

In the very first joke we analysed, there was a choice between 'Cook who?' and 'Cuckoo!' If you were out in the country in spring and that is what you heard, there is little likelihood of you interpreting it as 'Cook who?' or even a sequence of 'Oo-cucks', as a comic poem reminds us:

> 'The cuckoo!' cried my child, the while I slept;
>   'Sweet Pop, the cuckoo! O, its cries impinge!
> The harbinger is here!' And up I leapt
>   To hear the thing harbinge.
>
> I flung the casement, thrust the visage through,
>   Composed the features in rhapsodic look.
> Cupped the left hand and ... lo! I heard an 'oo',
>   Soon followed by a 'cuck'.
>
> Another 'oo'! A 'cuck'! An 'oo' again.
>   A 'cuck'. 'Oocuck'. 'Oocuck' ditto. Repeat.
> I tried to pick the step up but in vain –
>   I'd ... 'oo' ... missed 'Cuck' ... the beat.

> I'd missed the beat. And this would last till June
>> And nothing could be done now to catch up –
> This fowl would go on hiccuping its tune,
>> Hic after beastly cup.
>
> 'Oocuck!' ... 'Oocuck!' ... that was four weeks ago,
>> Four non-stop weeks of contrapuntal blight.
> My nerves are ... what was that? ... Ah no! Ah no!
>> Spare me the ingalenight!
>>> Justin Richardson, 'The Oocuck' (1959: 88)

A continuing sound like this – given, by the logic of the poem that 'Cuckoo' did go on uninterruptedly – is open to any division one cares to put on it. It could in just as likely a fashion be divided into a series that repeated 'Uckook' or 'Kooker'. There were those boys at school that invited one to go on repeating 'Kinellfer' without stopping. B. F. Skinner notes another school trick of the same kind: asking other children to repeat 'Bell-Eye-Mud-Dum' (Skinner, 1957: 282).

What is philosophically interesting about these examples is that they bring home the fact that the perceptual divisions that come down on the sound material, 'carving it up', as the current philosophical idiom has it, do not necessarily respect any 'joints' already there. Skinner's example will do as illustration: it seems to present four separate units, but, when the transformation takes place in the mouth of the luckless victim of this joke, becoming 'I'm a dumb-bell!', it turns into what is strictly five words, with entirely different lines of division – 'Eye' is not separated from 'Mud', and the vowel of 'Mud' detaches itself to become a word entirely on its own.

In this joke:

> Where do policemen live?
> Letsby Avenue.
>> (Ahlberg and Ahlberg, 1982: 56)

two words ('Letsby Avenue') forming a proper name turn into a sentence of five words, two of them elided ('Let's be 'avin' you!'). There is no necessary preservation of any 'units' or 'entities' or 'things'. Indeed, thing-making becomes a matter of perceptual choice, given the clues to the intentional context (Figure 16).

Again, notice how there is a distinctly unpleasant meaning in this riddle, exposing the Hearer again into becoming a joke, for it suggests that he or she is under suspicion from the law – hence its power over us. We are sensitive about decisions concerning boundaries since they are something that so often brings us up against the law, whether that of the land, that of language, or that of morality.

As extraordinary examples of how the provision of a series of Second Clues can transform the sound of a sentence so that it becomes an entirely different

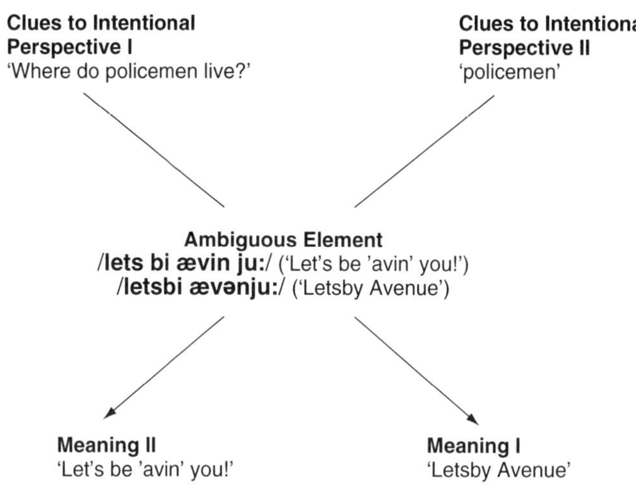

Figure 16

meaning with entirely different words one can take any of Frank Muir's and Denis Norden's performances in the BBC 'My Word!' stories. They were significantly titled because the game consisted of a challenge to transform the meaning of a familiar phrase or saying so that it changed its meaning completely, a special kind of Shaggy Dog Story. 'He who hesitates is lost' became 'He who has sad dates is last'; 'Discretion is the better part of valour' became 'This creation is Tibet, or part of Ella', using, as you see, various kinds of 'phoneme-chime' (e.g. 'lost' and 'last' was pararhyme (/l...st/ and /lɑ:...st/); 'hesitates and 'dates' was a rhyme). One of the challenges for Frank Muir was to transform 'Come into the garden, Maud'. He managed to tell a long story in which Second Clues were convincingly built up so that it was transformed into 'Carmen? Toothy Gordon? Moored?' The story depended on the unlikelihood of two yacht enthusiasts named Carmen and Gordon (called 'Toothy' because of his prominent front teeth) getting married – and 'moored' became well established long before the end of the story as yachting jargon for *married*. Both these examples well illustrate the absence of any necessity for the new interpretation having the same number of entities as the first ('Come into the garden, Maud' has five words, 'Carmen? Toothy Gordon? Moored?' has four) (Muir and Norden, 1976: 167–70).

The assumed stability of an entity is frequently called into question in the world of the joke. Here is a more subtle example:

> What's the difference between a cup of tea and a magician?
> One's a cuppa, the other's a sorcerer.
> (Ahlberg and Ahlberg, 1982: 80)

The Ambiguous Element is not an 'element' in this one, but rather a region with vague outlines, for the 'carving up' of what is heard produces entities with quite different boundaries, so there is a real problem about what to put in the middle of the diagram, There is no one 'thing' that conveniently switches from one interpretation to the other (Figure 17).

The philosophical point here about the number of entities is one of considerable importance, as we shall see. We may be tempted to assume that there is *one* thing in front of us *all of which* changes into something else when the interpretation changes, but that is most definitely not the general case. An overlap perhaps, but what it is of the original unit that is retained is entirely determined by the new intentional perspective. One cannot say of it that 'this' changed into 'that'; that the very same thing we had happily selected out of the continuum of sound that came to our ears was still there in its singularity after the changeover. The tendency to think that in all cases of a gestalt switch a *single* entity changed into another *single* entity perhaps arises from the unthinking use of Wittgenstein's 'Duck-Rabbit' as the paradigm example (Wittgenstein, 1967: 194e).

There is a feature of this joke that has relevance to what will be encountered later when we have a look at the Story. The fun of this joke does not depend solely upon the main switch as Figure 14 has shown. 'Sorcerer' would not have come so pat as the punchline of the joke if it had not been supported by a *rhyme*, 'cuppa' (/kʌpə/) and 'sorcerer' (/sɔːsərə/). It is not much of a rhyme, that final /E/, that common sound linguists call the 'schwa' – it is what most unstressed vowels turn into: in fact it is not even one the handbooks on rhyme have much use for, since it depends on so slight a similarity. *The Penguin Rhyming Dictionary*, for example, is dismissive of this kind of rhyme: of rhymes in '-er' it says, 'rhymes dependent on this syllable alone are unsatisfactory and should be avoided' (Ferguson, 1975: 17). A rhyme, you may recall, is produced when a syllable or syllables at the

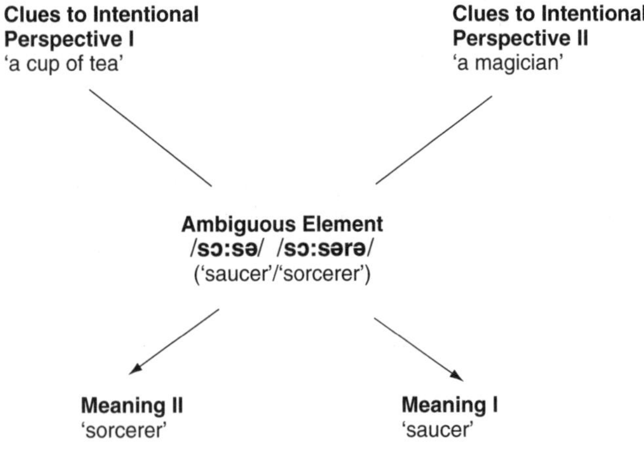

Figure 17

end of a word, that syllable or syllables *beginning with a vowel-sound*, is repeated with a change in the consonant that precedes them, for example:

'hat' (/**hæt**/) and 'mat' (/**mæt**/) – **æt**
'potion' (/**pouʃən**/) and 'ocean' (/**ouʃən**/) – **ouʃən**
'stationary' (/**steiʃənəri**/) and
'inflationary' (/**infleiʃənəri**/) – **eiʃənəri**

note that *absence* of a consonant before the key first vowel counts as a change ('potion' and 'ocean').

What is worth noticing here is that a rhyme seduces us with its pleasure precisely in the same way as a joke. A portion of a sequence of sound, which may be meaningless in itself (-ationary, /**eiʃənəri**/) turns up in two words with entirely different interpretations. This is just what an early analyst of rhyme, J. C. Schütze, influenced by Kant, concluded that every rhyme must have, that

> the identity of sound…can have an aesthetic significance only when, and only because, it covers a variety of meaning (*Morgen, Sorgen*). The principle of diversity in unity is here applied to explain the aesthetic effect of rhyming which otherwise…would result in unbearable monotony. (See Herbert, 1970: 275)

This is why the handbooks of versification reject a chime such as 'tin' and 'satin' as a true rhyme, because the portion (/-tin/) repeated does not begin with a vowel but with a consonant (/t/). In a joke, however, the change can slide on any overlap at all, given adequate clueing.

A rhyme can thus be justifiably viewed as a mini-joke – no wonder children make much of them:

> There was a man called Michael Finnegan;
> He grew whiskers on his chinnigan;
> The wind came out and blew them in again –
> Poor old Michael Finnegan!
> (Opie and Opie, 1959: 31)

The fact that there is no such word as 'chinnigan' doesn't disturb the children who chant this, indeed, anyone who does, or that only a part of the sound-sequence in the first rhyme makes sense ('chin-', /**tʃin**/), the rest being nonsense ('-igan', /**igən**/): it is enough that the structure now familiar to you goes through (Figure 18).

There is the same change of interpretation upon a continuum of sound, added to the satisfying spectacle of such an important facial feature as a man's whiskers, significant of the power of the patriarch, being blown back into his face by something as uncontrolled and impassioned as the wind, a little allegory of what the joke itself always does, snatch authority from the

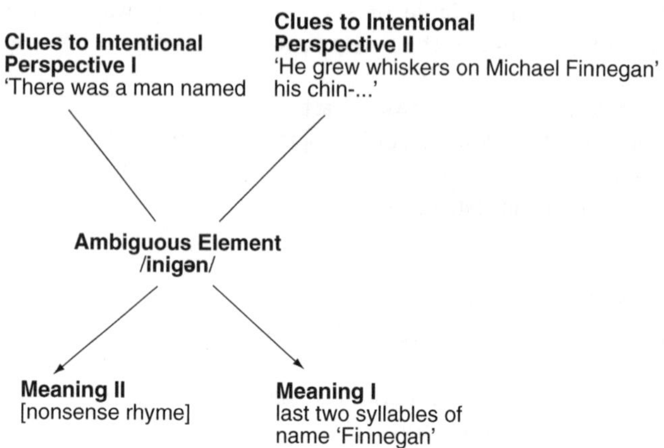

Figure 18

accepted meaning and transfer it to a new and unexpected one. (The jingle above was quoted in the 'Just for Fun' section of Iona and Peter Opie's *The Lore and Language of Schoolchildren*, pp. 17–40; the whole chapter, indeed the whole book, provides extraordinary evidence of the power of rhythm and the joke to command the attention of children.)

So Rhyme well illustrates the last philosophical point we discerned that it is not necessary that a single entity is transformed whole, for part of it or aspects of it may drop out of notice altogether. What forms the chime between interpretations may have no sense in itself at all ('-innegan'), or have no separate sense in one appearance and turn up as two entities in another ('in again'). The rest of the words of the line form the clues for memory to take up the intentional perspective that elicits the desired meaning, just as in the Joke.

So there has been a small but significant step here in discovering that Rhyme and the Joke have exactly the same structure.

Concerning this question of boundaries in the Joke, very often the Joker takes advantage of what he can assume is already in our memory and so he fails to deliver the boundary of the succeeding entity or entities – he or she presumes that a sidelong reference will suffice. The question of the link is openly fudged, but the effect is by no means diminished because we can see for ourselves exactly what the new entity or entities are to be. Take the following:

What happened to the cat that swallowed a ball of wool?
She had mittens.
        (Ahlberg and Ahlberg, 1982: 83)

Though the second meaning 'kittens', does not appear in the joke at all, this does not affect the comic effect of the whole. What has been produced is a rhyme, 'mittens', the appropriateness of which has been established by the reference to the ball of wool, a metonymic association, so the aesthetic delight of the metamorphosis of meaning is here doubled – we get rhyme and joke together for the price of one.

The manuals of versification used by aspiring poets introduce us to other chimings across words of consonant and vowel sounds (notice that spelling is not to be depended upon as a guide to sound for either vowel or consonant; in brackets I have given the International Phonetic Alphabet version of the actual phonemes):

INITIAL RHYME, where the first consonant and the first vowel are repeated, e.g. 'race' (/**reis**/) and 'reign' (/**rein**/);

PARARHYME, where the first and last consonants or consonant-groups remain the same, as in Wilfred Owen's poem 'Strange Meeting', e.g. 'laughed' (/**lɑːft**/) and 'left' (/**left**/);

ALLITERATION, where consonants are repeated, e.g. as in Shakespeare's Captain MacMorris's 'What ish my nation?', where 'sh' (/**ʃ**/) is repeated: 'ish' (/**iʃ**/) and 'nation' (/**neiʃən**/);

ASSONANCE, where the vowel-sound is repeated, e.g. 'whose' (/**huːz**/) and 'beauty' (/**bjuːti**/). Recall that ordinary spelling does not correspond to the sounds being uttered.

For all of these the same can be said of them as was said of rhyme, that a *meaningless* element forms the tie between two units that have different meanings. So we can add these to the list of linguistic features which share the same structure as the Joke. Unsurprisingly, we can find jokes that use them as frequently as straightforward rhyme:

[Initial Rhyme]:
What's purple and burns cakes?
Alfred the Grape.

[Pararhyme]
How does a witch tell the time?
With a witch watch.

[Assonance and Alliteration]
What did the father ghost say to his son?
Spook when you're spooken to.

[Assonance and alliteration]
A council worker was seen inspecting rabbit holes. What do you think his
    job was?
A borough surveyor.

But jokes are not to be simply categorized in this manner, for the linking of the interpretations can be achieved by all kinds of confusions, well illustrated by the howlers schoolchildren produce in examinations:

> Quinine is the bark of a tree: canine is the bark of a dog.

> Oxygen can be prepared by heating potassium chocolate.

> Socrates died from an overdose of wedlock.

> Aladdin was a man who had a wonderful lamp: every time he rubbed it, a Guinness sprang up out of the ground.

> A connoisseur is a man in a uniform who stands outside a hotel.
> (Richmond, 1936: 33, 34, 37, 40, 42)

It is relevant to notice that the misunderstanding on which the straightforward joke trades produces in mistakes of this sort an unintentional humour, the results of pupils' inattention and consequent mishearings. The links can be quite distant: 'connoisseur' (/kɔnəsəː/) does share some phonemes, as they are called, with 'commissionaire' (/kəmiʃənɛə/), /k/, /n/, /ə/, and the half-similar /s/ and /ʃ/, but the pupil was probably also influenced by the French character of each word. With the pair 'Guinness' (/ginis/) and 'genie' (and/or 'djinn') (/dʒiːni/ /dʒin/), the link is even more tenuous: one vowel /i/, one consonant /n/, and the spelling of each word with a letter 'g'. 'Quinine' (/kwiniːn/) and 'canine' (/kænain/) are closer, oddly given a double link by the pun on 'bark'. This last provides an interesting insight into the operations of memory which take up whatever sensory mnemonic offers itself in the circumstances, however false it may be. 'Chocolate' (/tʃɔklət/) and 'chlorate' (/klɔːreit/) share as much in the appearance of their spelling as they do in their sounds, the common phonemes being /k/, /l/ and /t/. The Socrates mistake (linking 'wedlock' /wedlɔk/ and 'hemlock' /hemlɔk/) achieves a chance appropriateness since Socrates was in fact blessed with a difficult wife, Xantippe, whose name was commonly used to mean a scold; but that is part of the unintentional humour since the pupil obviously could have no idea of that fact, since the word 'wedlock' is taken to mean a poison, introducing the further metaphorical interpretation of wedlock as something that could induce death, a thought that brings together the harmless and the threatening. So it is no surprise that misunderstandings can often be comic, and that the base of comedy itself is the resolution of misunderstandings, as we shall shortly be seeing.

4. Jokes on jokes

Since the Joker's aim is to defeat expectations, it is no surprise that one of the kinds of expectation he or she can defeat are those concerning jokes themselves. Once a pattern of joking is set up, so that Hearers are fore-warned of what is to happen, the Joker is stimulated to subvert the pattern of the Joke itself with another joke.

> A: Knock knock!
> B: Who's there?
> A: Doctor.
> B: Doctor who?

Some naïve children add 'You've just said it!' after this as an unnecessary Second Clue, but the more sophisticated just laugh at once. The inventor of this joke considered rightly that 'Doctor Who' was a sufficient clue in itself, thus cleverly making the Ambiguous Element provide its own clue to the memory (Figure 19).

Some jokes defeat the very expectation of the joke itself by making the ritual of joke-telling go wrong:

> What's green, lives in a field, and has 4000 legs?
> Grass – it was a mistake about the legs.
>   (Ahlberg and Ahlberg, 1982: 23)

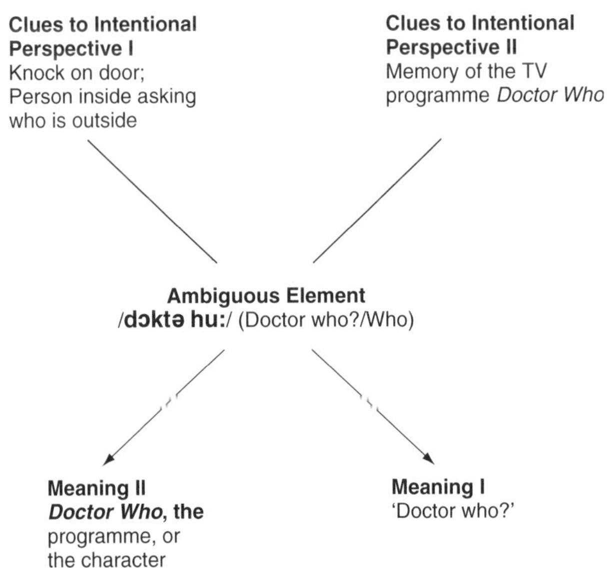

Figure 19

One might argue here that there is still a link in that grass could be seen metaphorically as having 4000 legs, but the Joker denies the transference. The same could be said to be true of the Shaggy Dog Story, the principle of which is to hold the hearers to a very long tale only to fob them off at last with the feeblest of puns. As an example, take the long story about a knight who, commanded by the king to set out on a quest, is subjected to a whole series of irritating obstacles which prevent him leaving the palace, these described in deliberately boring detail by the Joker, the last two of which are a terrible rainstorm outside and the discovery of his horse being lame, at which point the impatient king calls his servants to bring forth a substitute, which turns out to be a smallish Labrador dog: at this the exasperated knight protests: 'Who would turn a knight out on a dog like this?' But often the hearer is not thrown even a bone of this kind:

> What's big, red, and eats rocks?
> A big, red rock-eater.

A first analysis is shown in Figure 20. Here there is no excuse at all: the joke is nothing but a joke at the Hearer's expense whose willing engagement in the ritual of the joke is what is rendered ambiguous, his expectation foiled, which puts the Hearer at the centre of a second analysis, as in Figure 21.

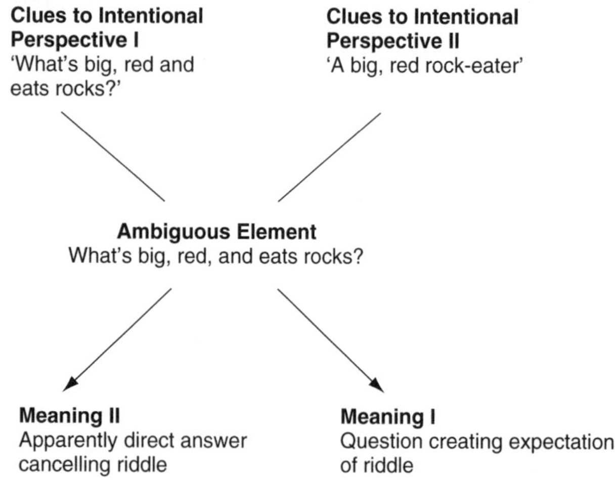

Figure 20

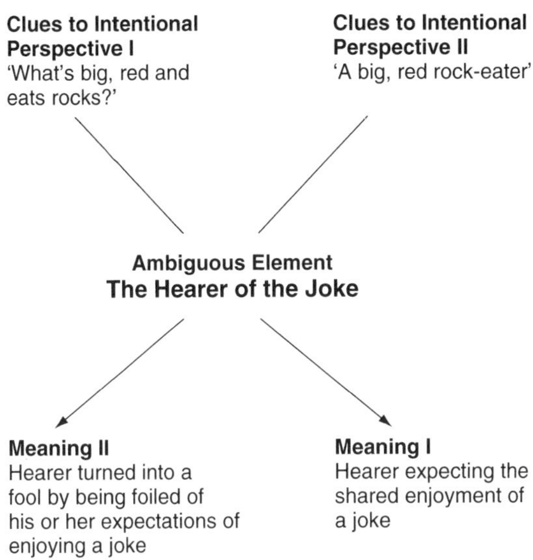

Figure 21

So a joke need not depend solely on the ambiguation of a series of sounds: the ambiguity can range over experience as complex as a person's own expectation, his or her very failure to interpret correctly.

A reminder here, though, that nothing can fail to produce its ambiguations. Dwell on the image and notion of a 'big, red rock-eater' and an endless succession of associations comes to mind. You might start with the 'rock' as one of an authoritarian regime in family or society and the big, red rock-eater becomes a rebel, the monstrous image all the stronger for its red colour and its intent being upon eating, fulfilling a rapacious appetite. So, strictly speaking, one cannot safely put 'Apparently direct answer cancelling riddle' in the spaces above, for intentions, desires, appetites, are too alert for meaning in whatever proffers itself to the eyes and ears.

Here is a variation on the 'Knock, knock' pattern that traps the hearer. Can you see how it is done? There are two jokes present:

A: Knock knock.
B: Who's there?
A: Banana.
B: Banana who?
A: Knock knock.
B: Who's there?
A: Banana.

B: Banana who?
A: Knock knock.
B: Who's there?
A: Banana.
B: Banana who?
A: Knock knock.
B: Who's there?
A: Orange.
B: Orange who?
A: Orange you glad I didn't say 'banana'!
   (Told by Ella Walding)

5.   Ranging outside a sequence of vocal sounds

So far all the jokes we have looked at have been ones that used words as the sound-medium over which interpretations can range. However, jokes are not limited to the sound of words. There is the story of the schoolgirl who had recently been taught about onomatopoeia by her English teacher (e.g. 'cuckoo' as the name of the bird). With some excitement she drew him and her class to the door of a cleaner's cupboard. She opened it to demonstrate something – the teacher thought that this was going to be merely a performance of how useful the word 'creak' was. To his and the class's amused surprise, the noise from the stiff and rusty hinges sounded exactly like a hoarse little voice saying 'Creak!' (Figure 22.)

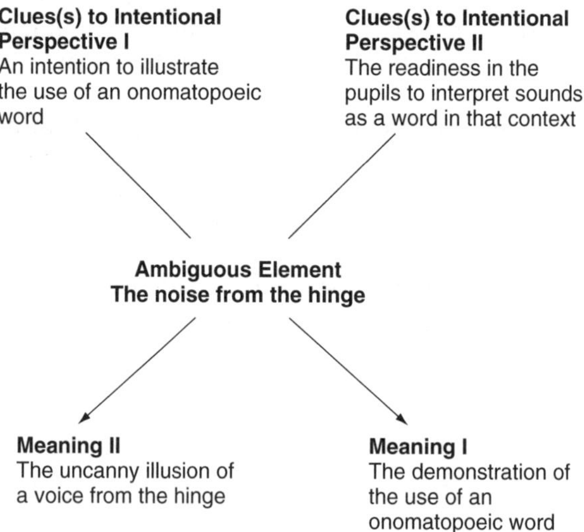

Figure 22

So there is no necessity for one of the interpretations of the Ambiguous Element to be a human word at all. Those linguists who have produced *verbal theories* of humour have been misled by the very limits of their discipline to ignore the fact that humour needs a wider explanation than that involving words only (Raskin, 1985; Attardo, 1994). Neither is there any limitation as to sound – an experience with any of the senses will do. The philosopher Bede Rundle thought that there could not be a Wittgensteinian Duck-Rabbit within the modality of the sense of smell, but a joker could tell you that he had spilled your precious amyl acetate – and you can certainly smell it – but it turns out that what looks like his tongue in his cheek was a pear-drop in his mouth all the time.

There are children's practical jokes that involve tactile ambiguities: there is the Christmas game in which you are blindfolded and various things are put into your hand: for example, you are told that you have a sheep's eye in your hand; after your dropping it in horror, you are shown that it was a peeled tomato – a true joke, for you move from a frightening interpretation to a harmless one.

But we can move across into jokes that are purely visual. Trick pictures often bring home the fact that when we change from one interpretation to another there is no necessary preservation of a boundary marking a single entity. Look at Figures 23 and 24 by Peter Brookes.

Figure 23

'Eustacia . . . that lonesome dark-eyed creature up there that some say is a witch. Call a fine young woman such a name . . .' **The Return of the Native: 9.3 pm**

Figure 24

There is a special point to notice here. Some people, probably those too ready to take the objective world as what it habitually appears, find it difficult to perceive a second perception in a trick picture. Assume that such a person for some moments only noticed the mouse: the black would then be just a random area of background, the outline of which having no significance whatsoever. Such a person is also likely to fail to see the upper set of whiskers as anything but some unimportant detail, if they are noticed at all. For those who notice the cat first, the boundary between the light-coloured fur and the dark is not a boundary that is relevant to distinguishing a separate entity, merely a division between two tints of fur.

As was pointed out in the last section, those who have taken the Wittgensteinian Duck-Rabbit as their favoured illustration of a trick picture have been tricked themselves into ignoring this key feature of visual illusions, namely, that one cannot depend on the whole of the picture embracing both interpretations, just as we saw that puns are no respecters of word-boundaries. In the example of the Duck-Rabbit from the Musée de Magie in Paris (Figure 25) it is the whole of the complete duck that changes into the whole of the complete rabbit (by turning one's perspective through 90 degrees; in the museum one can physically turn the picture). But it is quite easy to

Figure 25

take the Duck-Rabbit, place it in an ambiguous context and show that entity-boundaries are not secure (Figure 25). Now that clues to intentional perspective have been provided (for the Rabbit – the furry tail on the left, a glimpse of the forward part of the thigh, and the paws in the middle; for the Duck – the pointed tail on the right and the webbed feet immediately below to the left of the Rabbit's paws), the gestalt-switch produces a change of boundaries in this picture. A little more of the Rabbit's body becomes visible, which, in the Duck gestalt, disappears into the background of leaves, and vice-versa, a glimpse of the back of the Duck becomes perceptible that is nothing but part of the leafy background in the Rabbit gestalt and, one

Figure 26

must add, may have no attention paid to it at all, that is, it was *sensed* by the person looking at the picture, but not *perceived*, perhaps not even perceived as the edge of a leaf. It is often assumed – for it is comforting so to believe – that we have identified everything within our field of view and nothing is outside the range of our immediate knowledge, but that is plainly empirically false. This is a fact of considerable philosophical moment, and we shall be returning to it.

Children's books frequently include ambiguous pictures. There is the famous French series called the Devinettes d'Épinal ('The Riddles of Épinal') that contain the original of the well-known 'young girl/mother-in-law' illusion (Figure 27). This drawing, used by the psychologists E. G. Boring and

Figure 27

R. W. Leeper, came from a comic magazine called *Puck* (6 November 1915), the drawing made by one W. E. Hill (Boring, 1942; Leeper, 1935). What was not generally known until 1992 is that it was copied with certain features of disguise from one of the Devinettes (Wright, 1992d) (Figure 28).

One can play the same game with Hill's drawing as we did with the Duck-Rabbit. Put a mirror for the 'young lady' in the place where the apple was, and the 'mother-in-law' is a less likely first choice for the mind to select (Figure 29). Put a magic crystal ball for the 'mother-in-law' and it turns her into a fortune-teller and makes her a readier gestalt (Figure 30).

Many people on first seeing this picture, in fact, have difficulty in picking out the 'mother-in-law', perhaps because, having picked out the 'young girl', which presents itself in a realistic style, they cannot adjust to the grotesque caricature style of the 'mother-in-law' picture. With the crystal ball as a clear clue to the 'mother-in-law', that gestalt becomes more achievable. With both sets of clues in the Gombrich manner the illusion becomes a visual illustration of the fivefold structure of the Joke, two rival interpretations, each supported by a clue to an intentional perspective (Figure 31).

The Devinettes usually give one no visual clues to the second interpretation, only verbal ones. Sometimes the gestalt-switch is one the old gestalt

Figure 28

Figure 29

Figure 30

Figure 31

psychologists would have called a 'figure/ground' switch, in that an outline serves to mark first one side as substantial, the other as empty, and then changes them round, as in Figure 32, where one has to look for '*La France* crowned with laurels'.

This most obviously shows the failure to preserve a single entity from one gestalt to another. It cannot even strictly be called an overlap. There is no 'this' or 'it' that is kept the same, only an edge, which in a real-world example would not be a drawn line at all. Some of the Devinettes are very difficult. What is interesting is that, when a difficult one is given to children, they find quite convincing faces where the artist never meant them to find them.

Giuseppi Arcimboldi, who painted many such pictures in which a land scape or a bowl of fruit becomes a human face, did not need to alert his audience. In the picture by W. Hollar we are actually given the Second Clue in the title: 'A promontory of land, like a man's head' (Figure 33).

There have been several examples (the 'Doctor Who' is one) where the Joker can rely on our memories to initiate the rival perceptions and does not have to provide obvious clues to either interpretation. A remarkable instance is that of the drawing by the American artist Joseph Hirsch (Figure 34); he

Figure 32

does at least give a Second Clue in the title of the picture, 'Five Faces', which in view of our immediate 'seeing-as' of *one* face, is a challenge to us. Its method is not dissimilar to those of the Devinettes.

Another example is a photograph of some ducks in winter on the pond outside the staff refectory of Hokkaido University in Sapporo, Japan (Figure 35).

Figure 33

Figure 34

6.   Rhythm and play

In Section 3 we examined jokes based on rhythmic effects in language. Take the joke about the cat who swallowed a ball of wool – 'She had mittens', based on the rhyme 'kittens'/'mittens'. It can readily be seen that a rhyme, indeed all rhythms in words, music and gesture, share the Joke and Story pattern.

Figure 35

Consider 'mittens' and 'kittens' (/**mitṇz**/, /**kitṇz**/). One can say that the Ambiguous Element is '-ittens' (/**itṇz**/). The 'm' (/**m**/) and the 'k' (/**k**/) represent the clues to the rival intentional contexts, as in Figure 36.

This is not to suggest that the hearers of the joke are consciously aware of the Ambiguous Element as a separately repeated feature: they are only

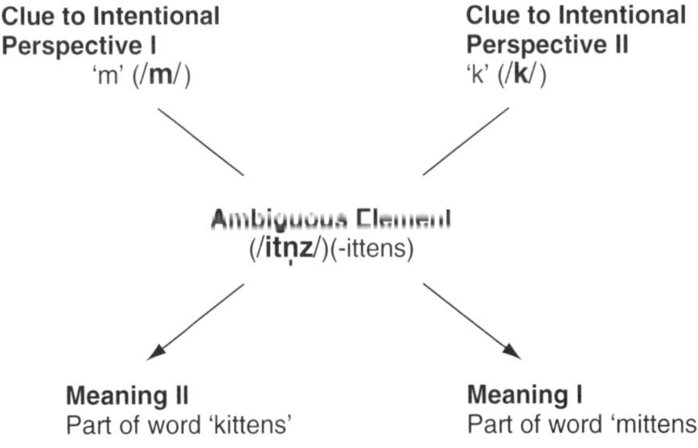

Figure 36

subliminally so, but, nevertheless, it is that upon which the pleasure of the word-play is based. Take the repetition of '-innegan' (/**ɪnəgən**/) in the 'Michael Finnegan' rhyme.

The point needs stressing. Say these two lines (the last two lines) from a poem of Gerald Manley Hopkins ('Pied Beauty'):

> He fathers-forth whose beauty is past change:
>   Praise Him.

The rhythmic pleasure in the play of the sounds is not consciously noticed. Compare an accomplished musician listening to a modulation in a piece of music and someone with no knowledge of music: the musician may be aware of the modulation, even of the actual change of key, but the person without musical knowledge cannot say as much – however, the effect of the modulation works aesthetically upon both in a similar way. In fact, it is possible that the ignorant listener is at that moment responding more sensitively to the music. So here in the lines of poetry, for, if we now examine the rhythm of the phonemes alone, leaving aside the effects of the rhythm of the metrical beat, it is surprising what subtleties of assonance and alliteration are in this line. Putting it in International Phonetic Alphabet brings out the interweavings of phoneme repetition:

/hi: fɑːðəz fɔːθ huːz bjuːti ɪz pɑːst tʃeindʒ preiz him/

> He fathers-forth whose beauty is past change:
>   Praise Him.

Look along the lines and you will see rhythmic repetitions that are not indicated clearly by the familiar printed letters, for, as we well know, the sounds we actually pronounce and the printed letters on the page do not correspond at all closely in English.

To take the vowels first. /**ei**/, pronounced like the name of the letter A, is spelled 'a' in 'change' and 'ai' in 'praise. The /**u:**/, pronounced 'oo', appears as 'eau' in 'beauty' and 'o' in 'whose'. Now ask yourself whether you were consciously aware of either chimings when you first read the line: you sensed and you appreciated their rhythmic contribution to the line, but you had not knowingly noticed them, not unless you were a poet yourself or a literary critic or an actor. Like any joker, I have drawn your attention to a feature you had clearly *sensed* but not perceived.

We need not pick out all the alliteration, the consonant repetitions; one will suffice. Were you aware that there are four /**z**/ sounds, all spelled 's', and, of course, the 's' in 'past' is not one of them.

One could also examine the metrical beat of the line and the effect of stressed syllables, and, even then, we would not have begun to consider how all these rhythms contributed together to the lines, and, thence, to the whole poem itself.

This is word-play at the level of the sounds of language. It could only take place if the sensory upon which it worked was meaningless to begin with, allowing perceptual freedom to range over the field of the Real. So what is *play*? It is significant that we use the word 'play' to describe the looseness of, say, a lock ('There was a certain amount of play in the lock which allowed us to get back in without the key'). There is the connotation in the word of there being some former rigidity which has now come loose, now moving about slightly. Is not this the pattern of the Joke, in that an initial under-standing, quite strongly held, has to undergo an unexpected transformation? If human communication, and human perception itself, are of this form, it is hardly to be wondered at that we all take a spontaneous pleasure in rhythms and visual patterns in all of which there is a simultaneous preserva-tion and transformation – especially in the dance where both rhythm and pattern work together, and more especially when we are the performers ourselves?

It is no surprise to find that children delight in rhythm and play, for both have at their core that which makes us human animals, delighting in the discovery that something familiar has become satisfactorily 'defamilarized' in Viktor Shklovsky's fashion (Shklovsky, 1965). I used the word 'animals' deliberately. My family once had a cat that even in advanced years retained its fondness for play. In our garden we had a small plaster cast of Lupa, the female wolf that suckled Romulus and Remus at the origin of Rome, the cast itself not much bigger than the cat. More than once we saw the cat pretend to stalk it, leaping at it with evident delight (possibly at being able to get off scot free!). So the cat was able to appreciate at its own level the transforma-tion of an apparent threat into something perfectly safe, or at least an inanimate object into another animal to play with. Karl Groos, a Swiss writer on the play of animals and of man, notes how common it is for animals, such as a kitten, *to treat* an inanimate object, such as a ball, *as* prey, even starting it up again in its travel by patting it with its paw in order to chase it at once, pointing out that there seems to be an deliberate engagement in make-believe (Groos, 1898: 132).

Gregory Bateson, the anthropologist, has a useful definition of play:

> Those actions in which we now engage do not denote what those actions *for which they stand* would denote.
> (Bateson, 1978: 152)

On observing monkeys at play in San Francisco Zoo, he noted that a playful nip was not regarded as an act of aggression precisely because the 'attacking' monkey had a special grin on its face. One could say that the grin was a Second Clue that changed the apparent attack into one of play. It indicated that the actions in which it was engaged did not denote what they usually would, namely, an attack. A duality of interpretation was being maintained. The grin established another frame for the Ambiguous Element.

Now one can generalize his definition in a way that allows it to apply to the common structure of the Joke, the Story, perception and communication, for in every case a denotation is shown to be ambiguous, a 'single' referent is shown to be a combination of referents, a single selection from the Real to be shown to be open to correction from the selection of another person. The novel interpretation 'does not denote' what it originally denoted, and yet the new meaning can be shown (at least, that is the claim of the corrector) to accord with our first intentions, those very intentions now seen to be uncertain, though necessarily 'taken as' mutually certain.

In play, the fun lies in *tricking* the other into relying on a 'strong wrong' First Clue. Take a gambit in chess in which one player apparently performs a move which appears to be a fault but in reality is a temptation to the opponent to move in a predictable and self-weakening way. What kinds of play gain the applause in tennis? – Surely when one player's shot has the character of a decisive win, say, a shot from the net which drives the ball down and across, but the opponent instantaneously realizes that a ball in just that very direction and with just that force can be turned into an unreachable lob to the back of the court. Do not masters in jujitsu show aspirants to the sport how to take advantage of their opponent's very own momentum and turn it to their disadvantage? It is as if, as in the Joke or the Story, one player is attempting to force upon the other his or her definition of the shot. The shot, like a protagonist's mistaken view of the situation, may be strong, but it can perhaps be shown to be wrong, and the applause is loudest when the Second Clue that forces the reversal of the definition is completely unexpected and yet ideally appropriate, just as we laugh loudest at the punchline of a joke that takes us by surprise and yet by the same token proves its rightness. What deep unconscious satisfaction do millions have watching a James Bond film when they see him over and over again outwit the villain by taking advantage of some chance feature of the situation and surprising his attacker?

When Plato said in *The Laws* (II. ii) that Apollo and Dionysus were the 'leaders' of the Muses we can interpret that, as Nietzsche would, in seeing Apollo as the inspirer of harmony and agreement, and Dionysus as the challenger and innovator. It recalls too Friedrich Schiller's distinction between the 'form-drive' and the 'sense-drive', the contestation between them resolved by the 'play-drive' (Schiller, 1967 [1795]: 95–7). These can be readily matched to what we have discovered, in that

(1) the 'sense-drive' is the sensory experiences that we have, the brute registrations of what arrives at our sense organs;
(2) the 'form-drive' is the taken-for-granted agreement in selections from that sensory registration;
(3) the 'play-drive' is the novel interpretation that hopefully corrects that agreement, called 'play' precisely because it takes what was treated as fixed as corrigible, and in a way that still appears to satisfy our original motivations, our desires and fears.

7. Retrospect

Before going any further, here is a look back at what has been discovered so far.

First, a basic structure has been discerned in *all* jokes and riddles, which may be made multiple, but which at base depends on the ambiguation of originally neutral material. Another way of putting it would be to say that the mind is encouraged to make rival intentional selections from a varied field of blank evidence presented to it though any of the senses and any of the memories that we have gained from our sensory experience. The mind is *motivated* by pains or pleasures, and by the memories of those now invested with consequent fear or desire to select portions from this evidence which it may or may not have done successfully, so the joke hangs upon a tension between the disturbing and the harmless, the embarrassing and the reassuring, the frightening and the delightful, both interlocked by the ambiguous link.

The pattern, as so far simply (and as yet inadequately) diagrammed, consists first of an Ambiguous Element. This is not necessarily constant across the interpretations, for it is free to change its boundaries, even to the point of vacating them altogether (as in the Rubin Vase example), although overlaps of various kinds are the most common form of transformation. It should really therefore be called an ambiguous *region* with vague outlines. There has been a repeated warning that it would be a great mistake to believe that it was always the case that one entity changed wholly into another – many a conjuror, in order to trick us, takes advantage of this habitual tendency of our perception.

Developing associations that enrich the joke by bringing in further suggestive contexts to transform our understanding lie as an indefinite aura of connotation around any joke. There is clearly no logical limit to the interpretations that can be derived from one. It is as if the sensory evidence can go on being mined for further meanings, produced by the succession of new selections from the region that has become salient. Just as Shakespeare produced six meanings from one word in that remark of the Fool's about Lear's servants ('Thy asses are gone about them'), so we as readers, hearers and spectators can take up the evidence and re-examine it for more. In this, what we hear and see is no different from any other evidence. Just as a geophysicist can take up some layers of clay from alluvial deposits and first find out when they were laid down; then, compare the climate of the years in which they were deposited; then, from measuring the magnetic-pole direction of iron particles laid down in them, discover in which position the Earth's magnetic pole was thousands of years ago – so evidence goes on being open to further investigation. Jokes, being evidence about motivations in human life, are no different in this respect. And just as we can say if we like, that there was 'information' about the movement of the Earth's magnetic poles in the alluvial clay, we can say there is 'information' in the joke, but the word is really being loosely used as a metaphor, for the 'information' has to be selected by a mind before it deserves that term. There are unknown indicators about us and our histories in everything we say, but it requires a mind motivated to search in special ways in order to attribute meanings to them.

2
The Story

Typically, stories should go through transformations.
(Roy Schafer)

1.   The joke pattern in the Story

It was said some time ago by a writer on irony, G. G. Sedgwick, that 'the comic is composed of just such elements...as are found in many a tragic situation' (Sedgwick, 1967: 26). A linguist with a primary interest in humour, Salvatore Attardo, has noted the similarity between jokes and humorous stories (Attardo, 1994: 254–70). The claim in this book is that all stories *without exception* – tragic, comic, tragi-comic, plotless, absurd, tragical-historical-comical-pastoral – all correspond to the Joke structure we observed in Chapter 1. This is a large claim, often denied, but, proceeding with the step-by-step approach adopted so far, let us see if we can establish its credibility.

For what is a story? Simply, someone is in pursuit of a certain goal, and everything in the situation appears to conspire to make them think that something or someone will either – if it is a tragedy – contribute to that end, or – if it is a comedy – hinder that end. From the hearer of the story's point of view the clues the protagonist is depending on are discovered to be wildly misleading, and there are others he or she is missing which point in a contrary direction. The conclusion, in the simplest case, comes when the protagonist realizes his mistake – the mis-*take*. Furthermore, as we have learned from looking at the joke, there will be occasions when the protago nist signally fails to realize the mistake, and even occasions when the reader (or spectator) does not realize 'everything' that could be realized. Let us take a brief example to begin with, from Aesop's fables:

A wolf thought that by disguising himself he could get plenty to eat. Putting on a sheepskin to trick the shepherd, he joined the flock at grass without being discovered. At nightfall the shepherd shut him with the sheep in the fold and made it fast all around by blocking the entrance. Then, remembering that he needed a specially fat sheep for the feast at his daughter's wedding, he picked up his knife and slaughtered the biggest animal, which happened to be the wolf.

Assuming a character that does not belong to one can involve one in serious trouble. Such play-acting has cost many a man his life.

(Aesop, 1971: 38)

The wolf is the protagonist in pursuit of a goal, the killing of the sheep. The core element subject to his favourable interpretation is his own false appearance in among the flock, which he regards as one that will guarantee an ample satisfaction of his desires. The rival clue in this situation, the one to which he was blind, was the perspective of the shepherd, that included all the sheep in a gaze that saw them as possible choices for the fattest of roasts. This was the tragic pattern, for, though the wolf thought he was going to achieve a high satisfaction, it led to the cessation of all his desires. Notice how important motivation is to perceiving, how it governs how one chooses what one sees (Figure 37).

There was something ambiguous, which from one point of view promised the satisfaction of the protagonist's desires and from another denied them. It was the shepherd's looking for the fattest sheep that led to his choosing the disguised wolf, a visual element to which the wolf had paid no attention. This intensifies the wolf's 'tragedy', for part of the very feature that was to

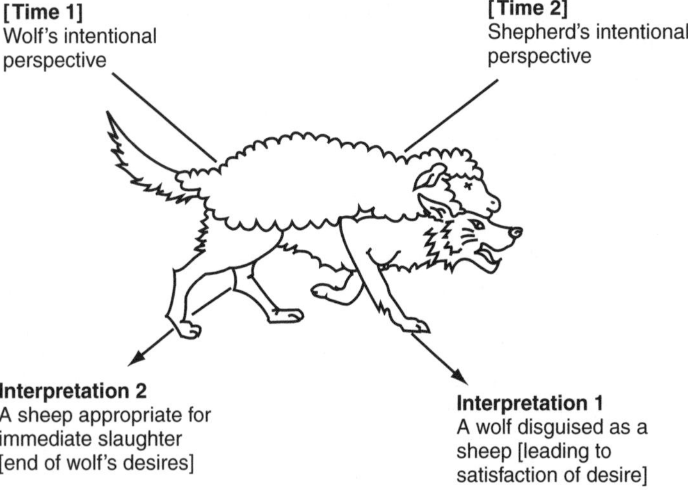

Figure 37

guarantee the plenitude of his desires, his disguise, became the salient one that ensured his death.

The structure is patently the same as that of the Joke, but with this difference, that, because this was of the Tragic Pattern (the protagonist under the belief that his interpretation would guarantee satisfaction of his desires and his commitment to it being the cause of the very opposite), the meaning shifts from happiness to catastrophe. The Joke, as we have seen, offers us an escape from the threatening to the harmless, earthing the dangerous potential; hence the laughter, being the physical release, in those convulsions of the diaphragm, of the energy called up by the fear in preparation for action. Of course, in the type of joke that results in the Hearer's discomfiture, this release is enjoyed by the Joker.

It is no surprise that the Story should have the same structure as the Joke, for we guessed as much when we considered the Fool's pun. Look at this from *Othello*:

> OTHELLO: Put out the light, and then put out the light.
> If I quench thee, thou flaming minister,
> I can again thy former light restore,
> Should I repent me: – but once put out thy light,
> I know not where is that Promethean heat
> That can thy light relume.
>   (*Othello*, V, ii, lines 7–13)

With what he spells out for us, the ambiguous structure of the first line falls neatly into the fivefold pattern (Figure 38).

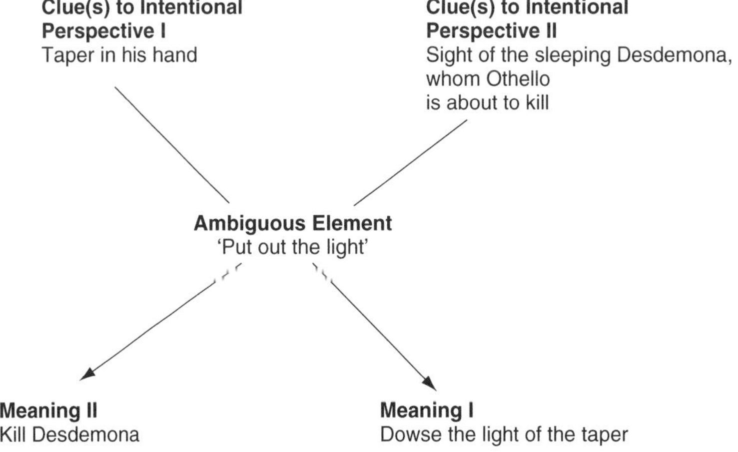

Figure 38

The contrast between the two meanings could not be sharper: the mere dowsing of a taper on the one hand, the killing of his wife on the other. Again we can pursue further ambiguities, for we know ahead that time is to render his reflection on the impossibility of 'reluming' Desdemona's life as one fraught with warning of which he takes no heed.

For a story of the Comic Pattern, one in which an Ambiguous Element is subject to ever better interpretations, is this Japanese folk-tale, 'The Crows and the Archers':

A flock of crows were gathered in a forest to try out the fledglings that were come of age to fly alone, to test their wit and determine whether or not they were worthy of being received into the company of their elders, and there were three young ones at the bar-of-question.

Said the leader of the flock to the first younker: 'Answer me this: What is of all things in this lower world the most dread and fearsome?'

The bantling replied: 'An arrow.'

Whereat all the crows flapped their wings *hata-taki* in august approval, and the sire of the hatchling preened himself in satisfaction. To this the examiner answered: 'Thou sayest sooth, and art a full-fledged member of the flock.'

Then he demanded of the second: 'What is thy answer?'

The candidate responded: 'I count the skilful archer more to be feared than the arrow, for without the archer to shoot it, the arrow were no more than this branch on which I perch!'

At that all the crows cawed *ka-a-ka-a* in admiration, while the father of the prodigy was speechless with pride. And the leader, scratching his poll with his claw, replied: 'Clearly thou art right, and I pass thee.'

Lastly he asked the third of the minors, 'What hast thou to say?'

Returned the junior: 'I count both wrong. It is the unskilful bowman that maketh my blood run cold and my pinfeathers stand up.'

When they heard this, all the assemblage sat dumb with astonishment, and the leader-crow asked: 'How sayest thou?'

'Why,' answered the crowling, 'with the skilful archer a crow hath only to flirt to one side or other when he heareth the twang of the bow-thong, and the shaft misseth him. But as for the archer who lacketh skill, when the cord twangeth, one knoweth not whether to sit still or fly, for which-ever one doth one hath no surety of safety.'

Now at this sapiency in one but three moons out of shell, all made obeisance before him, and the leader, deeming his headship in danger, took flight forthwith nor stayed wing till he was come to the next province; and as for the wise one, the flock made him their leader in his place.

(Wheeler, 1984: 5–6)

It can be analysed as in Figure 39. The elder crows have quite rightly taken a *dangerous* situation as their test example and wish to know which of the young crows will be able to produce the best account of it, that is, the interpretation that will guarantee the best course of action when it presents itself, namely, that of a human archer taking aim with bow-and-arrow. At each step what appears to be an adequate piece of advice is elicited: each young crow reflects on the situation and comes up with his own analysis. Interpretations are concerned with the future, what is to be done when what looks like the same evidence presents itself again. When we drew those arrows in the diagrams of the jokes, they signified more than a mere mental connection, for they pointed ahead in time as to how the evidence should be handled. This is what most human concepts are: recipes for future behaviour with some not-exactly-precise recurrence in the flow of the Real, outside us or inside us.

Notice the applause from the elders of the community at each stage of the story. That flapping of wings and noisy cawing were an acknowledgement that they had recognized *authority* in the interpretation presented, yet the story plainly shows how that communal approval was no guarantee of a final authority, for it passed from one young crow to the next. One is reminded of Hayden White's comment on narrative:

> And this raises the suspicion that narrative in general, from the folktale to the novel, from the annals to the fully realized 'history', has to do with the topics of law, legality, legitimacy, or, more generally, *authority*.
> (White, 1981: 17)

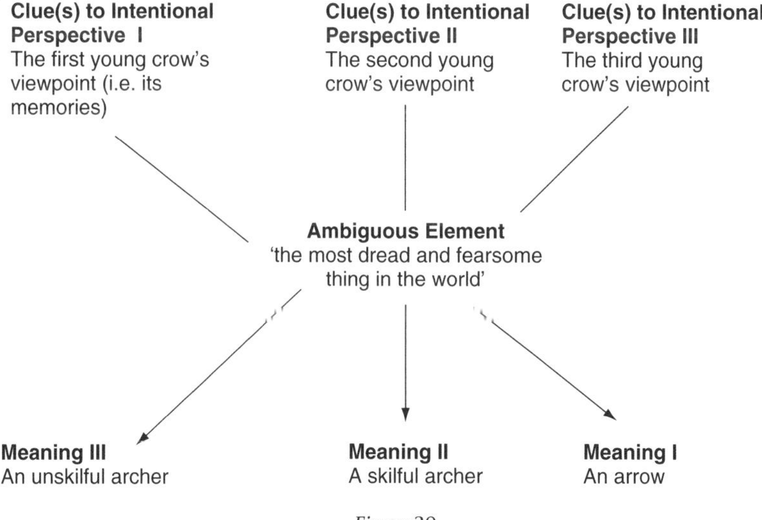

Figure 39

Anyone, for example, who is tempted to equate author*ity* with the author-*ities* will find an allegory here of how authority is rather something that is continually passed on from one to another like a baton in a race.

So Aesop is not to be mocked for the 'moral' that he attached at the end of each of his fables, as he did here, for it was the first step in the further interpretation of his story, a clue to a new intentional perspective on *the whole story* as Ambiguous Element, a story which already depended for its dynamic on the transformation of understanding. One can say that the core transformation at the heart of the Story or Joke provides us with the very same structure for seeing more in it that we saw at first glance. We can draw a 'moral' of our own. We must be like the succession of young crows: it was the last young crow that was deemed the wisest for recognizing the danger of uncertainty, the absence of clear and continuing interpretation in the threat of the unskilled archer, likely in his ignorance and lack of skill to produce the worst outcome.

This crow community are thus ready to see their story as one of the Comic Pattern since all are left in what is thought to be a better position of preparedness than at the start, though the third young crow's analysis, correctly interpreted, contains undoubtedly the message that the best laid schemes o' crows and men 'gang aft a-gley, / An' lea'e us nought but grief an' pain, /For promis'd joy!' So there is a shade of the Tragic too in this reminder of the inadequacy of all our concepts to capture the real.

2.   The Story in advertisements

We have seen in advertisements how advertising agents exploit the Joke, particularly in the form of a pun. It is no surprise to find that they are driven to exploit the Story in exactly the same way. To draw the passer-by into a story is to tempt him or her into taking up an intentional perspective favourable to the product: the very process of moving our judgement from one interpretation to another tends to encourage the fixing of the correction we have arrived at, especially if we have been induced to laugh. A laugh is a guarantee that we share and thus enjoy the superior position of having the better interpretation.

Take a television advertisement put out by one of the instant-coffee firms not so long ago. A man is entertaining an attractive girl, having persuaded her into his flat, and she expresses a desire for a cup of real coffee. A fleeting expression of dismay on his face reveals to us that he does not have any real coffee to give her, but he conceals this fact from the girl as he wishes to preserve an appearance of wealth and sophistication. We see him going into the kitchen out of the girl's sight, where he proceeds to boil a kettle and fill cups with powdered coffee. However, we see him turn on a hand-mixer which gives a whirring sound similar to that of a coffee-grinder and then make a hissing sound himself imitating the sound of a coffee-maker coming to the boil. These are the needful Second Clues which are going to govern the girl's assessment of the coffee when she comes to drink it: that taste is to be the Ambiguous Element. We see his gleeful expression all the time and are this seduced into sharing the mischievous enjoyment of the deceit. It is, of course, entirely successful, for when he brings in the coffee, the girl expresses her approval of the taste, the noises as Second Clues having ensured her false intentional perspective.

The advertising tactic is not so much that of proving to us onlookers that the taste of X's instant coffee is as good as that of real coffee, but of drawing us in on the pleasure of the irony of deceiving the girl. That pleasure of superiority of judgement (seeing the girl's false intentional perspective and being safely aware of the true intentional perspective) in the course of a sexual seduction is what is secretly drafted onto the brand of instant coffee, so that next time we are in the supermarket, this feeling will attach itself to that brand of instant coffee so that we buy it unthinkingly. What the advertiser distinctly does *not* want you to do is to see through the ploy yourself: he prefers you to be in the position of the girl – you are to remain unaware of the deeper ambiguity through being seduced by the surface one.

Next time you turn on the TV, look for advertisements that include a *visual transformation* of any kind. Having found one, look for the clues that establish the rival intentional perspectives. To give you an example, Rowntree, the chocolate manufacturer, produces a chocolate bar that goes by the name of 'Lion Bar'. The agent who created the advertisement looked busily for something to tie the bar to the name: he or she found it in the cracking open of the bar, for, when that is done, the rough edge and the glutinous strands of the filling could be said to have a rough resemblance to the opening jaws and teeth of a lion. So he or she instructed the film-maker to put in a lion's roar on the sound-track as a Second Clue to synchronize with the cracking open of the bar: *voilà*, a visual joke. It was surprisingly effective because the roar was a frightening enough one to transform those broken edges into a nightmarish jaw and the strands into teeth – indeed, its non-lionlike qualities gave it an additional monstrous unpleasantness that strengthened the joke. In any run of half a dozen advertisements some such transformation will be found. Be alert for the Second Clue or Clues that tempt the would-be buyer into performing the transformation.

These transformations illustrate a philosophical point that will be returned to later. One cannot specify a precise moment common to everyone when A turns into B, that is, the moment at which the breaking Lion Bar turns into the mouth of a roaring lion, for it is the judgement of each onlooker that effects the transformation. Just when one person notices the effect of the Second Clue will differ from that when another does. Note that the degree of similarity does not have to be very great if the Second Clues are powerful enough. As we have seen with the Joke, a fudge will work successfully, even if what appear to be obvious countervailing clues are present.

When next a prudish person accuses you of being dirty-minded for seeing the top of a bottle close to a model's mouth on the wine or male perfume advertisement as distinctly phallic, ask them to consider the following. Imagine a hundred pictures drawn to the following requirements. No. 1 shows the top of a bottle close to the model's mouth. All the ones between 1 and 100 show a gradual transformation of the bottle into a penis, No. 100 being unmistakable. Now these are now presented to two experimental subjects, one, A, who has them presented to him or her successively from 1 to 100 and another, B, who sees them successively from 100 to 1. Now it is obvious that it will be some time before A perceives the trick that is being played on him: it may not be until he gets to No. 75 that he calls out his realization of what is being perpetrated. On the other hand, B is likely to go on seeing the penis until No. 15 or so.

It is not very difficult, given this demonstration (which hardly needs an empirical test!), to understand the trickery that goes on in an actual story. It also lends support to the psychoanalysts, who maintain that we are affected by unconscious associations even when we may protest that we have no such thought in our conscious mind. Freud's 'cigar that is sometimes just a cigar' is never really just a cigar – what Second Clues are in the surroundings or in the mind of any observer or the smoker himself, consciously or unconsciously, cannot be ignored. So although the advertising agent who protests that he or she had no thought of any sexual connotation in the picture provided may be telling a truth on the *conscious* level, yet if he or she, after reading this, goes on protesting that no such *unconscious* intention was in their minds, we shall be right to call them disingenuous. If they tell stories in their advertisements, then they must accept the fact that the tale is not controllable by the Teller: it is an Ambiguous Element for which we as Hearers can provide unexpected Second Clues.

There are stories implicit in many advertisements. Take this one by NatWest (Figure 40). You as the tyro entrepreneur are part of this story, originally down on the ground fearful of the risks of the height of business activity. Here the bank has raised you up with a reliable system of pulleys and ropes, and, though you are high in the air, you now need have no fears, able to get on with your profitable venture. The pun in the slogan 'We'll help you get your business off the ground', is aided by the picture, which gives a First Clue to the *literal* sense of 'off the ground' by showing someone palpably off the ground; the Second Clues are the instructions given below on how to contact NatWest. There are also other metaphorical connotations in the picture from the cleaning of a window, suggesting that the view you now have of your business future is to be cleared; further still, there is shown a picture of a large and glossy office building – also 'off the ground' of its planning – which you will one day own and thus be able to employ such cleaners as these. There is also another minor Ambiguous Element: the letter 'O' in the word 'ACTION' across the bottom of the advertisement is

Figure 40

three things at once – the letter 'O', the NatWest logo, and an electric button, which gives the metaphorical impression of one's getting *immediate* service from the bank.

Sometimes, exceedingly irritated by advertisements in the cinema, where, unlike for those on the TV, one cannot turn the volume off – and the volume in some cinemas is often excruciatingly loud! – I determinedly focus

my attention on those portions of the screen on which I am not supposed
to be concentrating. It requires a good deal of conscious will-power, for the
designer of the advertisement is skilled at anticipating where one would
normally look next, for example, at the bright eyes or figure of the fetching
model, but after a while one can amuse oneself in this way, discovering all
sorts of interesting random detail that one was meant to overlook because it
does not contribute to the story's demands. Such detail cannot be ruled out,
for one can still choose to see something, an chance oddity in the background, a pattern, a rhythmic succession, some supposedly negligible
feature, that the director had consigned to the background everyone is
presumed to ignore; one can even see something as something else in the
manner of Hamlet and Polonius when they were looking at a cloud – were
parts of the cloud a weasel, a camel or a whale? (and each may have seen a
different part of the cloud as 'the' animal). The effort and interest of this
strategy is often successful enough to prevent me hearing the words I am
supposed to be understanding, so that they recede into a babble of
nonsense, ceasing to be words at all. It is pleasing to defeat the advertiser at
his own game, using the very same technique as he is practising upon me.

Here is another philosophically interesting point: one usually thinks that
one could never escape hearing words, especially blasted at one at a high
level of decibels, but it proves to be quite achievable. One would also loosely
believe that one is forced to see the obvious objects presented to one in the
visual field, but one can determinedly see something else instead, given
sufficient motivation – and you can imagine how angry I am in the cinema
on such occasions. Just as the psychoanalyst may give the patient a
'Rorschach' test, in which he or she, driven by inner obsessions, is encouraged to find pictures in the random splash of an inkblot folded over on
itself, so one can choose not to see what is in front of one's nose. What this
demonstrates is *the power of motivation* in the process of seeing and hearing:
the sensory input remains the same, but there is clearly a module in the
brain, guided by feeling, that does the choosing of what object-shapes to
project into it – camels, weasels or whales.

3.   The 'plotless' story

In all the stories we have looked at so far, the course of events has followed
the line of a plot: at its simplest, the protagonist or protagonists have a
strongly held false view to which they obstinately hold; *the faint right clues*
appear, becoming gradually obvious to the discerning hearer, reader or
member of an audience, and these clues point to a better assessment of the
situation; the story, comic or tragic, proceeds by intensifying *the strong
wrong clues* taken up by the protagonists and increasing the obviousness of
the countervailing clues; the story ends with what Aristotle called the
peripeteia (the 'around [*peri-*] -forcing' [*-pet*]), that is, the forcing around of

the intentional perspective) at which point the scales fall from the eyes of the protagonists and they, for better or worse, perceive both interpretations, if not all their implications.

But not all stories follow this sequence with the gestalt-switch at the end known to protagonist and reader alike. All that is minimally required is that the reader is made aware of the rival perspectives; there is no necessity that we witness a sudden, final discovery by the protagonist. On the contrary, the reader may discover the rival perspectives that the protagonist knew all along; or the latter may never become aware of them. Literary critics of *Othello* are generally agreed that Othello, though apprised of his major misconception about his wife, never achieves an understanding of why both he and she were so vulnerable to the kind of attack Iago mounts against them, nor to what degree they both carry a measure of blame for what happened. Thus one can say that, although *Othello* has a recognizable plot, is indeed perhaps the most neatly plotted of all Shakespeare's tragedies, it nevertheless retains something of a plotless character: an irony invests it which is outside the reach of the characters themselves and does not depend on the chronological progress, albeit devious, of their understanding.

A poem of Thomas Hardy's, 'The Shadow on the Stone', can provide us with an unusual example of a plotless story because of its own awareness of the basic ironic structure:

> I went by the Druid stone
> That broods in the garden white and lone,
> And I stopped and looked at the shifting shadows
> That at some moments fall thereon
> From the tree hard by with a rhythmic swing,
> And they shaped in my imagining
> To the shade that a well-known head and shoulders
> Threw there when she was gardening.
>
> I thought her behind my back,
> Yea, her I long had learned to lack,
> And I said: 'I am sure you are standing behind me.
> Though how do you get into this old track?'
> And there was no sound but the fall of a leaf
> As a sad response, and to keep down grief
> I would not turn my head to discover
> That there was nothing in my belief.
>
> Yet I wanted to look and see
> That nobody stood and the back of me;
> But I thought once more: 'Nay, I'll not unvision
> A shape which, somehow, there may be.'

> So I went on softly from the glade,
>   And left her behind me throwing her shade,
> As she were indeed an apparition –
>   My head unturned lest my dream should fade.

Here the persona in the poem, that is, the imagined speaker, himself plays with our familiar basic structure. The Ambiguous Element he chooses is a chance shadow thrown upon the 'Druid stone'. In his grief-stricken state for his beloved who has died he perceives in a random shadow thrown by some leaves her outline as if she were gardening there, standing behind him. Knowing full well that it cannot be such a shadow, he plays with the ghostly possibility of her being there. This, on a higher level, is the same trick of the imagination that allowed me to subvert the advertisements in the cinema, turn the outer world into a Rorschach test, and see what the desiring mind prefers to see. Hardy's persona in the poem says that, to subdue his grief, he deliberately does not turn his head to prove to himself that she is not there. He has a moment in which he is tempted to do so, and then resolutely does not, leaving the garden without looking back. The analysis of his own imaginative play is thus as follows in Figure 41.

He is aware of the rival perspectives, but, to give himself the false impression that she is still there, he refuses to turn his head, ostensibly *denying*

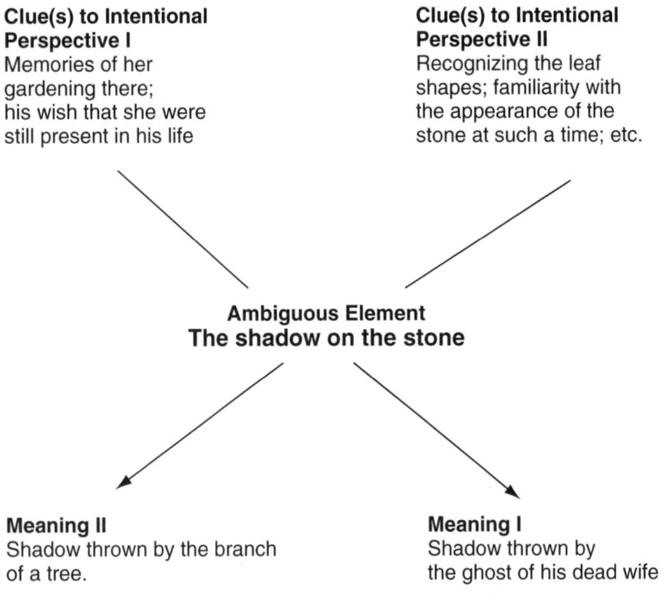

Figure 41

himself the Second Clue. Of course, this is a pretence, since there are plenty of other Second Clues that prove the same thing, a fact of which he is perfectly well aware, so one can draw a diagram for that clue itself as an Ambiguous Element as in Figure 42.

Hardy the man already had made ghostly associations with this stone. It had been found lying in his garden under three feet of earth with some signs of a fire and half-charred bones (see Bailey, 1970: 412–13). He had had it dug up and upended like a monolith. When a friend, Clive Holland, visited him in 1898, Hardy took him out to it for a photograph to be taken, and while this was in progress Hardy asked, with a smile, 'Do you believe in ghosts? If you do, you ought to see such manifestations here, on a moonlit night.' The second Mrs Hardy once told a friend of hers that Hardy one day found his wife burning all his love-letters to her behind this stone. This poem was begun in 1913, a year after his wife's death and completed in 1916.

This context of composition leads one to interpret further. There is an inconsistency in the persona's attitude: on the one hand he claims that he

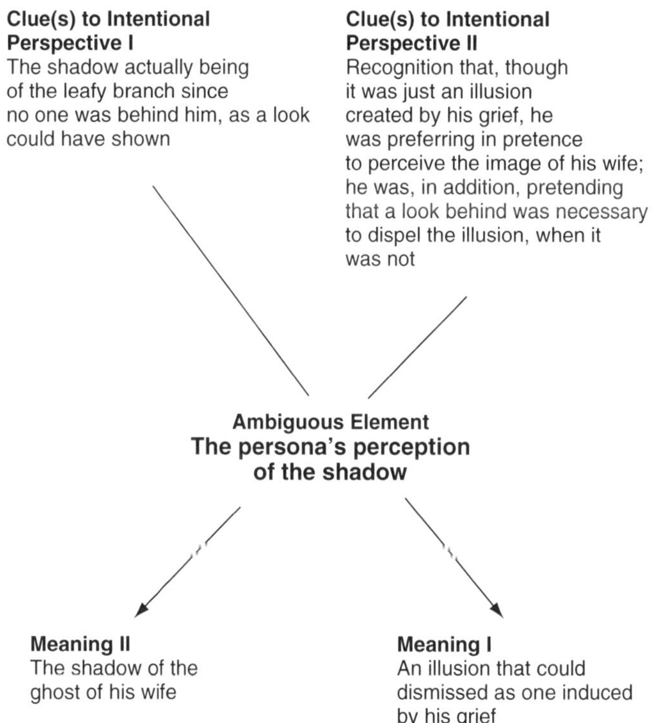

Figure 42

had 'long learned to lack her', that is, his grief was now under control; on the other, his very refusal to turn his head betrays a unexorcized wish for her presence. The writing of the poem, if taken as an act of the persona, shows a wish to be guided by 'dream', by imagination, and thus to play with interpretation and its dynamic structure, so the persona becomes a poet himself, so skilled in the ambiguating of sights and situations that he can disambiguate too, in the imagined withholding of a clue. He transforms other aspects of the moment: (1) that it is the 'Druid stone' makes the shifting shadow take on a ghostly association, and Hardy himself has contributed to sharpening those very associations, not merely in the exchange with Holland in the garden, but in his other poems and novels (consider Stonehenge in the penultimate chapter of *Tess of the D'Urbervilles*); (2) he addresses a question to one he knows is not present as if she were, as guaranteed by the shadow-shape; (3) the fall of a leaf is 'a sad response' to it, an image that ingeniously takes advantage of the customary connotations of autumn's passing; (4) he professes not to know how 'somehow' the shape is there, when he himself is the maker of it; (5) he goes on 'softly' from the glade as if not to disturb the ghost. For each of these the basic ironic structure is evident. There is no advance of 'plot', for the rival meanings are co-present throughout, intensifying the significance of these minor ambiguities. Our pleasure in the poem arises both from sharing the persona's deliberate ambiguous play and then turning our own intentional perspectives on what he does with that play. There is no one moment of *peripeteia*, no sudden final realization for persona or reader: the aesthetic effect grows with the depth of our interpretation, stimulated by the persona's own aesthetic expertise.

4. 'Nonsense'

'Nonsense' has been put in inverted commas to make plain that, in any written presentation of something ostensibly with 'no sense', it will in fact produce sense, even if it was written by someone insane. The mind cannot help but impute meanings to it, consciously or unconsciously. It could only be meaningless if the circumstances were such that attention was withdrawn by some quirk of motivation, when the printed page would not even be seen as a printed page, as blank of meaning as if it were before the eyes of a newborn baby (imagine someone lost in a brown study, considering something of immense importance to them, with a newspaper by chance open in front of them). We treat nonsense in the manner of an artist who produces some 'found art', calling some fragment of driftwood she has picked up on the beach 'Eagle in Flight', in that we are at once tempted to project meanings into a random array. Just as we see faces in the fire, so too nonsense works upon us to work upon it. We have already seen how apparently nonsensical jokes can nevertheless carry a hidden potential for disturbing us.

Indeed, though human beings have laughed at many a joke, it has needed philosophers from Hobbes onwards to point to the concealed threat in a joke, the hint of insult, embarrassment or fear. Take this misprint from a newspaper:

> She was married in Barnoldswick, Lancashire, to Arthur Wormsley, and to this onion were born three children.

Is it a child's story with onions as people? Is it an insult to the Wormsleys, calling him or her an 'onion', suggesting that a stinging smell emanates from them or that there are layers of concealment in their natures or that they were as negligible as persons as this humble vegetable? It even starts to ignite the syllable 'Worm' in his name into some kind of literalness, the onion harbouring a worm, a fault, an unpleasant threat. Sense will invade the 'nonsense', do what we will, for it will resonate somehow with our most intimate fears and desires, the more so, as the psychoanalysts remind us, for getting at us in this indirect fashion. Shakespeare was quite happy to use 'nonsense' when it suited him:

> ENOBARBUS [speaking of the unlamented death of Antony's wife, Fulvia]:…
> the tears live in an onion that would water this sorrow.
> (William Shakespeare, *Antony and Cleopatra*, I, ii, 171–3)

Naturally, we at once make sense of this by figurative association: 'onions make you cry; such tears express no emotion; therefore, there is no need to cry for Fulvia since you are really happy to be free of her' – but the words are strictly nonsensical, for can tears 'live in' an onion? How can tears living in such an onion water sorrow as one would water a plant? Enobarbus, being well aware of Antony's intentional perspective, can have no fear that his 'nonsense' will go uninterpreted. So 'nonsense' does not resist interpretation: it merely awaits a human intentional perspective. When Pyramus and Thisbe called upon the wall 'to stand aside' they knew what they meant. As we shall see later, figurative expressions are based on the same structure as that of the Joke.

Here is an absurd story by a Russian surrealist writer which is significantly named 'Optical Illusion':

> Semyon Semyonovich, having put on his glasses, looks at a pine tree and sees that a peasant is sitting in the pine tree and shaking his fist at him.
> Semyon Semyonovich, having taken off his glasses, looks at the pine tree and sees that nobody is sitting in the pine tree.
> Semyon Semyonovich, having put on his glasses, looks at the pine tree and sees again that a peasant is sitting in the pine tree and shaking his fist at him.

> Semyon Semyonovich, having taken off his glasses, again sees that nobody is sitting in the pine tree.
>
> Semyon Semyonovich, having put on his glasses, looks at the pine tree again, sees that a peasant is sitting in the pine tree and is shaking his fist at him.
>
> Semyon Semyonovich doesn't want to believe in this phenomenon and decides it is an optical illusion.
>
> (Kharms, 1971: 68)

A reader who has read this book up to here comes armed with an intentional perspective to make sense of this, for the word 'illusion' in the title fore-warns you. It is actually about the alternation of intentional perspectives, presumably from a false one to a true one. At first sight, as we say, because one usually sees better with glasses than without them, the peasant in the pine tree shaking his fist is the genuine undistorted sight. But since nothing is genuine in the strict sense here, what can we take a hostile peasant in a tree to be? A turn to the psychoanalysts will give us what they call a 'return of the repressed', particularly because it occurs with such obstinate repeti-tion, under a 'repetition compulsion'. This is a state in which the neurotic person is driven to repeat the circumstances which surrounded a traumatic experience in the vain hope of bringing it under control, even though the repetition is a painful one. Here the image of the threat being high in a tree indicates a phallic height and dominance; the fact that it is a peasant, someone not important in the social order, of a type who has rebelled in the past, also emphasizes the libidinous charge in the image. Semyon even has a name that reminds him of his place in the social-familial order: Semyon 'son of Semyon' (Semyon-ovich), expected to be the same as his father and yet not (in not being allowed to desire the mother). The taking-off of the glasses becomes the neurotic's resistance to the return of the repressed; the putting them on again an acknowledgement of its presence. Semyon is like someone who alternates between wanting to laugh at a joke and then refusing to because he discovers a threat in it not to his taste, that is, he accepts the two rival intentional perspectives that create the joke and then rejects one of them in order to deny that there is a joke at all; someone who is the victim of a joke or someone too embarrassed to admit to the recogni-tion of some obscene meaning often does just this. Semyon finally deceiving himself with his declaration that it is 'an optical illusion' can represent the neurotic's desperate refusal to accede to what is trying to emerge from his unconscious. No doubt other interpretations could be found for this story, but the one above is certainly defensible (for a compa-rable analysis of Edward Lear's nonsense verse 'The Owl and the Pussy-Cat' see Elizabeth Wright, 1999: 13–17). The uneasy humour of the story comes from the apparently nonsensical situation and the (uncertain) security of the reader who feels, because he is the reader of a nonsense story, that such helpless crossings-back-and-forth are not for the likes of him – which unfortunately has the result of turning the joke upon the reader, who has no right to feel so secure, and who has often been in a situation in which he or she did their best to pretend that an unwanted fact was not stubbornly factual. So nonsense does not protect us from ourselves, the would-be-detached readers, becoming Ambiguous Elements in our turn, as Laurence Sterne, the author of *Tristram Shandy* well knew. It does appear that jokes and stories have an insidious way of getting under our skin. They are like dreams forced upon us and have the same power as dreams do of unearthing unconscious forces that we would prefer to keep buried.

5.   The long story

Finally we come to the long story. The structure is exactly the same, and, furthermore, the structure is the same as that of all the stories you as reader find within the story.

In the standard realistic novel, one is presented with the protagonist pursuing his or her *strong wrong clues* while you are delicately provided with the saving hints, the *faint right ones*, the Second Clues, that save you from such a predicament. The skill with which the author slips in the faint right clues may defeat you for a while, so that it is not until you are well within the text that you suddenly become aware of what is happening, at which point faint clues you have missed, if not all of them, become retrospectively obvious to you. At that point, being comfortably out of the predicament that surrounds the protagonist, you can, from your position of superior knowledge, enjoy the rival perspective denied to him or her.

For this same technique of indirection in classical literature Jane Austen's novel *Emma* offers a prime source, both at the level of the main plot and at the level of detail. One could say that even to an unskilled reader the book's opening paragraph itself is a faint Second Clue to the forthcoming ambiguation of the character Emma herself:

> Emma Woodhouse, handsome, clever, and rich, with a comfortable home and happy disposition, seemed to unite some of the best blessings of existence; and had nearly twenty-one years in the world with very little to distress or vex her.
>
> (Austen, 1960 [1816]: I, 1, 5)

The skilled reader knows full well that what is to be looked for is someone with a penchant for strong wrong clues, that is, someone who is likely to stick stubbornly by their view of themselves, one who has not experienced those challenges to one's picture of one's own personality which render them better able to handle the disturbing shifts of self-understanding that come to haunt us all. Notice that Austen begins with what looks like the end of a book, the only thing missing being a husband, equally handsome, clever, and rich, but that list has an overweening look of hubris about it. Only the word 'seemed' gives the faintest of warnings about this idyllic concatenation of qualities, plus the fact that any parent or even future husband would have the right to be highly suspicious of someone who has reached twenty 'with very little to distress or vex her'.

And the first chapter has not gone by before there are soundings of the danger that will accrue to Emma from a dubious predilection of hers for trying to engineer wedding matches between people in her circle, for which she is reproved in due form by the 'sensible' Mr Knightley, of whom we soon come to know that we have to regard him as our moral touchstone. There is also a warning from her hypochondriac father, who sees it as a disturbance of reassuring habit, even though his judgement of his daughter, that she 'never thinks of herself, if she can do good to others', is wildly adrift from that of the perspicacious Mr Knightley's judgement of her, who specifically warns her off the next attempt she proposes, with Mr Elton, the local parson, of whom he says, 'Depend upon it, a man of six-and-twenty can take care of himself.'

The first half of the novel is largely taken up with the course of Emma's campaign to marry Mr Elton off to one Harriet Smith, the illegitimate daughter of someone unknown, who had been placed as a parlour-boarder at a school run by a Mrs Goddard, whose company at cards was often in request by Emma's father. It is when she is described from Emma's point of view that faint clues to the unsatisfactoriness of Emma's judgement of her become plain to the discerning reader. If you take Emma's plan to marry Elton off to Harriet as the Ambiguous Element, then her valuing of Harriet will be a significant part of her Intentional Perspective on that plan (Figure 43).

Observe then the faintest of Second Clues in the following, when we are given some insight into how Emma assesses Harriet:

> She was not struck by anything remarkably clever in Miss Smith's conversation, but she found her altogether very engaging – not inconveniently shy, not unwilling to talk – and yet so far from pushing, showing so proper and becoming a deference, seeming so pleasantly grateful for being admitted to Hartfield, and so artlessly impressed by the appearance of everything in so superior a style to what she had been used to, that she must have good sense and deserve encouragement.
>
> (Austen, 1960 [1816]: I, iii, 23)

What is slyly betrayed here is Emma's own vanity. As one who enjoys being deferred to, who likes the gratitude expressed for what constitutes very little effort on her part, and the aura that surrounds her from the effect of her surroundings, the splendid mansion she lives in, she is too quick to come to her final conclusion that Harriet has 'good sense'. It is the very strength of her

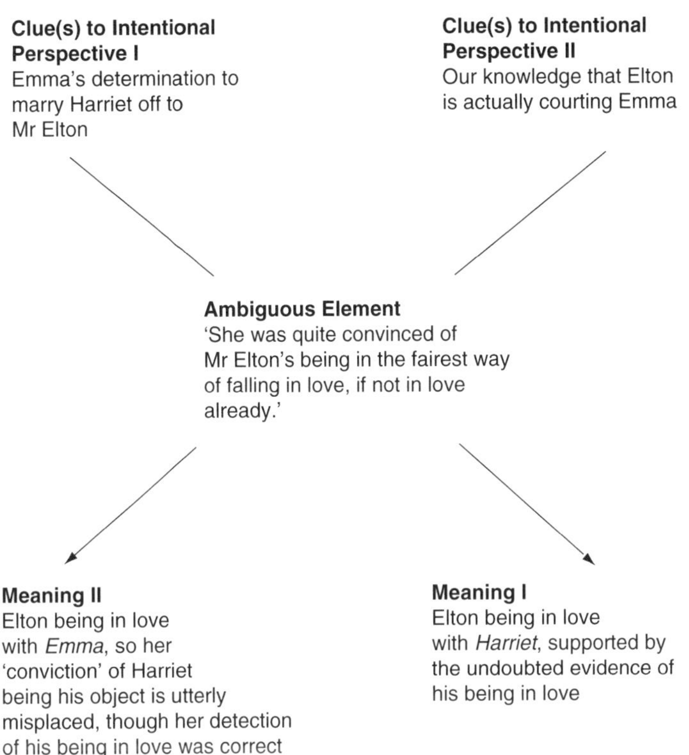

Figure 43

deference to Emma that is to prove one of the causes of Emma's undoing, as Austen continually reminds us. The deference is taken by Emma as a strong wrong clue of the 'good sense', whereas it is a faint right one, pointing to an imbalance in their relationship, with Harriet perilously taking Emma's counsel as gospel.

From the point of view of this book one of the most fascinating of Emma's rationalizations occurs when a real *riddle* is in question. Here we have again the tendency of the tribe of authors and poets to embed in the detail of their works demonstrations of the very structure they are exploiting at the level of their plot, made all the more powerful here since the clever Emma credits herself with being a good solver of riddles, just as Oedipus did. Harriet, as one of her amusements, was given to the collecting and transcribing of riddles, and Emma had set about assisting her in the project. The riddle is one that Mr Elton had written himself to add to that list, though he coyly claimed that it was the work of 'a friend of his', and specifically says that he 'does not offer it for Miss Smith's collection' since it is his friend's, but pushes it across the table *to Emma* 'with a look of deep consciousness'. It reads as follows:

To Miss ——
CHARADE

My first displays the wealth and pomp of kings,
    Lords of the earth! their luxury and ease.
Another view of man, my second brings,
    Behold him there, the monarch of the seas!
But, ah! united, what reverse we have!
    Man's boasted power and freedom all are flown;
Lord of the earth and sea, he bends a slave,
    And woman, lovely woman, reigns alone.
Thy ready wit the word will soon supply,
    May its approval beam in that soft eye!
        (Austen, 1960 [1816]: I, ix, 71–2)

Before considering Emma's own reading, let us analyse it in the familiar way (Figure 44).

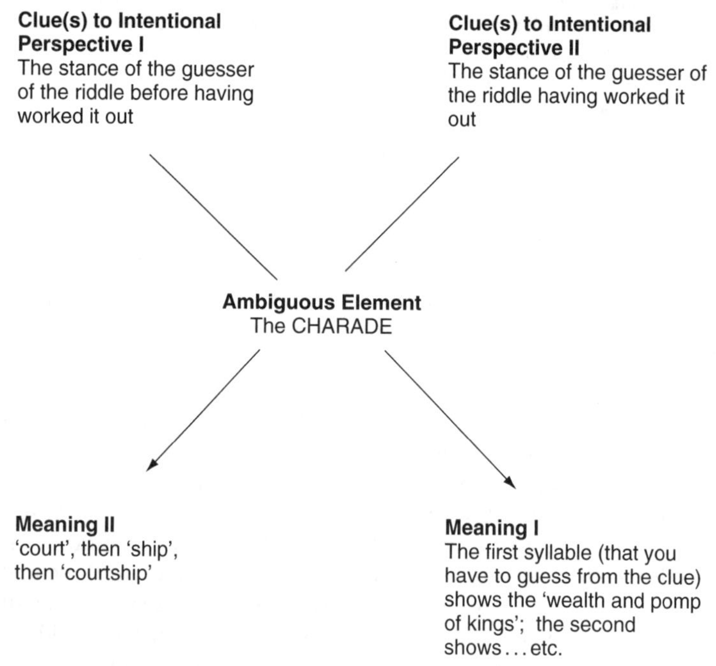

Figure 44

Emma gets the meaning at once, a proof of her own 'ready wit'. Again, her cleverness in interpretation is displayed, but it is blind to itself in this regard, for she cannot help but note that the term 'ready wit' is singularly inapplicable to Harriet: 'Humph –' she thinks, 'Harriet's ready wit! All the better. A man must be very much in love indeed, to describe her so' (1960 [1816]: I, ix, 72). The Ambiguous Element, this phrase in the riddle, is being determinedly exposed to Emma's false Intentional Perspective, so that its actually being a Second Clue to the major ambiguity of the situation, that the riddle is addressed to her, plus the fact that it was pushed towards her with that 'look of deep consciousness', is as determinedly misread. The reader sees immediately that Harriet is quite unable to solve the riddle, and, what is more, she is hardly to be persuaded at first that it is addressed to her, showing a disinclination to copy down the last two lines as having special significance for her – she may be 'dull', but not so dull as not to be able to sense that 'ready wit' is a quality she does not possess.

The riddle sequence comes to a close when later in the evening Elton returns and discovers that 'his friend's' riddle has been copied into Harriet's collection, Emma having said that the 'friend' may be 'sure of every woman's approbation while he writes with such gallantry'. Elton's response to this. which he can only interpret as encouragement from Emma, is given with a special emphasis:

> 'I have no hesitation in saying – at least if my friend feels at all as I do – I have not the smallest doubt that, could he see his little effusion honoured as *I* see it' (looking at the book again and replacing it on the table), 'he would consider it as the proudest moment of his life.'

Emma is glad to see him go, feeling that 'there was a sort of parade in his speeches which was very apt to incline her to laugh', at which point she 'ran away to indulge the inclination, leaving the tender and sublime of pleasure to Harriet's share'. That she should be tempted to laugh reveals the presence of ambiguity, but the 'parade' at which she laughs would not have been such a source of mirth if it had been given its correct interpretation. The excess she detected was that of his very seriousness concerning her, but also a sign of the hypocrisy of the man which betrays itself to her although she does not know the cause, for his professions of love are false, as the final outcome proves only too readily.

This first part of the novel comes to its end with Mr Elton's outburst of 'violent' professions of love for Emma in the carriage returning from the Westons' Christmas dinner (1960 [1816]: I, xv, 129). Emma was not in the least prepared for it, had even dismissed the warnings of John Knightley, Mr Knightley's brother, that Elton was paying her a great deal of attention which she seemed to be encouraging, her reaction being to be amused at 'the blunders which often arise from a partial knowledge of circumstances, of the mistakes which people of high judgement are for ever falling into'. Austen sees that we shall at once apply Emma's strictures here to Emma herself, an 'amusement' at which we are amused, the riddler again become a riddle to herself. That phrase, 'the blunders that arise from a partial knowledge of circumstances' you can see applies to all stories, the 'circum-stances' being the Second Clues. The second part of the book follows precisely the same pattern until Emma finally discovers what Austen regards as a sound intentional perspective, particularly upon herself, which fortunately happens to coincide with Mr Knightley's. Of the fact that we as readers might have our own intentional perspective on that denouement Austen seems amusingly ignorant. Even the most adept of spinners of narrative is not beyond having a narrative woven about herself (for example, in betraying her own fascination with the supposedly weak character Frank Churchill, and her unconsciousness of the possibility of our not sharing her idol Knightley's dismissal of him).

So we may say that, unbeknownst to Jane Austen, her enthralment with the riddles of daily human existence, contained an injunction to solve them and to go on doing so. However confident understanding may be in its categorizations of the world, there is that in the world which will inevitably play a joke upon it, see them as riddles in turn. There are always unintended consequences which the self's or someone else's later intention may come to encompass. There are always new discoveries to be made in the most familiar of things and persons and selves, elements to be categorized that never were so before since they had gone unnoticed in our mutual haste to agree upon something. Paul Ricoeur has written that all we refer to together should be seen for what it is, '*co*-reference' (Ricoeur, 1983: I, 78, my emphasis), and that can produce disagreements as unexpected as Emma's discoveries about herself, however satisfied she may have been with her picture of herself. When Harriet and she discussed 'the riddle', they were happily co-referring, but we and they all interpret 'its' significance differently. The same is true of *Emma* itself, indeed, of any story, which can go on being transformed by its readers. Though there may be a 'closure' in the plot as stable and blissful as Emma's and Knightley's union, the author cannot defend it from our plottings, for we know there are no such 'closures' in life itself, nor even in death.

6.   Retrospect on the Story

So the Story is thus of exactly the same pattern as the Joke. In both there is a change of interpretation, governed by at the least two Intentional Perspectives with differing emotional charges, and the greater the difference in that charge the greater the relief – or the shock.

A story can proceed in a purely formal manner, the strong wrong clues that the protagonist is impressed by being slowly undermined for the reader by the faint right ones, until the final *peripeteia*. In the Comedy, the protagonist is under the impression that all is turned to his or her disadvantage, and in the

Tragedy all is turned to his or her advantage; for both equally, the strong wrong clues are attended to and the faint right ones ignored with greater and greater determination. Malvolio in *Twelfth Night* is blind to the absurdity of being asked to wear yellow stockings cross-gartered; Oedipus in Sophocles' *Oedipus Rex* will not accept Tiresias' description of his incestuous state even when it is spelt out to him in plain words. Like Emma in the Harriet sequences, they turn the Second Clues themselves into Ambiguous Elements in order to preserve their favoured interpretation. All these are stories that work through the course of the interpretation in a sequence that matches the protagonist's experience, but, as we have seen in the so-called 'plotless' stories, the rival clues may be present throughout and never be seen together by the characters themselves. This latter is true, for example, of most of James Joyce's stories in his collection *Dubliners* and in several of Ernest Hemingway's short stories.

The director who took Shakespeare's stage direction in *Othello* – '*He puts the handkerchief from him; and she drops it*' – and asked the actor of Othello to move so brusquely that he became the one to cast it to the floor, unnoticed by both himself and Desdemona (though not by Emilia), dramatically sharpened the irony by making Othello ignore a Second Clue *of his own making* that would subsequently have saved him from Iago's machinations with that very handkerchief. But even when he is finally and shockingly apprised of what has happened to him, it is blatantly obvious that Othello does not understand what it is in himself and his wife and his society that has laid him open to such deception, so, as was noted earlier, there is an element of 'plotlessness' in what is regarded as one of the most tightly plotted of Shakespeare's plays. There is always a plot for some onlooker that does not correspond to the manifest sequence of revelation: this is why another's interpretation can open one's eyes to a story with which one thought oneself utterly familiar.

So it is not surprising that there is hardly a play of our greatest dramatist that lacks a figure appreciative of the irony of a riddling situation, whether an openly 'all-licensed fool' or some other character given to reflecting on the ambiguity of life, from Richard the Third, amused at the extravagance of his own duplicity, to Autolycus in *The Winter's Tale*. In *Hamlet*, as we have seen, the riddler is the main protagonist himself. The Russian Formalist Viktor Shklovsky saw the Story as 'a riddle in extension' (see Martin, 1986: 46), a view wholly in keeping with the theory of this book.

They are all dealers in nonsense, ready to find a meaning that escapes the 'wise' about them, and to share it with the audience, with whom they share the spectatorship: 'Edgar!' cries Edmund in *King Lear* to us, 'pat he comes like the catastrophe in the old comedy.' Edmund is narrating his own 'old comedy' in order to deceive Edgar and his father, and he is well aware of the irony of what he creates. But we can play the joke on Edmund in turn, Edmund who mocks at his father for thinking that the stars determine men's characters and then immediately gives away the fact that he considers his own self fixed by nature as something beyond his control, but who, at the point of death, admits that he can do some good 'despite of [his] own nature'. Authors are great riddlers, but they and their creations, however subtle and persuasive their irony, are open to endless ambiguation themselves, as their very tales remind us. But this was just what we found in the Joke, that the Joker himself was vulnerable to being joked upon, unaware of a Second Clue to a new Intentional Perspective that would reveal another meaning showing through, like the fiendishly gleeful mouse in the centre of the stupid cat's face in Peter Brookes' drawing. Just as we saw in the case of the Joke, there was not even the security of the very same object being the focus of the transformation (in outline the mouse was not the cat), for part of the joke may readily consist in changing the very boundaries of 'what' is being transformed. The same can be said of the transformation of a 'person' for what constitutes a self, a personality, may be very different after the transformation from what 'it' was before, and may even remain, as with Othello, in a divided state. There is a throw-back here as a kind of etymological joke on all of us, for the word 'person' originally meant a theatrical mask through (*per*) which the sound (*son*) of the voice was heard.

It would appear that, in principle, interpretations are endless, but we still have to propose them to each other. Whose is to be accorded the baton of authority, as it was in the case of the Crows, is a matter for debate and of test against the Real outside and inside human beings, but, as the story of the Crows well illustrates, even when understanding is out in the open and mutually shared as much as it can be, there is no absolute guarantee of a single and happy outcome.

7.   An addendum on narratology

It would not be appropriate to address the subject of the Story without a reference across to the discipline of narratology that exists within literary theory. Narratology is a relatively new field of inquiry that has taken as its subject-matter the characteristics of narratives of all kinds, with especial emphasis upon the relations of author to text, internal narrators to text (especially their point of view), the relation of the incidents on the story to the order of their narration, the modes of construction of character, effects of time and duration, the common patterns found across stories of different types, the construction of characters, the varying types of narration of events, dialogue, and internal thoughts (excellent accounts of narratology can be found in Shlomith Rimmon-Kenan's survey, 1983; Peter Brooks, 1984; Mieke Bal, 1985; Steven Cohan and Linda M. Shires, 1988; and, most recently, H. Porter Abbott, 2002). There have been a number of theories about the structure of plots and interesting analyses of texts have been made on the basis of them. It is useful to consider what their aims are and whether what is being done bears upon our present philosophical concern.

The Russian Formalist Vladimir Propp was able to show that Russian folk tales could be constructed according to a limited number of elements, that he calls 'functions', in varying combinations but always in a strict order (Propp, 1979). Many of the tales, for example, have a 'helper' for the hero or heroine, who provides an indispensable 'magical agent' whose use at a critical moment allows them to overcome the challenge of an enemy. The analysis is fascinating and of great value to those whose area of investigation is confined to tales of this type. Hints of a wider generality can be seen in what the order he picked out in his analysis shares with that of Tzvetan Todorov, who detected in stories a progession from a state of equilibrium through a disruption of it that comes to be acknowledged, to a final new equilibrium (Todorov, 1977: 111). The similarity to the pattern of the Joke diagram is obvious: it is a case of the first Meaning being replaced by the second. The idea resonates with Shklovsky's 'defamilarization', a breaking through the conventional and habitual with a fresh interpretation (Shklovsky, 1965).

A great deal of attention has been paid to the relation between the events that any story recounts and the order in which they appear in the text. A writer can produce all kinds of ironic effects by anticipating and/or withholding contextual clues about the events. This simple device of the flashback is an obvious illustration which provides Second Clues for the reader often not available to characters in the text; as a result there are many subtle effects that can be achieved. The series of events is sometimes known as the 'story' or the '*fabula*', and the actual account of them the 'narrative discourse' or '*sjuzet*' (Russian Formalist terms; see Lemon and Reis, 1965). This is of considerable help for the literary theorist and critic as the text may deviate from the course of events for particular aesthetic reasons. Notice that the analysis does assume that identifiable, singular, objective events pre-exist their narration, and, as we shall see, this is a doubtful premise from the point of view of what lies at the basis of a story. As an analytic tool for the examination of an individual text, however, it is of very great use.

Those who have examined plot as such have drawn attention to the fact that 'closure' is performed in many stories, and have drawn attention to it. Closure is taken in the sense of the problem set up by the plot having reached a satisfactory resolution. What is interesting is that it has been taken for granted, so that, although many individual stories have been examined, the general nature of what is going on has nowhere been teased out. Take for example, what H. Porter Abbott says about this story:

Taboo

His guardian angel whispers to Fabian, behind his shoulder: 'Careful, Fabian! It is decreed that you will die the minute you pronounce the word "doyen".'

' "Doyen"?' says Fabian, intrigued.
And he dies.

Porter is obviously aware that the trajectory of this story depends on 'suspense', 'surprise' and 'expectations', but he gives no analysis of them and how they relate to each other (Porter Abbott, 2002: 52). What is required here is a making plain of the fact that it all hangs on the ambiguity of Fabian's utterance of 'doyen'. By this point in the book the reader should have no difficulty in the fivefold pattern clearly enough, and notice that the rival intentional perspectives are as motivationally contrasting as could be wished, with harmless curiosity on one side, and death on the other. It is, in fact, a nice little allegory of the danger that lurks in the most familiar identifications.

The same can be said of Steven Cohan and Linda M. Shires in their book *Telling Stories* (1988: 55). Though what they say about a story they discuss – it is a four-picture comic strip – they do not home in on the core ambiguities of the story (for there are more than one). They trace its course in great detail, and mention all the rival interpretations, and acknowledge that a 'transformation' has taken place, but they do not attribute the cause to the intentional perspectives that we and the agents in the story are encouraged to take up. In particular, no *general* conclusion is arrived at from their analysis, except by describing what happens as a 'syntagmatic enchainment of events', without explaining what the 'syntagm', that is, the basic narrative structure common to all stories, is.

Wallace Martin has made a similar criticism of French proponents of structural narrative analysis (Claude Brémond, A. J. Greimas and Gerald Prince). He suspects that 'a plot, like a sentence, has a structure we intuitively apprehend'; this is an insight that our later investigation into the Statement (Chapter 5, section 2) will endeavour to sustain. He also complains of the group that:

> What is lacking is an explanation of how the actions [in the plot] interlock with each other to create a plot, and how the formal patterns are related to the story's content. (Martin, 1986: 97)

Shklovsky is closest to the stance taken up in this book for he did detect as essential elements in a plot a moment in which a *riddle* is proposed and one in which it is solved (see Todorov, 1977: 231).

Someone who does recognize the part played by motivation in interpretation is Peter Brooks, and he sees that interpretation is an intersubjective affair:

> The narrative act discovers, and makes use of, the intersubjective nature of language itself, medium for the exchange of narrative understandings.
>   (Brooks, 1984: 60)

This is to be the central theme of Chapter 5, below. Brooks views interpretation from a Lacanian stance, as driven by a desire that by its very nature cannot be gratified, since it is a perpetual want of what never can be achieved, the final unity (originally imagined with the mother) that will satiate all longings. Motivation for specific needs can become distorted, turning immediate goals into metonyms for the further unachievable satisfaction. *The Thousand and One Nights* as an endless metonymy, a narrative upon narratives, is a fitting analogy for the process of all stories.

In the next chapter is an explanation of the theory of perception upon which this analysis is based, moving in Chapter 4 to the theory of knowledge it implies, both exhibiting the narrative pattern as at the core of human understanding – and misunderstanding.

3
A Theory of Perception

1.   The pattern of Ernst Gombrich's diagram

Look again at Gombrich's diagram (pp. 4–5), which reminds us in turn of the five components, the Ambiguous Element at the centre (the lines), the two Clues to Intentional Perspective (the flowers and the ears) and the two Meanings or Interpretations that result (the vase and the two profiles).

An extreme example of two persons endeavouring to gain some kind of superimposition of their understandings occurs where sensory elements themselves differ. Here is another story-poem that illustrates such a situation. It is called 'The Fog', by a much-ignored but excellent poet, W. H. Davies.

'The Fog'

I saw the fog grow thick,
Which soon made blind my ken;
It made tall men of boys
And giants of tall men.

It clutched my throat, I coughed;
Nothing was in my head
Except two heavy eyes
Like balls of burning lead.

And when it grew so black
That I could know no place,
I lost all judgment then,
Of distance and of space.

The street lamps, and the lights
Upon the halted cars,
Could either be on earth
Or be the heavenly stars.

> A man passed by me close.
> I asked the way; he said,
> 'Come, follow me, my friend' –
> I followed where he led.
>
> He rapped the stones in front;
> 'Trust me,' he said, 'and come';
> I followed like a child –
> A blind man led me home.
>   (Davies, 1951)

This speaks on many levels, but I think one relevance to our present concerns will not have escaped you, namely, that sensory systems are tuned to particular environments. Should the environment change, what may be conceived as a strongly embedded evolutionary advantage may turn out to be useless: a sensory skill developed for a particular niche may turn out to have wider application. The sighted man in the poem is at a disadvantage: he was led safely and accurately home by the blind man, normally thought of as severely limited.

This story tells us something about perception and something about stories. It reminds us of four critical features of the evolutionary scenario: (1) organisms are constantly faced with new challenges from the environment, because systems and percepts that have proved viable may suddenly become maladaptive; (2) hence, it is necessary to have a mode of changing systems and percepts, either through species-adaptation or more immediate behavioural modification; (3) in order to achieve this, a degree of individual variance is required to allow for continual recategorization; (4) consequently the rate at which recategorization can be carried out will be critical with respect to changes in the environment.

What is clearly not a good policy in the evolutionary game is to become fixed on a particular strategy – indeed, to forget that it is precisely that, a strategy. The pattern of a good strategy, as we shall see, is one that bears a great deal of resemblance to that of a story. It is one of the central contentions of what is called 'genetic epistemology' that percepts and concepts remain ineradicably provisional, for this allows for a rapid reconfiguration in the new circumstance (Piaget, 1970; von Glasersfeld, 1984; Hooker, 1995).

Now if we are taking the poem as an allegory of adaptation, let us see how the four evolutionary features apply to it. The first was about the new challenges that an organism must be ready to face, in this case the fog, rendering the existing sensory equipment of the speaker in the poem useless. The second was the ability to change system and/or behaviour, this being the speaker's yielding up his own decision to another. The third was individual variation, the fortunate existence of the blind man with his special ability. Finally, the rate of change of adaptation in this case was immediate, for the speaker allowed the blind man to lead him home, even though he had no idea of the special advantage possessed by the one offering help.

The degree of difference as regards individual variation is very marked. Consider how the blind man found the way: by tapping with his stick he produced characteristic echoes from the surrounding walls, fences and hedges which would not even have corresponded to the visual entities that the speaker could pick out. Even where the two, say, passed 'a lamp' and the speaker saw it clearly, the blind man might not have known that he was 'passing a lamp', for all he sensed was a change in the character of the echoes typical of that area of street. So the two were not even matching portions of the continuum of the real external to them, and yet by their own judgements they were acting successfully. It would be difficult to be precise at all about supposedly common 'referents' – and we put that word 'referents' in inverted commas to indicate its dubiousness – but nevertheless this did not impede their co-operation in a practical act. In fact, there may have been gross mismatches of reference-fixing, *but since none of these emerged as relevant to the activity in which they were both engaged*, neither became aware of the differences, which anyway they would regard as negligible for that context of interest. The philosopher Willard Van Orman Quine, however, believes that 'an absolute standard' can be arrived at by drawing in all the speakers of a language, adding in a footnote:

> This qualification allows for occasional deviants such as the insane or the blind. Alternatively, such cases might be excluded by adjusting the level of fluency of language whereby we define sameness of language.
> (Quine, 1987: 27)

It was fortunate for W. H. Davies that there had been no commissar of language who had already 'adjusted the level of fluency of language' in order to declare 'deviant' the blind man's use of it.

Notice that we have used the words 'interest', 'concern', 'relevant', 'judgement', and could not avoid doing so. It is easy to see why: no action is undertaken unless motivation is involved. The speaker did not want to be lost in a fog in a Jack-the-Ripper London. The blind man was motivated by a fellow-feeling, his opportunity to repay acts of comparable kindness that he had met with himself, say, when people helped him across the road. Thus life-and-death issues are involved in sensory selection and the guidance our systems afford us animals and human beings. Both perceptual and conceptual knowledge cannot be detached from fear and desire, pleasure and pain, however much our systems may work to conceal the fact. One of the awkward consequences of that temptation to conceal, the cause of

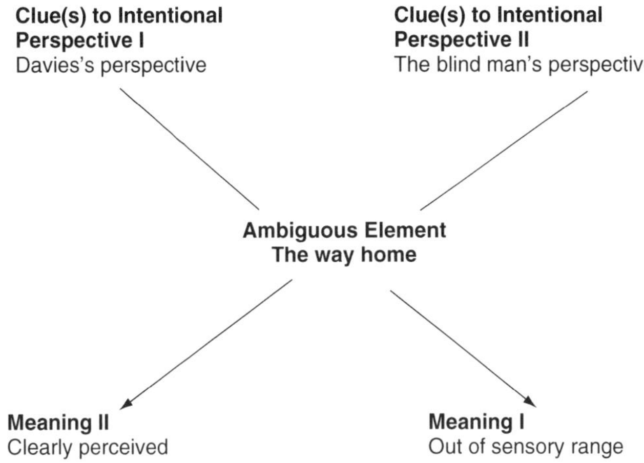

Figure 45

which I hope to make clear, is that we are too often encouraged to think that our categorizations are all as they should be.

The story takes the form of the speaker's poor interpretation with its threat of danger, being replaced by a better one from an unexpected source (Figure 45). What is philosophically interesting about this example is that there is no preservation of any referential boundaries across the two of them for 'the way home', even though both participants managed to maintain a successful co-ordination of action. Although it was necessary for them to speak as if they had achieved coincidence of their referential selections, there was no requirement that they had really done so.

The mismatch here is at the level of sensory registration. Far more common are the misunderstandings that result from differences in intentional perspective, what it is that desire, fear, interest, concern, have trained the person to select as significant from the enormous range of input from the senses. The pattern is precisely that of the Joke and the Story, for they are prime examples of it themselves. All the examples worked over in the first two chapters exhibit the pattern. It is time to examine what the theory proposes as explanation of this pattern of endless correction.

2.   Proportional variation or 'structural isomorphism'

In the December 1999 issue of *Behavioural and Brain Sciences* is a paper that considers an unusual neurophysiological claim about the nature of human sensing (Palmer 1999). It argues for the possibility of what is called 'structural isomorphism' between the input to any sensory organ and the inner brain's response to it. The claim is a simple one: that the only similarity between the incoming source of sensory excitation and the presentation that the animal organism experiences is in form of a ratio of proportional intensity. The first person to put forward the notion was the American philosopher Roy Wood Sellars (Sellars, 1922: 37), taken up later by myself, Barry Maund, and Louis Allix (Wright, 1986a: 13–14; Maund, 1993: 57–8; Allix, 2004: 155). It is not too difficult a notion to explain.

Consider the relation between the infra-red *heat* coming to cameras that are set to night-time vision (as, for example, when battlefields are being filmed at night) and the *green* colour we see on our television screens transmitted from those cameras. Heat is not *like* green colour, but there is no doubt that they are *varying in proportion to each other*. The structure is the same, hence the use of the adjective 'structural', and the form (*-morph*) is the same (*iso-*), hence 'isomorphism'. Louis Allix, whose work on perception is perhaps the most recent I can quote, puts the point thus:

> En outré, un rapport d'homologie structurelle entre la réalité et nos perceptions est indispensable pour que nous puissons découvrir quoi que ce soit sur la réalité.
>
> [Above all, an affinity based on a structural homology between reality and our perceptions is essential if we are to be able to discover whatever reality consists of.]
> (Allix, 2004: 155)

Notice that this proportionate match of intensities and variations through time definitely does not carry any *information* about what those sounds stand for or what that green colour means. After all, it needs an audience in the cinema or in front of the television set to do the interpreting. One cannot say, strictly speaking, that 'words and music' are being transmitted by the system or 'pictures' by the other.

There is obviously no limit to what might be discovered, given the possibility of tracing causal connections. Climate changes over a millennium can be worked out from the state of the tree-rings of ancient sequoias. But equally, someone dining at a table made from ancient sequoia wood may see those very same tree-rings and gain no knowledge from them whatsoever. The structural isomorphism does not of itself convey knowledge or information: it is merely evidence from which knowledge might be derived.

The philosopher H. P. Grice has the useful notion of a 'natural sign' (Grice 1967: 39). He gives a simple example to get his definition going: a doctor sees some red spots on a child's skin and diagnoses measles. The red spots are a 'natural sign'. What Grice wants to make clear about a natural sign is its difference from a 'non-natural' one. His example of a non-natural sign is that of the three rings a bus conductor might give on a bus's bell to mean that the bus is full. This is dependent on the establishment of some understanding of a sign as within an established convention or habitual gestural symbol-system. His article is in fact devoted to extending the definition of meaning in the sense of its theoretical place in human communication, so beyond giving his measles example, he says no more about natural signs since that was not his remit.

However, the notion is worth pursuing. First of all, it is strictly imprecise to call such a sign 'natural', as his own example demonstrates. There is nothing natural about the doctor having the skill to interpret the rash as one of measles. In the past, perhaps all our ancestors were able to do was diagnose illness; further back still, it was perhaps not noticed at all, or, if it were, no one attributed anything to it. So a natural sign in itself contains no *information* as such: it is merely *evidence* that someone who has attended to various causal successions and contiguities in the past or is attending to in the present can take to be an accompaniment of some other occurrence. What is significant about the 'natural sign', as one can see from the measles example, is that there is no definite limit to what they can yield as clue.

Take a footprint, often the clue for a detective. Perhaps all that the detective need interpret to solve his case is that fact that someone had actually walked in that place; or, that a woman had walked in that place; or a woman weighing nine stone; or a woman weighing nine stone who wore shoes bought in Belgium; or a woman weighing nine stone wearing shoes bought in Belgium three years ago, etc., etc. There is clearly no limit as to what 'information' that footprint will yield to the appropriately informed eye, but no one would say that knowledge of all those things was waiting about in the shape and texture of some muddy soil. Evidence, yes – but not information. Sometimes we remain Dr Watsons and never reach the Sherlock Holmes level.

Take those television viewers among my readers who were not aware that an infra-red camera is being used for those night-time broadcasts from a war front? They have been *sensing* perfectly well what was before them, but they were unable to read the 'natural' sign. They are reading other aspects, say, 'the firing of tracer bullets', but not that the relative strength of infra-red rays is being presented to them. If they came into a room where someone had turned the TV-set upside down, they might not be able to interpret anything at all except 'green flickerings on a TV screen', and perhaps, if they were Brazilian natives, not even that. Yet the connection between camera and screen might contain all sorts of sophisticated circuitry.

It is plain that the situation is in no way altered if the causal link between the evidence and the natural sign is highly complex, as many a detective story shows. Of two events utterly remote in character one might be taken as natural sign of the other if there is a complex causal link between them. Those comic machines dreamt up by Heath Robinson connected, say, the tossing of a pancake – by a fantastic series of levers, cogs, balls rolling down chutes, exploding balloons and the like – to the setting-off of a firework: so one could say that the lighting of the firework was a natural sign of the tossing of the pancake.

For an example closer to the animal one, there might be a circuit in a television system that, we might say, 'sharpened the edges of objects'. Now in processing the evidence, which we have seen contains no information, this 'sharpening of edges' does not handle information either. In fact, David Marr, an investigator of the last century who endeavoured to analyse what is going on in robot vision, made a gross error in talking of what one of the circuits was doing as 'recognizing edges' (Marr, 1982); all it was doing was altering pulses in a circuit that produced *a narrowing of transition regions* on the matrix of phosphor cells on the cathode-ray screen, a matter of the switching that produced a change of distribution of intensities on a matrix, no more – certainly not an 'edge', for 'edge' is an *interpretation* of what that distribution of intensities is evidence of. One would have had to have already picked out 'an object' from the field in order to speak of 'an edge'. Those Brazilian natives would certainly not have seen 'edges of objects' on the upside-down TV when they came into that room, perhaps not even ourselves, for all the sophisticated circuitry inside it. It would be like saying that the green colour on the screen provided an automatic recognition of the heat reaching the infra-red camera. Compare my game with cinema advertisements (p. 52). There has to be an active interpreting system in play, guided by a motivated memory. No one would say that 'information' was being passed to the screen by these 'smart' systems. They are no smarter than a smart card.

There are theorists who have examined the amount of evidence that can be transmitted through communication systems such as the telephone system. C. E. Shannon and W. Weaver were the first to produce mathematical theories to assess the quality of such transmission (Shannon and Weaver, 1949). They were working for the Bell telephone company and thus it was natural for them to use the word 'information' for what they were reducing to numerical understanding. But the word is strictly inapplicable. It is a metonym, the figurative device where we use one item to stand for another that is often found with it, that is, just as we use 'the pen' to stand for *all that can be written* in the epigram 'The pen is mightier than the sword', so Shannon and Weaver used 'information' for what could be said to be transmitted on telephone wires. But there is no actual *linguistic* information in that system unless there are human beings at each end who can interpret what is being sent and what is being received. As regards the material nature of what was happening in the wires, that was no more than evidence. Shannon and Weaver's mathematical theory applies in exactly the same way to variations being conveyed along wires that have nothing to do with human words, for example, as between parts of some automatic system such as a robot in a car factory. So 'information' is actually a misnomer, though they have a perfect right to use it as a metonym.

The conclusion is that, because our sensory experiences are structurally isomorphic, moving in concert with the intensities and frequencies and pressures, etc. which excite our sensory organs, the result is as real as what causes them, brute nature. They are, therefore, definitely *not mental*, except in the sense that they are in a brain. Blind sensing comes first, for all recognitions are learned. No*thing* of itself comes labelled or sorted. We select from the real in our heads. This is another reason why the claim that sensory experiences take place in the brain does not imply solipsism, that such a belief entails that all experience is a private dream. They are as real as the phosphor glowings on the back of a TV screen even when no one is making anything recognizable of them.

So what is the point of this long explanation about 'structural isomorphism'? The claim is that our sensory systems work on this very principle. This is exactly the kind of evidence, a field of proportional variations, upon which the motivation system works with its changes of intentional perspective to produce those interpretations we call 'persons' and 'things' and 'properties'. The fact that this allows for endless correction and readjustment is precisely its evolutionary advantage – we are not stuck with one selection. It is what lies at the centre of the Joke and the Story, and, if it is true that narrative is the key to all understanding, of communication and thought, and, therefore, of all that is human itself.

John Locke in his *Essay concerning Human Understanding* (II, ix, 8) quotes from a letter that he had received from a Dublin lawyer, one William Molyneux (or Molineux), which put the following question:

Suppose a man born blind, and now adult, and taught by his touch to distinguish between a cube and a sphere of the same metal, and nighly of the same bigness, so as to tell, when he felt one and the other, which is the cube, which the sphere. Suppose then the cube and the sphere placed on a table, and the blind man made to see: quaere, *whether by his sight, befor he touched them, he could now distinguish and tell which is the globe, which the cube?* To which the acute and judicious proposer answers: *Not. For, though he has obtained the experience of how a globe, how a cube affects his touch, yet he has not yet obtained the experience that what affects his touch so or so must affect his sight so or so; or that a protuberant angle in the cube, that pressed his hand unequally, shall appear to his eye as it does in the cube.* I agree with this thinking gentleman, whom I am proud to call my friend.

Neither Molyneux nor Locke, though, have the benefit of your understanding of structural isomorphism, Sellars' 'differential correlation' that vision works by. Which of the two diagrams in Figure 46 is called 'Mellowflow' and which is called 'Cricketycrack'?

Since you found the question easy, ask yourself why. A clue: notice that you were comparing sensory experiences in two different modalities, sound

Figure 46

and sight. Why should structural isomorphism offer you an answer? Think about that, and then see if you can cast some doubt upon what Locke and Molyneux say about whether the blind man who newly regains his sight has any help towards distinguishing the sphere and the cube.

3.   There is no direct similarity between the input and what is experienced, only a proportional one

If Palmer's hypothesis is correct, that the only similarity between the input to a sensory organ and the sensory experience is a structurally isomorphic one, then there are several implications.

First, the sensory experience does not directly resemble the input. To give an example: some snakes have two small pits just below their eyes which are responsive to infra-red light, that is, they, like the infra-red cameras on the battlefield, pick up a field of intensities that corresponds to the *heat* in the space before them, enabling the snake to experience a corresponding field of intensities. Now it is plain that the part of the snake's brain containing that sensory experience is not itself *hot*; there might be something burning in front of the snake, but there is nothing of a burning temperature inside the snake's head. In other words, the only resemblance or correspondence between the infra-red ray input and the presentation in the snake's brain is in the *proportion of intensities* over the field.

In exactly the same way there is no *pictorial* similarity between your sensory experience of a colour such as green and the electromagnetic waves that arrive at your eye. Roy Wood Sellars put it this way: 'sensuous contents are not *like* that which controls their rise', in that there is only a 'differential correlation' (Sellars, 1919: 414, his emphasis). The experience of light is an internal affair of the brain; the intensity and distribution of it will correspond in a complex and not necessarily direct way to the intensities that arrive at your retina (for there are many automatic refinements), but that will be the only correspondence. Just as for the snake, the sensory presentation in the brain is not itself hot, so the visual presentation is not a matter of light-waves. One might call the experience in the brain by a kind of metonymy an 'inner light' (Alroy 1995), but no one is sitting in your head looking at light-waves: we merely sense the external light-wave distribution *by means of* this internal colour-distribution, which strictly speaking, of itself has nothing to do with real light except varying in proportion with it. We do not need another pair of eyes in the brain because eyes have evolved to respond to light-waves, and there are no light-waves in the brain. This, interestingly, was part of what Hobbes maintained, that all sensory experience was made up of 'phantasms … perpetually generated within us', and if we ask 'by what sense do we take notice of sense', Hobbes would answer, 'by sense itself' (Hobbes 1839: 389), as it is a direct experience. In fact, it quite commonly occurs without the open-eye stimulus altogether, as in dreams, migraine 'fortification' patterns, hypnagogic and other mental imagery, or even from simply rubbing the eyes vigorously.

Now some philosophers, it cannot be disguised, have resisted this notion of internal sensory experience. Over a hundred years one argument that has not changed is the parodic one produced by F. H. Bradley against Thomas Case (who had argued for internal presentation of sensory qualities in his *Physical Realism* [1888: 25]). It has been repeated by A. C. Ewing (1930: 137), Daniel Dennett (1992: 28) and Michael Tye (1992: 159). Roderick Chisholm (1954: 46–7) quoted Bradley approvingly: 'when I smell a smell, I am not aware of the stinking state of my own nervous system' (Bradley, quoted by H. H. Price [1961: 127]). But an American empiricist philosopher, Roy Wood Sellars, has already effectively answered the attack (1932: 141–2), made by A. C. Ewing, who objected to the notion that part of the brain could be blue:

> Now if by 'mental' is meant that they [the immediate objects of perception]...are *qualities of the mind*, this statement is clearly false unless we are able to maintain that our mind is blue when we look at the sky and round (or elliptical) when we look at a penny.
>   (Ewing, 1930: 137)

But since Sellars had always distinguished the sensory features from what they are attributed to, this accusation cannot stick. He rejected the notion of internal copies of things – the Mirror-Copy Theory (Locke's mistake); he argued instead for a 'differential correlation' between the distribution over the sensory (e.g. visual) field and the 'surface elements of surrounding objects' (1932: 86), which we can now see was an argument for a *structurally isomorphic* relation. The only copying, he says, is of relations, mediated by causal ratios (1932: 86, 427), the only 'resemblance' a matter of structure and connection (1922: 37; 1932: 281). He uses the metaphor 'contour' for what is matched (1965: 238) between input distribution and sensory field.

Here he distinguishes himself from traditional empiricism, for he points out that Locke 'did not see the possibility of similarity between cause and effect on the lines of a reproduction of pattern' (1932: 111), and that is what structural isomorphism is, a reproduction of pattern not a copying of sensory features. Though common sense may clothe the physical world with sensuous qualities – we take the external 'door' to be 'green' – the physical and sensory contents are not identical: there is only a concomitant (indirectly traceable) variation between the input distribution and the one over the field. The light-rays coming from that door are no more green than the infra-red rays coming to the night-vision camera. The result is that the continuum of the internal field is an indirect effect of the continuum of the external distribution at the receptor: there is no match of external 'object' to internal 'datum'.

Daniel Alroy and I have added another scientific argument which seems to clinch the matter (Wright, 1981; Alroy, 1995). It has been well attested that when blind persons for some medical reason have had electrical probes put into the part of the brain responsible for the sensory presentation they have experienced 'flashes of light'. Now it is possible to connect the wires to that probe to any kind of input: they could go to a microphone in another room, in which case the blind person could tell you when a sound occurred in that room even though it was out of earshot for you; or it could be connected to a pressure-pad under a mat at the door, in which case he could tell you when someone or something was at the door; and so on. Clearly, as long as the blind person knew or could find out what he was connected to, these would be reliable perceivings, even though there was no possibility of a resemblance between the experienced flashes and what was at the beginning of the causal chain. So all that is required for sensing is a structurally isomorphic field with some kind of sensory character, but, not only is there no need for 'closer resemblance', it is actually impossible. So even if the connection for the blind person were made to a photo-electric cell (that is responsive to light-waves) there would still be no resemblance between the light-waves and the inner experience other than Sellars' 'differential correlation'.

Notice that, if the blind man *did not know* to what the connection had been made, the flashes would be utterly meaningless to him, quite 'knowledgeless', evidence that he could not interpret at all, a fact which constitutes an empirical disproof of what Donald Davidson and others claim, that knowledgeless sensory experience is an impossibility (Rorty, 1980: 154; Davidson, 1989: 170; Harman, 1990: 39–40; Putnam, 1993: 186: McDowell, 1994: 24–45). You will recall that it was the chime of a meaningless portion of words that produced the enjoyment of rhyme (hearing 'innegan' repeated in different contexts in the verse about Michael Finnegan). We can unconsciously enjoy the repetition of the meaningless across two meanings, of real sensation across two distinct perceptions – as in all jokes and stories.

There are some blind people who regain their sight. It is well attested that what they first experience is a chaos of uninterpretable sensation. It is quite common for normal people to experience such 'flashes of light' as Alroy mentions, for example, when there is pressure on the brain, as in a coughing fit. For example, I myself when coughing in the dark experience the sight of four small bright semi-circles, curved upwards, each with a dot where the centre of the circle would be, with four more matching them below, but upside-down. They are entirely non-epistemic, knowledgeless, of course, except that I now know what they are caused by, though I did not as a child. It is a nice empirical indication that sensory experience can exist devoid of ordinary information (as it did in my childhood), however accurate it may be as matching some input pattern of variation, and however much later, as a grown-up interested in things sensory and perceptual, I learned to read 'entities' in it. (For another empirical proof, see Smythies and Ramachandran, 1997: 437–8.)

When Dr Johnson kicked at a stone to disprove Bishop Berkeley's claim about all sensory experience being in the mind, saying 'I disprove him *thus*!', he did not prove that the sensory evidence was not in his *brain*. Incidentally, because he was going on bare evidence and not given information, nor did he prove that it was a stone, for it easily could have been a brick and not a stone, or a piece of metal and not a stone, or a part of the rock stratum beneath his feet and not a stone, etc., etc. When you apply a word like 'stone', you are interpreting evidence, and as with some detectives, you can get it wrong. Evidence is not information.

One last stubborn objection that is presented against this case is that concerning the 'private three-dimensional space' in which the colours and sounds and feels are supposed to occur if this theory is correct. This can now be summarily dealt with. If sensory experience is brute, meaningless, can exist without a mind (though not without a brain), then the internal stereoscopic sensory 'space' is equally real and equally devoid of objective information (proved in the empirical possibility of the extreme case of a mutation born without any neural connections between its pleasure/pain module, its sensory modules and its memory). The stereoscopic experience, as with all the other sensations, is only structurally isomorphic to the input and therefore *does not pictorially resemble external space*. One can then ask 'Where is the 3-D "space" that one experiences when looking into a stereoscope?' I have an old Victorian one that provides fascinating views of Snowdonia: where is the 'space' I clearly see down through the gully of 'The Devil's Kitchen' on the Idwal Crags, with Llyn Idwal 'far' below? Only in my brain – and one has to accept that this sensory experience of 'distance' is not a picture of real space, only a 'structural homology' of it, as Allix says.

To end with a quotation; the 'thee' referred to is the body:

> To thee, secluded one,
> The dark vibrations of the sightless skies,
> The lovely inexplicit colours run ...
> (Alice Meynell, 'To the Body', 1923: 89)

4.   The Ambiguous Element

The Ambiguous Element at the centre of the Story diagram represents a portion of our sensory fields. The sensory fields by this theory are structurally isomorphic with what arrives at the sensory organs, something we can do little about, beyond putting our fingers in our ears or closing our eyes. To quote Wordsworth,

> The eye – it cannot choose but see;
> We cannot bid the ear be still;
> Our bodies feel, where'er they be,
> Against or with our will.
> ('Expostulation and Reply', v. 5)

There is a consequence here that has not been sufficiently acknowledged. These fields, since they vary automatically with the input, are beyond human control. As we have just seen, they are basically not mental, in the sense that *they could exist without a mind*. They are not *subjective*. Perhaps some unfortunate animal mutation has been born without the experiences of pleasure and pain; if so it would not have the motivation to pick out any-*thing* from its sensory experiences and would therefore have nothing in its memory, would know nothing even though it would be sensing perfectly well. It would have sensed fields but they would have no intentional perspective bearing upon them, selecting portions to guide action. This gives us reason to consider that the sensory fields are fundamentally material in nature, or, as was noted earlier (Chapter 3.2) a part of the Real, out of our control. In the view of Roy Wood Sellars, they were 'rather peculiar characteristics of neural wholes and inseparable from them' (1922: 317). He followed Lloyd Morgan (1923) in taking sensory experiences to be an emergent novelty, dependent on the complex structure of evolved neural architecture and having no existence apart from it – a series of dynamic events taking place within it and serving an adaptive function which provide the 'stimulus' for a 'complex interpretative response'. Sir Ernst Gombrich is moving towards the acknowledgment of this with his remark that 'the optical world . . . is really part of the physical world' (Gombrich, 1982: 176).

Among philosophers, of whom Daniel Dennett is a good example, there has been an enormous prejudice against seeing the sensory experiences as part of the material furniture of the world, but it is really an ostrich avoidance not to admit their existence. The reason for the prejudice is that they fear that to acknowledge the fact would be to open the door to the idealism of Bishop Berkeley's kind together with all the relativistic horrors that come with it, that is, not only would we have no way of proving our contact with the real world, but we should be lost in a solipsistic world of private experiences. The 'idealism' trouble we shall deal with in due time, but the other has already been dismissed. We have already seen that, if the sensory fields are material, varying in a causal way with the intensities at the sensory organs, they are not subjective at all, but real existences in their own right, that can exist apart from a thinking mind, and so they occur without any solipsistic self (*solus-ipse*: 'solitary self') being present. They are as real as *the light-rays* reflected from a raindrop on the bonnet of a car flickering in concert with the vibrations of *the noise* from the engine inside.

If this requires a rethink about what constitutes the fundamental nature of matter, *so be it.* One of the outcomes of this theory is that knowledge is never complete, so the view that all reality can be reduced to a collection of precisely singular objects is clearly still open to revision, for something does happen in the complexities of neural organization to produce these 'dynamic events', as Sellars called them. There are more things in heaven and earth, Daniel, than are dreamt of in your philosophy.

Furthermore, there is a crucial advantage in having the sensory fields present mere evidence, a knowledgeless distribution varying in accordance with the input. Like Sherlock Holmes, we can go on finding out more and more from them as from a footprint, and this is what enables us to adjust our responses when we get feedback from new challenges in the environment. If we were stuck with one set of interpretations, particularly of what we take to be a single object, we could never *learn*; we would be moving on instinct, and such automatic responses can turn maladaptive at any moment. So the Ambiguous Element, which is evidence of a portion of the always untrustworthy material continuum around and within us, has to present itself as bare evidence. So it is no surprise that from a joke or a story we can go on discovering more and more meanings in them.

One psychologist of perception of the last century, James J. Gibson, tried to argue the sensory fields away. Ernst Gombrich has always been suspicious of his claim that visual experience was an epiphenomenal 'luxury' (Gibson, 1971: 31), saying that he could not 'swallow Gibson's theory whole' (Gombrich, 1969: 43). Gibson should have heeded Ludwig Feuerbach's warning long ago that sensation is no 'mere luxury or trifle' (1966 [1843]: 50). Feuerbach's target was Hegel, but there are many philosophers today who seem not to appreciate that the world is first of all sensed and not known. Gibson even argued that 'visual perceptions are not necessary for visual perception' (1971: 31). Although we now know from the 'blindsight' experiments (Weiskrantz, 1999) that minimal adaptive assistance can be derived from low-level registration of input, nevertheless, to deny that sensation is not necessary for active perception amounts to a *reductio ad absurdum* of Gibson's own case. However, it is easy to see why this assertion is being made, because Gibson, more than any other psychologist of perception, has drawn attention to automatic processes that alter the input in significant ways. He insists that the intake is not passive because there are automatic alterations to it that render the result apt for successful perceptual and motor interaction with the environment. However, he has made a simple logical error concerning this processing of the input before it gets to the sensory field.

Let us take as a representative example, one that we have mentioned before concerning David Marr's vocabulary (p. 76), the production of sharper 'edges' for outlines of regions within the field. The result is to produce the equivalent of turning up the contrast knob on the TV screen.

But, as we saw, it is certainly not the case that producing such a change in the distribution on the screen is an automatic enhancer of information. Consider two persons looking at the bark of a tree: one is an expert on moths, rather short-sighted; the other is one of his students, with excellent eyesight. In spite of these differences in sharpness of focus, the disadvantaged expert can nevertheless make out a camouflaged moth on the tree and accurately name its species, whereas the moth remains outside the perception of his sharp-eyed student.

A modern American painter called Chuck Close paints pictures that entirely consist of a mass of small cells of colour. If you are close to the painting you can only see the cells of colour, which in themselves produce fascinating patterns that intrigue the eye. If, however, you move away from the picture and view it from a distance of ten feet or more, the cells resolve into a face (with apologies to the artist, one can't help seeing a pun here, that one has to chuck a close view to see the face). Or one can screw up one's eyes to *blur* one's vision to see it. If that Chuck Close painting were on TV, it might be better to turn down the contrast in order to see the face better. So *discriminability* at the level of the field bears no logical relation to *accuracy* of perceptual identification. People who think that things are come to us already sorted (and probably labelled) seem to think that the clearer one's vision the more 'information' one is getting, but this little demonstration shows that perceptual information has no given relationship with clarity of vision. Although on many occasions acuity of vision is adaptively helpful, there are others in which it is not. Consider Figure 47. It is in screwing up your eyes *to blur* your vision that you see 'who' it is. Acuity is not the same as acuteness.

Hence, no enhancement of *knowledge* is provided by an 'edge'-improver: it is entirely a contingent matter. So the most that can be said is that such a Gibsonian process renders the field often but not always more apt for current selection, but does not provide any information whatsoever. On top of that, since it is automatic, it is always open to being maladaptive in some novel situation. Gibson did not realize that he was using that treacherous metaphor 'information' when talking of the visual field. The new theory of perception insists that the field is entirely knowledgeless – in philosophical terms, 'non-epistemic' or 'non-conceptual' or 'non-doxastic' (from Greek for 'no notion') or 'anoetic' (from Greek for 'no mind'); others have described sensing as 'raw feels'. What portions of that bare evidence are taken to mean is another matter altogether.

A word now about the nature of a sensory field itself, based on the research of the Australian philosopher of perception Barry Maund (1975: 47–8). It is not yet known how the field is built up but a reasonable assumption is that it is made up of a matrix of some kind, with some neural circuit that produces the effect of continuous variation. That a real picture can be built up in this way can be readily illustrated by what is called a 'Movitype' screen (this analogy was first used by Roy Wood Sellars 1969 [1916]: 237). A Movitype

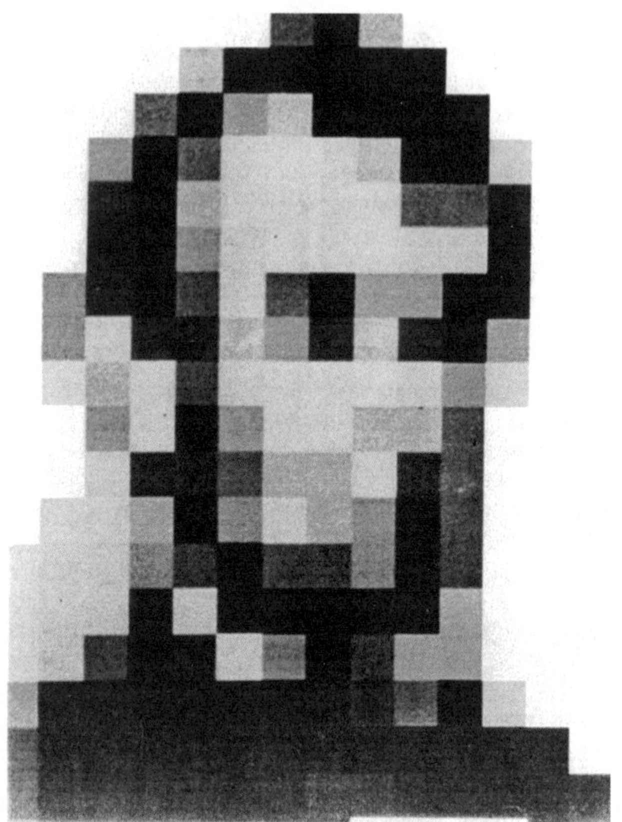

Figure 47

screen consists of a matrix – or 'raster' as the neuroscientists prefer to call it (from the Latin *rastrum*, a 'rake'; think of the lines on a TV screen as 'raked' across) – that is made up of an array of tiny light-sources in the manner of a Chuck Close picture. A computer-led input can excite these lights so as to give the impression of letters passing from right to left, or even, on the more advanced forms now commonly used in advertisements, to show moving pictures. Let us suppose that you are watching an advertisement such as the one I saw recently at the railway station at Munich, which showed a sequence of statements in German that ended up with the slow appearance out of random sparkles of a picture of a Seven-Up can.

Now Maund's point is as follows. It is obvious that there are two ways of describing what you are seeing. We could either adopt the everyday public language and say 'I saw some German sentences, followed by a picture of a Seven-Up can.' Although that is a perfectly adequate way of describing the sight, nevertheless, there is a scientific way of describing it which bears no relation whatsoever to this commonsense description. One could ask the electronics engineer to provide us with a computer print-out staged across the seconds that you were watching it of the point-states of the raster of lights. This would no doubt be a long and complex document, with the state of each tiny light-source given its place in the sequence. The interesting aspect of this list is that, although it would give a comprehensive and point-by-point detailed description of the state of the screen, nowhere in that list would there be a mention of 'German words' or 'a Seven-Up can'.

What this makes clear is that there are *two* ways to describe such a screen, which I have called (1) an *'object-*determinate' description, the 'commonsense' one, in which publicly recognizable objects are mentioned, and (2) a *'field-*determinate' description, which gives an accurate point-by-point account of the actual state of the field, but makes no mention of what any passer-by would make of it. For example, because my German is limited, I was unable to translate much of what appeared. As regards the picture though, I might have an advantage over a German-speaker who had just arrived on the platform – since the advertisement endlessly repeated itself, it became possible for me to recognize 'the' Seven-Up can as it formed out of the random sparkles *before* someone who was seeing the sequence for the first time. To put it in a simple form, I might, as we say, 'see the can' before there was for the new arrival on the platform any 'can' to see, which is a Joke or Story situation, for I was interpreting the same Ambiguous Element in a different way from them. Notice that they would not even be counting *one* thing as being present in the picture.

It provides a proof that objects do not pre-exist the selection of them. Nevertheless, in spite of these variations in recognition from person to person, the state of the raster on the advertisement board was roughly the same for both, and could be given the same field-determinate description. Incidentally, the first philosophers to argue for the field-determinate/object-determinate distinction were some Buddhist philosophers in India in the eighth century, who spoke of the infinitesimal points that made up a visual scene and the objects that constituted the scene (Matilal, 1986: 359–71).

As one last illustration, you may have seen an example of the new 'light-shows' that up-to-date computers can accompany music with. They consist of ever-changing light-patterns that represent nothing at all, the rhythms of which bear a close relation with the music. Now the electronics engineer and the software designer could no doubt provide us with a list of all the changes that took place over a small sequence of one of these, but nothing in that list would correspond to some chance 'percept' that your brain happened to project onto that sequence. You might momentarily 'see' a 'catherine-wheel', but no such 'object' exists in the sequence. If an opponent retorts 'But you know it's a light-show', then it is easy to arrange that a sleeper has a virtual-TV-hood put over their head during sleep and they be subjected to such a light-show as they wake. They would have no idea that 'it' was a light-show; they would just sense non-epistemically, a condition those opponents deny the existence of.

Feuerbach, who was mentioned before as not underestimating the senses, that is, *what the body contributes to our access to the Real*, was strongly opposed to Hegel's attempt to reduce the world to the activities of reason, of the mind alone, or as he would have put it, existence to thought, and, consequently he lauded the senses as essential to the process of knowing:

> We read the Book of Nature with the senses, but we do not understand it through the senses. The understanding is an act through itself, an absolutely independent act... *The senses give us riddles, but they do not give us the solution, understanding.*
>   (Feuerbach, 1903–11: Vol. II, 144; my emphasis)

So Feuerbach unconsciously with his remark about the senses giving us 'riddles' was acknowledging the actual nature of the case, that, as in any riddle, we are presented with bare evidence and rival clues that only our memories, primed with our always tentative desires and fears, can help us to interpret. This is why he insisted that to think was to be 'dual' (1903–11: Vol. IV, 304).

So what are the empirical consequences of the distinction between 'object-determinate' and 'field-determinate'? – for the analogy is taken to go through for human sensory fields in the cortex, which is where many modern neuroscientists now place them. What is it then that the field-determinate description describes? Notice that it certainly does not describe the world in terms of things, objects, persons, selves. It is no more than a record of a distribution of intensities, as we would expect from a structurally isomorphic field.

Because a cartoon appears on the TV screen we are not thereby led to think that the phosphor glowings have suddenly become illusory. Because sometimes we dream with our visual field does not make it any less real in such a state than the TV screen showing a cartoon. It is common for people who are very tired but who are forced to remain awake *to dream with their eyes open*, that is, they go into a dream using the input from their open eyes as the material to reinterpret (I myself once in such state of tiredness and not wishing to fall asleep since I was with an acquaintance in a car at night, dreamt that I was watching a firework display – the acquaintance suddenly spoke to me, woke me, and I saw the 'fireworks' change before my eyes into the raindrops on the windscreen, illumined by sodium-vapour lamps, being rhythmically disturbed by the wipers). The same applies to those semicircles I see when I cough in the dark. Is a TV screen less real when it is showing interference? And to mental images – is the TV screen less real when it is showing a video instead of a live broadcast? And to hallucinations – is your computer screen less real when it is showing a screen-saver? One give-away about hallucinations is that those desperately trying to dismiss the claim that vision is a real experience within the brain always limit their discussion to hallucinations of given objects, like Macbeth's dagger; but the truth is that frequently some people can have hallucinations that are like modern painters' abstract pictures, endless kaleidoscopic changings of colour and form that are not of any-*thing* at all (rub your eyes now for a while to get one!). There is a systematic ambiguity here that has been overlooked by the too-logically minded, and there is a special reason for their ignorance, that we shall come to later (pp. 111 ff.). So even a dream has a real aspect in the field in which we experience it, so it is obvious that those sensations inside the brain, called 'qualia' in the current philosophical literature, are no mask between us and the real world.

There are further considerations that lead us to the conclusion that the field remains remains basically knowledgeless, non-epistemic evidence even for the mature observer, and, since this is such an essential part of the argument, it is worthwhile having a look at them – and they are curious and interesting in themselves.

(1) Take, first, the difference between the fields of the two eyes. The perspectival difference, as those computer manipulators of the new 'Magic Eye' 3-D patterns well know (Horibuchi and Inoue, 1994), is not specifiable in the everyday terms we apply to the entities we select. Only at the level of the individual point, the 'pixel', is the difference describable. This renders inapplicable the objection of such philosophers as Gilbert Ryle (1966: 107) and George Pitcher (1971: 41), who tried to claim that when looking at a candle we squint and see two candles, we are, to quote Pitcher, only 'seeing one thing twice'. Again, the neurophysiologist, like the computer programmer, may be able to give a precise description of the state of the point-states of the sensory field traceable to each eye, the field-determinate description, but that description at the level of the field is to be distinguished from the description that the experiencing subject may give, the object-determinate one. I have just looked at the front cover of a book of 'Magic-Eye' 3-D illusions, squinting in the required manner: I saw a bas-relief of the number '3' and the letter 'D', but that description is utterly useless if what was wanted was a description of the detail in the pixels of the picture which allowed my internal cortical circuits to project the stereoscopic experience. That level remains knowledgeless, *non*-epistemic to me.

Hold these Julesz squares about 15 inches away from your eyes (Figure 48). Now, if you can, squint them together. You will see in 3-D a triangular hole in the middle. Now ask yourself 'Where is that space?' And the answer is obviously 'Not in external space, but in the space your brain creates from the differing inputs of your two eyes.' If you are skilled

Figure 48

enough, try the squint close to your eyes (it helps to angle the page at first to get the two images to click into superimposition, and then draw it slowly away a little): you will then see a triangle *above* the background. Neither of these spaces is external, but they are both real at the level of sensing. Now try to see where the two squares differ at the level of the field – you will find it very difficult though not impossible. With larger squares, more precisely printed, one can easily do it; however, your automatic systems inside your brain have no difficulty in assessing the differences at once in order to produce the 3-D sensation (Julesz, 1960).

At its simplest, one can say to those that deny the existence of the knowledgeless field that they have only to open one eye and close the other alternately, for differences can be detected that owe nothing to the way in which the field is described at the level of the objects or persons seen. I can do this with my present visual field and at once I can pick out the fact that my right eye sees a little more round the side of a pen on the desk than the left eye. But the difference I thus describe with reference to my pen affects the whole of my right eye's field as distinct from my left, every point of it, that is, beyond my powers to describe it consciously.

There is a further point about double vision: because of the constant readjustment of the focusing angle of our two eyes, much of our visual field, that part we are *not* focusing on, *is always overlapped with double images*. This fact was first pointed out by Hermann von Helmholtz, the distinguished German psychologist (Warren and Warren, 1968: 176–7). It takes considerable introspective attention to become aware of them, but it is the same effect that shows up plainly when one holds a finger close to the eyes and then focuses on a distant point. None of these double images is cognized, so the conclusion is that much of one's vision is normally in a state of confusion, always non-epistemic for this reason alone.

  A simple experiment you can do now will also prove the point: without moving your head, try to recognize what is to the left and right of you; you will easily discover that all round the periphery of your vision is an undoubtedly sensed region which is outside your ability to recognize. A hard-headed Australian materialist, on hearing this, tried to claim that those regions were merely ones of what he called 'faint belief', but that objection falls down because it assumes that those regions of the continuum causing those distributions have already been inspected and recognized, which is far from being the general case.

(2) Helmholtz also pointed out that the whole of one's vision is always affected by the after-image effects of *what one was last looking at* (Helmholtz, 1901: 254–62). Butchers take advantage of this effect when they surround the meat in their windows with green paper, for the complementary colour of green is red, and the result is that the meat appears redder to the eyes of prospective customers than it otherwise would. Thus one's vision is continuously altered by a feature that plays no part in the normal assumptions of recognition, a knowledgeless element lying over our whole visual field all the time. Perhaps that illusory effect tipped the balance on whether a piece of meat was bought or not – a woman who had been looking in the window for some time buys the meat against her husband's wishes, he having in boredom been gazing round at the traffic. The difference remained entirely unknown to either of them, outside the range of their mutual cognition, and yet part of an intrinsic feature of their experience.

(3) After-images also have the feature of being as apt as any other sensory record for the provision of knowledge. An after-image which until time t^1 had been utterly unnoticed, that is, entirely non-epistemic, can at time t^2 be noticed as having been caused by something of significance (e.g. I become aware of an after-image which I realize has been for a few moments just off the centre of my visual field; I have no recollection of how it got there, for I may have glanced in the direction of the dazzling light and had to glance away again so immediately and automatically that I had no opportunity to register what caused it; but, after a few moments in which it remains outside my attention altogether, its characteristic shape makes me now aware that my wife has brought me up a cup of tea on our hexagonal silver tray which she had placed on the windowsill in the sunlight. This is an undeniable counter-example that proves

(a) that parts of our visual field can be non-epistemic;
(b) that they may *subsequently* become inspected as evidence;
(c) the experience from which I obtained this information about an external object was *entirely internal* (for everyone has to admit that after-images are an internal experience). So if we can learn from one internal experience, why not all?

(4) Fit a virtual-reality hood on someone's head while they are sleeping and, as they are waking up, unaware of what has happened to them, make the input to the screens an entirely random one produced by some computer such that all that is on the screens is a phantasmagoria of rapidly changing shapes and colours. No *thing* will be recognized. But one need not go to the trouble of virtual-reality hoods. One can refer to the experience of the nineteenth-century psychologist Gustav Fechner. George Henry Lewes quotes Fechner's experience of waking up in a strange place: opposite his bed was the black funnel of an iron stove, and very often on waking in the morning he reported himself as being in a state of not being able to make out what he was looking at, 'subjectively unconscious of the objective fact', the chaos of sensation thus existing apart from recognizable percepts (Lewes, 1874: 94–5).

Then, too, a large number of people have 'hypnagogic' imagery as they go to sleep and 'hypnapompic' imagery as they wake up, and the best description of these experiences is to say that they correspond to a computer randomized output on a monitor screen, rather like a screen-saver – indeed, it is possible that they may have something of that very function, so it is perfectly common and normal experience to sense and not to perceive. Of course, as one wakes one may begin to play a sort of 'faces-in-the-fire' game with them, as I often do, as I have them regularly, but it is not necessary, and often the speed of transformation defeats the gestalt-module's attempts to fix a percept on the changing field. Nor is it necessary that memory is already at work in these transformations. It is a subtle but I think definite point: if I happened to catch a glimpse, say, in a turmoil of purple convexities, of a portion that looked like the face of Samuel Johnson, it would not necessarily mean that an image of Samuel Johnson had emerged from my iconic memory that I might have missed perceiving – no, Samuel Johnson is no more in that passing show than he would be if I caught a likeness of him in a chance distribution of pebbles on a beach. As I wrote this, I caught sight of an expressive face among the leaves of the clematis outside my window – no one is going to say that the face was there before my gestalt-module picked it out.

Leonardo da Vinci counselled young painters to stare at an old wall covered with patches of damp and moss and lichen until they begin to see the outlines, say, of a battle. It does not seem to be counter-intuitive to believe that in their emotional excitement they might forget that they were looking at a wall. Many people who are under emotional stress do just this with faces in the fire. In Dickens's *Great Expectations*, Pip, as he went downstairs to steal the pie, heard the wooden steps of the stairs say 'Stop thief!' and 'Get up, Mrs Joe!' Some philosophers – J. L. Austin is a good example – always imagine that perception is taking place within very limited conditions, devoid of any motivation. Their error is to presuppose that the difficult business of learning has taken place, and everyone is safely and securely agreed to the point of the impossibility of any future disagreement on an unthreatening, unexciting, already defined portion of the Real. In their view of the world, everything has already been learned about. Why they should be tempted into such a secure view of the world is to be examined later (pp. 219–21). To quote the American philosopher of rhetoric, Calvin Schrag, 'there seems to be a bit of the incommensurable in each chunk of commensurability' (Schrag, 1986: 104), that is, there is always something outside the objectively agreed measurement, enumeration, identification, that escapes the whole mutual procedure of reference to 'entities' in the word, and that is the non-epistemic sensing that our *differing* bodies provide us with, 'against or with our will'.

5.   The source of the Intentional Perspectives

Sensory fields do not of themselves mark out 'objects', 'persons', 'selves', or 'properties'. The sensory, as a Gricean 'natural sign', is thus explorable evidence, like tree-rings, footprints, or, for the geo-physicist, the varve deposits in Sweden, and like them are not given *information* at the object-determinate level. Some neurophysiologist of the future may no doubt be able to trace the field-determinate correlation between input and cortical response in the brain, just as an electronics expert might be able to trace the correlation between intake at the TV camera and the distribution on your TV screen, but what that screen showed in terms of persons and objects would not be his concern. In any case, whatever we have selected as significant from the fields in the context we judge ourselves to be in, there is always more there that we are ignoring *because it does not concern us at the moment*. Recent psychological experiments have shown that subjects, with sufficient attention having been directed onto one part of the field, can ignore something as blatantly obvious as a man in a gorilla suit walking across in front of them. There is no hope of our attending to every momentary aspect of the sensory fields, and it is *attention*, driven by motivation, that produces the selecting.

Motivation is traceable to need, to the organism's requirements for the maintenance of life and the reproduction of its species. Pain and pleasure, in hunger and thirst, sexual release and deprivation, health and bodily damage, warmth and cold, are the immediate sources of the drive. Drive is significantly named. It propels the organism into those actions that will satisfy it, but this cannot be done unless there is either instinctual guidance embedded in the brain as an automatic response or the organism has been able *to learn*. It is also not without significance that the word 'mind' when used as a verb – as in 'Never mind!' – means *to be concerned about*.

According to Jean Piaget, learning proceeds by a feedback process (Piaget, 1955). As soon as the organism experiences pain or pleasure as a result of its interaction with its environment, the sensory field is subject to a sorting process in which certain regions become fastened in memory with a marker of desire or fear, encouragements to approach or withdrawal together with those actions that ensure the repetition or avoidance of the experience. Such desire or fear produces 'attentional pulses' that direct what is now able to be noticed if it recurs. Continual encounters with what produced the initial memory refines and corrects the percept, a process that Piaget calls 'accommodation' and 'assimilation', accommodation being the ever more precise adjustment of the percept under varying circumstances and assimilation the embedding of the percept and its accompanying motor movements into memory for future guidance. Piaget calls them 'mobile object schemata' (1955: 93), terms that match Ernst Gombrich's 'scheme and correction' (1977: 231). As Ernst von Glasersfeld (1984: 25), following Piaget, insists, what is achieved is no more than an adaptive fit with its perceptual construct, which cannot in any way be a replica of part of the environment. This meshes with the argument as it has so far proceeded, since the non-epistemic field is entirely open as far as the selection of gestalts is concerned.

This is not to say that in some higher animals a wider curiosity has not evolved that induces exploratory behaviour apparently 'for its own sake', for curiosity has served its forebears well in the past – it clearly does not kill the cat on the majority of occasions. One can instance those species which, as well as man, successfully turn up in an impressively extensive range of habitats: the Rat and the Raven are good examples of such inquisitive animals. As sensory experiences in themselves, pain and pleasure intrinsically do not convey knowledge. A new-born child may feel a pain in what we would call its 'foot', but the child has no knowledge of any such 'thing' as 'a foot', experiencing only a certain intensity in a portion of the body-image field. One even has to learn how to conceptualize the body-image. Only when in an organism pain and pleasure are linked with the sensory fields *such that portions of those fields are placed in memory marked with fear or desire* can any learning begin. As was mentioned before, it is empirically possible for a random mutation in a species to occur producing an organism in which there is no such neural link between the pain/pleasure experiences and the other sensory experiences; thus the organism would have all these experiences without any opportunity of gaining any knowledge, and would no doubt soon die. A mind, even one in the higher animals, only comes into being when the pain/pleasure system begins to embed portions of the fields into memory marked with fear and desire.

This is where a remark of Montesquieu's becomes applicable, that it is the 'allurement of pleasure' and the aversion from pain that enforce the first 'singlings' from the sensory fields that are remembered. For those that do begin to learn, those portions do constitute a first singling out from the field, but whether that particular unifying of sensory criteria will be satisfactory as a guide to action only further action can decide.

It is not as if there were some-'thing' already 'single' to pick out, only a fuzzy region that may or may not serve our current purpose fully. You recall that Feuerbach criticized Hegel for trying 'to equate existence and thought' (Feuerbach, 1966 [1843]: 51); he would agree here that the 'singling' and the action it attempts to guide can never capture the '*in-fin-*ity' (the *no-limit*-ness) of the sensory experience, its remaining utterly irreducible to the tentative boundaries of the concept. Oddly, it also reminds us that we can indeed remember incredible detail given the motivation, and the eye of the imaginative among us can discern 'affinities in things / Where no brotherhood exists to passive minds' (Wordsworth, *The Prelude*, Book II).

One old empiricist, George Henry Lewes, drew very close to what is argued here: with Montesquieu he believed that 'It has long been observed that we only see what interests us...The satisfaction of desire is what both impels and quiets mental movement', from which he concluded that this 'discredits the old idea that the senses directly apprehend – or mirror – external things' (Lewes, 1874: 121–2). It is the basis of the 'open horizon of unexplored content' implied in the 'Et Cetera Principle' of the ethnomethodologists among the sociologists (Cicourel 1971: 148), that in any common reference that two or more people make there is always more than is openly expressed or could be expressed, as if we carelessly said 'et cetera' after every statement that we make.

Some of those who have attacked empiricism on the ground that it believes in an internal mirroring of external things (e.g. Merleau-Ponty, 1970: 52; Rorty, 1980) conveniently forget that there were empiricists who did not hold to such a view. William James, too, wrote of 'the transformation of the world of our impressions' being effected 'in the interests of our volitional nature'. Or take Roy Wood Sellars, who argued for a basic internal field of pure sentience, but with this difference, that his evolutionary bent prevented him from ignoring the part played by feedback in adjusting our percepts – he called it a 'from-and-to' relationship, thus anticipating Piaget – so that he proposed a cortical sensory field that was responsive not to external *things* but to the *energy-distribution* of light-waves over the whole of the retinas (Sellars, 1970: 125).

Now if it is the motivation of initially pain and pleasure, and subsequently fear and desire (as well as the evolved curiosity) that induce selections from the sensory fields, this implies, firstly, that each animal, each human being performs its own Piagetian 'accommodations' and 'assimilations' on its own fields. We can now see the reason for the Story pattern in the W. H. Davies story of the Poet and the Blind Man. Differences, first, in sensory response can be significant in human communication and co-operation, unsuccessful in the former case, successful in the latter.

Secondly, differences in what has been learned and therefore in intention and attention, produce the kinds of story that we examined in Chapter 2. So there is a double possibility of difference in understanding even when the people concerned believe that they are talking about exactly the same 'thing'. *Sensory registration* will remain different, and what has been learned, *the intentional selection*, will remain different.

In the case of animals the draconian judgement of evolution will sort out the one who successfully differentiates the input from the one who does it unsuccessfully. In the human case, there is always the possibility of one person communicating what he or she has learned to another. This was successful in the case of the Poet and the Blind Man: although their references only very roughly coincided upon the external continuum of matter, their common venture, that of reaching the Poet's home, was carried through to its desired end. Co-reference, no matter how long it has proved its trustworthiness, is always no more than a *viable* affair. It is time to examine just how it is that two human beings frequently manage, not only to get their differing selections to coincide in useful co-operative action, but also to take full advantage of those differences in order to achieve that co-operative end.

6.   An analogy and a summary

To give a final clarification to the doubled nature of perception when two or more people are involved, here is an extended analogy. It uses the notion of a television display, but, as we have just seen this is acceptable as long as we keep in mind the differences between a television screen and the display in the brain (particularly that the former is strictly speaking not coloured and the latter is).

You will have heard of those machines used by bomb-disposers which are equipped with a TV camera and robot arms and hands. At a safe distance the bomb-disposers can send the machines to look at a bomb, and, if the task is one that robot-arms can perform, the operator can make those arms and hands carry out the task of making the bomb safe. Imagine that there are *two* such machines and *two* operators, both examining the same bomb which is two hundred yards away, and, because of some special reason, the operators are themselves some distance from each other and, therefore, since they cannot see the other's screen, they have to communicate by telephone. Take it too that the bomb is of an unfamiliar type.

Now this *is* analogous to the human situation when two people are examining what they call the same object, for there are several respects that match even if there are many that do not.

(i)   For both this case and the perception case, the access to the external is *indirect*, via a causal system that is structurally isomorphic. The distribution of intensities on the TV screen roughly matches that picked up in the camera, just as the distribution on the retinas (the 'camera') roughly matches the distribution on the presentation field in the brain ('the screen').

(ii) In both, there are 'circuits' that produce certain automatic processing between the 'camera' and the field (consider the contrast controls in the TV set, and Gibsonian 'edge'-enhancers in the brain).

(iii) In both, there is no actual *perceptual information* passing from the 'camera' to the 'screen', only *evidence of a distribution of intensities*, the structurally isomorphic pattern.

(iv) In both, mutual decisions have to be made about what is to be *regarded as, taken to be* objects in the field. Let us take it that the bomb is of an entirely new design, so that the bomb-disposers have the difficult task of making out what they are looking at. Their final decision illustrated a move from one entity to two *for virtually the same sensory input*, as in the Joke.

The commonest objection to using a television screen as an analogy for inner sensing is that of a 'vicious regress' objection, and, before continuing, it is worthwhile making its inapplicability clear. This objection is very old, having been first put about by the nineteenth-century German philosopher Hermann Lotze, that it would be impossible to have a visual screen in one's head because that implied that there would have to be a little person inside your head looking at the screen, and he (or she) would have to have a screen inside *their* head with another homunculus (or 'mulierula') looking at that screen, *ad infinitum* (Lotze, 1884: 492–3). This antiquated objection has been repeated countless times (for example, Hirst, 1966: 178; Ryle, 1966: 173). It is often backed up with the false assertion that using it implies that the proponent believes that colours *inside* the head match colours *outside* the head (Tye, 1992: 159; Dennett, 1992: 28, 49), but, if one accepts that the only similarity is a structurally isomorphic one, that of proportional variation, the 'colours' inside the head are only matching variations of intensities and frequencies, and not anything 'pictorial'. Remember that structural isomorphism includes the idea that what arrives at the eyes is in fact *colourless*, that the external real is not coloured at all. There are no light-rays inside the head, so eyes there would be useless. Colour in the cortex is directly sensed. So with the 'ground' of the metaphor limited as above and this ancient objection finally laid to rest, we can proceed with the Television Analogy without fear of being accused of making a 'howler', as Gilbert Ryle would have said.

Now this could be a typical snatch of conversation over the phone between the two bomb-disposers:

A: Can you see the wire bent like an N?
B: No.
A: Over to the left.

B: Oh, I see what you mean. To me it's a Z, because I'm seeing it side-
ways.

A: Well, can you get hold of what's next to it on the left?

B: Yes. [B operates his robot's servo-hands.] Got it.

A: Now give it an anti-clockwise turn while I hold the base. [A operates
his own robot's servo-hands to hold the base.] Good. There it goes...
No –

B: Careful! Now I have turned it, I see that it's *two* nuts, not *one*. I saw the
sides flash.

In this short interchange A and B together obtained a satisfactory mutual fix
on what they both called 'the nut' (that is, 'an object', an 'invariant', an
'originary *it*', a 'determinable *x*', 'a thing'), and they both successfully
homed in on 'it' and commenced the next stage of their task.

Here are the Story diagrams for the various levels of ambiguity for the
human case and for the Analogy; they have been combined on the same
diagrams to show the comparison more clearly.

First, the level of human sensing in which two seeing brains are
confronting roughly the same portion of the Real (Figure 49). Second, the
level of perceptual interpretation (Figure 50).

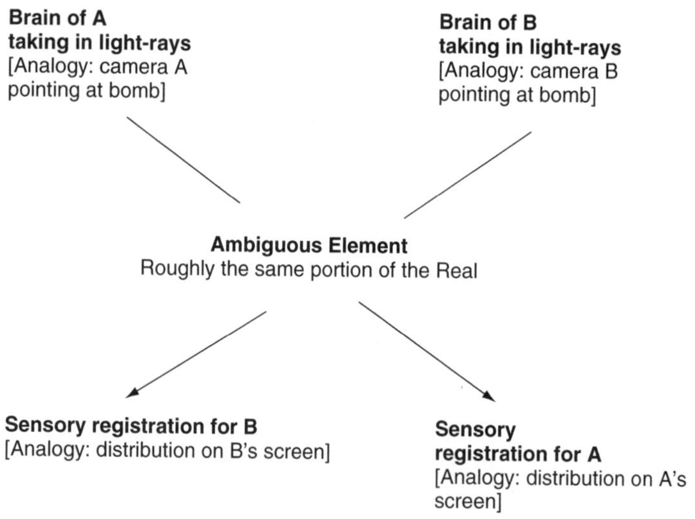

Figure 49

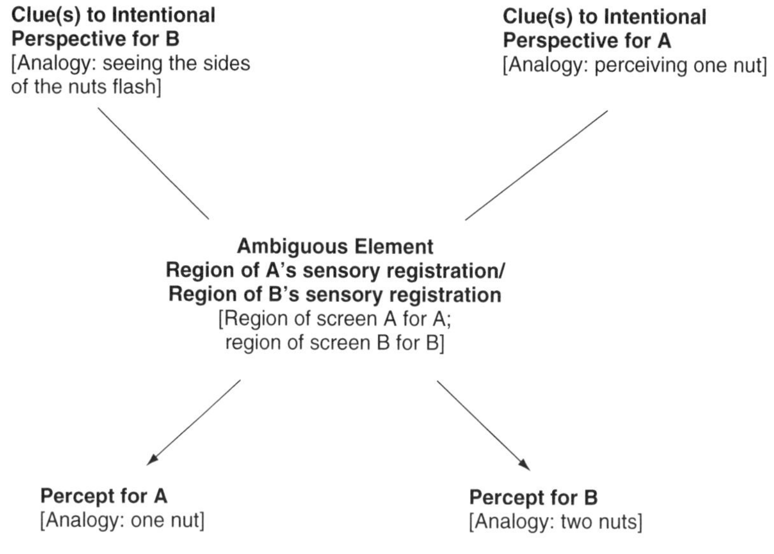

Figure 50

If the Joke and the Story are to be used for the human intersubjective situation in perception and communication, the features that match this analogy for the human case are these:

(A) A sensory registration system that is empirically private to each (empirically private, because we do not know what the neurophysiologists of the future might be able to achieve in examining sensory fields, perhaps even sharing a pixel or two). This means that two persons' selections are always from a numerically different field with its own characteristics. The fivefold structure is obviously present at what we might call by analogy the 'sensory' level.

(B) The causal links between external region and internal field are direct ones, except for any Gibsonian pre-sensory adjustments, but the field is only structurally similar to the input, making it only indirect evidence of it. The recognition of entities cannot fitly be described as either direct or indirect since one cannot speak of a link between some 'given object' and internal 'sensum'; we can only say that the part of the field's distribution so far selected by the perceiver does vary in proportion with a part of the real outside, but whether that selection will go on proving viable is another matter. This rules out any accusation of solipsism for this theory, since sensing is viewed as non-subjective, capable of existing without a mind. What we sense in the brain is no phantasm, but a brute portion of the Real in a most intimate form, one we can escape in blank unconsciousness (for even the illusion of dreams takes place on real sense-fields). Qualia are no 'veil of perception': they are as real as what they are varying proportionately with, the equally real, non-sensory input.

(C) The registration is *caused by energy- and/or mass-distributions*, emanating either from overlapping regions of matter arriving at detectors sensitive to input external to the brain or from sources internal to the brain. A field-determinate account of the distributions of the registration could in principle be given (e.g. digitally) without any reference to what the observer might select as an 'object' therefrom. For example, a television engineer could give one a digital print-out of the state of the 625-line system on a screen at any one moment without any reference to what a viewer might take the 'picture' to be of. It would be a scientifically punctiform account of the caused condition of the phosphor cells of the TV screen. This, it will be readily seen, is the 'field-determinate' account of the condition of the field mentioned earlier (pp. 87–8) to be distinguished from any 'object-determinate' account that the observer himself might give. Similarly, the neurophysiologist of the future could in principle give such a punctiform account of the state of the internal cortical field, though the structure of each point or pixel is open to further investigation (so too the way in which an analogue effect as of a continuum is obtained).

(D) Pragmatic selections, known as 'objects', 'persons' and 'properties', are made from the fields on the basis of the methodological assumption of single sources within those fields that can be responded to successfully again at a later time, a postulate of identity that enables two separate experiences to be regarded for the time being as one in order that a mutual fix of the two perspectives may be maintained in harness upon the external mass/energy region in the service of the guidance of purposive action. To quote the old American idealist Josiah Royce, who has already sketched out the possibility of non-epistemic fields (Royce, 1976 [1899]: Vol. I, 24), the idea that objects are the same for all of us is part of the 'necessary folklore of a realism that believes objects to be given' (Royce, 1976 [1899]: Vol. I, 73). The diagram for this level matches all those we have applied so far, in all the jokes and stories, because we have reached the *perceptual* level, that at which the selection of entities takes place at the behest of motivation.

(E) This methodological assumption is retained by the participants in order that negotiated mutual correction may be performed to improve the super-imposition of their perspectives. This correction is in the service of judged utility, ideally mutual, but itself open to negotiation. F. C. S. Schiller pointed to this with his notion of 'correlation of sense-spaces' coupled with the 'postulate of logical identity' (Schiller, 1902: 113); the same emphasis can be seen in Alfred Sidgwick's attack on 'verbalistic tendencies' (Sidgwick, 1934).

This allows what are in fact two different selections from the Real on two different 'screens' to be *treated as* one so that a possible correction of that very 'oneness' can go through if required. Another way of putting the methodological principle is to imagine the participants saying 'We shall agree to ignore the negligible'. Now just what is strictly negligible the agents cannot securely define together, particularly when they are saying 'Let us neglect it', which means that they are also ignorant of what each happens to be ignoring as 'negligible'. One might be regarding something as negligible which for the other is significantly criterial and vice versa. Not all the sensory that is being responded to has been verbalized at the level of mutual understanding. The success of the posit is only always partially achieved, even when all in a Wittgensteinian 'form of life' appear to assent to it: it actually never could wholly be so for the sensory experiences remain obstinately different and words can never wholly capture their richness. There is no guarantee that for some few agents or even one agent a separate sensory criterion was in operation which, given a change of environment, would prove specially adaptive, whereas all their fellows in the form of life would be at a disadvantage. Saul Kripke has pointed out that Wittgenstein's concept of 'aspect-blindness' needed investigating (Kripke, 1982: 46–8): one should now be able to see why, for aspect-blindness is none other than the non-epistemic nature of sensing, from which others may be drawing better conclusions than oneself.

(F) Mutual corrections, as in the Joke and the Story, provide a triple proof (I) *of the existence of the external source of distributions* from which the object-selections are made; (II) *of the existence of the sensory-fields as such* in which those uncertain object-selections are being made. Corrections from A accepted by B (and vice versa) and sustained by subsequent satisfaction in utility prove to both A and B that, first of all, (i) the partner was able to invade the supposed privacy of his or her sensory fields and reorganize it in a way that revised his or her intentional selections from it (*two* nuts not *one*), forcing even a retrospective re-ordering (thus his or her *self*, which is made up of the particular fears, desires, interests and concerns which a body has learned to construct and pursue). Secondly, (ii) it proves that the partner has *an existing sensory field of their own changing in proportion with that existing external source of distributions*, that is, a structurally isomorphic field, for otherwise they would not have been able to bring the change about. Thirdly, (iii) and this is a strong philosophical claim since it purports to solve the 'Other Minds' problem ('How do we know that other minds exist?'), *minds as selectors of entities and properties must exist* since they have to be able from outside to effect an internal change of one's very selfhood. One must add that all our objects and persons and properties only have reality in so far as they remain *viable* co-ordinations of our intentional selections from the undoubted real. One odd feature of this analysis is the fact that a 'correction' may prove to be mistaken, that is, the proposed *objectivity* is wrong, but the actuality of the change of gestalt by someone else still proves the independent *existence* of both the experience of sensing and the input with which it is varying. So this is what philosophers call a 'parsimonious' realist position, since it claims no more than a realism of the material base without any commitment to there being 'a sum of things' or 'given selves'. Even selves are not given singularities: on the contrary, the argument indicates how selves are constructed, namely, by projecting a singularity in concert with others just so that the continual correction of oneself and the participation in the correction of other selves can proceed – which happens every time we speak or are spoken to.

Our next concern will be to analyse this 'triangulation' on the Real, tracing its origins in philosophy, and this will lead to proposals about the nature of language and the faith that underlies it.

4
A Triangle with Fuzzy Corners

1. The Triangulation

At the point we have reached, it appears that the transformation of one person's understanding by another of how to act with regard to the real outside and inside them may reach down to a deeper structure. It is this to which the Joke and the Story may both bear witness. Just what is it *to propose* a meaning to another person, to endeavour to get them to accept another interpretation of the world?

The philosopher Donald Davidson also drew attention to the updating of one person by another, calling it a 'Triangulation', in which the two people and the object they are confronting are at the three corners of the triangle (Davidson, 1991: 159–60). The metaphor of Triangulation connotes an attempt to arrive at a reliable map of a problematic terrain, and thus provides a good analogy for what is in progress when two people compare perceptual experiences. Now a triangle is what appears at the top of our fivefold diagram, in that there are two views of ostensibly the same region of the world, with the second being a hopeful correction of the first. The lower corners of the diagram represent what construction is to be put on the evidence, how it is best to be dealt with.

It is plain that we talk about the problematic, for we most often want to update our hearers whom we take to be misconstruing the world; of course, sometimes we do repeat to hearers what they already know, but that is usually with the aim of ensuring they keep it in mind, which still falls under the definition of a problematic situation from our point of view – though that may not be their judgement! So the terrain of the real is not wholly mapped out, and adjustments with our theodolites across the triangle lead to continually enhanced corrections. In the metaphor too is the connotation that the fact that there are two involved in the matter develops the whole process incrementally, a kind of stereoscopy that makes for settling to a (hopefully) common judgement. It seems to be a straightforward case of two heads being better than one.

Human beings have the advantage of animals in that we can communicate new adjustments of interpretation to each other and have them independently assessed for adaptiveness and utility. Of course, the 'stereoscopy' depends on each member having a differing access to the region of concern, just as literal stereoscopy depends on the differing views of the two eyes from which the brain is able to construct a better guide to the shape and distance of external surfaces. Plato acknowledged such differences with the example of a wind appearing cold to one man and warm to another (*Theaitetos*, 152d). Davidson in the article quoted above writes of these 'differential' reactions to the incoming stimuli. Gareth Evans is another philosopher who is prepared to admit to the fact of this perceptual relativity, that there is no requirement that a speaker and a hearer think of an object in the same way or even approximately (Evans, 1982: 337). We may quote the great Immanuel Kant on the topic: 'To one man...a certain word suggests one thing, to another some other thing; the unity of consciousness in what is empirical is not, as regards what is given, necessarily and universally valid'(*Critique of Pure Reason*, B140). The Poet and the Blind Man provide an extreme example.

As regards *sensory* differences alone, as we saw in Chapter 3.6 there is an abundance of evidence that each of us differs in all kinds of respects (e.g. in frequency and intensity ranges in both hearing and sight, in reaction to tastes and smells, in responses to heat and cold, etc.). There is no denying the differences at sensory level as Quine is tempted to do: there are no 'innate similarity standards' between one person's sensory registration and another's, only a more or less good overlapping of their tuning (Quine, 1987: 37).

Because of the differences in our learning histories, neither can we be using exactly the same criteria for 'the same thing', a fact which the psycholinguist Ragnar Rommetveit has established, which implies that we each have a different cardhand of criteria for perceptual identification (Rommetveit, 1974: Ch. 4). There is, therefore, undeniable relativity both at the sensory and at the perceptual levels. The fact is admitted by Daniel Dennett when he is discussing the 'Baldwin Effect' in evolution, the fact, mentioned above, that each organism has different wiring and that this enables evolutionary selection to proceed, winnowing out those whose sensing and state of learning are inadequate for the new environmental challenge (1992: 185–7).

So the advantages for the Triangulation are plain and are conceded on all sides. When a communication is successful, one human corner of the triangle induces a change of percept in the other in the direction of willed action, which entails the fact that the human corners are adjustable.

2.   What is at the object corner of the triangle?

A move is customarily made in the current philosophical analysis of this Triangulation which seems intuitively justified and, because of that, has escaped analysis. Let us take Gareth Evans' use of it. He is prepared to admit to the facts of sensory and perceptual relativity, that there is no requirement that a speaker and a hearer think of an object in the same way or even approximately so, but he adds that all that is needed is that *they are both referring to the same object* (1982: 337).

Now I should like to draw attention to what is probably the reader's own reaction on reading this, namely, to feel that there is nothing suspect about that italicized assertion. After all, it seems plain that, though the two human corners can be in a state of indefiniteness, the corner occupied by the external real has no such vagueness about it, for is not that what the percepts are trying to home in upon? Bertrand Russell was quite definite about it: in the real, he declares, 'there can be no such thing as vagueness or imprecision; things are what they are, and there is an end of it' (1923: 85).

The psychologist James J. Gibson also sees the world as already consisting of recognizable 'invariants', his word making plain the fixity of the object which perceivers are endeavouring to grasp (1977: 67). It is clear that no doubt of that fixity entered Evans' head, nor perhaps in that of the reader too. We can find a similar assurance in John McDowell's and Michael Tye's conviction that entities that are 'thus-and-so' await our perception (McDowell, 1994: 9; Tye, 2000: 46–7). Quine, although he was prepared to allow 'inscrutability of reference', was insufficiently general, for he confined his inquiry to an obstinately *singular* 'gavagai'/rabbit, when it would not have taken a conjuror long to induce him to see portions of other objects as 'a' rabbit (Quine, 1960: 26–46).

One might at first point out an inconsistency in this claim. The term 'entities' includes persons as well as things, and we have already conceded that the human corners of the triangle are not fixed. There is no denying this because an adjustment of one person's selfhood by another can easily bring about an unexpected, even traumatic, change in that self to the point that the receiver of the correction finds himself well nigh unrecognizable (take Othello, who, after hearing the truth from Emilia, is unable to inhabit the selfhood that placed him as a worthy servant of the Venetian republic, an identification that was the core of his social being, a fact made plain in his speech before his suicide).

Well, then, one might say at this point, persons perhaps constitute a special case. It is as if there had at first been only the two ends of a line, but now a triangle has appeared, because the corrected self finds itself distinct from its earlier manifestation. Surely, one would think, there is no comparable uncertainty when it comes to objects? Is it not obvious that the object pre-exists our attempts to define it?

Take a statement from the latest book on perception, one which exactly parallels that of Evans'. A. D. Smith is attacking what is called the 'Indirect Realist' position in the philosophy of perception which takes it that each person has only an indirect access to the external real via some kind of inner sensory experience. It strikes him as obvious that there must be a common object for the two persons in dialogue, finding it impossible to understand how someone believing in presentations of the world inside the brain has therefore any right to talk with anyone else of a common object before them such as a page in a book. To strengthen his case, he carries the accusation to an example in which two people are indeed using an apparently indirect path to the object, two physicists talking of an electron whose presence has left a track in a Wilson cloud chamber. The access is indirect certainly, but there is no doubt whatsoever in Smith's mind – and perhaps in the reader's – that there is a *single* electron as their target, and, furthermore, they had access to it via the direct access of seeing the photograph of a *single* track in the cloud-chamber. It makes clear, in Smith's view, that anyone trying to deny this is left with the impossible task of providing reliable reference to objects for which he has no means within his theory. He regards this as a convincing argument, for it shows that one cannot escape *taking the existence of external objects for granted.* To try and put objects at one remove from us, Smith assures us, 'infringes the requirement that an empirical world contain public objects susceptible to common reference' (2002: 16). What sort of a 'requirement' is this?

It is exceedingly common for objectivists like A. D. Smith to express their conviction that the world consists of singular entities by saying that we have to *take for granted* that they exist. Bernard Williams is the most recent, typical of many, whilst talking about the truth that we all accept about 'everyday objects':

> The *assumption* is that the identification of such everyday objects . . . plays such a basic role in human thought that our interpretations of other actual societies, and hence our understanding of human beings in general, can *take* it *for granted.*
> (Williams, 2002: 53, my emphases)

This assumption is part of what he calls the 'State of Nature *story*' (my emphasis) upon which his recommended virtues of Sincerity and Truthfulness depend. The same insistence that we should 'take for granted' the existence of commonly identifiable entities recurs in the current work of many philosophers (Evans, 1982: 40–1; Blackburn, 1984: 20; A. C. Grayling, 1985: 3, 12–13; Ben Ze'ev, 1989: 537; Heller, 1990: xi; Van Inwagen, 1990: 6; Hoffman and Rosenkrantz, 1997: 151).

Compare now what is said by some earlier philosophers. I shall quote a short representative group, although there are more.* Nietzsche, for whom ' "Thingness" is created by us', asserts that our judgements of this ontic kind in the world work 'under the *presupposition* that identical cases exist' (Nietzsche, 1968: note 29, 307, 289). It is the second assertion that opens up the real issue. Notice the echo in what Roy Wood Sellars says: 'No two individuals can possibly have numerically the same thing-experiences, even though it works ordinarily to make that *assumption*' (Sellars, 1969 [1916]: 57), my emphasis in both quotations). F. C. S. Schiller prefers to use the word 'postulate' as bringing out the fact that we are dealing with a *methodological fiction* and not with an absolute given:

> We stand unalterably committed to the *postulate* that identity shall be, though everywhere we have to make it and by force to fit it to the facts.
>   (Schiller, 1902: 104, my emphasis)

Now what these philosophers and scholars from other disciplines are saying looks very similar to what Williams and the others are saying. Place these side by side, the first from Aaron Ben Ze'ev, the second from Humberto R. Maturana and Francisco J. Varela:

> Instead of thinking that the perceptual system encounters isolated atoms from which a meaningful object is constructed or imagined, we can *assume* that at a certain level of description the perceptual system is sensitive to that object.
>   (Ben Ze'ev, 1989: 537, my emphasis)

> If it appears acceptable to talk about transmission of information in ordinary parlance, this is because the speaker tacitly *assumes* the listener to be identical with him and hence as having the same cognitive domain which he has (which never is the case), marvelling when a 'misunderstanding' arises.
>   (Maturana and Varela, 1980: 32–3, my emphasis)

---

*The philosophers Friedrich Nietzsche (1968: 289, 307); William James (1977: 139, 333–4, 433, 449–61); Fritz Mauthner (1923: II, 117); Josiah Royce (1976 [1899]: I, 73, 586); Roy Wood Sellars (1969 [1916]: 57); C. I. Lewis (1929 [1916]: 21); F. C. S. Schiller (1902: 103–4; 1929: 163–4, 223; and Humberto R. Maturana and Francisco J. Varela (1980: 32–3); the linguists Alexander Bryan Johnson (1968 [1828]: 72); and Sir Alan Gardiner (1932: 80); the psychologist Hermann von Helmholtz (1977: 140–2); the sociologist Alfred Schutz (1962: 3–47); the social theorist Theodor Adorno (1973: 14); and the psycholinguist Ragnar Rommetveit (1978: 31).

Look now at the two uses of the word 'assume'.

Ben Ze'ev's application of the word 'assume' clearly implies that he actually *believes* that 'the perceptual system is sensitive to *that object*'; indeed, the whole of Ben Ze'ev's work is based on that belief. It is something of which he is *convinced*. He was only using the word 'assume' to make plain that this was a kind of axiom about the real situation which one's overall theory of perception must include *as a given actuality*. The fact of the existence of singular objects is not to be doubted at all; in fact he believes that not to be convinced of it lands one in a philosophical morass.

Maturana and Varela, on the other hand, are using 'assume' differently, but just as acceptably. It is plain from what they include in the parenthesis that they reject the notion that two persons speaking to each other and co-operating in action have the same percepts and concepts of what is at the centre of their concern. Indeed, one can say that persons would not be concerned to be talking at all if they had the impossibly perfect agreement. As Wilhelm Dilthey pointed out,

> Interpretation would be impossible if the life-expressions were totally alien. It would be unnecessary if there were nothing strange about them.
> (Dilthey, 1913–67: Vol. VII, 225)

that is, we could not talk if we had nothing in common and we would not need to talk if we totally agreed on everything. As Graham Dunstan Martin puts it, 'the *difference* between individual consciousnesses' assessments of reality is ... a vital factor in evaluating and enlarging our own knowledge' (Martin, 1981: 32).

The ambiguity comes out well in a recent article on the topic of representation in perception. Charles Travis, concerned, I believe rightly, to argue for sensory experience as 'dumb', that is, bare evidence devoid of any *given* knowledge, states the following:

> It is making out, or trying to, what it is that we confront that we *take* things, rightly or wrongly, to be thus and so.
> (Travis, 2004: 65, his emphasis)

Is he agreeing with Ben Ze'ev or with Maturana and Varela as regards a given reality of 'things'? There is the familiar apparently postulatory phrase, 'take ... to be', and he rightly admits that we are 'trying to' make out 'things', but it is far from clear whether he thinks the 'things' pre-exist our selection from the flux. Look at the second use of the pronoun 'it': does it mean a given pre-existing public 'thing', or a current selection from a stuff without any pre-fixed boundaries, one that allows an individual selection at will, or does it mean the stuff of the real itself? Judging from the rest of his article, it appears that it never occurs to him, particularly in his discussion of the logic of the term 'looks', that, when one person's eyes pick out a single thing, another's (equally 'single') may only overlap with his, or may be two-and-a-bit samples of something else, or may even not be picked out at all.

A feature of evolutionary advance becomes relevant here. The 'Baldwin Effect' Dennett described draws attention to the fact that members of natural species have different 'wirings' in their responses to stimuli, and this is what allows a species to adjust to the environment, for those with an inadequate set of criteria die off (Dennett, 1992: 186–8). Dennett draws a little diagram of a pack of upright rods, each representing a species-member, with a group that tops all the others, with one particularly successful member out-topping them all (Figure 51).

What Dennett also acknowledges is that the environmental niche may change. However, what he did not make clear is that the successful group, made up of members each with a slightly different set of criteria, that were for a time responding adaptively to 'an object' in the world outside them, are now winnowed out anew because that 'object' is no longer what 'it' was. It is plain that there was no 'single' object that was the same for them all. So nature's scheme is best described, not as selecting and holding to invariants, but allowing for *the tracking by the species of rewarding features of the real as they change their sources*. These features may obviously not respect any *singularity* that might be attributed by us to the original choice of any one of the group: after all, to give a specific example, after the passage of time some members of it remain alive because they had included as the identified 'prey' what others had not recognized as such, prey that had been insignificant in its numbers before the change but became so after it.

At any time, any species will present a fuzzy set of responses to external stimuli, so that one cannot speak of 'one' object to which the species as

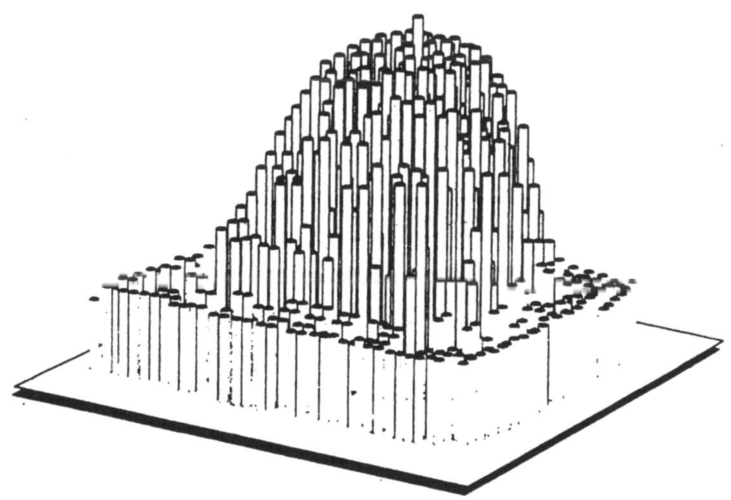

Figure 51

a whole is tuned but rather of a number of overlapping ones. Dennett's diagram should be seen, not only in motion through time, but with a set of rods above pointing downwards representing the dangerous real and these would be changing in length as we looked. It never occurred to Dennett to see the real as anything other than already conveniently sorted out into discrete objects awaiting recognition.

Now human beings in one sense are no different from animals in that they also gain by passing on new versions of the world, but, in language, they have a much more evolutionarily efficient mode of doing it. Following Dilthey's suggestion, it is plain that one talks only when one wishes to update other members of the species, when one thinks one has discovered that what has been *taken to be* an 'invariant' by us both as a guide to action has turned out not to be so. Or one asks a question, which is plainly a directing of the other onto the portion of the world that one requires updating on (or one gives or obeys a command, which is a way of obtaining action directly to produce change in such a portion).

Now I (and Travis) used the term 'taken to be' of the 'invariant', that is, the two participants in the minimal communication situation, *take it for granted* that they have both focused on the same area of concern, that involves the motivations of both of them (their fears, desires, pains, pleasures). There is an immediate oddity here for the would-be informant believes that he or she knows more than the hearer, so they are *not* focusing on exactly the same portion of the real. Indeed, the updating may produce a complete restructuring of the boundaries of the putative single object, qualitatively or spatio-temporally (in the case of the Rubin Vase illusion (Fig. 5, p. 6) a *single* candlestick turns into *two* human profiles and one full-face drawing and the gestalt-switch preserved nothing of the original save the outline).

There is no logical or empirical guarantee of singularity over perceptual changes like these: one bird-watcher might easily say to another, 'You know the bird you just counted – well, it was two-and-a-bit leaves.' To quote Dinnaga, a sixth-century Buddhist philosopher: 'Even "this" can be a case of mistaken identity' (quoted by Matilal, 1986: 332). Man may be 'the measure of all things', as Protagoras said, but he is *measuring*, counting, and that is an intersubjective idealization. It never disposes of the ever-present Kuhnian 'incommensurability' across from one person's 'referent' to another's (Kuhn, 1970: 198–204). Even the most recent substantial philosophical investigation into the relation of reference and consciousness never questions the singularity of 'the' object (Campbell, 2002).

One last indication that analytically minded philosophers have misconstrued what singularity is shows up when they try to account for gestalt-switches, such as Wittgenstein's 'duck-rabbit'. They always characterize the switch of interpretation as a move from 'seeing the picture as X to seeing it as Y': 'seeing-as' for them is always a 'seeing X as Y', but, as we have just seen, there is no guarantee that the singularity of the first interpretation will be preserved in the transformation. Even the duck-rabbit can with a little imagination be seen as more than one entity, a lake with a small island, say, or a stalactite seen through a cleft above a pool with a bubble on it, or two fungi growing on a rotting apple, etc., etc.

3.   Taking for granted: its place in the Statement

The Two Bomb-Defusers, and the Poet and the Blind Man, *took for granted* that they were referring to the 'same things' when they referred to 'the nut' and the 'way home'. The very act of 'taking for granted' itself discourages enquiry into its own nature, which is, in my view, one of the chief causes of the disinclination to regard it as worthy of analysis. After all, if two people are taking something for granted together, it would appear distrustful to the other if one of them set out to enquire into the nature of that compact. However, without being in any degree distrustful, we have a right here to make such an investigation.

Consider the phrasal verb 'to take for': this means (I quote from an earlier article of mine):

> *to accept one thing* as if *it were another* (e.g., 'It was so foggy I *took* him *for* his brother'); and 'granted' means *allowed, permitted, exposed to no expectation of opposition of will and desire from the other*. So 'to take for granted' means *to accept an illusion of real agreement as a perfect agreement, an apparent blending of motivation with another as a perfect fusing*. And what is this illusory agreement the illusion of which is to be temporarily ignored? – that a *single* object is before the agents concerned.
> (Wright, 1985: 86)

and they are concerned agents. So, in order to obtain a rough-and-ready mutual fix on a portion of the real, a *partial* overlapping of their differing selections, they have to behave *as if* they have a *perfect* one. The psycho-linguist Ragnar Rommetveit puts it thus: we 'take a *perfect* intersubjectivity for granted in order to achieve a *partial* one' (Rommetveit, 1978: 31). Alfred Schutz, another of the group listed in the footnote above, calls it a 'reciprocity of perspectives', 'the idealization of the interchangeability of the standpoints', the taking for granted that, if I were in your shoes, your standpoint would seem to be the same as mine, and you and I see things with the same typicality (Schutz, 1962: 11–12).

My own way of describing this trick by which we get a rough mutual grasp on the Real has been to say 'It is by a PRETENCE of *complete* success that we *partially* capture THE REAL' (Wright, 1978: 538).

In my view this set-up must have been an essential feature of the first successful language utterance. Two of our early hunter-gatherer ancestors must have been in a situation where one of them realized that the other was focusing its attention on roughly the same portion of the real as itself, and yet was failing to respond appropriately – that is, an updating of its fellow's percept was called for. Of course, there is no requirement that the *ur*-speaker was consciously aware of the notion of the overlapping of their perspectives: it probably believed that 'an' object was indeed 'exactly the same' for its partner. Nevertheless, the structure is one that looks like trust, for the pattern is as follows (ignore the fact that we put it in modern English, for they may have used gestures and noises): it is as if A indicates to B 'You know that bush that we are both seeing in the same way?', and then takes B to be acknowledging this somehow; and then A adds, 'But we are not seeing it in the same way, for it contains a deer.' In order for the statement, for that is what this is, to go through, first, there has to be first an apparent agreement on some portion of the real, which is then followed by a hopeful correction of it.

But this is the pattern of the Joke and the Story. Two people *assume* that they are referring to the 'same' entity only for one of them to discover that they were not. One could say that they have acted out a paradox, in that they first gained Rommetveit's mutual assumption of perfect intersubjectivity only to accept that it was only a partial one. To call *S is P* a 'proposition' reminds us that an informative utterance is precisely that, for the hearer has to consent, that is, adjust his or her motivation, to the change *proposed*. Propositions are thus active adjustments of existing agreements (of course, as I mentioned at the start, they are sometimes uttered with the aim of renewing or reasserting an agreement already made). They are certainly not static – except in the mutually imagined 'reciprocity of perspectives'. By this dynamic movement in the 'space of reasons' (W. Sellars, 1956: 289–90), new information is passed from one agent to another. Why else did Wilfrid Sellars (the son of Roy Wood Sellars) call it a '*space* of reasons' if not to allow for movement? (W. Sellars, 1956: 289–90). The proposition is thus the core element of language, prior to the grammatical units that make it up; as Benedetto Croce put it, 'the sole linguistic reality' is the proposition (Croce, 1909: 240). Questions and commands, as we shall see, are outgrowths of it; even exclamations, which do have an instinctive base, blur into propositions at times.

But to act on the putative perfect coinciding of their perspectives does demand what has the form of trust, the reason being that there is the implication that one's so-far-reliable percept is going to be subjected to a possibly risky transformation by one's language partner. I say only the form of trust, for no one could say that this lucky performance was carried out with open-eyed understanding of what was in progress; hardly, since it looks as if Nietzsche was the first to get a grasp of the *practical* necessity of this key assumption, to see it as a methodological fiction. If one listens to Plato, it is impossible to know and not to know simultaneously (*Theaitetos*: 191–2), but that is virtually what one is doing when, as hearer, one enters into the Idealization, for one is saying that you know something together with the speaker which, at the same time, you are prepared to allow him to transform into what you did not know. A mythical way of putting it would be to say that the laws of Apollo merged with the desire of Dionysus. A more down-to-earth analogue (that is more than an analogue) is to cite what goes on in a democratic parliament, where existing laws are altered so as to become new ones, strictly a patently *illegal* act. Within the terms of the philosophy of perception, one can say that both parties have to behave as if they are *seeing that* in order to enable their individual *seeing-as's* to be brought into some kind of mutual harness.

Notice here that it does not strictly matter for the argument to go through whether what we experience are goings-on in the brain, what philosophers today call 'qualia' or are colours, sounds, smells, etc. actually in the world external to us. Even if one believes that colours and sounds and smells, etc. are part of the public furniture of the world, they still are only a 'big blooming buzzing confusion' that has to be interpreted in co-operation with others (William James's phrase, that he had borrowed from 'someone'; James, 1977: 233).

Our use of the verb 'to count' can be given a new explanation as a result of what is argued here. It has two meanings: *to reckon up the number of a group of things* and also *to esteem, to value*. This association is not without significance, for it could be said within the theory that picking out a numerical unit is in fact a performance involving our desires. As Aristotle said, what counts as six apples for the seller may not count as six apples for the buyer. How often have you heard someone rejecting a classification with the phrase 'That doesn't count.' It appears that that purest of activities, mathematics, has a very impure origin in the hidden ambiguity of a mutual play with the Real.

To remove one last objection. It might be said that the two engaged in communication may be well aware that the other has a different understanding of the object outside them, but that very mutual awareness does not prevent them believing that a single object is before them, utterly independent of their differing views. However, there is nothing to sustain this belief other than their projection of that singularity, for how could one possibly gain a logical guarantee of such singularity in detachment from all human access? We can even say that we do not know whether the flux consists of discrete entities or not, or even a mixture of the two, but, whether it does or not, that makes no difference to our acts of discovery and communication, which must proceed on repeated initial *assumptions* of the ultimate possibility of perfect co-reference, and which can proceed successfully from our point of view without really committing ourselves to such an unsustainable claim. What indeed it is *to commit oneself to the process of mutual hypothesis* is something to which we shall return. We have come closer to agreement with Alexander Bryan Johnson's dictum:

> *Estimating nature by the oneness of language is a fallacy which enters deeply into every system of philosophy.*
> (Johnson, 1968 [1828]: 72, his emphasis)

4.   The projection of singularity

> The fool sees not the same tree that the wise man sees.
> (William Blake, 'Proverbs of Hell', No. 8)

>   difference
> Perceived in things, where, to the unwatchful eye,
> No difference is
> (William Wordsworth, *The Prelude* 1850, Book II, ll. 299–301)

Now we arrive at the first important outcome of this analysis: there is no need *to believe* that the two engaged in dialogue are focusing on a perfectly singular thing, only that they act *as if* they are. They are to *take for granted* that they are counting up to one together. Another way of putting it is to say that they are to treat what is in fact merely an overlap of two choices from the real, more or less close, as one and only one thing. If the overlapping of their obviously different selections from the real does not produce any realization of cross-purposes in the current situation, then both will be content to view what is before them as one and the same entity. But how ironic this is! – since in order that information should pass from speaker to hearer there had to be such a difference. This makes plain that, although there was an undoubted and undoubtable portion of the real in front of them, the *singularity* of the entity was only hypothesized in a kind of blind collusion. We can now declare safely that Evans and the others were turning the practically necessary regulative idea of there being singular entities in the world into an unsupported actuality. One might call the error 'Reifying the Thing'.

If this still seems strange to you, the strangeness can be removed by recognizing that this is how we deal with money every day. Last week at a conference I held up a euro coin and said, 'Don't we all agree that the value of this coin is the same for all of us? Yet because of the actual bargaining over buying and selling that is going on around us now its value is changing as we speak. I saw a Wall Street commentator on TV last week and a Movitype strip was showing the changing value of the dollar as he spoke. So you [the audience] can imagine a Movitype strip behind me showing the changing value of our words as I speak to you now. The belief that the coin has a stable value is only a catalyst that really takes no part in a commercial exchange but enables it to go ahead.' The Schutzian 'idealization of the interchangeability of standpoints' is that catalyst for language.

There is one objection here that I have already dealt with in other places (Wright, 2001: 11–12), that put forward by David Wiggins, the erstwhile Professor of Logic at Oxford University, that it is obvious that the object 'is there to be found' because if there is an aura of vagueness around the object, everyone's individual vaguenesses are the same because of the very fact that they are vague (Wiggins, 1986: 95). One can see how strong the prejudice is in Wiggins' argument because, while he is prepared to assert that 'there are no lines in nature', which would appear to admit that nature does not come already sorted for us, he cannot help thinking that 'we' are homing in on a pre-existing singularity. The weakness of the argument lies in its failure to see its *intersubjective* character as his use of 'we' betrays, for he never analyses the triangulation – he sees two ends only: an 'object' awaits 'us'. But his remark about vagueness actually gives his argument away, *for it is patently not the case that each person's vagueness is the same as another's*, for what one person considers too negligible to mention at time[1] might emerge as highly relevant for her at time[2] and what the other considers negligible equally so for him – but each at time[1] had failed to make salient those different criteria.

Wiggins, in believing that such vaguenesses are the same for each, was really doing no more than *exhorting us to join with him in Schutz's idealization*, the initial stance of an apparently perfect co-reference needed for the making of a statement. To exhort someone in this way is actually a call to uphold the mutual faith without which language cannot proceed. So on one level there is nothing wrong in Wiggins encouraging us to join in the idealization, for that is what we all have to do: what *was* wrong was to believe that each person actually has the same perspective on something identical in the same way for both of them. The Poet and the Blind Man *had to* talk of *one* 'way home'; the Two Bomb-Defusers, of 'the nut'.

Wiggins is really saying something like this: 'What is vague to us both is of no account, because we trust each other, and therefore, if any mismatch turns up, we can sort it out amicably.' Of course, Wiggins does not see it like this because he views his remarks as a call to fall in with reason, to rely on 'common' sense. Jürgen Habermas makes the same error: he understands that a mutually trusting idealization lies at the base of the human communication when he argues for his 'ideal speech situation' but what, like Wiggins, he does not take account of is the element of play that allows the updating of that idealization to be carried through. Typically, he gives away the fact that the idealization is a presupposition but without seeing what that implies:

> The objective world is *presupposed* in common as the totality of facts, where 'fact' signifies that a statement about about the existence of a corresponding state of affairs, *p*, can count as true.
>
> (Habermas, 1984: 52, my emphasis)

He is prepared to say that we each have 'individual maps' (1984: 79) but regards the idealization as normatively binding. One can draw attention to the fact that he sees 'jokes, fictional representations, irony, games, and so on' as 'category mistakes' (Habermas, 1982: 271), and so his mind is closed to the possibility of the proposition being of the Story pattern. The philosopher Willard Van Orman Quine makes virtually the same kind of error too, for he believes that all fineness of individuation depends upon the language, in which are available 'all distinctions' (Quine, 1960: section 12), which matches Wiggins' exhortation to us to join in the public faith. It is a case, as we shall see in the final chapter, of not accepting what a proper faith entails. Reason depends upon trust and not the reverse. He should have recalled F. C. S. Schiller's version of the idealization, that it is a 'postulation of the irrelevance of differences' (Schiller, 1929: 348), and for two people to *take* differences *to be* irrelevant as to engage in an act of trust, to take a joint risk that they know might produce conflict.

So when someone says to us with Bishop Butler 'Everything is what it is and not another thing' (Butler, 1970 [1726]: 14, para. 39) or, in more up-to-date philosophical fashion, with Alvin Plantinga, 'Everything is self-identical is true in every possible world' (Plantinga, 1974: 57), or, with Robert Kirk, the fact that we each make different constructions of the sun, does not mean that they are not about the same sun (Kirk, personal communication, 2005), then we shall agree with our tongue in our cheek, knowing that all they are actually saying is that we should join with them in the imaginative projection of the singularity of things and persons.

5. Ontology

Therefore, there is neither a *singular* object at the third corner nor *singular* selves at the other two corners. There are portions of Real existence there which for the time being are judged as satisfying the current purposes of the two in dialogue, for the ability of one to correct the other proves that. There is no doubt of the realism of the flux or *materia prima* or ὕλη or 'being' at the corner, for we get a shock when the other proves his or her access to it by inducing a change in our perception, as any joker does, but there is doubt about each of us making the same 'objective' selection from it – the other could not have induced the shock without that difference. What it does not prove is that something that is timelessly 'thus-and-so' for both of them inhabits that corner, nor that they themselves are timelessly 'thus-and-so'. To correct someone's view of the world is to alter *them*. But this is what we would expect from the evidence of the Joke and the Story, for there is nothing to guarantee either the interpretation or the singularity of the Ambiguous Element. We are ourselves Ambiguous Elements. People (and philosophers) have been confusing singularity, what we claim to *know* mutually, with what *exists* at all three corners, that to which singularity cannot be mutually applied with logically perfect precision. To quote Andrew Seth, 'Existence is one thing and knowledge is another' (Seth, 1887: 126), and that applies to both things and persons. Another philosopher who has stressed the *plurality* of our separate views of the world is Michael Lynch.

He draws our attention to the variation in perspective, the conceptual and perceptual scheme, that each of us has (Lynch, 2001).

A picture of what is going on would help. If we take the top three positions of our familiar diagram they will represent the Triangulation that allows for one person to update another about the world. The 'intentional perspectives' are, of course, those of two human beings, themselves open to being updated in their view of themselves by each other. What they are focusing on, the Ambiguous Element, is some fuzzy portion of the Real and each has his or her own view of it, so the corners of the triangle consist of overlapping regions that are, at the beginning of any communication, *taken for granted* as singular and common to both, one might say, as *Dinge-an-Sich* in the Kantian noumenon. Take all the circles as selected from the background of the Real in Figure 52. The fact that there is an uncertain multiplicity at the corners has to be *trustfully* ignored. The trust has to be entered into willy-nilly, whether it is realized or not: otherwise there would be no possibility of getting the two *differing* viewpoints into some kind of temporary lock with each other, a lock that enables the hoped-for correction to go through.

However, I am not going to express this view by saying that 'There are no objects' as Wilfrid Sellars has been tempted to do (1981: 57). There are certainly objects in the sense that for our social group at this time our overlapping selections have produced and are producing guides to action that are serving us in varying degrees of reliability at the moment, and these are

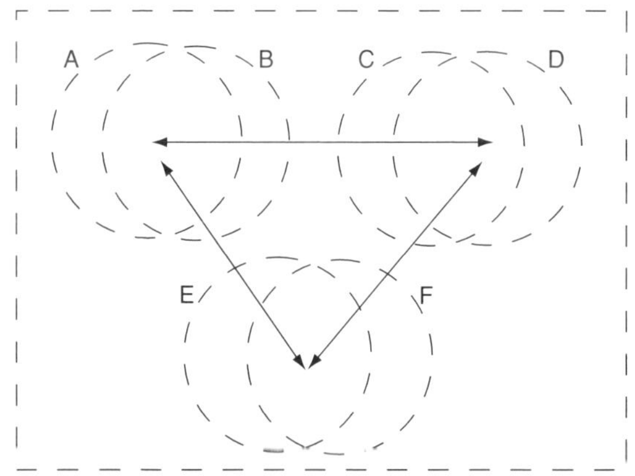

A: First Subject's concept of himself.
B: Second Subject's concept of A.
C: Second Subject's concept of herself.
D: First Subject's concept of B.
E: First Subject's concept of the Object.
F: Second Subject's concept of the Object.

Figure 52

what we call 'objects' (and 'persons'). We need to hold to the system to keep going, and this is the core sense that one can give to Peter Strawson's insistence that a 'descriptive metaphysics' must include the concepts of 'basic particulars' and 'persons' (Strawson, 1959). But none of this escapes the essential requirement that we have to keep in mind that these entities are still only entities *imagined as singular out of the Real by co-operating persons*, and they all basically remain contestable. So, once we understand the trusting trick – and I do mean trick – by which 'common' sense is established, then we can enter into its *taking for granted* with open eyes. The Trick has exactly the structure of the Joke and the Story. We have to hold to common sense while recognizing the trust that is its foundation.

If it still strikes you as bizarre, the oddity can be made less so by a reassuring implication. One can apply the philosopher's tool, Ockham's Razor, here. William of Ockham, a medieval philosopher, argued that, in one's view of what constitutes the basic elements of reality one should commit oneself to as few as possible, for then one will rest on the simplest hypothesis; to have a multiplicity would give too many hostages to fortune in the great contest of philosophy. One's ontology, that is, one's picture of what makes up what underlies everything, should be as economical, as frugal as can be, given one's beliefs. So here one can ask 'Which is the more frugal ontological commitment of these two? – to be convinced that the world consists of endlessly countable singular entities (things and persons) or merely *to act as if there are such.*' The answer is obvious – the latter, for that commits one's belief to only three components, the very ones we discerned from our look at the Bomb-Disposers analogy:

(1) *the existence of the continuum*, flux, matter, or *hyle*, what the Ancient Greek philosophers called the 'wood', the stuff of which everything is made, the Real, and this includes both the Real external to the mind and all sensory experiences in their knowledgeless, non-epistemic state;
(2) *human agents* engaged in this language-game (who, remember, are not singular either, their perceived singularity being only virtual, though their sensing and what it is isomorphic to is part of the Real); and
(3) *the game itself*, which moves through time as an ongoing, needful, experimental process performed by those agents. This is the best sense to be given to what the social theorists call 'structure' (Archer, 1995; Bhaskar, 1978; Giddens, 1977).

To use Michael Jubien's words, we can have as many things 'as we *like*' (Jubien, 1993: 1, my emphasis) but without any of the ontological baggage that philosophically committing ourselves to an actual universe of them would bring. The word 'like' is important because, as was noted before, no one would pick out, 'single' any-*thing* from the stuff of the world unless motivated to do so. Ernest Sosa has pointed out that anyone embracing an ontology of ordinary physical objects is liable to this very charge, namely, that they are faced with 'an explosion of reality', since there is no limit on the number of entities that one could pick out (Sosa, 1987: 155–87). It reminds us of one of Bertrand Russell's comments, that finally, to banish all difference from the 'common' referent, one would have to have a word for every infinitesimal instant of every object, an *apax legomena*, a language of 'once-only-names', achievable only by the character in one of Jorge Luis Borges' stories, Ireneo Funes (Russell, 1923). Borges' character has a memory so extraordinary that he can remember every instant of all his sensory experiences, and so fix a name to each one of them. He was metaphorically drowned in the impossible richness of his selections his memory made from his sensing. One is also reminded of John Locke's warning that we could not name everything (*Essay*, III, iii, 2).

Joshua Hoffman and Gary S. Rosenkrantz have endeavoured to counter this part of the argument by a claim that, among entities, organisms would not be liable to such endless division since they obviously fall into given 'natural kinds', but this is no more than a last-ditch reiteration of Schutz's idealization as applied to 'natural kinds' (Hoffman and Rosenkrantz, 1997: 177–8). This is no surprise if one recalls that evolution produces a system in which species do not fixate themselves upon 'invariants', but track rewarding features that inevitably are changing even as they are 'singled'. It is curious that some philosophers try to attach fixation to natural kinds, for, if anything should remind us of evolutionary change, natural kinds should.

If you think about it, since our sorting of the Real is the result of past and present negotiations about how it is to be viewed, there is no likelihood of our homing in on some given timeless, perfectly singular thing. The Real is there sure enough (both in our sensing and in what our sensing is changing in proportion with), for it is what will reward us if we get our interpretations right and punish us if we get them wrong, though what constitutes that 'right' and 'wrong' is itself precarious, since what was right for us today in one context may not be so tomorrow in another. However, to keep the social feedback process going we have to behave as if all the objects exist as we take them to be while knowing that, though we have selected a 'thing' out of what exists, out of the Real, its 'objectivity' is a mutual hypothesis.

Objectivity and existence come apart. What is, therefore, also entailed is that one cannot say '*Cogito ergo sum*' for that is an illicit attempt to declare that they – in this case singular *subjectivity* and existence – are one.

Figure 52 shows clearly that, though your 'object' exists as a choice from the Real, and my 'object' exists thus too, the two choices rest on our (tentative) trust that they both overlap without any mismatch according to our judgement of the outcomes relevant to my assessment of the purpose, my judgement of what it means for me, and yours. There is no guarantee available that will banish the possibility of future disagreement about some outcome. This is why trust is prior to logical agreement, as we have seen in this chapter. This is a poetic, not a logical, epistemology.

Before concluding, there is one set of objections to be dealt with which is likely to be levelled at this analysis and also some general remarks to be made relating it to other views. Since, as an epistemology, it is of what is called the 'naturalized' kind, then it must have an answer to what the philosopher Hilary Putnam has asked about naturalized epistemology. Naturalized epistemology claims to give a scientific account of what knowledge is, that is, as an act of knowledge it presumes to consider what knowledge itself is. Though that may seem at first to be equivalent to gazing at one's own navel, it is apparent that the investigation is not ruled out as an inconsistency. There is nothing logically objectionable in enquiring into how knowing and reason might be seen as features of an evolved organic system of regulation of action. Putnam has made three objections: (1) that it relies on the Correspondence Theory of Truth; (2) that it has to presuppose reason; and (3) that it cannot account for normativity of any kind (Putnam, 1982).

The present argument has answers for these three accusations. First, as regards his claim that it relies on a Correspondence Theory of Truth: if the system is one in which such correspondence is mutually projected as a useful *make-believe*, then his objection loses its force. Second, in saying that naturalized epistemology 'presupposes' reason, his very own words point to the answer, for within the Triangulation argument reason is indeed essentially constructed through an active *presupposing* of universally agreed unities and deductive validities. Instead of being a weakness of the argument, this is one of its strengths, namely its bringing out into the open the trust in that mutual presupposing upon which knowledge is based. Putnam, like those other philosophers I have mentioned, was himself presupposing without realizing it. Lastly, he said naturalized epistemology can find no base for normativity because it is driven back to a circular argument in which the subject strives to be his own guarantee of reliability (Putnam, 1982: 245). But the Triangulation argument yields verdicts whose reliability requires *mutual co-operation* to establish, and sees all 'entities', selves, others and things as inescapably intersubjectively established. The normativity lies in its placing faith at the core of knowledge, even at its most 'impersonal', for all 'impersonal' means is that we are all – so far – in agreement.

5
Language

1. How do people make their differing perspectives converge on a region of the Real?

Although the Poet and the Blind Man did not have the same sensory access to the real outside them, that is, the material continuum in all its incalculable variations, nevertheless, they were for a while able to act in a way that satisfied their immediate concerns. The fact that the coincidence of perspectives was strictly incomplete did not prevent an agreement being reached which appeared to satisfy current interest. That is not surprising, because attention of its very nature is selective, and, *if what is selected by two or more persons serves that particular interest, it does not matter for that moment that it may not satisfy some other interest.* Through further experience, when the relevance of other issues is to the fore, those differences may become salient to one or other of them. Emma and Mr Elton were both happy to think they had reached the same understanding when talking of 'the riddle' about court-ship, but the scene in the carriage later in their narrative was to prove it otherwise.

A comment from nearly 180 years ago is relevant here:

Two men, who assent to the same general proposition, may possess very diverse meanings.

In the use of general propositions, much misunderstanding occurs from the identity of language and the diversity of nature. If I assert that George is good, you may assent. Under this verbal identity, I may refer to actions of George that are unknown to you; and you may refer to actions of George unknown to me. Nay, the actions to which I refer might cause you to reprobate George.

(Johnson, 1968 [1828]: 91)

What, then, is the structure of this hit-and-miss co-operation, for the risk will not go away? One could, of course, begin like Wittgenstein, and say that once a rule has been publicly agreed upon then all judgements coincide and that anyone who claims to have a subjective view of the rule is making a queer mistake. But mis-*takes* are exactly that – 'queer', precisely because they upset the comforting *takings*-for-granted everyone has been making. It was very queer indeed for Pip when Magwitch visited him in his lodgings and started to evince a peculiar fatherly manner. It is much more consoling to believe that the world is made up of familiar things and persons, entities that remain reassuringly singular and reliable.

John Heil, who realizes that there exists a kind of triangulation between two observers and 'an object', nevertheless cannot make the move to considering the possibility that, though each observer regards what he sees as an object, it might be the case that the object for each is a different selection. He takes an iceberg as an example and claims that it is more accurate to say that 'perhaps, the line runs between me and some state of affairs of which the iceberg is a component' (Heil, 1993: 216). In this he is still talking of 'the iceberg'. We should rather heed Peter Unger's insistence that it is likely that there is no fact of the matter about whether entities are determinate or not; he reminds us that there is 'an enormous amount of gradualness' in the world (Unger, 1988: 294). As an iceberg is melting all the time, and is thus exceedingly 'gradual', we have to ask what is *to count* for us as part of it or not, or the 'same' or not, and that means consulting my desires and fears and your desires and fears about just where we shall agree to draw the line.

There can therefore be no so-called 'Correspondence Theory of Truth' in which the proposition in a statement actually corresponds to some external 'state of affairs' since there are no objective *singularities* beyond human choice, only the incalculable Real. I have always thought that there is a give-away in that familiar phrase 'state of affairs', for affairs are things that involve desires and fears, but the phrase is used as if such impure matters were furthest from the thought of the speaker dealing in the high question of 'Terewth', to use Mr Chadband's version. Truth-as-troth, on the other hand, takes them very much into account.

Nor can there be a pure Coherence Theory of Truth for that still begs the question of what sustains the agreement across persons. That too is part of the general trust that all that has been identified fits into a non-contradictory whole, but that is no more than a shadow cast by our social hope. The Pragmatic Theory of Truth ignores the problem of who is to decide whose needs and interests are satisfied by the outcome, which is also a begging of the question of how to deal with the risk involved in entering into an agreement, and it also signally ignores *the need to idealize fictively the final outcome*, an idealization present whenever we speak (as we shall see abundantly confirmed in the next chapter). Tarski's Semantic Theory of Truth ties truth to a logically rigorous formal system of 'object-sentences' or 'token-sentences' that are generated according to constraints and rules in a metalanguage (such as ' "Snow is white" is a true sentence if and only if snow is white'): this should be able to be seen at once as a formalizing of the 'taken-for-granted', one in which the risk of mutual trust has vanished in a complacent identification of the idealization with the Real (Tarski, 1983). The Performative Theory of Truth (Strawson, 1949) is nearest to acknowledging the risk, since to second what another says, even with the word 'Ditto', is to commit oneself in an act of faith, and then what that faith is to consist of becomes ethically crucial; the proponents of the Performative Theory, however, do not see the relevance of faith to the argument – for to say 'Ditto' is to commit oneself to the fictive idealization, whereas they take it merely as a perfect repetition of what was said before.

What we can see so far from stories is that a mutual co-ordination of reference that serves a practical end can exist when the actual selections made by two or more observers do not match. It is when a correction goes through, successfully or unsuccessfully, that the real outside the triangulation proves its existence; the triangle doesn't have sharp corners. Not for nothing did Robert Frost start his poem 'Mending Wall' with the lines,

> Something there is that doesn't love a wall,
> That sends the frozen-ground-swell under it
> (Robert Frost, 'Mending Wall', ll. 1–2; Frost, 1951: 53–4)

Indeed, we can be sure of the existence of that 'frozen-ground-swell', the Real, under our 'walls', our words, at the very moment when a change in knowledge takes place that is of concern to our living purposes, altering them and us in the process, that is, exactly when the *certainty of some identification of ours is shown to be dubious*, even of our own 'self', we can be *certain of the existence of the real*. A correction applied from outside can alter the very objectivity, not only of objects, but of the self observing, since the particular selection it is making was a directing of its own desire or fear.

So brute existence, both of (A) *the internal sensory field* to which another has shown him- or herself to have had a disturbingly intimate access, and of (B) *the external distribution of energy* to which it is proportionately tied, has been shown to be present by the very shifting about of what we take to be 'an object'. Objectivity remains provisional and uncertain precisely because it is only the outcome of an essentially fallible co-ordination game, but what it works on is unmistakable being, the Real, inside and outside the brain. So this is *a philosophy of realism*, but not a realism of given objects and persons, but one of a real that lies outside our tentative projections.

It was noted before that there is no inbuilt assurance of inevitable progress in this correction scheme. Richard Gregory is right in his claim that all our percepts are hypotheses (Gregory, 1993: 232–62). Some philosophers, for example, Richard Woodfield, have questioned his theory that all perceptions are hypotheses constructed from a separate sensation-level: it is on the ground that gestalt-projection bears no resemblance to logical inference. As Woodfield says, 'Monkeys do not make guesses when they leap from tree to tree' (Woodfield, 1996: 11). But one has to see the *metaphorical* point of Gregory's use of the word 'hypothesis'. As we have seen, the essential feedback provided by the motivation system is automatic (when we feel a pain our memory is stimulated at once), but, nevertheless, memory has a key advantage in that it can be updated at any time, either immediately as a result of some further motivation-feedback, or, in the human case, by communication. (Of course, for the latter, there may be, on some highly self-conscious occasions, processes of logical inference literally involved.) So a selection from the Real does partake of the nature of a hypothesis in that it is only *viable*, open to adjustment at any time should the feedback of an unexpected pain or pleasure result, or should a social partner give us warning of pain or promise of pleasure. So, although it is counter-intuitive to think of a monkey 'making a hypothesis' as its jumps from tree to tree, nevertheless, whatever its systems are automatically doing, they are not guaranteed a *certain* success. Lower down the evolutionary ladder automatic systems that fail are not reproduced. For we human beings all communication of knowledge works on a basis of warning or promise; and rhetoric upon the dialectical skill of indicating those contextual clues that will suggest the needful change of our gestalts to ward off failure.

What is it then that leads philosophers – as well as hard-headed men of commonsense – to go on claiming that the world of everyday recognizable things and persons is what actually exists? It is because to achieve the co-ordination of our separate selections, we have to behave to each other *as if that were what was really the case*, that all objects and persons were indeed common in the same way to us all, or, to put it in the philosopher's language, we had *already* achieved a logically pure singular reference. In view of the huge prejudice, perhaps the most powerful form of prejudice there is, it needs reiterating that all these philosophers are doing is exhorting us not to question the trust that binds us together. But to question it *philosophically* is not to question it *ethically*. They are too blinkered to see this distinction.

It is part of the essential structure of communication that we *dramatically perform* a perfect coincidence of reference even when we know full well we have not achieved any such thing. The fact that we have made different sortings from the real, so that what we really have is a practical overlap and nothing more, will not prevent us together carrying out much of what we wanted to do. An adequate convergence of our separate selections is all we need, but how adequate it is is up to the real.

That this 'fictive' method has to be adopted can be readily understood: unless we acted to bring our differing perspectives on the real into some measure of overlap, we could never effect any corrections whatever. So, with Quine, we can agree that language does need an 'absolute standard', but it is one that is hypothesized, maintained mutually as a useful regulatory idea, a practically useful 'let's-pretend'. That it is a fiction tends to conceal itself, because each of us is making his or her own selection from what is undoubtedly real, that is to say, one could claim that each person's individual selection of an object or person or self was real in the sense of being just that particular selection from existence, but whether the criteria that person was applying are going to remain successful or not is another matter. Of course, the longer the success continues, the more recognition becomes a familiar habit, the more we are tempted to take 'the object' as existent in the same way for us all. The basis of this co-operation is thus an act of trust, and to that important fact we shall return.

In Chapter 4.3 meanings were conceived of as existing in 'a space of reasons' (W. Sellars, 1956: 289–90), a space in which there was dynamic movement for that is the purpose of communication, to allow the hopeful updating of one person by another to go through. Two people *take for granted* that they have one referent, one entity, person or thing before them just so that a correction may go through. It is obvious that, if they did not make that first hypothetical move, they could not get even a rough mutual grasp on the flux in which they are wholly immersed, even to the tiniest cell of their own beings. The triangle does not have singularities at any of its corners. So, as we saw earlier, each proposition is indeed a proposing of a change in the way the world is to be perceived, and hence in the way a word is to be understood.

The Triangulation Argument does not need an ontology of subjects and objects, which is a problem both for anyone like Bertrand Russell who thought the world consisted of a totality of facts, and those, like the idealists, for whom the subject was dominant over reality. The argument only needs 'subjects' and 'objects' as part of our method of handling the world when some difficulty turns up. To quote Calvin Schrag again, the whole subject/ object dichotomy is bogus: 'reference can no longer be depicted as the mirroring of honest-to-goodness entities in the external world' (Schrag, 1986: 32–3). Social selection of those imagined singular entities *from* the incalculable Real goes on all right, but their use can only proceed on its sufferance. Certainly the game of playing with them really goes on, just as a performed drama in progress in the theatre has a source in the Real apart from the fictions of its plot and characters, but that does not make Hamlet real. So the mundane familiarity of the *singularity* of our selves and of the things about us remains ultimately *fictive*, a virtual appearance of objectivity mutually projected onto the Real, however much habit has seemed to take the tentativeness out of 'them'. As part of our daily method of thought and communication they retain a real aspect, just as the performed drama does. It is that 'reality' at one remove that gives them their 'transcendental', even 'spiritual' character. Our prejudice for the safety of certainty keeps backing them up, but nothing can turn those singularities, those *finite* entities, into the continuum of the *infinite* Real which is what actually engages with our desires and fears. Nor are those desires and fears entirely free from correction, though the resistant Real can surge up through them too.

2. The Statement and its origin

An informative statement in language, one that updates a hearer, can thus be said to conform roughly to Friedrich Schiller's tripartite division that was mentioned before (J. C. F. Schiller, 1967 [1795]; see Chapter 1.6, p. 41):

 (i) There is first the 'sense-drive', the sensory registrations in our brains that provide the bare evidence, different for each person. We can see this as the Ambiguous Element.
 (ii) Then there is the 'form-drive', in which we can now say that two or more speakers of a language engage in Schutz's 'idealization of the reciprocity of perspectives', taking for granted that they are singling out what is exactly the same entity in the Real. We can see this as the First Intentional Perspective, the First Clue, taken to be identical for both.
 (iii) Then there is the 'play-drive' which can stand for the ironic correction induced by the would-be corrector of the hearer. We can see this as the Second Clue.

Let us take a representative statement, one actually made in a real circumstance. Note that we are not looking at a 'sentence', which is rather an idealized abstract from the hurly-burly of human life, but something really spoken that conveys a new understanding to the hearer.

Take a speaker A saying 'The cat is on the mat' to a hearer B and updating their understanding thereby, part of a conversation about a real cat. They begin with the mutual presupposition: that Speaker and Hearer have already achieved a perfect coinciding of reference upon the flux, that they have singled out exactly the same portion together, that it exists as a numerically single, objective entity in a way entirely independent of their own views of 'it'. The Hearer knows well that his view needs updating: in being prepared to listen, he is readying himself for an updating of his selection from the continuum, moving nearer to a proper notion of that 'single' thing with which they are concerned. This then is the essential first move in a communication, that, unconnected from their own partial understandings, as an ideal goal for them, there exists a logically single entity upon which their differing perspectives can focus. The *assumption* is that a perfect co-reference awaits the refining of their separate, limited conceptions of the thing. It is like two people peering through fog *taking for granted* that *one* tree, identical for both, is the target of their vision.

So let us suppose initially that they both are focusing on the cat with which they both are familiar. Now A is aware that it is on the mat and adds to the presupposition 'The cat' the words 'is on the mat'. This latter portion of the statement produces the updating of B's selection. It is as if A says to B, 'You know that (single) cat which we have both come across in our differing experiences?' – to which B replies 'Yes' (the interchange that establishes the necessary collusion about there existing a logically perfect referent as goal for them both) – 'Well,' says A, 'it is on the mat.'

The process is like the Liar Paradox – 'Epimenides the Cretan said, "All Cretans are liars."' It starts by maintaining that A and B both 'speak the same language', that is, have all their referents worked out in logical commonality, in ideal mutual knowledge, all signifiers matching all signifieds in complete detachment from all users of the language, whatever fuzzy perceivings and conceivings they may individually have. It ends by admitting that they had not reached that ideal stage, that their language had not been the same, the reason being that there was one cat that they did not have identical understandings of since part of its existence included for A its being on the mat at that time and for B it did not. What is strictly a fictive act enables an advance of interpretation of the Real to take place: to quote Paul Ricœur, 'fiction is the privileged path for the redescription of reality' (1981: 142). What he says about play may fitly be applied to the Statement:

> In playful representation, 'what is emerges'. But 'what is' is not longer what we call 'everyday reality': or, rather, reality truly becomes reality, that is, something which comprises a future horizon of undecided possibilities, something to fear or hope for, something unsettled.
> (Ricoeur, 1981: 187)

And also this of Calvin Schrag's, the American rhetorician:

> Saying is the relating of a narrative or the telling of a story. The German *sagen* highlights this originative sense is saying more pointedly than does its English equivalent. *Sagen* is the activation of a *saga*. It is a story or a tale being told. It is a narration of that around which the saying turns, and it is a narration implicating the narrator.
> (Schrag, 1986: 123)

At the end of each statement we resume that idealization of our 'referents' which constitutes our 'everyday reality', but knowing full well that that 'everyday reality' remains 'unsettled' since the Real can upset it at any time. The puzzles of the Real are all about us, and it is only by entering the story of the Statement that we can try to cope with them, as Richard Kearney says:

> It is precisely because we are beings who know that we will die that we keep on telling stories, struggling to represent something of the unpresentable, to hazard interpretations of the puzzles and aporias that surround us.
> (Kearney, 2003: 231)

The Real is always 'unpresentable', part of it being the meaningless sensations we try to order together, themselves structurally isomorphic to other parts of the meaningless Real outside them. Stories are our only mode of handling it. Don Cupitt, in his book on the Story, points in the same direction: 'language usually works by endlessly seeing one thing in terms of another', which is what we have seen the Story to be (Cupitt, 1991: 57).

The pattern is reminiscent of Freud's 'Fort–Da': he observed his son, aged one-and-a-half, playing with a cotton-reel that he had on a string and amusing himself by alternately allowing it to disappear, saying to himself 'Fort' (*Gone!*) when it disappeared and 'Da' (*There!*) when, as he pulled it back, it reappeared. Freud attributes to the game the unconscious meaning of enacting the disappearance of his mother and her subsequent reappearance. For us this is immediately evocative of the structure of the Joke and the Story in that an unpleasant interpretation is succeeded by a pleasant one. In the Statement the hearer is subjected to a challenge to an apparently safe agreement with the other that is at once reinterpreted as a restitution of that safety (Freud, 1985: 283–5).

Another way of bringing out the paradoxical nature of the Statement is to liken it to Geoffrey Bateson's notion of the Double Bind. Bateson's own definition is as follows:

(1) When the individual is involved in an intense relationship: that is, a relationship in which he feels it is vitally important that he discriminate accurately what sort of message is being communicated so that he may respond appropriately.

(2) And, the individual is caught in a situation in which the other person in the relationship is expressing two orders of message and one of these denies the other.

(3) And, the individual is unable to comment on the messages being expressed to correct his discrimination of what order of message to respond to, i.e., he cannot make a metacommunicative statement. (Bateson, 1978: 180).

It is strange to see how the definition applies, for the first two criteria fit the Statement perfectly, in that we begin by assuming an identity of understanding and then allow it to be exposed to an unexpected transformation in the narrative mode. As in (1), we are in a vital relationship with the speaker and we do seek to respond appropriately: as in (2), there are 'two orders of meaning', the one, supposedly agreed with the speaker, and the one he or she uses to subvert the first. The third criterion does apply in the case where the updating is unacceptable to the hearer and circumstances, such as when an inferior social position, or some other obstacle, prevents us from expressing our opinion on the putative updating of our understanding.

Bateson was applying the notion of the Double Bind to schizophrenic patients, but it turns out that their predicament shares a structure with that of normal people in dialogue.

In Chapter 2.7 we noted that Viktor Shklovsky defined art as a 'defamiliarization', in which the artist made objects strange to us, renewing our perception. He detected it in lyric poetry but also in the Story, particularly in the plot. It is a definition that applies readily to the Statement if it is seen as this transformation of a hypothesized agreement. He sees habitual associations being stripped away so that the object can be re-experienced (Shklovsky, 1965). What he did not see was the practical necessity of beginning with a taken-for-granted agreement, those habitual associations. It can also be seen that Todorov's picture of the progession in the Story from equilibrium through disruption to a new equilibrium projects the pattern of the Statement onto the Story (Todorov, 1977: 111). Roland Barthes anticipates this claim:

> The narrative is one big sentence, just as every statement is in some sense the outside of a little narrative.
> (Barthes, 1977: 84)

There is an obvious objection here which springs from the desire to hold to the singularity of the referent, not as *assumed* but as *believed*. *The whole point of a language, goes the objection, is to have agreement on the rules, whether of the meaning of words or of the workings of syntax. A dictionary, surely, cannot be a matter of continuously changing meanings, for how would anyone understand anyone else if meanings changed all the time? If the syntax had no accepted rules, the words would lose their relationship with other words and we could make no sense of any statement, unable to tell a noun from a verb or one tense from another. We would have anarchy and chaos: no one would be able to communicate with anyone else. We would have collapsed into the most currently hated of all states, relativism. Since the investigations of the linguist Ferdinand de Saussure, we have known that there has to be 'synchrony', that is, a fixed set of rules that govern* la langue, *independently of any user, and it is obvious that the rules can be codified, both in the dictionary as regards meanings and in the grammar as regards syntactical relationships. Or we might use Noam Chomsky's terms and speak of the 'competence' of speakers of a language, their acquaintance with its rules, not necessarily conscious, as distinct from their 'performance', the actual way they use it. Saussure does admit that language changes as a result of usage over time, for in* le parole, *spoken and written language historical changes do take place, producing 'diachrony', but this does not disturb the basic tenet that rules must apply.*

One can at once concede that 'rules must apply', but the character of the present theory lies in the desire of speakers to project the agreement of those rules. It is not that the rules exist independently of the speakers, for we have seen that there is no way in which the 'objective singularity' of entities outside us (and within us) can be established apart from the Triangulation. As Horst Ruthrof says, 'A dictionary does not contain any meanings, only verbal substitutions' (Ruthrof, 2000: 150), which implies that the dictionary is blindly within the idealization, as if words could be substituted with other words without reference to anyone's motivations. Ruthrof is someone who cannot ignore the contribution the body makes to the meanings of the language.

Of course, Schutz's Idealization of Reciprocity of Standpoints is not something of which the speakers are actively conscious: it has arisen out of an evolutionary success with one person's facilitating the endless correction of percepts and concepts in the other. However, although the acceptance of 'rules' is essential for language, no statement could be made if we adhered to them slavishly. What Catherine Bates says of a whole text can be applied to the Statement: 'A text makes a contract between writer and reader who agree for a period to play the same game', and, as with all games, the winner is the one who transforms the course of that game through applying the rules in a novel way (Bates, 1999: 73). A contract, of course, implies an act of trust between the two speakers, so the trust is the basis upon which the proposition is based, a trust that will allow itself to be surprisingly subverted. Stanley Fish, who allows that all objectivity is mediated, nevertheless believes that 'convention' is what guarantees the assumptions we make together (Fish, 1981: 10–11). This can now be seen to be a half-truth, because, while it is indeed true that we have to hold to agreements together, that must be in faith that allows for a correction from the other that might not be 'mediatable'.

You may recall the account given by the blind and deaf Helen Keller of her first entrance into language. The teacher had for a long time been pressing on her hands the signs for things, but Helen had not understood the use of the signs. She explains that she had a sudden revelation of what she could do with a sign as she ran her hands through the water coming from a tap; the teacher signed 'water' at that moment. It seems likely that what she unconsciously realized, as the water ran over her hands was not that she had just 'come to understand what a name was' (Aitchison 1996: 96), but that language began with the understanding that the other's attention was focused, through the word 'water', on *roughly the same* portion of the Real as her own, even though she and her teacher had markedly different perceptions of 'it', her teacher having normal sensory access to the world, she herself being deaf and blind. At that same moment she could have employed the sign in communication about that very water. Though she could not see or hear the water from the tap that she was feeling, she nevertheless could have updated her teacher's understanding of it, for example by saying 'Warm'. It is a parallel case to the Blind Man leading the Poet home. And the useful coincidence was achieved by both behaving *as if* they had focused on a single entity. Again it is a case of the 'trust' being willingly open to subversion.

There may be still a temptation in some readers to say 'But there must be real water out there, quite apart from Helen's feeling of it and the teacher's seeing and hearing of it!' No one is denying that some imprecise region of the Real is before them both, but there is no *logically singular* object there. Take up the implications: such an objector has already admitted that he or she believes that water, identical for both, is existing outside both of them *apart from how it feels, how it looks, how it sounds, how it tastes, how it smells,* which is to concede what has been argued for, namely, that the Real does not possess the sensory features the brain ascribes to it, only structurally isomorphic characteristics that are responding to intensities, frequencies, molar shapes (for touch) and molecular ones (for taste and smell) – so the Real is colourless, soundless, 'touch-less', taste-less, and smell-less. So what is left for water to be? Why, obviously, as the scientists tell us, the molecules made up of two atoms of hydrogen and one of oxygen – but that is not to be relied upon. As J. van Brakel has reminded us, liquid water contains some H_3O positive ions not found in steam, and steam contains H_4O_2 molecules not found in water (van Brakel, 1992), and one might add there will be a few atoms of deuterium oxide thrown in and perhaps lots of calcium carbonate, and dissolved oxygen and nitrogen, and hosts of bacteria and other animalculae, etc., etc. And on top of that we do not know whether these molecules, of whatever kind, are to be thought of as made up of waves or particles or something else, and who is to say where the 'water' ends and the 'water vapour' being given off begins. If at this point the objector falls back on appeals to human use, we are back with the problem of two or more persons judging by their desires and fears whether a particular sample is to be called 'water', which is exactly the plight of the Two Bomb-Defusers.

A communication from one person to another is much more like translation from language to language than has been generally admitted. George Steiner is an exception to this general disregard, for he makes the case that each of us speaks an 'idiolect' of the 'common' language (Steiner, 1998), our own private version of it. We all know the truism that there are always concepts that are not translatable from one language to another: it should be as familiar a truism that in our idiolects there are always concepts that are not translatable. The reason that we speak is to try and correct this imbalance wherever we perceive it.

If the essential move is from a mutually hypothesized agreement to an updating of that agreement, we can gain a picture of a scenario that could fairly represent the origin of language, for the key insight is plain. It must be that one of our early ancestors, in some situation where both were focusing on what appeared to be the 'same' entity, cottoned on to the fact that the other needed updating about it, that they were not seeing it the same way, and so a change in the other was required if co-operative action was to be successful. So what did the *ur*-speaker need if he was to effect that change? Surely a Second Clue in this story to alter the *ur*-Hearer's perceptual take on that portion of the Real that was the focus of their desires or fears.

Let it be a male and a female, and it is the female who recognizes the need to update her partner. Our speaker is to use what has so far been a non-symbolic sensory element – she has 'to utter' it. It may be an action she performs with her body, say, a manipulation of objects around her, or a mere foregrounding of them before the 'hearer', a proffering, circumscribing, limiting. Somehow she must create an awareness of a relation between the intentional context and the so far non-symbolic thing so that the 'hearer' will make a similar interpretation to her own. If the situation is such that the two beings are sharing a common intention, for example, both are hungry but it needs *two* of them to weigh down a branch to get some fruit, the updating required will be clear enough to her. One chimpanzee's reaching for food is often seen to stimulate others to do so, but that action cannot be taken to be symbolic: it is no different from the birds mentioned in Chapter 3 flying off together when one of them observes danger. The originality of a speaker is to select something initially *non*-symbolic in this case that will indicate what must be done. And it is precisely at this stage that its non-symbolic character disappears and it becomes symbolic. The speaker's intention must, through some association which the hearer can recognize, be indicated in that movement or sound – so that it becomes symbolic, a *gesture*, a *word*.

As the linguists would say there has to be some kind of 'transparency' in what she does. To take examples from language today, in the word 'crash' there is an onomatopoeic transparency that contains a clue to its meaning, the sound of the word reminding us of the sound it means: in 'the *foot* of the hill' it is a metaphorical one, the foot being the *lowest* part of the body: in 'bureau', the original French meaning was 'desk', so this is a metonym, that is, the figure or trope that makes the memory move from one item to another closely associated with it (from the desk to the office where the desk is commonly found and where most of the business concerned with it goes on). You can see that the word 'transparency' itself is transparent because one can metaphorically 'see through' to the meaning of the word. As the linguists would say we are 'motivated' to understand the word: the new word has to have something in its form that is not arbitrary at all. You will no doubt have tumbled to the fact that a transparency is itself a story, a joke, for two meanings are residing in one element (Figure 53). So one essential feature of the moment of first speech is that there has to be a transparency in the movement or sound to excite the memory of the hearer.

Of course, once a successful communication has been made, the movement or sound may be remembered just for being successful and the original transparency be forgotten. You have used the word 'bureau' for *office* many times but perhaps this is the first time you realized the connection with the desk, but the jogging of the memory had to be there for the first users of

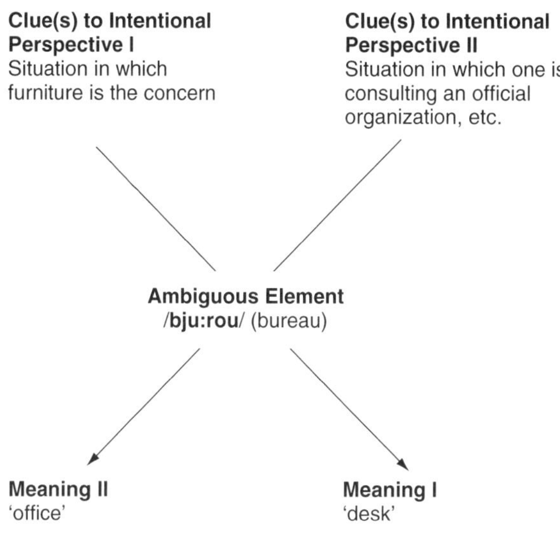

Figure 53

'bureau' for *office*. How many slang-speaking Americans who use 'broad' for *woman* are aware that it is a (slighting) reference to the breadth of a woman's hips, and hence, by a further metonymic leap, to woman as a sexual object? Saussure, in his emphasis on the arbitrariness of the words we use in language, that is, he believed that any word could have been chosen for any meaning, forgot the moment of word-creation (Saussure, 1977: 67–70): he even went so far as to say that 'no one disputes the arbitrary nature of the sign' (1977: 68), an extraordinarily conservative thing to say. Even in a code two people have to get together to set up the transparencies: otherwise no one receiving the message could 'see through' to the concealed meaning! To repeat, once a symbol has been successfully used, the original transparency can be forgotten as the speakers and hearers now have a memory of its successful use: the pick-up of meaning can take place virtually automatically. Did you, for example, have to think of someone physically *picking up* something in my use of 'pick-up' in the last sentence? It is plain that Saussure confused arbitrariness with the mundane familiarity of the word that has lost its initial transparency in becoming part of memory's prompt response. Jacques Derrida points out that it is characteristic of language to 'efface its origins', but there is a price:

> The rhetor accedes to objective truth, denounces error, deals with the passions, but all by virtue of having lost the living truth of its origin.
> (Derrida, 1976: 271, 277)

So back to our first speakers. In our postulated case, the fruit-on-the-branch problem, let the sight of bats hanging up in their sleeping cave be familiar to both of them, and also the high-pitched cry of the bat. She pushes her companion under the branch, pushes up his arms, then leaps up uttering the cry of the bat. She is increasing the Second Clues to the new interpretation of situation, that of both of them hanging on the branch. The sight of bats hanging in rows is a very familiar one for the 'hearer': he remembers the sight: the earlier one and the present one could share the feature of creatures hanging. He leaps up to join her: the branch comes down – they get the fruit.

In the 'speaker's' movements, an imitation of those she wished the 'hearer' to perform, there was a transparency of visual similarity. In her uttering of the bat's cry, itself an onomatopoeic likeness, there was the metonymic evocation of bats hanging in a row. All these associations were familiar to them both. With the bat-cry and the leaping up to hang there, she had used transparencies, converting the non-symbolic into the symbolic. She became one who means in the use of them – interestingly whether her partner understood or not, or even whether he only picked up one of them. She turned something non-symbolic into something symbolic by that action, and, in our stipulated case, thus created a word and *communicated* for the first time. Whether it was a statement or a command is open, for she might have interpreted it as meaning 'Jump up and hang there!' and he might have taken it to mean 'Hanging on there brings down the fruit', which is another example of how communication can go through without there being perfect mutual understanding.

The linguist Leonard Palmer notes this point well. Of two speakers who actually have differing understandings of a situation in which nothing in their act of communication brings those differences into mutual salience, he says:

> What is important is that the speaker cannot correct this misapprehension in the hearer *because he does not know of it*: for it is only from the behaviour of the hearer that the speaker can know whether he has been successful or not. Since in this case the behaviour evoked is precisely what the speaker intended, the hearer exhibiting awareness of the intended situation, there is nothing to show that, though the answer is right, the 'arithmetic' is wrong.
>
> (Palmer, 1972: 321, his emphasis)

This is the same point as was made by Alexander Bryan Johnson (see the previous section, p. 121). It is worthwhile noting that our *ur*-speaker might have experimented with several signs in the hope that one transparency would be effective. It would be odd to say that she did not mean each time. There might even have been a chance success: she might have picked up something by chance which she was about to reject as having no transparency, but which happened to work for her 'hearer'. In her haste to find a suitable object she might have picked up a twig which had two leaves dangling from it. The sign works (that is, *becomes a sign*) because the 'hearer' now imports a transparency into it which she had failed to notice. The pragmatic success goes through and the food reward is achieved together, and so this sign may become mutually used. But it is still possible that, even if she thought that the leaves now recalled the bats for him because of their hanging down, perhaps he never thought of the bats at all but merely picked up the notion of hanging down, having made no sense of her 'bat' squeaks. If that is what happened, this might be called the first example of what the linguists call 'folk-etymology' or 'popular etymology', which occurs when the hearer remembers the meaning of a word because of a reminder that had nothing to do with the speaker's original transparency (for example, we may be very ready to associate 'an *ear* of corn' with a human ear, because of the way the grain of corn is attached to the stem, but in actual fact 'ear' in its corn sense is related to German *Ähre*, 'spike', whereas 'ear' in its other sense is related to German *Ohr*, meaning the human or animal ear).

What all these various cases illustrate is that *a new sign has to be effected via a transparency, a story*. Anything may be taken as a sign, provided that the 'speaker' is relying on its effectiveness. The hearer might take up the meaning using that very transparency, or, as we have just seen, may, all unawares, take up some other chance indication to memory. And we have learned that once a sign is successful, the original transparency becomes of less importance and might disappear from immediate recognition. The word becomes a mnemonic for everyone, immediately – though still hopefully – bringing out of memory what is required. This is why a joke can easily be made with transparencies that have almost passed out of notice, for all one has to do is to provide a Second Clue to the first meaning:

> He was so anxious he ran down the platform and leaped into the compartment of the waiting train. His nerves were on the rack.

Can you see the First Clues to 'on the rack' and the Second Clue that undoes the metaphorical effect, that is, interferes with the transparency?

English school textbooks of the past used to call transparencies that have grown inactive 'dead metaphors', but that is an inadequate name because the effect occurs just as well with metonyms:

> His knowledge of the Iron Age is somewhat rusty.

The rival clues are present with the result that the metonym 'Iron' in 'Iron Age' flickers into ambiguity. One can see the analogy with comedy and tragedy: one finds it difficult, given the presence of both clues, to move easily to a fresh meaning.

Plato in his dialogue *Cratylus* centred the argument on the question of whether names fitted their meanings in some natural way or whether they were solely conventional. Socrates spends much time discussing the fitness of names, and finds possible intriguing matches, such as, for σῶμα, *soma* ('body'), an origin in σημα, 'sema' ('grave'), the transparency being that the body can metaphorically be looked upon as the grave of the soul, but comes to the conclusion that, because such associations cannot be traced rigorously across words, 'custom', that is, convention, is the dominant influence. The solution is to accept that names begin with transparencies (onomatopoeic, metaphorical, metonymical, synaesthetic [a structurally isomorphic similarity across the different senses: see pp. 77–9], or combinations of these, for one does not rule out another), and, when the word has been accepted into the language, the continued use renders the original transparency redundant and 'custom', convention, takes over.

Conventional use, however, as we have abundantly seen by now, does not rule out different uses by different individuals. V. N. Vološinov has an amusing example from Dostoevsky's story 'Diary of a Writer', in which the all-too-familiar worst of expletives is used in nine different senses, altering according to the context around it (Vološinov, 1973: 103–4).

Ludwig Wittgenstein, eager to reject Bertrand Russell's notion of a world made up of given facts, a view he had at first adhered to, came to argue that language use was the arbiter of meaning. He had moved in the right direction, but he made the error of thinking that, once agreement had been reached, people's judgements were the same too, and any divergence from them could only be unjustifiable:

> If language is to be a means of communication there must be agreement not only in definitions but also (queer as this may sound) in judgements.
>   (Wittgenstein, 1967: 88e)

One can agree with the first part of his claim, in that it is true that people wishing to communicate must begin by acting as if they have agreed in definitions, but no communication could be made if they agreed in judgements, because the whole purpose of the communication is *to change* the judgement of the hearer. This is the usual error of seeing language as static, not dynamic, arising from the fear of disturbing the common trust – as well as the current cosy view of the Real. So we can say that in the ordinary informative statement where one speaker wishes to update another about a change in the character of 'a' referent, then it is fair to say that every statement depends upon a transparency for the meaning of a word is changed by its utterance: the new context, the Second Clue, the 'logical predicate', as in the Joke or the Story, induces a change in the 'logical subject'. This shows the Statement to have the same structure as the Trope, which is why, as was mentioned before, making a statement turns us all into Cretan Liars.

Saussure, like many another writer on language, was only exhorting us into the needful mutual trust without seeing that it is maintained only to allow for that very change.

Furthermore, since Saussure thought of *la langue* as 'synchronic', that is, timelessly fixed in some real sense, he never could explain how language change came about, how the diachrony ('through-time') actually occurred, a gross weakness of his theory. Although he acknowledged with his notion of *le parole*, actual speech as used in time, that use of the system did not correspond to the idealities of *la langue*, the abstract system that he took as his scientific investigation, he provided no link between the two. For example, he knew that the Old Latin *necare* 'to kill' had, in the Vulgar Latin of the fourth and fifth centuries changed to meaning, 'to drown' (from which French *noyer*), admitting that 'the bond had loosened' between word and concept, but he never enquired into the process of that loosening, which must have arisen from some actual person's new interpretation of the word: the situation in which that occurred would have had the Story pattern, for he or she moved the meaning from 'kill' to 'drown', perhaps as a result of a misinterpreting someone else's use through the presence of some strong countervailing clue.

So if the 'immutability' of the system is one that is mutually projected as a *regulative* ideal, an indispensable method of ensuring that different people can bring their understandings into some sort of partial focus, then the problem of language change has a solution. Saussure, like many other writers on language, mistakes the indispensability of a useful tool for a logical necessity. It led him to make his claim that the meaning of a word (what he called the 'concept' or the *signifié*) and the word itself (what he called the 'sound-image', the *signifiant*) were like two sides of a sheet of paper, the front the thought and the sound the back (Saussure, 1977: 113). What is strange is that in making the *concept* a half of his pair, it never occurred to him that concepts are had by persons and are not identical from body to body. He draws a diagram of the communication situation (1977: 12) with two heads both showing inside them 'C' for *concept* and 'S' for *sound*, but his blind embracing of the idealization prevented him from seeing that neither the concept not the sound are the same in each head! Saussure, as was pointed out by Émile Benveniste, neglects what is referred to, the Thing, but Benveniste is still as much trapped as Saussure was for he is convinced that the Thing is something given in its singularity to both speaker and hearer (Benveniste, 1939: 24). It is all very well to say with Edouard Pichon, another French participant in the debate over Saussure's theory, that 'the signified idea and the signifying word coalesce with each other in a perfect adequation for the speaking subject', but, like Saussure, he ignored the fact that each 'speaking subject' has his own 'idea' and his own 'word' (Pichon, 1941). We shall see later that to be convinced of the 'perfect adequation' between the word we use and the meaning we attribute to it, as well as their adequation with the logical fixity of the entity it applies to in the world, leads to a dangerous misapplication of the idealization, which should be only a useful tool, grasped only to be immediately laid down again in each genuine act of communication. Benveniste, it must be said, did give precedence to actual discourse over the fixity of the word, and thus put the Sentence before the Word: he should have put the *Statement* before the Word (Benveniste, 1971: 104–5).

We are *playing* with this logical ideal, and have to, but there is no need to believe it. Paul Ricœur puts it well:

> Words are proposed in the mode of play. The analysis of play thus enables us to recover in a new way the dialectic between the suspension of didactic reference and the manifestation of another sort of reference, beyond the *époché* of the former.
> (Ricœur, 1981: 186)

We start with 'didactic reference' that is, we assume together a perfection in our 'common' identification of a portion of the world, but this is only to allow to take place in the hearer the playful transformation that 'manifests itself' as a result of the speaker's Second Clue. He applies Edmund Husserl's term *époché* to the initial idealization, for that means a 'bracketing out', a mutual hypothetical ignoring of something. And what is it that is ignored? – the actual *difference* in the portions of the Real that each of us are selecting at the corner of the triangle that we are for the time being calling 'the same'. Ricœur like Gadamer, whom he praises for his 'magnificent pages on play' (Ricœur 1981: 93; Gadamer, 1975: 101–31), has grasped the need to recognize what play is, the recontextualization of a *supposedly* fixed 'event', 'thing' or 'person' that renders its 'identity' anew. This is the dynamic core of every statement we make. Don Cupitt sums it up: 'It is as if every conversation were really a contest of narrative hypotheses' (Cupitt, 1991: 69).

Ricœur also praises I. A. Richards for his emphasis on the importance of *context* in the determination of meaning. Richards, in fact, foreshadows the thesis of this book, although he does not link transformation with narrative as such. His assertion that words express 'the large-scale rivalries between contexts' could have been used as an epigraph for the chapters on the Joke and the Story (Ricœur, 1978: 76–83; Richards, 1936: 40).

The Two Bomb-Defusers, and the Poet and the Blind Man, had to behave *as if* there was *one* portion of the world that both were focusing on, and it is not ruled out that in an actual case the one who is being led might still have to correct the other. Saussure is like Wiggins: all he is doing is exhorting us to make the first move in a statement, that is, to take the entity as fixed for speaker and hearer, without realizing the purpose of that 'taking as', which is to achieve that partial superimposition of understandings that permits a dynamic change in the relation of word and meaning, *signifié* and *signifiant*, to go through. This is why Saussure came to contradict himself because he argued at the same time for the 'immutability' and the 'mutability' of the sign, without having any explanation of how one got from one to the other, particularly as he insisted that the humble speaker of a language had to take words as he or she found them – 'No individual, even if he willed it, could modify in any way the choice that has been made' (Saussure, 1977: 71–8, 71). Yet when Saussure drew a diagram of what the 'thought' and the 'sound' were chosen from (1977: 112), he always showed them as waving flows, that is, fluxes: he never considered that each individual might be making slightly different choices from those fluxes.

The linguist Sir Alan Gardiner criticized Saussure in precisely this respect. Of two persons using the same French word *bœuf* ('ox') when faced with an example of that species each will gain a new, if infinitesimal, contribution to the meaning of the word (Gardiner, 1944: 109). Each person is sensing differently through the different sense modalities, the ox itself has features not possessed by all its fellow-species members, so there can be no precise meaning common to both speakers *other than the imagined one they are working with to focus on that portion of the Real before them.* Here are two more linguists who say the same thing as Gardiner: 'Every time we apply a word…we transpose its semantic value' (Karcevskij, 1964: 208); 'Each fresh act of communication with language is a metaphor, applying something known to something unknown to create an original synthesis' (Shopen, 1974: 788).

The psychologist Jerome Bruner's characterization of the function of the Story can now be seen to fit that of the Statement, the building-block of language:

> *The function of the story is to find an intentional state that mitigates or at least makes comprehensible a deviation from a canonical cultural pattern.*
> (Bruner, 1990: 49, his emphasis)

That 'intentional state' is the Second Clue of the Story and the Joke, the logical predicate of the Informative Statement. Roman Jakobson the linguist also drew attention to this novelty of the Statement:

> The very act of speaking is the marking of the unusual from the usual.
> (Jakobson, 1987: Ch. 2, pt. 4)

And from our point of view, the 'usual' is the taken-for-granted convergence on a singular entity, and the 'unusual' the transformation induced in the hearer by the provision by the speaker of the Second Clue.

Hans-Georg Gadamer, whose focus is on hermeneutics, enlarges on the idea:

> A person who speaks – who, that is to say, uses the general meanings of words – is so oriented toward the particularity of what he is perceiving that

everything he says acquires a share in the particularity of the circumstances he is considering. But that means, on the other hand, that the general concept meant by the word is enriched by any given perception of a thing, so that what emerges is a new, more specific word formation which does more justice to the particularity of that act of perception. However certainly speaking implies using pre-established words with general meanings, at the same time, a constant process of concept formation is going on, by means of which the life of a language develops.
(Gadamer, 1975: 428–9)

It will at once be seen how this dovetails with what Gardiner claimed about the use of the word *bœuf*, that each actual use contributed something new to the meaning.

One can refer across to the philosophy of science and say that it would explain Thomas Kuhn's characterization of scientific advance as the replacement as a result of a 'crisis-state' of a 'paradigm' in 'normal science', that is, an accepted interpretation, by a new theory (Kuhn, 1970: Ch. 10). *Scientific advance thus has the structure of the Statement, and, hence, of the Story* for the Statement moves from an existing mutually projected 'normality', via a 'crisis-state', to a new 'normality', a *crisis* because a change of motivation has to be negotiated between speaker and hearer. Nor should it be a surprise that Kuhn used a gestalt-switch as an analogy for what happened: 'What were ducks in the scientist's world before the revolution are rabbits afterwards' (1970: 111). The diachronic progress of a language thus comes about through such Story-like situations, for the new perception made by one of those speakers may come to prove its worth across the population of language-speakers.

Fritz Mauthner, a German philosopher of the nineteenth century, would have agreed with Gardiner and Gadamer:

We do not recognise a correct language, any firm and tyrannical general use of language, only countless usages of language of which there are as many as members of a people. Every one of them has a slightly different usage, *which he regards as correct.*
(Mauthner, 1901–2: II, 155, my emphasis)

Mauthner, however, did see that, if each regards his own use as correct, he is likely to think that his own use represents everyone else's. As he pointed out, anticipating the Schutzian idealization:

Two individuals communicate with each other, because each one of them *sees* the speech-habits of the other *as* similar to his own.
(Mauthner, 1901–2: II: 117, my emphases)

Significantly in our Story context, Gardiner saw words 'mainly as *clues*' (1932: 34, 65: my emphasis) to enable a Hearer to focus on the 'thing-meant', and, furthermore, the thing-meant, as we would expect the Ambiguous Element to do, escaped the final definition of both Speaker and Hearer: 'the thing-meant is always outside the words, not within them' (1932: 50), that is, indisputably knowledgeless, non-epistemic – not even safely fixed as a 'thing'. This is no surprise if we only have a structurally isomorphic access to the flux of the Real and the 'thing-meant' is a tentative mutual superimposition of two differing 'referents' at the object-corner of the communication triangle. Gardiner was aware that he was treading on exciting and unexplored philosophical territory but he somewhat timidly withdrew from enquiry. Of his two partners in dialogue, James and Mary, he says:

> Was the thing seen by Mary really the same thing that James had meant? In this question are involved deep metaphysical issues upon which, for all their interest, we must resolutely turn our backs.
>   (Gardiner, 1932: 81)

An interesting and unexpected outcome here is that the one who lights on the new meaning may not be the one who publicizes it, for he may not realize that he is using the word differently from his fellow-speakers, and it may be one of them who notices the useful mismatch! We shall return to this unusual point again when we come to consider metaphor.

To pursue a thought of Steiner's. He argues convincingly that the very life of language would be lost if a language were to be regarded as a matter of strict analytical definition. There is a danger of a chasm opening between 'individual perception' and the 'frozen generalities of speech'. He explores interestingly the Romantic rebellion against the imposition of public rigidity upon meaning (Steiner, 1998: 180–95): what he does not explore is the need for us to project in faith – with the mutual open-eyed acknowledgement of risk – that 'public rigidity'. What the Romantics, and those modernists who in their 'difficult' handling of words have made much of the metaphoricity of language, do not see is that a proper faith in a 'common' language cannot be escaped. What they were really attacking, without knowing it, was the recurrent superstitious tendency to reify an existing synchronic view, not the notion of a public language *per se*.

To conclude with two brief comments on cruxes in contemporary philosophy that are solved if this theory is correct. The American philosopher Saul Kripke has produced a theory of reference called the Causal Theory of Reference. He argues that, once someone has fixed a name by an act of 'baptism' upon something or somebody, the name gets passed 'from link to link', from speaker to hearer, from 'giver' to 'receiver':

> the receiver must, I think, intend when he learns it to use it with the same reference as the man from whom he heard it.
>   (Kripke, 1980: 96)

It should be seen at once that to argue that there is a single referent that remains the same apart from our human choices is no more than Wiggins' error, in that it is a disguised exhortation to us to join with him in the Schutzian idealization.

Another lies in a thought-experiment of Hilary Putnam's, used in order to show that what our words mean depends on what we engage them with (Putnam, 1975). He imagined another world on which the substance we know as water was not H_2O but XYZ. The people on that planet called it 'twater': it corresponded in all other respects to water, looking, feeling, tasting, etc. exactly like the water we have on Earth. He maintains that, since the scientific fact is that it is a different substance, the meaning of our word 'water' and their word 'twater' was ineradicably different, which proves that meanings depend to an important degree on what we apply our words to and are not primarily determined by our intentional choice. 'Water/twater' is thus an extraordinary Ambiguous Element, for as regards all ordinary human (and alien-being) uses it is identical, but as regards scientific enquiry it is utterly different. What is amusing about Putnam's example is that it can be taken as an analogy for all reference across persons, for each of us does have a different concept of 'what' is being referred to. 'Scientific enquiry' has no difficulty in establishing the fact of such perceptual and conceptual relativity. Of course, Putnam has a measure of truth in what he says because the Real can subvert any person's concept and percept; it invades our language all the time – since that is why we speak at all, to adjust the referrings of others so that they may move more smoothly in harness with the Real. However, it is forgotten that the Real can disturb human agreements from within the human beings themselves. One person's 'water' is not another person's, though they both have to use the word 'water' of 'it', that portion of the Real, to talk at all (although it is also easily forgotten that we each pronounce the word 'water' differently). It is this latter practical necessity, the needful idealization that keeps us in rough co-ordination, that hides the facts of difference. Putnam's puzzle, like Kripke's, can only be set up if we remain inside the idealization, believing that H_2O and XYZ exist in perfect singularity apart from human choice, which is obviously to engage blindly in the idealization of a mind-independent *objectivity*, when all we can be sure of is that there is mind-independent *existence*. Putnam tries to make appeal to 'experts' who know all about 'natural kinds' like water, but that, as with Hoffman and Rosenkrantz, is only a dangerous rhetorical appeal to authority that also disguises the underlying performance of mutual trust (Putnam, 1975; Hoffman and Rosenkrantz, 1997: 177–8).

3.   The Question and the Command

The early twentieth-century logician, John Cook Wilson, used to make a clear distinction between the logical and grammatical subjects of a sentence. He illustrated his point effectively by pointing out that the substantial meaning of a sentence in use, that is, an actual statement, depended on the *question* in the mind of the Hearer, whether openly expressed or not. For example, let us suppose that before the informative statement 'The cat is on the mat' by a Speaker, the Hearer had asked (1) 'Where is the cat?' Then the new information is contained in the words 'is on the mat', which makes 'The cat' both the logical and the grammatical subject of the sentence, and 'is on the mat' both the logical and the grammatical predicate (Wilson, 1926: 123–6).

But suppose that the Hearer had asked (2) 'What is on the mat?' In that case the new information is contained in the words 'The cat', with the result that the logical subject is now the state of the mat as regards what is on it, and the logical predicate is 'The cat', while the grammatical subject and predicate remain as before, subject 'The cat' and predicate 'is on the mat'. Note that the very intonation of the Speaker's answer would differ in answering question 2, for, instead of the stress being on 'is on the mat', it would be upon the informing words 'The cat'.

We need not stop there. Consider further possible questions. (3) 'Which cat is on the mat?' The answer in this case puts the stress on the word 'The', even probably changing the pronunciation of it from /ðə/ (matching the last syllable of 'wea*ther*') to /ði:/ (rhyming with 'see'), for this stress on the definite article enhanced by the change in pronunciation would mean that *it was the cat they had been referring to before* that was on the mat, and it is this cat that is the logical subject.

(4) 'Which mat is the cat on?' Here in the answer it is the second 'the' which changes in stress and pronunciation to bring out the fact that it is the mat they have referred to before on which Tabby is now to be found.

(5) 'What is the relation of the cat to the mat?' Here the new information lies in the preposition 'on', that state being the logical subject.

(6) The Hearer could even ask '*The* (/ði:/) what is on the mat?', making clear that he knows that it is something that was referred to by them both before that is on the mat, but he does not know of the many that were which it is.

Once the statement has been made in response to the question, the Hearer could go on to enquire the time in which it occurred ('When was the cat on the mat?'), the place ('Where...?'), the reason ('Why...?'), and for clarification on further subtleties ('In spite of what...?', 'On what condition...?', 'In what manner ?', 'With what result ?', etc., all elements that would be described in formal grammar as 'adverbial').

Whatever the question, the Hearer is endeavouring to point to the blind spot in his or her knowledge, making salient the aspect of their 'common' entity in which they need updating. It is interesting that Shakespeare commonly uses the word 'question' to mean *problem*: 'To be or not to be – that is the question' (*Hamlet*, II, I, 56). Notice that there is still the taking-for-granted by both that there is a *single* entity in the Real upon which

Speaker and Hearer can hope to converge in their understandings but, as we have seen, this is no more than their method of obtaining the rough superimposition of their perspectives that enables the updating required by the 'problem' to go through. It is a kind of ideal goal that has to be put up in imagination, there being no necessity that we take it for real. There is an inter*play* between the static logical subject, the presumed agreement, and the dynamic logical predicate, which is how Sir Alan Gardiner saw them, the subject being his what the speaker vouchsafes 'as a help to the listener' and the predicate his 'interest and principal aim' (Gardiner, 1932: 20); we can now see that that 'help to the listener' was the mutual *presupposition* of co-reference, and the speaker's 'interest and principal aim' his desire to update his hearer with a novel transformation of his understanding.

The Joke is not far away here, for the speaker may not be aware what question is in the mind of the hearer, and so may convey information that has an important difference from what he the speaker imagines. This is why a liar cannot be sure that he is not speaking the truth. Take this story from China. A Chinese peasant heard that the Emperor's taxman had called all peasants into the village. When he was brought before the taxman, he burst out with the claim that all his seven cows had just died in a fire that very week. The taxman looked at him oddly and dismissed him, saying that he would inform the tax-gatherer who was due the following month. On his return home he discovered to his horror that indeed all his cows had died in a fire while he was away in the village. He was all for rushing back with a witness to prove his statement to the taxman, but, when he approached his neighbour for help, he learned from him that the taxman had not been interested in whether he had any animals now, but merely whether he had had cows or sheep or goats *in the preceding year and how many*.

The English philosopher R. G. Collingwood even formalized what we have been talking about, giving as his first key dictum about what we do when we 'propose' statements to each other,

> PROP. I. Every statement that anybody ever makes is an answer to a question
> (Collingwood, 2002 [1940]: 23)

This is perhaps an exaggerated way of putting the point about the updating that hopefully goes on when we pass on information to each other. Of course, we must add the point just made, that there remains the question of, in whose view, what question is really being asked. The Speaker may be the one who believes that the Hearer needs updating on something, though the Hearer, of course, may be very unwilling to be updated and refuse to believe it. Nor is it to deny that speakers often repeat things that they know that their hearers are already aware of but are repeating them for safety's sake, and again that is often not the view of the hearers themselves:

> HAMLET: There's never a villain dwelling in all Denmark –
>   But he's an arrant knave.
> HORATIO: There needs no ghost, my lord, come from the grave
>   To tell us this.
>   (William Shakespeare, *Hamlet*, I, v, 24–7)

Mikhail Bakhtin, in his incarnation as Valentin Vološinov, saw each statement as a response to a question, and thus characterizing all language as 'dialogic':

> Any utterance – the finished, written utterance not excepted – makes response to something and is calculated to be responded to in turn.
>   (Vološinov, 1973: 72)

The German philosopher of hermeneutics Hans-Georg Gadamer figured the goal of ideal agreement as a 'fusion of horizons' (*Horizontverschmelzung*), in which the individual's interpretation fused with the tradition that is passed on to him. This blends with our notion of the Joke and the Story in that a former concept is transformed yet maintained in a new grasp of that region of the Real in *question*. One would not say, for example, that Hamlet and Horatio achieved a new 'fusion of horizons' because it was obvious they both knew that every villain in Denmark was an arrant knave, for, as a result of Hamlet's remark being deliberately and thoroughly uninformative, no advance was made.

Gadamer, like Collingwood, saw communication as involving both question and answer:

> Part of real understanding, however, is that we regain the concepts of a historical past in such a way that they also include our own comprehension of them. Above I called this 'the fusion of horizons'. With Collingwood, we can say that we understand only when we understand the question to which something is the answer, but the intention of what is understood in this way does not remain foregrounded against our own intention. Rather, reconstructing the question to which the meaning of a text is understood as an answer merges with our own questioning. For the text must be understood as the answer to a real question.
>   (Gadamer, 1975: 374)

That 'fusion' can only come about, that is, our understanding ought not to remain incompatibly separate from the originally accepted meaning (the First Intentional Perspective) but, as a result of our questioning, should be shown to be newly combined with it as the Second Clue produced the metamorphosis of meaning. This is not a counsel of perfection as each act of communication, each answer to a question, is part of an ongoing, unending process towards a final fusion of all these three, rule and motivation and Real, a fusion that can never be achieved. The fact that a mutual trust is involved in this inescapable process will, as I have already indicated, form the major theme of the conclusion of the book.

The Command, the Imperative Mood as the grammarians call it, is in a way different as regards the hoped-for convergence of understanding than the Statement and the Question. If you look again at the snippet of conversation Leigh Hunt quoted at the beginning of Chapter 1, it is as easy to subvert a command as a statement:

A: Incorrigible dog! come now; be serious.
B: [*comes closer to A., and looks very serious*].
A: Well, what now?
B: I am come, to be serious.

'Come now' is in the imperative mood and in this use has a metaphorical meaning: *Give up your opposition, fall into agreement with me*, and the like; B does what can always be done with a metaphor – pun on it by introducing a clue to its literal meaning, in this case his action in response to the command (Figure 54).

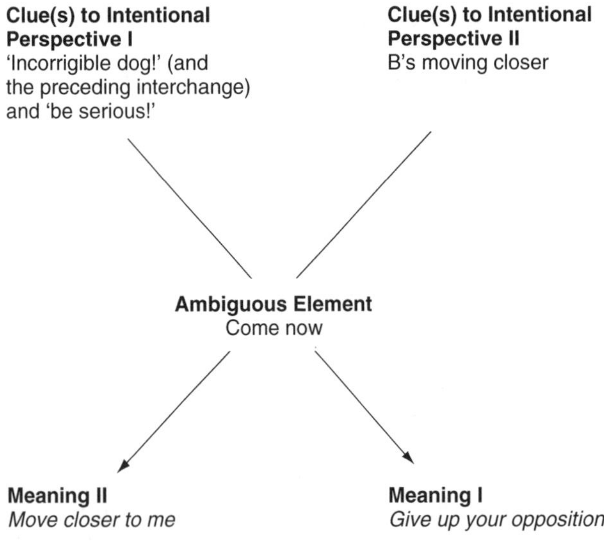

Figure 54

The same analysis can be made of 'Be serious', for A wanted B to give up his deliberate game of misunderstanding and join in the more important language game, whereas again B took the phrase as referring to the state of his facial expression. It is the principle behind the comic novel *The Good Soldier Schweik* by the Czech satirist Jaroslav Hašek, in which a guileless private in the Austro-Hungarian army causes havoc by obeying orders precisely. Hans Georg Gadamer underlines the fact that commands cannot specify all that the master requires:

> The comic situation in which orders are carried out literally, but not according to their meaning, is well known. Thus there is no doubt that the recipient of an order must perform a definite creative act of understanding its meaning.
> (Gadamer, 1975: 298)

So it must be plain that, from all that has been said, strictly speaking, even with the best will in the world, no command can be obeyed precisely. No human will can match another's since no human understanding of the world can match another's. To borrow a phrase from the psychoanalyst D. H. Winnicott, we can only be 'good enough' (Winnicott, 1965: 187). So the Command, as much as the Statement, raises the insistent question of the nature of the trust existing between partners in dialogue. For the Command, in particular, it takes the form of what action is taken to match the command given, therefore, what is to constitute obedience and loyalty. All these are profound moral questions.

4.   Transparency

> Thus every metaphor so formed is a fable in brief.
> (Vico, *The New Science*, II, ii, sect. 404; 1970: 87)

> ...examine Language; what, if you except some few primitive elements (of natural sound), what is it all but Metaphors, recognised as such or no longer recognised; still fluid and florid, or now solid-grown and colourless? If those same primitive elements are the osseous fixtures in the Flesh-Garment, Language, – then are Metaphors its muscles and tissues and living integuments.
> (Thomas Carlyle, *Sartor Resartus*, Ch. I, xi, ll. 75–80;
> Carlyle, 2000 [1833–4]: 56)

It is this synthesis of the heterogeneous that brings narrative close to metaphor. In both cases, the new thing – the as yet unsaid, the unwritten – springs up in language. Here a living metaphor, that is, a new pertinence in the predication, there a feigned plot, that is, a new congruence in the organization of events.

(Ricœur, 1983: I, ix)

In section 2 of this chapter we touched upon the workings of onomatopoeia, metaphor, metonymy and synaesthesia, that is, the imagery that appears in language, the 'tropes', and saw, as Vico claims above, that the structure of the Story applies to them as well. That they are called 'tropes', then, is no surprise as 'trope' is from the Greek τρεπειν, 'to turn' (compare the words 'tropic' [where the sun turns], 'heliotrope' [flower that turns with the sun]) in that the meaning of the word is *turned*, producing an unexpected result, which makes it itself a metaphor. Here is an example as a reminder. It is from John Keats' poem 'Lamia', taken from the description of how Lamia was transformed by the god Hermes from her serpent form into that of a beautiful woman:

> Her eyes in torture fixed and anguish drear,
> Hot, glazed, and wide, with lid-lashes all sear,
> Flash'd phosphor and sharp sparks, without one cooling tear,
> The colours all inflamed about her train,
> She writhed about, convulsed with *scarlet* pain.
> (Keats, 'Lamia', ll. 153–7; Keats, 1947 [1820]: 152)

Here a likeness is found between something visual, the colour scarlet, and the bodily experience of pain. This is a synaesthetic likeness, one that works across two sense modalities, sight and bodily pain; it is, therefore, a *structurally isomorphic* likeness that captures the sharp insistence of the pain through the conspicuous quality of the colour. Keats has also punned on the word, as Lamia's transformation, as we have learned from preceding and succeeding lines, involved the disappearance of all the *colours* of her serpent skin. So the fivefold pattern of the Story applies (Figure 55).

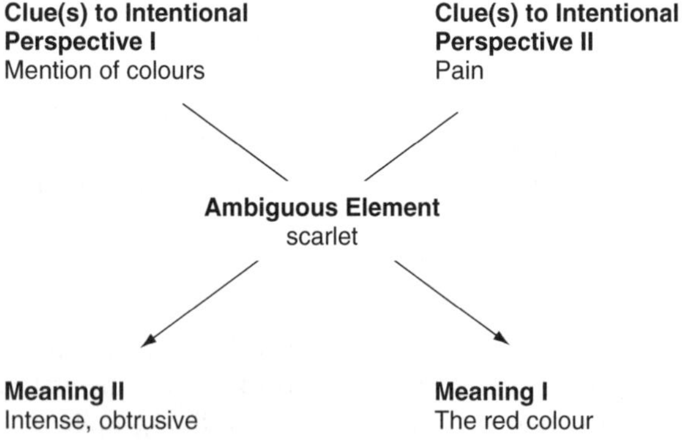

Figure 55

You may recall the discussion of Molyneux's Problem in Chapter 3 (pp. 77–8), the solution to which was found to lie in seeing the structurally isomorphic similarities that exist across sensory modalities. We are enabled to move from colour to pain here because we cannot find an appropriate colour interpretation when that adjective 'scarlet' is written as qualifying 'pain' and are forced by the context (the Second Intentional Perspective) to find something that justifies the novel use. Just as scarlet attracts the attention so often by its contrast with its surroundings (as the poet George Herbert puts it of the red of a rose, an 'angry' colour that 'bids the rash gazer wipe his eye', 'Vertue', ll. 5–6; Herbert, 1971 [1634]: 65), or as someone else has said, is as noticeable as the sound of a trumpet, so too the pain she feels.

Keats could have been the very first person to notice this structurally isomorphic similarity, so it did not exist as a known fact beforehand. Metaphors depend on sensory elements outside the world of words. Take using the word 'cloudy' for English apple juice: no one has to trace the similarity to the facts of the suspension of particles in the juice and of the suspension of water-vapour droplets in the air and their both producing an interference with clear sight before he can understand the metaphor. Immediate *sensory* memories of the experiences suffice to effect the leap in thought. It is not a matter of the application of a rule without reference to the sensory context. There is a relevant point to be made here from another discipline, that of the law:

> Even when verbally formulated general rules are used, uncertainties as to the form of behaviour required by them may break out in particular concrete cases. Particular fact-situations do not await us already marked off from each other, and labelled as instances of the general rule, the application of which is in question, nor can the rule itself step forward to claim its own instances. In all fields of experience, not only that of rules, there is a limit, inherent in the nature of language, to the guidance general language can provide.
>
> (Hart, 1961: 123)

Keats's pun, of course, prevented us editing out the Colour meaning. In the normal use of any trope, the Second Clue enforces an editing out of the existing meaning. Here is a normal metaphor, where the First Clue is edited out by the Second: 'I know we've had trouble, but the important thing is *to look on the bright side.*' The analysis is given in Figure 56.

The metaphoric similarities and metonymic associations on which the troping swivels are many: a well-lit scene providing quick discrimination of visual differences, improving access to recognition; the pleasure afforded by brightness of colour; light as associated with the warmth, pleasantness and vigorous growth of spring and summer; the cross-associations with metaphors of height-as-value, the sky being the source of light, etc. (see further on such

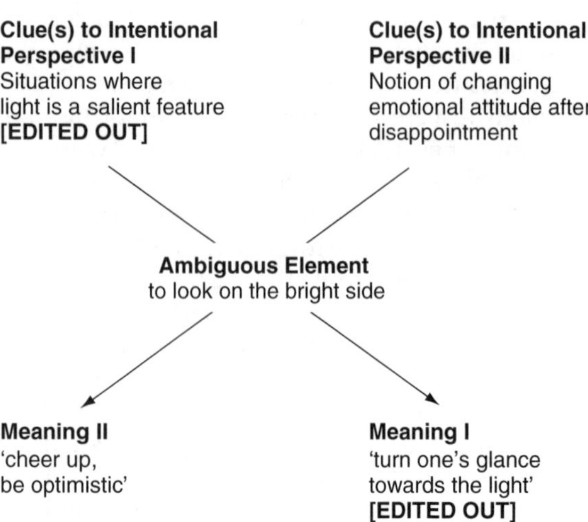

Figure 56

connotations in Lakoff and Johnson, 1980). Metaphor can challenge any former categorization and leap across the most unexpected boundaries redrawing them in the process; to quote Ted Peters:

> In the event of metaphor we break through previous categorizations and establish new logical boundaries on the ruins of the old ones.
> (Peters, 1978: 368)

In section 2 of this chapter we saw that a trope can always be interfered with by a reminder of the meaning that is normally edited out, so that we cannot avoid the more established meaning, as here:

> In determining the floor-space, a ceiling of 15,000 square feet should normally be the limit (from a government regulation). (See Figure 57.)

Here the reference to *floor*-space produces a reminder of the original meaning of 'ceiling' and thus interferes with the smooth operation of the metaphor by preventing us editing it out.

In English textbooks of the past such interference was known by the name of 'mixed metaphor', but this was a distracting name since the same effect can occur with metonyms:

> They are going to strike at the casino because the shop steward *got given his cards*. (See Figure 58.)

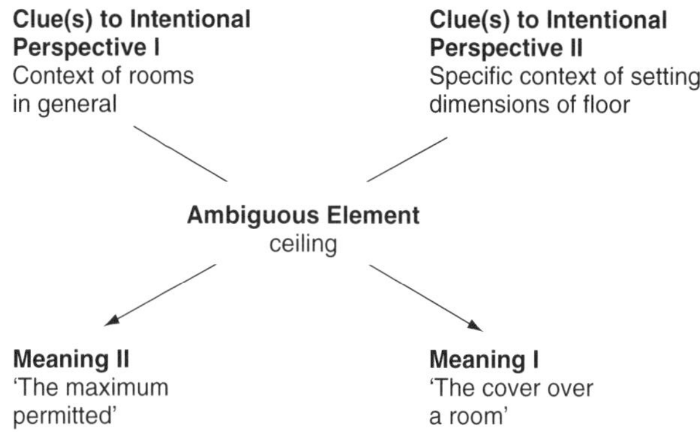

Figure 57

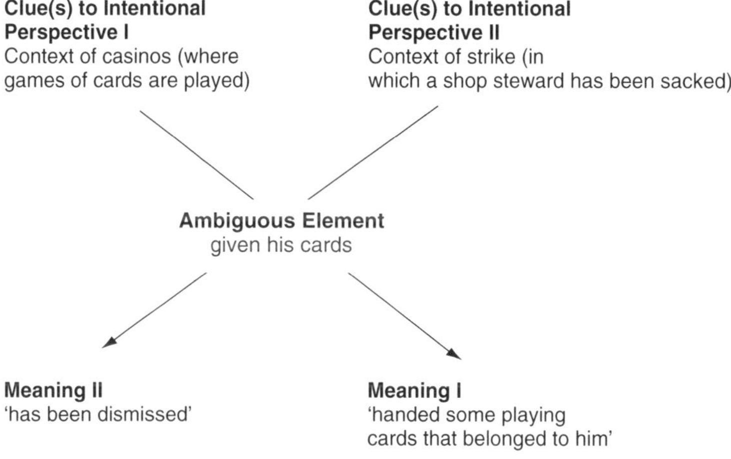

Figure 58

The metonym depended on the notion of being handed back at dismissal the official documents that are required for employment standing for the whole act of dismissing a worker. Here the editing-out of the notion of cards as the key meaning is prevented by a reference that brings in another meaning of cards, namely, the cards played with at casinos.

The argument in Chapter 5.2 was that all words began their history with a transparency even though that transparency could drop out of notice once the word had been mutually established. One way of putting this would be to say that *le parole*, actual speech, precedes *la langue*, the language as an abstract system common to all, but that would be to forget that, to begin a statement, one has to act as if complete agreement has already been reached, which puts *la langue*, at least in imagination, before *le parole*. Those seventeenth-century 'natural philosophers' like Thomas Sprat who were suspicious of tropes and recommended all scientific writers to avoid using them were making the Wiggins error in not realizing that they were only exhorting those in communication to hold to the idealization of reciprocity of standpoints (Sprat, 1922 [1667]: 271–2).

What is undeniable, however, is that every new word must have begun with a transparency; something has to jog the memory of the hearer so that he changes his concept, moves through the story. None of this rules out different people importing their own transparency into what they hear to help them remember, which is the point made earlier (section 2) about folk- or popular etymology (as in the '*ear* of corn'/ 'animal or human *ear*' case); it is something like what happens in a game of Chinese Whispers in that each uses what appears to them to be effective.

There are the obvious onomatopoeic words where the sound of the word matches the sound that it means: we all can readily produce examples – 'crash', 'whistle', 'thump', 'thunder' and so on. What is not commonly realized is how conventional those words have become, for it is plain that they are nothing like exact imitations; but even the very first use need not have been exact, for all that is needed is that the hearer of a new word gets a clue that works in the given context, and the hint might only have been slight. It would indeed be very strange if such an impossible criterion as exact likeness were necessary, for all that is needed is a vague reminder, and the advantage of a vague reminder is that it can easily apply to a wide range of sounds. I found it uncanny one day last month when I was sawing some wood when suddenly my brain took the sound of the sawing as a strange voice saying 'Fever, fever, fever'; no doubt a psychoanalyst could tell me why this word came into my mind – a further story.

Since we began with synaesthesia, let us take another version of it that is exceedingly common since it also finds a likeness between the sound of a word and its meaning, but in this case the meaning is not that of a sound as it is with onomatopoeia. If you look back at the 'Cricketycrack/ Mellowflow' drawings in Chapter 3 (p. 78), you will see how promptly you named the two, thereby illustrating to yourself your skill in detecting structurally isomorphic similarity. If 'Cricketycrack' as spoken were to appear on the sound-track of a film, examining the sound-track on the reel of film where it occurred would show *sudden variations in intensity*, whereas 'Mellowflow' would show *smooth variations*. It is that similarity that you detected between the sounds and the drawings, matching sudden changes in direction of line with the jerky sounds of 'Cricketycrack', and the curved lines with the smooth changes of the sounds of 'Mellowflow'. Now since the medium by which we communicate as human beings is sound itself, it is not unexpected to discover that such similarities were capitalized upon by the first speakers. If on some remote planet in the universe, the intelligent beings can communicate through light signals (as apparently certain species of squid can do, changing the colour of the skin), the imagery of light will be similarly capitalized upon in their languages.

One of the earliest words that etymologists have endeavoured to reconstruct by hypothesis from those that can be definitely traced is the Indo-European root AK, which means 'to be sharp', 'to pierce'. It is not too bold to see the synaesthetic likeness between the sudden change of sound as being like an edge of some sort, as in 'cricketycrack'. There are many words that can be linked to this original root:

'ακρος' (Greek), pointed.

'*acuere*' (Latin), to sharpen.

'*ecg*' (Anglo-Saxon), 'edge', giving the Modern English word 'edge' (compare the German *Eck*, 'corner, angle').

'acacia', a *thorny* tree.

'acme', originally a *sharp* peak, used metaphorically for the 'highest' achievement.

'acrobat' from 'ακροβατικος' (Greek), literally 'sharp-walking', one who originally *walked on tiptoe*.

'acid', from Latin '*acidus*', sour, originally pronounced /**akidus**/ with a 'sharp' /**k**/; note the four-way synaesthetic imaging here, from the *sight* of a sharp object to the *sound* of /**k**/, to the *taste* of something sour, and sometimes to the burning *feel* of acid.

'acute' (from Latin '*acutus*', 'pointed, shrill'), used in English for the *sharpness* of an angle, as well as metaphorically for *intelligent*, for an intelligent person can distinguish, i.e. 'cut between', one thing and another. It is interesting that in the Latin the word retained the onomatopoeic sense of 'shrill' (a sound-to-sound likeness, not a synaesthetic one).

'eager', originally 'keen' with the metaphorical sense of cutting easily through to something.

'to *egg* someone on', originally to prod with something sharp like a spur.

'paragon', from 'παρακοναειν', to rub against a whetstone, that is, metonymically, to test for excellence, hence, something that is excellent; 'ακονη', a whetstone, for *sharpening* knives.

[and, further, 'axe', 'cut', 'scrape', 'scar', 'scale' (of fish, etc.; and also, related, 'shale'), 'scratch', 'hack', 'science' (from Latin '*scire*', to know, originally 'to cut [between]'), 'score' (the *tally* meaning coming metonymically from the habit of cutting marks in wood to keep score), 'sharp' (originally Anglo-Saxon *scearp*), 'shell' (from Anglo-Saxon *scell*); 'chop' (related to Low German *kappen*, 'to cut'); and many more].

As can be seen from 'acme' and 'acute', once one transparency has been established, the /k/ for the sharp point of the peak and the edge of a knife can be further developed as a *metaphoric* transparency for another meaning, 'acme' giving the 'summit' of achievement, and 'acute' the ability to distinguish, that is, 'cut between' things that are confused to others. For the metaphor of height as a measure of worth (the 'summit of achievement', 'high quality', 'You're the tops'), see again George Lakoff's and Mark Johnson's book on metaphor (Lakoff and Johnson 1980: 15–19).

Metonymic transparencies (those that use one thing found in a situation for something else found in the same situation, like 'the Crown' for the monarch) turn up in 'acacia', the tree so named because of its *sharp thorns*, and in 'acrobat', named from one of his salient features, that of *walking on tiptoe* (presumably on a high rope).

Poets are well aware of synaesthetic likenesses of this type, for they make the sound of the verse match something in the meaning that is *not* a sound. Here is Robert Burns getting us into the swing of a dance:

> The piper loud and louder blew;
> The dancers quick and quicker flew;
> They reel'd they set, they cross'd, they cleekit,*
> Till ilka carlin swat and reekit[†] ...
>> ('Tam O'Shanter', lines 145–8)
>> *'joined hands'
>> [†] 'till each witch sweated and steamed'

And Tennyson:

> And, like a downward smoke, the slender stream
> Along the cliff to fall and pause and fall did seem.
>> ('The Lotos-Eaters', lines 10–11)

And John Clare:

> There lies a sultry lusciousness around
> The far-stretched pomp of summer which the eye
> Views with a dazzled gaze.
>> ('The Heat of Noon', lines 1–3)

It is evidence of the power of the unsaid that the structural isomorphism between the sounds of /vjuːz wið ə dæzłd geiz/ and the sight of a quavering heat haze in a leafy summer quite defeat any attempt to specify common criteria. Carlyle's remark (quoted at the start of this section) about language being founded in poetry is apt: we can see each new word as a poem in little. From Ricœur's we can add that each is a story.

As we saw in the 'hang-down-on-the-branch' illustration of the use of transparency to establish a new word, there is no requirement that only one transparency is at work, that metaphor and metonym and the rest should operate separately from each other. The memory can be stimulated several ways at once, and thus speakers have a right to hope that more than one clue effects the realization of their meaning. To take an example: 'What the board has been saying is just *sabre-rattling*.' Now the immediate figure here is a metaphor: the board's words are *like* the sabre-rattling that would represent a threat on the battlefields of the past, and so the word suggests a threat about which there is some doubt of its force. However, the rattling of a sabre as a warning to one's enemy is a metonymic symbol, in that the noise is supposed to stir the memory of the enemy about the danger of the whole threatened attack, not merely the danger of sabres as such, so the sabres, a part of that whole, stand for all of it. Here is another: 'scatter-brained' – 'scatter' is a metaphor for the disorganization of someone's mind, its chaos *similar* to what happens when things are scattered; '-brained' is a metonym for the possession of a mind, because the mind is in the brain – a highly illogical combination to make a metaphorical adjective qualify a metonymic noun, yet it poses no decoding problems for our memories.

One unusual feature of a transparency that creates a new meaning arises out of the fact that Harry S. Leonard drew attention to (Leonard, 1967: 266), that persons in dialogue may consider that they have reached a perfect mutual understanding when their perspectives on the entity in question contain differences that may surface later. Because of this inescapable irony, it may be that of two persons in dialogue, A and B, one of them, say A, is *already* understanding the circumstance in a more valuable way than B. The difference may not appear until later and – what is even more ironic – it may be *B* who notices that A is saying or doing something unexpected. This is how a new metaphor or metonym may come into the language: it may be A's imagination that has made the poetic move to a new meaning, *but it is B who brings it to everyone's notice*. A was under the impression that everyone understood the entity in the same way as herself! Many a trope may thus have appeared with the speaker quite unaware that their own meaning was at odds with those of others. One can be a poet and not know it. This is inevitable since the initial move in a statement is *to take for granted* that others are working with the same 'objective' meanings as oneself.

The philosopher Donald Davidson has written about metaphor (Davidson, 1978, 1986). He is right from one point of view to say that metaphors come suddenly and unexpectedly into the language-game and then become so familiar to everyone that they settle down as what we call literal; what he misses is that a metaphor (or a metonym), precisely because it is part of a *game* – and thus falls into our familiar Joke/Riddle/Story pattern – need not have been so to one speaker, who had been already using that transparency for a long time, with everyone else unaware of her doing so. Its emergence is only unexpected for her in the sense that she discovers that everyone else had been playing the game differently. He is also wrong then to say that metaphors have no meaning, for the reason he gives is that they are *not* part of the language-game. I am afraid here he still is under the inhibiting influence of the twentieth-century's idolatry of 'logical analysis', for a game deals in ambiguities, which logicians abhor. The 'metaphor' certainly had meaning for its user long before anyone else saw from her actions in some critical circumstance how she was using it, so it was indeed part of the language-game, even though officially not part of *la langue*. She was no Humpty-Dumpty (but even he could have defended his use of 'glory' to mean a *nice knock-down argument* on the strength of a metonymic shift). Because it is a game, that is what you can do, whether you know you are doing it or not! You don't win at chess by knowing the rules, but by seeing new gestalts among the arrangement of the pieces that your opponent does not – no one would say that the one who sees the new and perhaps winning gestalt is 'not playing chess', not in the game, for seeing such things is just what *playing* is! And we have seen that every new word has to come into being this way; it is how the meaning of a symbol begins, how something non-symbolic becomes a symbol.

So the Trope exhibits exactly the same play between persons as the Statement, and is therefore bound up with the issue of faith and risk that we discerned in the operation of the triangle at the end of Chapter 4, section 6. To quote Paul Ricœur on the subject of play:

> In this risk of an unknown partner lies the 'charm' of play. Whoever plays is also played.
> (Ricœur, 1981: 186)

5.   Rhetoric

> Wherever there is persuasion, there is rhetoric, and wherever there is 'meaning', there is 'persuasion'.
> (Kenneth Burke, 1962: 696)

> Rhetoric ... is the study of misunderstanding and its remedies.
> (I. A. Richards, 1936: 3)

Armed with our new analysis, we can confront current theories of rhetoric and see which it helps us to oppose and which it helps to defend.

Looking back over the past twenty-five years or so of theorizing about rhetoric what is found is a debate over the very nature of rhetoric itself. On the one hand, there is a group for whom rhetoric is to be seen as arising out of objective situations in which some urgency of decision is called for, and thus is a matter of arriving at the external truth that for some reason is misconstrued. In this view the orator or speaker is concerned to bring his hearers' understandings closer to the existing array of facts. On the other hand, the opposing view sees rhetoric as a process in which the speaker is recommending novel conceptualizations of the world, which makes rhetoric a part of the ongoing adjustment of our knowledge structures in face of the unexpected contingencies with which nature presents us, resulting in a succession of disclosures and transformations. This makes rhetoric an epistemic enterprise, a 'communicative praxis' (Schrag, 1986), in which the speaker endeavours to revise the judgements of his hearers about what is to be considered as known. The former group sees the latter as relativists purveying an unreliable take on the world and themselves as secure within a philosophy of certainties that are at least accessible in principle: the latter see the former as rigid authoritarians and themselves as courageous experimenters prepared to challenge outdated formulations of thought.

The rhetorician Jeffrey Bineham sees this conflict as marked by the degree to which the contestants share or disavow the anxiety that Descartes was subject to, namely, his desire to find some secure foundation for our claims to truth (Bineham, 1990). In philosophy at large there is a strong current of thought that rejects any such foundation and pours scorn on the foundations suggested in the past: for example, Jacques Derrida attacking the 'metaphysics of presence' (Derrida, 1973), François Lyotard 'grand narratives' (Lyotard, 1984), and Richard Rorty the 'mirroring' of things implicit in the empiricist project (Rorty, 1980). Equally, there is a reaction against such moves in a desire to prove that human beings are indeed capable of apprehending things that are 'thus-and-so' (McDowell, 1994; Brewer, 1999; Tye, 2000). The dispute can be traced back to Ancient Greece with the Sophists on the one hand and Plato on the other. Can we effect a dialectical resolution of these two positions or are we condemned, as some fear, to live with irresolvable 'conundrums' (Cherwitz and Hikins, 1986: 163)?

Let us look in more detail at the way the dispute shows itself in the field of modern American rhetorical studies. Among those most eloquent as rhetoricians themselves in favour of our being able to derive knowledge of a pre-existing objective reality are Lloyd F. Bitzer, Richard A. Cherwitz and James W. Hikins. Bitzer, in a key article in the very first issue of *Philosophy and Rhetoric*, pointed incontestably to the fact that, if one examines any situation in which rhetoric is in play, in that situation is some 'exigence' or other, some matter of urgency, major or minor, that requires co-operative action. He defines a 'rhetorical situation' thus:

> A complex of persons, events, objects, and relations presenting an actual
> or potential exigence which can be completely or partially removed if

discourse, introduced into the situation, can so constrain human decision and action to bring about a significant modification of the exigence.
(Bitzer, 1968: 391)

An exigence is 'a thing which is other than it should be'. Where there are no exigencies, there is no rhetoric. One is here reminded of Wilhelm Dilthey's saying that, if we were all in absolute agreement, we would say nothing, and added that, if we were all in absolute disagreement, we would not be able to say anything (Dilthey, 1913–67: Vol. VII, 225). This neatly encapsulates what has been proposed about the Statement, in that, to initiate a statement two people must reach an *agreement* over something together, but that is only done so that that element of *disagreement* of which the speaker is solely aware may be transmitted to the hearer. The world, says Bitzer, presents objects to be known; for some of them our point of view is unsatisfactory in some respect, and it requires the co-operation of others to put them right. It is up to the rhetor who has perceived this imperfection to seek the propitious moment to persuade those of whose assistance he is in need to join with him to bring it to perfection. The audience must be possible 'mediators of change'. This, in Bitzer's view, rules out both science and poetry from rhetoric. As he puts it,

> The scientist can produce a discourse expressive or generative of knowledge without engaging another mind, and the poet's creative purpose is accomplished when the work is composed.
> (Bitzer, 1968: 387)

He is not saying that scientific statements and poetic ones do not have audiences, but that the audiences are not ones that the speaker is trying to use to assist in the correction of some exigence. What he is quite sure of is that there is a touchstone to distinguish a genuine rhetorical statement: if it bears the marks of anything *fictive*, it can be rejected:

> Real situations are to be distinguished from sophistic ones, in which, for example, a contrived exigence is asserted to be real; from spurious situations, in which the existence or alleged existence of constituents is the result of error or ignorance; and from fantasy, in which exigence, audience and constraints may all be imaginary objects of a mind at play.
> (Bitzer, 1968: 390)

Such a confident distinction between fantasy and reality, though we all perhaps would hope to share it, is not so easily achieved. Nevertheless, one must concede to Bitzer that in ordinary life we are all naïve realists at a certain level, and might even agree that we are surrounded by 'bare facts'. It is confessedly not easy to adopt enough philosophical detachment to acknowledge that a feature of rhetoric itself is persuading us of the 'objective reality' of those 'bare facts'.

But why are we naïve realists at a certain level? We have only to recall what was said about the necessary faith in Chapter 4.5 (pp. 118–19): the Triangulation Argument only needs 'subjects' and 'objects' as part of our method of handling the world when some difficulty turns up. That difficulty can be seen as Bitzer's 'exigence', but his 'bare facts' are only the sedimentation of the success so far of our mutual hypothesizing of perfect singularities, coupled with the sufferance of the Real. At no point do our individual corners of the triangle coalesce in absolute timeless superimposition, except in the real game that we are *playing* together. To be fair to Bitzer, he does concede in a later article that the current consensus is not always right (Bitzer, 1980: 91). Our ordinary objects and selves do not possess this perfection, and thus there is no empirical guarantee even of their singularity when to talk of the Real at all we must project an imaginary fixity onto its fuzzy portions. We have to play at being naïve realists, but we never can become them. This is where the 'exigences' come from; they are the problems, the Shakespearean 'questions' that call for statements: see Brutus's 'How that might change his nature, there's the question' (*Julius Caesar*, II, 1, 13).

To borrow Bitzer's own words above, they are in a sense the 'imaginary objects of' – not 'a mind at play', but *minds* at play. The needful fixity of 'bare facts' is only a part of our trusting method. Ernesto Grassi, an Italian rhetorician, is thus on the right lines when he says (with his countryman Giambattista Vico) that it is 'fantasy that…lets the human world appear' (Grassi, 1980: 7). However, it is not only as Vico thought that the first men were poets in the making of language and their myths, but we continue to be poets in handling language together every day (Vico, 1970: 74–9). What is more, it is that imaginary fixity of the logical subject that we throw away with the appearance of the logical predicate of every informative statement in order to pick that fixity up again in its adjusted form by the end of the statement as if there had been no adjustment whatsoever. The agreement slides on and we are hardly aware in many cases that our mutual counting went through a transformation as surprising as that of a story. It seems to be the same as before, even in spite of the possibility that what we counted as one entity now might be two-and-a-half.

This is where the *inventio* of the rhetor's world comes from. *Inventio* is the rhetoric's term of art for the novel input that the speaker is responsible for, the 'Second Clue' that induces the new interpretation in the minds of the audience. Cicero said that the first thing the orator must do is to invent what is persuasive (*De Oratore*, 99–306). But that is precisely what new thought is, the inward realization that what had been viewed under an old intentional perspective, now, like a joke, suffers a transformation under a new one, hopefully one that, as in Hegelian dialectic, performs an *Aufhebung* on the Ambiguous Element; an *Aufhebung* is a 'repeal' or 'rescindment' that is at the same time a 'lifting' into a new and better version of the old. Just as we saw with the metaphor, the first user of the metaphor may not be aware that they are using it, that they have a novel take on the supposed singularity which has not yet come into mutual salience because action has not yet produced a moment of criterial difference; as we saw (p. 155) the first user might be the originator of the new thought but not be the one to publicize it. The motivation behind the invention we can identify with Bitzer's 'exigence', the matter of urgency that forms the impulse to transform the hearer's understanding. This is why there really is no distinction between what the rhetoricians call 'proof' and 'persuasion', the 'apodeictic' – that is, the 'clearly demonstrated' – and the metaphorical (Leff, 1999), for the first is but the handle of the Statement which we have to turn with the second. To refer across to the conversation of science, one can say with Thomas Kuhn that invention, innovation, comes as the overthrow of a paradigm, but add that it is not only within paradigms that puzzles are solved, but the movement to a new paradigm partakes of the structure of a puzzle, or a riddle, or a story (Kuhn, 1970: 97).

The arguments of Richard A. Cherwitz, James W. Hikins, Earl Croasmun and Kenneth Zagacki are subject to the same criticism (Cherwitz and Hikins, 1986: 124, 13; Cherwitz and Croasmun, 1982; Hikins and Zagacki, 1988, 1993). Like Bitzer, they see the world as 'created of numerous particulars', 'discrete facts', but we can now trope the word 'numerous' as bringing out the process of human mutual *counting* being what enables us to handle the resisting Real, as Kenneth Burke calls it (Burke, 1962: 255). We can trope it because that counting does not guarantee the pre-existence of such ideal-logical distinctions, only uses them as hypothetical constructs to obtain a tentative coinciding of our separate referents, turning the multiple corners of the triangle temporarily into single ones. Their view is that such facts are ideally '*discrete*' before any *discerning* has gone on by co-operating motivated beings. Cherwitz and Croasmun are, like Bitzer, drawn into dismissing fictive entities from their ontology; as they say, 'they are not conceived to be real just because there is discourse about them' (Cherwitz and Croasmun, 1982: 2); in contrast, they add, undeniable facts, such as the sun being at the centre of the solar system, are guaranteed by what lies outside agreement (compare Robert Kirk, p. 116). Lloyd Bitzer's distinction between what he calls 'public knowledge' and 'private knowledge' rests on the same confidence (Bitzer, 1971, 83). The apparent 'common' sense of such declarations, however, gains its plausibility only from the same impulse as motivated David Wiggins: they are exhorting us to join in the common *faith* that maintains such 'objectivities', one that still relies unthinkingly on the sufferance of the Real. Such blind exhortations hide from their utterers the risk that all 'objectivities' universally retain. There is nothing wrong in entering the taken-for-granted of language in order to state one's theory; after all, one is just taking it for granted and one could not speak otherwise.

They also fall back on a very common argument, that of claiming that those who question the truth and certainty of our statements are committing a practical self-contradiction: for example, they accuse Raymie E. McKerrow of using 'the tools of rationality' when he is supposedly questioning them (Cherwitz and Hikins, 2000: 382). The attack takes the form of implying that people who argue in this way, that objectivity and truth are not as reliable as had been made out, have no right at all to argue thus because they are committing a form of practical self-contradiction. Why is this? Because, in the first place, they are relying on the objectivity of everyday things and selves to speak. How can you argue that your argument is *true* if you claim that truth is not to be relied upon? The point has been made succinctly by two psychologists, Stephen Wilcox and Stuart Katz, who said that people claiming to prove that we do not have direct access to given things and persons are involved in a contradiction because they have to refer to things and persons to make that very claim, even a reference to themselves when they say '*We* believe that this is true'. As Wilcox and Katz put it, someone who tries to say this is ignoring the very 'presuppositions' of their own reasoning (Wilcox and Katz, 1984: 153). This is an extremely common objection levelled at anyone who holds to a social constructivist view of human knowledge. The philosopher of religion, Alister McGrath, a realist, uses it against Don Cupitt, an anti-realist, claiming that Cupitt has no right to use the deliverances of science against religious realists because he is depending on a realist view of natural science to make his point (McGrath, 2004: 155; Cupitt, 1985). Another philosopher of religion, Paul Griffiths, tries to discountenance the claim that narrative lies at the heart of religion by saying that 'a pure narrativist program is self-referentially incoherent' (Griffiths, 2001: 231). John Searle has complained that those who propose alternatives to realism are at last obliged to presuppose the truth of realism in order to make their point (Searle, 1999: 20–6). But Searle gives the answer away: we are perfectly ready *to presuppose* the logical idealities that are things and selves – it is just that we do not wish to make the super-stitious error of believing in them as existing in transcendental perfection. As a response to Cherwitz and Hikins' latest article put it, it has been said that 'the self-exempting fallacy is thus a chimera' (Schiappa et al., 2002: 118). One cannot turn something that is only taken for granted into a mutual certainty; this is to misuse the 'tools of rationality'. Such ignoring of risk is a theme we shall return to in Chapter 6.

They do make a move towards acknowledging the differing perspectives people bring to a situation by saying that, once the relational factors that govern each perspective are teased out, then the objectivity before them emerges. This certainly looks like a move away from the Cartesian anxiety that Bineham spoke of, in that the perspectives of subjects are now to be made part of the total evidence, but subject and object are still to be taken as separate entities without any attention paid to that phrase 'taken as'. They actually give away their adherence to the Schutzian idealization of reciprocity by stating it in full *without seeing what they have said*. As with Aaron Ben Ze'ev (see p. 107), the slippage occurs in their use of the word 'assumption':

> We do make the *assumption* that a reality exists independently of individuals. This *assumption* is not arbitrary. It is *presumed* in the use, if not always in the theory, of communication.
> (Cherwitz and Hikins, 1986: 19, my emphases)

The answer to this should now be plain: yes, we *do* make this assumption, and it certainly is not an arbitrary one, because, if we did not presume it, no statement could ever be begun and carried through, but it remains an *assumption* and not a *belief* for all that. And, yes the Real does exist independently of individuals, but not as pre-given discrete entities, for even those 'individuals', so hopefully named, are not pre-given entities either, but require the assistance of other persons similarly placed in the imprecision of the Real to help them continue the endless process of identifying themselves. The present theory avoids both what Richard Harvey Brown has called 'positivistic objectivism' and 'romantic intuitionism' by 'transvaluing' them through a 'narration of the world' (Brown, 1983: 155).

Cherwitz and Hikins also attempt to back their position up with the usual claim that their opponents are lost in solipsism, but that attack, you will recall, has also been rendered futile (pp. 83, 99–100) (Cherwitz and Hikins, 1986). It is here, too, they say that they want to leave 'philosophical conundrums aside' (p. 23), but it is precisely an investigation of the Conundrum (see Chapter 1) that will release them from their confusion. The answer to all their objections was already implied in George Steiner's remark:

> Part of the answer to the notorious logical conundrum as to whether or not there can be 'private language' is that aspects of every language-act are unique and individual.
> (Steiner, 1998: 46)

They have forgotten what I. A. Richards asserted, that ambiguity is a natural property of language (Richards, 1936: 40), and it is that ambiguity across persons that is the source of every informative statement as it updates both its hearer and the language itself. In Robert L. Scott's words (another American rhetorician who sees rhetoric as intimately connected with the struggle of knowing):

> Ambiguity is simply the natural consequence of finite acting in the face of the infinite.
> (Scott, 1993: 16)

Or, in the terms of this theory, in our having together in the endless dialogue to adjust our imaginary, timeless singularities of language in their co-ordination upon the boundaryless Real.

By way of contrast, a word about those rhetoricians whose theorizing is upheld by the Triangulation Argument. Barry Brummett is noteworthy among those who see rhetoric as recommending ways of seeing the world, as he puts it, it being an 'advocacy of realities' (Brummett, 1976: 31). He borrows from Michael Polanyi and Floyd W. Matson the idea of a 'complementarity of rival perspectives', the idea that others whom we regard as having our interests at heart often urge meanings upon us, as we upon them (Polanyi, 1969: 125; Matson, 1964: 136). This is what constitutes the rhetorical act, the aim being a sharing of meanings: 'today's social reality is yesterday's rhetorical vision', a view which dovetails neatly with the Triangulation Argument in seeing the world of 'reality', of mundane things and persons, as an apparently settled array of mutual selections from the Real habitually taken for granted. So it can be said that the Statement is an act of rhetoric, for there is persuasion in it, the turning of the *intentional* perspective of the hearer in order that his or her entity-selection is updated. Persuasion (Latin *persuadere*, literally 'thoroughly to sweeten') is directed at motivation, and we have shown that motivation is in every concept as used, although we affect its absence in our initial act of trust. Is it not bad form to draw attention to one's own motivations when entering into a pact of trust with another? This, of course, can go along with Richards' remark about the universality of ambiguity, for it is out of the discordance of interpretations that hopefully better general understandings are arrived at. No observations are value-free; those which constitute no Bitzerian 'exigence' for us are those for which the shared meanings have been tested out in practice over time and have so far survived the challenges of the Real. The most familiar are those which seem most harmless and thus devoid of motivation, but, as any joker can readily demonstrate, the ambiguity may allow the harmful to scare us at any moment. In stories about the uncanny, it is always the most unthreatening entity that produces the most powerful fright when transformed (consider the fourth story in the disturbing film *Dead of Night*, in which it is a ventriloquist's dummy that becomes the object of fear – the ventriloquist hauntingly played by Michael Redgrave). It is not that the objective is free of motivational charge: it is just that familiarity has rendered us complacent about it, seeing it as neutral, *im*-personal, and thus risk-free. Yet they are only *im*-personal because we are assuming sameness of personal intentions and sameness of sensory access.

Brummett is convinced that all entities are marked with intention: 'what . . . objects are for humans always includes what we mean them to be' (1982: 426), but what he does not make clear is whose intentions he is talking about or whose bodies are doing the sensing. He ought to have pursued his thought that sensing is, as this theory maintains, 'meaningless', that is, non-epistemic (Brummett, 1976: 28), for he should also have insisted that it is different for each body which is precisely why the collective word cannot capture it. He believes that those for whom truth is justified true belief as judged by the individual forget that it is finally consensus that determines 'justification' and 'sufficiency'. Objectivists assume that what is called 'objective reality' is keyed to singular physical referents, but there are no such 'things' and thus they have difficulty in explaining how one interpretation comes to be succeeded by another, which is the second part of the rhetorical-narrative act, the first being the projection of the ideal agreement. This matches the difficulty Saussure faced in linguistics, of explaining how one got from the rigidity of *la langue* to the flexibility of *le parole*, from the timelessly unchanging 'synchronic' to the endlessly becoming 'diachronic'. But that transformation is performed in each statement.

Brummett as a *philosopher*, however, is overly optimistic about the inter-action of public consensus with the individual judgement, a point that must here await clarification until the conclusion. No one objects to his being optimistic as a *person*, as long as that optimism is held with full under-standing of the implications of the risk that faith in the other entails.

One rhetorician who has come close to what is being argued here is Walter Fisher, who claims specifically that 'All forms of human communica-tion need to be seen fundamentally as stories' (Fisher, 1987, xi). He even coins the term *homo narrans*, man as a story-telling animal. He takes from Alasdair MacIntyre (1981), Hayden White (1981) and Paul Ricœur (1981) the notion that in some way narrative is central to the nature of human being and endeavours to relate it to communication as such. He defines narrative capacity as the ability to infer 'states of mind from symbolic clues' (Fisher, 1987: 66). There is no escaping from the assessment of value when we take effects of action into consideration, which is as much as to say that our perspectives are intentional, and any 'good reasons' we apply to a situation of urgency must be tested against our motivations for they are what is offered in support of an *ought* proposition. He does not pursue the notion of 'symbolic clues' which might have led him to perceive the ironic structure of the Story and the transparency behind the symbol, and so he does not produce a theory of narrative as such, but he is convinced that a formal logic cannot deliver any morally valuable notion of truth. He correctly suspects the divide between fiction and truth, *mythos* and *logos*, but gives no explanation of their inextricability.

The ethical inadequacy of logic is a theme in Richard B. Gregg's book on 'symbolic inducement' (1984). With Ernesto Grassi he recommends our searching for 'a logic of invention and not deduction' (Grassi, 1980: 97–8) and with Kenneth Burke sees rhetoric as something 'continually born anew … the use of language as a symbolic means of inducing co-operation in beings that by nature respond to symbols' (Burke, 1962: 567). Gregg would agree with our characterization of language as an endeavour to get tentative holds on the recalcitrant flux; as he puts it, language is 'a means of fixing existence' (1984: 91), and he realizes that we all of us differ in our understanding of that 'fixity', citing George Steiner's belief that 'each communicatory gesture has a private residue' (Steiner, 1998: 47), which has as its consequence that 'meaning is not confined within language' since private meanings can exist easily within a public language. Certainly, as Wittgenstein maintained, there cannot be a private language, but it is actually the general case, as Steiner insists, that *there are private understandings of the public language*. Rhetoric is thus aimed at inducing choices in ways of symbolizing reality, either inducing new ones or stabilizing old ones. It appears that Gregg should be able to embrace the theory presented here without difficulty.

The rhetorician whose work is closest to the Triangulation Argument is Calvin Schrag (Schrag, 1969, 1980, 1986, 1997). For him 'praxis' is the key to rhetoric, the hermeneutical process conducted by human beings in communication from which their view of 'reality' emerges. He refuses to detach truth from method as Cherwitz and Hikins would have us do; indeed, he sets himself against all modes of foundationalism, whether the given entities be 'the' observing persons or 'the numerous facts'. Praxis lies at the intersection of discourse and action. With Richard Rorty he rejects the whole idea of a mirroring of entities in the mind – reflection, a word Cherwitz and Hikins use, is the last he would appeal to. There are no foundational referents: the whole web of facts is something that has to be penetrated, and what is required is the use of metaphor and narration. As he says, there has to be a conjoining of narration and reference. It is not that the entities lie around ready for our observing – it is rather that we have to tell each other stories which are then put to the world to be tested in action. There is an overlap with the Cherwitz view that there has to be an independent reality which must play its part in the resulting 'communicative praxis', but he is not prepared to accord it the discreteness they believe in. In particular, the *subject* is not to be accorded that discreteness; the decentred subject is just as much a part of that praxis as the decentred objects.

We must now add here, of course, that to speak we must begin by *treating* them *as* 'centred', that is, being the logical units our language-game requires. Surely this is what Jacques Derrida means when he says that the centre is 'a function, not a being' (Derrida, 1991: 67). Schrag comes very close to our view of the Statement when he maintains that there is 'a dialectic of repetition and novelty' undertaken by communicating agents which involves them intimately in their own self-definition (Schrag, 1986: 109); the 'repetition' can be seen to be the imagined perfect agreement of the logical subject, and the 'novelty' being the updating afforded by the logical predicate supplied by the speaker. Significantly, he images it as happening in a 'play-space' (1986: 6), in that we cannot accord primacy to either text, perception or action – the 'interplay' among them that results from our rhetorical interchanges with each other is what constitutes the movement of life and thought. Make the further addition of the definition of play that the present theory contains and Schrag's 'communicative praxis' becomes a favoured account of what rhetoric is. As one would expect, his definition of truth differs markedly from that of Cherwitz and Hikins:

> The truth at issue in a rhetoric of truth is not that of an epistemic corre- spondence of a reified proposition with that of an equally reified state of affairs, but rather truth as the disclosure of possibilities for agreed upon perspectives on seeing the world and acting within it.
> (Schrag, 1986: 187)

Tweak this by saying that 'reification' is what two language-users have to begin all statements with, and that the 'disclosure' is what resets that fixity to a new – but equally temporary – state.

Schrag's is a hermeneutical approach to rhetoric, owing much to Heidegger and Merleau-Ponty. Rhetoric is not a description of reality but an endless *re*description. To do this we bring the idealities of our thought mutually to bear upon the world, those that we have already accomplished together and project them in order that a critique of them can be performed. We test out the commensurable, what we have so far *regarded as* the same, *as* identical, in order to discover its incommensurability, to *re*measure it. He will thus have nothing to do with divisions between *langue* and *parole*, understanding and explanation, logic and metaphor, the scientific and the humanistic. As far as subjects are concerned, the participation in the rhetoric that is communication produces what forever distances us from ourselves – there is self-risk in every utterance. That is an anxiety we all have to learn to put up with. Of course, this is what stories are all about, dialogues in which subjects learn new definitions of themselves and the world from each other.

All of this is consonant with what is being argued for in this book, and the hope is that Schrag will see that the Triangulation Argument provides his account with a credible philosophical base. It is worth noting that he moved towards the theory of perception presented here in his insistence that sensation itself was 'dumb', non-epistemic, lacking in information about the mutually hypothesized 'things', a view that follows Kant's 'Intu- itions without concepts are blind' (Schrag, 1969: 8; Kant, *Critique of Pure Reason*, A51, B75).

To conclude this disquisition on rhetoric, one needs to look at the work of the philosopher Paul Grice, for there have been strong appeals to it made both in the debates about rhetoric and in linguistics itself; in the latter particularly there has been a theory about humour which places great reliance on Grice and which is thus very relevant to the topic of this book.

Paul Grice has made two contributions to the philosophy of language that have been made much of, both in philosophy as such and outside it where language has been subjected to analysis. The first was to give a definition of meaning, the second to make clear the presuppositions made by persons in dialogue that are necessary for that dialogue to proceed without ambiguity. The rhetoricians Marcelo Dascal and Alan G. Gross rely on Grice for their formulation of what constitutes rhetorical persuasion (Dascal and Gross, 1999) and the linguists Victor Raskin and Salvatore Attardo rely on Grice's 'conversational maxims' in their theories of humour (Raskin, 1985; Attardo, 1994).

His definition of meaning begins by distinguishing two types of meaning, that he calls 'natural' and 'non-natural'. The first applies to those cases where we take a natural occurrence to be a sign of a further happening, such as seeing a dark cloud on the horizon as being a sign of rain, or seeing a certain kind of spot on the skin as being an indication of measles. These are clearly non-symbolic, a taking of something in the world of mundane reality as evidence of the likelihood of something else. Non-natural meaning, on the other hand, is achieved when the utterer intended by his utterance of something to induce a belief in the hearer *by the hearer's recognition of that intention*. It has been generally assumed that Grice was the first to propose this explanation of meaning, but that is not the case, as I pointed out long ago (Wright, 1976: 513–14). Sir Alan Gardiner was the first to elucidate the symbol situation as essentially concerning the take-up of the speaker's intentions by the hearer:

> *The thing meant by any utterance is whatever the speaker intended to be understood from it by the listener.*
> (Gardiner, 1932: 82, his emphasis)

However, he differs significantly from Grice in refraining from identifying the thing meant as the speaker understands it with the thing meant as the hearer understands it. As I pointed out earlier (p. 141), he was aware that 'deep metaphysical issues' hung on this distinction.

Grice falls into the same temptation when he spells out the presuppositions that he considers persons in dialogue must make in order to communicate successfully at all. According to Grice, what distinguishes *bone fide* from non-*bona fide* communication is adherence to four 'conversational maxims'. These are as follows:

(1) *The Category of Quantity*: 'Make your contribution as informative as is required' (for the current purposes of the exchange) and possibly 'Do not make your contribution more informative than is required.'

(2) *The Category of Quality*: 'Try to make your contribution one that is true', with two more specific maxims 'Do not say what you believe to be false' and 'Do not say that for which you lack adequate evidence.'

(3) *The Category of Relation*: 'Be relevant.' [Grice admits that 'foci of relevance' may be difficult to fix in any particular case.]

(4) *The Category of Manner*: 'Be perspicuous', which includes as sub-maxims, (i) 'Avoid obscurity of expression'; (ii) 'Avoid ambiguity'; (iii) 'Be brief (avoid unnecessary prolixity)'; and (iv) 'Be orderly.'
(Grice, 1975: 67)

With these maxims in place and observed by the speaker, the communication is guaranteed to be *bona fide*, and it is obvious that 'lying, play-acting and joke-telling' are ruled out, as is fiction in general. The sub-maxim alone 'Avoid ambiguity' prevents the trigger of the joke being used at all in normal dialogue. If a psychoanalyst or a literary theorist were to protest that unconscious elements of meaning cannot be ruled out, the answer would be that in the philosophical and scientific analysis of communication we are not centrally concerned either with neurotic invasions of speech or with poetic or fictive elaborations of it – rather with what constitutes 'normal' utterance, which obviously must be the main topic in the investigation of language.

To anyone not acquainted with the Triangulation Argument none of this appears to be immediately questionable. There is no doubt that normal communication could not take place unless all parties involved made Grice's assumptions. But it can be seen at once that all that Grice has done is to spell out the Schutzian Idealization of the Reciprocity of Standpoints, but without the necessary qualification that all these are regulative ideals which have to be played *as if* they could be achieved. Like Cherwitz and Hikins above, Grice has not seen what his use of the term 'presuppositions' actually implies, that these are what we must pre-*suppose*, take for granted, while being fully aware that they cannot and must not apply. The information in a proposition could not even be proposed if they were strictly adhered to, for the 'truth' as conceived by the speaker can never wholly coincide with that of the hearer: it is that very mismatch which allows the communication to be set up in the first place. Ambiguity cannot be 'avoided', as it is at the core of the proposition.

Notice Grice's sub-maxim that one must 'not make one's contribution more informative than is required'. This is impossible of achievement, for subjects cannot know what they are revealing of their deeper intentions to their hearers. Criminals in telling a lie can easily give away a truth unawares, as we saw in the story of the Chinese peasant. Grice is reifying the Subject as well as the Object and is thus open to all the objections that have been levelled against turning the 'taken-for-granted' as gospel. The allusion to gospels is not irrelevant since the question of faith, the *bona fide* status of the speaker, his 'ethos', is precisely what is at issue. There is no way in which the good faith of the speaker can be attributed to the fixity of *la langue* for that is to turn the tentative mutual hypothesis into a rigid, pre-ordained deliverer of truth. Speakers and hearers have *to hope* that their private interpretation of the public word may guarantee all outcomes as happy, but it is grossly narcissistic to attempt to shift one's moral responsibility onto what is *believed* to be a given 'true' meaning in that word that the other can never challenge under any circumstances.

The failure to see this point comes out clearly in Dascal and Gross's effort to turn Grice's maxims into a support for a theory of rhetoric. When they say that 'co-operation is presupposed', they are using the word 'presupposed' to mean that actual pure co-operation is some kind of unchallengeable axiom as in some mathematical system, not merely an essential part of the *fictive* method of dealing with the Real (Dascal and Gross, 1999: 110). One illustration of their mode of argument is sufficient to show its flawed character. When they consider the likelihood of a person not being conscious of all their intentions at the time they speak, they are happy to claim the following:

> They may not be conscious of this intent at the time of utterance, but they would acknowledge that it was their intent if it were pointed out to them.
>   (Dascal and Gross, 1999: 115)

This is to play the omniscient god with someone's intentions, for, when at some later date new circumstances force the person to realize that some part of their deepest desires was compromised in the statement they made before, the outcome could be comic or tragic; the two speakers involved in a promise, perhaps, could not see at the earlier time just what was implicit in their mutual undertaking. Such a comic or tragic outcome is a *surprise* to the person concerned; she never imagined that she had such an intention. There is an excellent little poem by Frances Cornford that nicely sums up the point:

> In my dark mind you kicked a stone away.
> There in the light, a full-grown Purpose lay;
> And half in terror, half in glad surprise,
> I saw his unknown coils and sleeping eyes
>   (Cornford, 'Revelation', 1954: 70)

This is where my dictum comes into play: *What is implicit for each cannot all be explicit for both*. To claim that all intentions could have been mutually and harmlessly made salient is precisely to exhort us into the Idealization of Reciprocity of Standpoints. Again we find the Wiggins error, of turning the 'taken-for-granted' into an inflexible actuality binding across the persons in dialogue. That is what in good faith they must indeed engage in, but knowing full well that time, that is, the contingencies of the Real, can subvert the best intentions. It is noteworthy that they make appeal for support to the philosopher Robert Brandom, but he makes the same error, in believing that all can be made explicit, as the very title of his book, *Making it Explicit*, declares. This assertion of his, for example, typical of many such in his book, falls to the same criticism just made:

> Norms that are explicit in the form of rules presuppose norms implicit in practices.
> (Brandom, 1994: 20)

Yes, they are pre-*supposed* all right, but two persons with a proper trust in each other do not and cannot believe that the word alone contains all its meaning and thus completely encapsulates the 'norm' – and *that the other's 'practices' will be exactly what you expect according to your initial interpretation of the 'explicit' word.*

At the present moment in the world of humour research a dominant approach is based on the work of a linguist, Victor Raskin, as a glance at the issues of the periodical *Humor* over the last decade will make plain. He places a key reliance on Grice as establishing the difference between *bona fide* and non-*bona fide* utterances: jokes, of course, falling into the latter category. Both their theories are purely verbal theories of humour of a type that identifies incongruities between existing 'scripts' as the basic source of humour in language. Notice that speakers and their motivations have disappeared, for humour is presented as being explicable by the clash of given opposites in language. It is no surprise that it is *la langue* that is presumed to be the ground of these clashes of 'scripts'. Raskin makes much of mundanely accepted oppositions, the three major ones being actual/non-actual, normal/abnormal, possible/impossible. What he does not see is that jokes are often aimed at undoing those very oppositions, for the Triangulation Argument shows that all those distinctions are what constitute the very hinge of the transformation that a statement effects, a transformation that *was not in the language until that moment.* To talk of a script already existing to challenge a 'normal' view is to ignore the diachronic parameter of language within which, as we have seen, language is endlessly re-created.

Raskin's misuse of the term *bona fide* can be briefly shown by examining the way in which he treats an actual joke. He argues for a clear distinction between a non-joke (*bona fide*) and a joke (non-*bona fide*); this is a joke he chooses to put forward as an example:

> A: My wife used to play the violin a lot, but after we had kids she had not much time for that.
> B: Children are a comfort, aren't they?

He comments as follows:

> In [this joke] as well, for *bona fide* communication, the transition between the two sentences is two [sic] sharp, and the non-*bona fide* communication becomes preferable and certainly not inevitable.
> (Raskin, 1985: 102)

Raskin with his last phrase, 'certainly not inevitable' allows for two possibilities of meaning as precise *alternatives*, in that B's comment could *either* mean (1) that B is lucky to be escaping the noise of his wife's violin playing (which is, of course, the joke interpretation) *or* (2) that children are a comfort to parents. Raskin thus does allow for a choice between the *bona fide* version (2) and the non-*bona fide* one (1). But it never occurs to him that B could happily mean two things by his remark, (1) the joke interpretation, and (3) that A's wife's playing is generally regarded as bad, and certainly by B. It might have been the very first occasion that B made the point in (3) to A, and the very first time A realized the fact, having thought up to that moment that she was a very good player. The ambiguity here could have been specifically intended by him, as he capitalized on the *la langue* assumption that jokes and non-jokes are clearly separate in given 'scripts' (we don't find jokes being played on us in the Oxford Dictionary!). By Raskin's argument such an ambiguous remark is impossible, being *bona fide* and non-*bona fide* at the same time. Salvatore Attardo has pointed out how this is perfectly possible (Attardo, 1994: 287). So they cannot be taken as given opposites in the analysis of jokes, even though the question of *good faith* is central to that mutual hypothesis of identity of meaning across persons that is part and parcel of the first move in the Statement.

In addition, it is worth asking the not-irrelevant question whether Raskin was being *bona fide* when he used the word 'two' in the phrase 'two sharp'. We can make the leap of transparency between 'two' and 'too' easily enough because we have come across such errors with these words before, but, if we were to be confined to what the 'script' provides, which is unmistakably the word 'two', then Raskin, by his own argument, would be speaking nonsense.

6.   Logic pure and applied

If the Triangulation Argument goes through, the conclusions about faith being the foundation of both language and truth have strange consequences for logic. It is obviously marked off from ordinary language if that is governed by a narrative structure, one that deals in transformations. Jerome Bruner points out the dichotomy:

> The very speech act involved in 'telling a story' – whether from life or from the imagination – warns the beholder that its meaning cannot be established by Frege-Russell rules relating to sense and reference.
> (Bruner, 1990: 61)

Let us take pure logic first, where the relationships of symbols to each other are considered to work without persons to operate them and without any relation to the Real at large. It should be plain now that what is happening in pure logic (and pure mathematics) is that the symbols are regarded as corresponding to no referents at all, which is the same as saying that the 'taken-for-granted' singularities can *never* change because they have no contact with the Real whatsoever. The arithmetic books can ask us to add six apples to five apples to get an invariable answer, but why is it we might watch with care a suspect greengrocer putting the extra five we have bought into our bag? In logic and mathematics it is as if we have mutually agreed that we have moved out of time and the Real into a no-space in which nothing could ever disturb our agreements over meanings. Logic freezes the proposition so that it loses its transformative power, paradoxically by *playing at not playing*.

When we go through a syllogism such as the following,

All Higgs bosons have never been observed.
This is a Higgs boson.
So this has never been observed.

we discover that this is a *logically* valid argument, in spite of the fact that it is a self-contradictory one, but the self-contradiction arises from outside the logic sustaining the syllogism, something that is a matter of reference, and, since we have accepted a self-denying ordinance that our terms shall have no referents, we as logicians cannot complain. It emerges that *pure logic and pure mathematics are the most fictive of symbolic activities*, for we have decided beforehand that nothing real can invade their hermetic universes of ideal relationships. We really ought to say that they are not *linguistic* symbols at all, except in some figurative sense, since we do not use them to update each other about the Real. One could even say that, strictly speaking, the term 'logical proposition' itself is a self-contradiction, for in ordinary language a proposition is a proposal to change the language, and, when successful, enacts such a change, and within logic the language can never be changed. Of course, as a practice among pure logicians logic has a place in the Real, just as a play on a stage has a real aspect as an actual performance, but its nature is essentially fictive whereas the play, for all its fiction, has some relevance to our lives. In this pure logic and mathematics markedly differ from words in use, for the fictive aspect of words is employed in our game of updating ourselves in the Real. One could say that they demon-strate what happens to fictions when we give them no purchase on reality. They are purely imaginary agreements that are carried out as performances in the Real by agents capable of communicating. If one asks where their beautiful structures come from (since they can discover them) and why they are bound together with the mysterious logical 'must', then we turn to their being imaginary structures based on the notion of agreement borrowed from our motivated negotiations with each other about the Real and their 'must' comes from our own decision never to disturb their interconnections, given the rules we ourselves have set up. Chess masters can 'discover' wonderful new ways of making things difficult for their opponents, but no one is tempted to claim that these patterns were laid up in some chess heaven before they were created; similarly with the discoveries of mathematics and logic. As for the logical 'must', that is an example of what happens to agreements about fears and desires when for fun we take fear and desire out of the *equation*. A clue to this lies in the logicians being unable to avoid using words like 'satisfies' as they trace their deductive patterns in a situation where nothing is *satisfying* anybody. The fact that logicians and mathematicians cannot resist using aesthetic terms like 'beautiful' for the structures and proofs that are created is more evidence that their activities are an elevated form of play.

This is why it is foreign to the spirit of pure logic to quarrel with the syllogism for ignoring the acquisition of knowledge. For example, in the syllogism

> All men are mortal.
> Socrates is a man.
> Therefore, Socrates is mortal

it is *de rigueur* not to ask how we arrived at the truth of the universal proposition 'All men are mortal' if we had not *already* examined Socrates and found he was mortal, for he is obviously included in 'All men'. If logic is not only timeless, so is its supposed 'knowledge'. Of course it is the case that all logic is tautology, as is so often said, for, since we are supposed to be in perfect agreement, logic can say nothing of any point to anyone!

As soon as we try to transfer logical relationships into our active language, they have to fall back on our mutual trust just as any other feature of our utterances to each other has to. The Greeks, early on, detected in everyday argument a feature they called the 'enthymeme', which was any syllogistic reasoning that depended on a premise but which was not openly expressed. Christopher Lyle Johnstone in the *Encyclopedia of Rhetoric* gives a clear and simple example:

> Imagine a public meeting at which an election will be held for the office of city treasurer. A citizen rises to speak: 'I support Philopolis for he is an honourable man and a wealthy one, and a lover of the city.' This statement, for all its brevity, represents a rather complicated reasoning process in which most of the argument remains implicit. Such a proof can only

work if the audience will provide the missing elements, and thereby follow the reasoning and find it persuasive.
(C. L. Johnstone, 2001: 249)

It is obvious here that certain facts are taken as given, for instance, that a wealthy man is likely to be a better handler of money than a poor one. Aristotle puts it thus: 'it does not have to be stated, as the hearer supplies it' (Aristotle, *Rhetoric*, 1357a). Since by our very human being we have entered into the trust of language, the 'taken-for-granted' reality of things and persons about us and all their interrelationships, that 'nest' our forebears have handed on to us, in which we live at the sufferance of the Real, it is not difficult for a speaker *to take for granted* something already deemed to be in that trust, for that is already the taken-for-granted. This is the actual source of the hidden premises of enthymemes, though they remain as open to the subversion of time as any other verbal agreement (in Johnstone's example, it may be that some electors are convinced that the wealthy are the very last persons to be trusted with public money).

The very 0 and 1 on which all computing depends relies on our trust in each other, for they are no more than 'Yes' and 'No', and 'same' and 'different'. A taken-for-granted singularity depends on the background from which we together distinguish it. A boundary is taken by speaker and hearer to have two sides existing independently of those observing it, but that is exactly what has to be mutually imagined. As I put it in an early article, ' "Same" is a word that confirms the sharing of intentions' (Wright, 1976: 523), but one has to recall the impossibility of fully defining one's own intentions, never mind those of others. Sir Alan Gardiner confessed himself in awe of the 'depth of intention' problem, the 'things meant by speech' being 'susceptible of never-ending analysis' (Gardiner, 1932: 52).

One interesting conclusion here is that, for this reason alone, the computer's 0 and 1 can never alone be the source of an 'artificial intelligence' – a computer could not be a mind that is, unless, at the level of dialogic communication, its favoured noughts and ones that determined action were up for negotiation with another mind and could be transformed as a result of it. This implies, of course, that the artificial mind would have to have the equivalent of a sensory system upon which a *motivationally* guided perceptual module could lodge gestalts in its memory to guide action. That alone would bring it to an animal level, and then it would have be able to engage in the Idealization of Reciprocity of Standpoints in order to update another mind in language exchanges before it could be human.

By the same token the logical operators *if...then, either...or, and, all* and *some* cannot of themselves resolve ambiguity when the propositional varia-bles (interestingly named) that they 'govern' are given real application, for it is we who have to decide upon the direction of that governing. 'To govern' was originally *to steer* and steering needs a steersman and people to set the course, and the human motivations of fear and desire impel the ship. These empty forms make up a system which enables us to match our intentions – as we judge it – on many occasions without wasting time, allowing us to go on with what we hope will satisfy 'our' desires and avert 'our' fears. The fact that some of our intentions have been satisfied is itself part of nature's surprise, though we must remember that most of those whose sensory and perceptual powers were ill adapted for the task disappeared early in the evolutionary history of our species. What obviously must be added on the other side is that evolution is also responsible for the development of a set of mutually adaptive behaviours for intention-matching across the members of the species, or, one might say, for the innocent disguising of mismatching, an innocent disguising that subserves those deeper regions of intention where a common calculation of the future can only be *taken on trust*. None of this implies, of course, that this evolved ability to communicate necessarily means that some favoured 'progress' is guaranteed as a result, however much humankind in the past has been tempted to think of itself as the 'crown of creation'.

What we must now say about our actual use of logic – not our playing with it while it is out of gear with our daily work – is that the element of *play* is never absent. If what is implicit for each cannot all be explicit for both, every utterance that is involved in real action aimed at the satisfying of intentions must contain an element of hypothesis – or to put it more frankly, pretence. We are pretending that our intentions wholly match as inner experience when the truth is that they will only partially match in action. If the word 'pretence' still retains too much of a pejorative cast for you, let us replace it with 'let's-pretend', the harmless, open-eyed pretence of the sensible child who is as aware as any professional actor that what he pretends is not in fact quite the case, however good the match appears to be. This bears out Ludwig Feuerbach's insight:

> What the demonstrator [of logic] shares with me is not the thing itself... He is only an actor. He only presents to me, in perceivable form, that in which I should imitate him. Expository, systematic philosophy is dramatic, theatrical philosophy...
> (Feuerbach, 1903–11: Vol. II, 173)

It is not only possible for differing individuals and groups within one society to have intentions that lead to unforeseen clashes, but a single individual, of whom Oedipus can be the type for us, may have concurrent intentions that produce unexpected conflicts in the future. Henry W. Johnstone, the philosopher of rhetoric, asserts

> ...a fully reflexive self is no more a possibility than is a self completely aware of the ramifications of its own commitments.
> (H. W. Johnstone, 1959: 129)

Since intention-experience always has these fuzzy edges, our use of the logic-system will always have this pretence-element, this play-feature at work in it. Indeed, as has already been said, the play-feature is at its greatest when we withdraw the logic-system from its engagement with the world entirely and pretend that what it refers to is exactly the same for all of us, in other words, nothing at all. Precisely because it does not refer to anything – and must not if it is to remain 'pure' of the taint of human impulse – we can follow out its implication structures without fear of ambiguity. As soon as we make the system apply to anything, *even itself*, it runs into ambiguity: when it applies to itself that ambiguity becomes paradox.

Our intention-matching system enables us to treat the infinite as finite, to set limits on the continuum of the Real, limits on which, *as a result of practical tests*, we can mutually agree – and we must remember from the Triangulation Argument that there is no pure mutual knowledge. Mutual knowledge is a topic that exercised philosophers in the last century and, before proceeding with our enquiries, it is useful to look at the notion for a moment.

Let us look at Ludwig Wittgenstein's explanation of the notion of mutual knowledge. We may start from his own version of it: he gives the example of a pupil told to continue the series 2, 4, 6, 8…etc. We find him, after 1000, going 1004, 1008, 1012…etc. When the teacher stops him, he says, 'Yes, isn't it right? I thought that was how I was meant to take it' (Wittgenstein, 1967: section 143 et seq.). Wittgenstein's comment on this proceeds as follows. He is very careful to stress that there is no mentalist 'grasping in a flash' of the whole correct series before it is actually carried out. The truth is, he says, that we cannot obey a rule once only. His argument runs on as follows. A rule is a practice, a custom. The paradox that every course of action can be made out either to accord with a rule or to conflict with it can be dissolved if the implications of this are borne in mind. There is no paradox if we realize that a variety of interpretations is ruled out by the very fact of the rule being obeyed as a continuing practice. There are further implications he would like us to accept. We cannot talk of varying interpretations in the sense of the pupil's mistaken one. There is only the right interpretation, so the word *interpretation* should be restricted to the substitution of one expression of the rule for another: that is, an interpretation can only be a synonymous paraphrase for a single meaning. There are no other interpretations. That is why it is impossible to obey a rule privately. One cannot go on asking for justifications for the following of a rule. In the end one has to give up and say 'This is simply what I do' (Wittgenstein, 1967: section 217). I have no choice in the matter once I have been correctly taught: 'I obey the rule blindly.' There is even a reference to obeying rules on someone else's orders:

> When someone whom I am afraid of orders me to continue the series, I act quickly, with perfect certainty, and the lack of reasons does not trouble me.
> (Wittgenstein, 1967: section 212)

Notice that here it is Wittgenstein and not the bemused pupil who is placed in the position of obeying orders backed up with what the rhetoricians call an 'appeal to force'. It is fortunate that Wittgenstein not only knows how to continue the series correctly, but knows that his interpretation is a synonymous paraphrase for the actual rule. We shall not enquire what would have happened to the bemused pupil in the circumstances.

It is ironic to see in these very same sections the Master himself being corrected by his editor. In section 226, the manuscript read 'Suppose someone gets the series of numbers 1, 3, 5, 7, ... by working out the series of numbers $x^2 + 1$.' The editor corrected this to read 'Suppose someone gets the series of numbers 1, 3, 5, 7, ... by working out the series $2x + 1$.' How do we know that this is what Wittgenstein meant? Perhaps he meant 'Suppose someone gets the series of numbers 1, 2, 5, 10, ... by working out the series $x^2 + 1$' – which takes the variable x to move through the values 0, 1, 2, 3, ... etc. Or perhaps he meant '... the series 1, 2, 5, 26, ... etc. by working out the series $x^2 + 1$ – taking the value of the variable x to be first 0, and thereafter the number produced by the formula. Or perhaps...

We are to accept Wittgenstein's assurance that, because rules are practices and are taught, because 'to understand a language means to be 'a master of technique' (1967: section 199), because the only game to be played is the public one, it is impossible to have a private interpretation of a rule. Since he has redefined 'interpretation', it is not clear now just what it is the bemused pupil does have before he is taught the practice. Wittgenstein has no word for it. On the evidence of section 28 we might assume that he would have been happy with *supposition* since he there speaks of a person slow to pick up the meaning of 'two' as 'supposing *two* to mean a group of nuts'. But suppositions were not analysed in the discussion of Continuing a Series: they were processes too queer to be worthy of investigation, errors to be practised out at the earliest opportunity so that our pupil should reach the happy state of 'following a rule blindly'.

At one point it seems that Wittgenstein might be making a step towards an analysis of meaning less bound to the concept of *la langue*, the synchronic ideal. In section 224 comes this: 'The word "agreement" and the word "rule" are related to one another; they are cousins.' If we were to think that he was going to explore the notion of agreement, with its overtones of reciprocity, our hopes would be speedily disappointed by the sentence that succeeds it: 'If I teach anyone the use of the one word, he learns the other with it.' But this is ambiguous. One sense we can accept, that of making agreement between two parties play an essential role in the establishment of a rule: in another sense, agreement becomes merely the pupil's unprotesting obedience, as if, when he had learned to follow the rule laid down by the teacher, then he will have come to realize what 'agreement' means!

The same emphasis is detectable in section 231:

'But surely you can see...?' That is just the characteristic expression of someone who is *under the compulsion of a rule.* [my emphasis]

A more extreme example is section 240:

Disputes do not break out (among mathematicians, say) over the question whether a rule has been obeyed or not. People do not come to blows over it, for example. That is part of the framework on which our language is based...

The reference to mathematicians seems to insure him against the thought of real hostility, an opposition of wills over the meaning of a word, but one cannot confine this to mathematics. One might mention in passing that hostility between logicians is not ruled out: I once witnessed at Oxford in the 1970s an aggressive clash between the logicians Peter Geach and Dana Scott over the interpretation of two lines of logic that Professor Geach had written on the blackboard which led to Professor Scott storming out of the lecture room in high dudgeon at what he obviously considered to be an illogical move. But, in view of what has been said above, logic and mathematics do work on the principle of an unshakeable ideal meaning, whereas natural language works on the principle of trust in an unshakeable meaning, a trust that may well be unexpectedly put to the test. Does not the victory in an argument so often depend, not only on whose terms are being used to define the situation, but on *whose interpretation of those terms*?

There are two comments made by Alfred Schutz which are of special relevance to the Continuing a Series Argument and which qualify Wittgenstein's approach:

'rational action' on the commonsense level is always action within an unquestioned and undetermined frame of constructs and typicalities of the setting, the motives, the means and ends, the courses of action and personalities involved and taken for granted.
(Schutz, 1962: 32)

As we saw when discussing the enthymeme above, speakers and hearers come with a great range of 'common' understandings which they can dip into when using language. Wittgenstein would have seen the similarity here to his own insistence that the 'form of life' is so all-embracing that we take for granted the rules we follow within it. Here is a clear echo of his 'Now I know how to go on' (Wittgenstein, 1967: section 179). The 'typicalities' are those shared judgements which form the basis of our rules in common, but it has to be kept in mind that 'sharing' implies taking the multiplicities at the corners of the triangle *as if* they are singular. As Feuerbach insisted, 'The sharing of thoughts is not a material, actual sharing' (1903–11: Vol. II, 173). That is how a 'form of life' is constructed and maintained according to Schutz:

> Thus we may say that on this level actions are at best partially rational and that rationality has many degrees. For instance, our assumption that our fellow-man who is involved with us in a pattern of interaction knows its rational elements will never reach 'empirical certainty'...but will always bear the character of plausibility, that is, of subjective likelihood (in contradiction to mathematical probability). We always have to 'take chances' and 'run risks'.
>
> (Schutz, 1962: 33)

Schutz has carried his argument to the point where Wittgenstein's Continuing a Series Argument becomes relevant. What Wittgenstein described was exactly a risk that was run, a chance that was taken by two communicating agents who were conveniently assuming an 'ideal rational interaction'. It is logically possible, though, because of that failure of 'empirical certainty' for two agents *within the same form of life* to discover that their 'mutual knowledge' does not attain the ideal completeness that they had all along believed it did. Mutual knowledge is only mutual with respect to the overlapping of the speaker's and hearer's intentions.

In the last century the term 'mutual knowledge' or 'common knowledge' appeared in Stephen Schiffer's book *Meaning* (1972) and David Lewis's *Convention* (1969). Both books follow Wittgenstein in neglecting the possibility of one agent's meaning being distinct from that of another but yet overlapping in the sense of continually being provisionally confirmed in the co-ordination of behaviour. Nevertheless what they describe is the application of what Schutz calls 'complicated mirror-reflexes' which arise out of the idealization of reciprocity of perspectives. The regress of 'I know that you know that I know that you know that...x' is only dismissed by the fact it disappears into *trust*: we do not pursue such a ridiculous extension of our mutual knowledge for the simple reason that we accept the risk of x not being precisely the same for both of us. We cannot even make the first move in this regress because the other's knowing always retains an opaqueness that language cannot penetrate, for we cannot see as the other sees, hear as the other hears, and so on, that is, have the sensations that his body has, feel the emotions he feels. Another way of putting it is to say that, although we must go about telling each other that there is only ONE *word*-meaning, we know perfectly well that there are TWO *speaker's*-meanings, and it is just because there is this fertile contradiction that the Statement can be carried through at all, enabling *la langue* to be updated into *le parole*.

But a pure mutual knowledge is what pure logic must take as its axiom, which brings to the fore this strange feature of pure logic that it is rendering perfectly fictive what was only a partial fiction employed as a necessary method of getting as much co-ordination as possible between agents with differing understandings of the world. Its rule, as was made clear at the start, is *never to refer*, never to take its variables as having any correspondence with any entity whatsoever, for that would bring in the conflicting perspectives of us all as well as the incalculable Real of which those perspectives are themselves a part, and the smooth articulation of its purity would be sullied by the failure of mutual knowledge. It is significant then that the infinite regress above, 'I know that you know that I know that you know … *x*' in pure logic *does go on to infinity*, which should arouse our suspicion. Suspicion has also been stirred up whenever logicians have been tempted in dubious situations to make pure logic refer, try to use it in its pure form when two people are in dialogue about the Real. This is a case in which something purely fictive is being illicitly applied to something real. The result, unsurprisingly, is paradox, because it is the equivalent of saying 'I am pretending' and 'I am not pretending' at the same time.

Now we can see a new kind of explanation of Zeno's riddles. Take Achilles and the Tortoise. This is the well-known puzzle in which Achilles has to run a mile race with a tortoise and gives it half a mile start. The story (and it is a story) goes that, since it takes Achilles a measurable time to reach the half-mile point, the tortoise will have moved forward – say three yards. Then Achilles has to run that three yards, which also takes a measurable time, however small, so by the time Achilles has reached that point the tortoise will have moved, say, an inch further. You can see how the story goes from here – by the time Achilles reaches that point of half a mile plus three yards plus an inch, the tortoise will have moved further still, admittedly by a tiny distance, and Achilles must take up some time, equally small, to cover it, etc., etc. … to infinity, with the outcome being that Achilles never overtakes the tortoise.

We start applying our intention-matching system. It enables us to set limits on the continuum, limits on which, *as a result of practical tests*, we can mutually agree. Now we have just seen that there is no pure mutual knowledge, only an overlapping of intentional perspectives in the manner of a story; there is an ineradicable irony, an ambiguity, which, though it may be revealed as a mismatch by a later conflict, will nevertheless in the present be concealed in the fuzzy 'objectivity' of our 'common' entity. Ask now a simple question: when we have applied our definers, our words, our limit-setters to the decreasing distance between Achilles and the tortoise, are we not at some point – and *point* is a word that I do not really want to use! – going to pass beyond a defining that we can test mutually in the real world? Are we not going to pass beyond the possibility of real measurement, however subtle and refined our measuring device? Let us say that someone does invent some photo-finish micrometer that can measure the remaining distances with lower tolerance, there will still be a *tolerance* – significantly named! – for are we not dealing with purposes? At this stage, with two agents havering about whether the temperature has or has not affected the measurement at this finest of all fine practicable points, we have reached the situation where we onlookers throw up our hands in amusement at the comedy of an argument where no practical outcome can decide the issue either way. 'Sure,' we cry, 'how else could you be satisfied? You are, *to all intents and purposes*, fully agreed. There is no other test you could perform. So to try to go beyond this into the infinitesimal is to take the logic-system out of its useful task of intention-matching altogether. Own up! – you will be wholly pretending if you try to take the calculation any further. Beyond this stage you will have no way of fixing any limits on which you can mutually agree. You are pretending to have an interest in common with someone else on something which is impossible for you both together *ever to separate out for mutual identification.*' Another way of putting it would be to say that there is no Ambiguous Element that the two in dialogue can have some hope of overlapping on since neither can make their own 'objective' selection from the Real, and, hence, there can be no hope of any updating of one by the other, no communication of any kind – logic, in fact, taking a leap out of language. The logic-system, if taken beyond this stage, is put out of engagement with the real world, and you would be doing nothing else but playing with it. It would no longer be applied logic but pure. There would no longer be any projection of useful truth involved, but only fiction. The paradox of Achilles and the Tortoise is as fictitious as Achilles himself. In every context where agents apply words together, each agent can only apply his skill where a cross-referencing link, provable in intention-satisfying behaviour, can be established with the other. In the Achilles–Tortoise case and all others like it (Zeno has more examples) such a cross-referencing proof is being believed in *when there is no possibility of ever arriving at one*. It is really a sneaky way of trying to extend the taking-for-granted of there being singular entities common to us all into a situation where taking-for-granted has been ruled out. That is what pure logic depends on, the turning of the taking-for-granted into a given reality. In pure logic no actual *granting* must go on (and granting is a serious matter concerning human desires and fears) – the mathematical point has to be, as it were, *superstitiously* reified outside all human doing.

The key point in the argument above is not my own. I owe it to Alexander Bryan Johnson:

> 'Whilst Achilles passes over the hundredth of a mile, the tortoise moves on the ten thousandth of a mile.' The ten thousandth part of a mile is between six and seven inches. It names a sight and a feel; hence the tortoise is not yet overtaken: – but the proposition proceeds, – 'Whilst Achilles passes over this ten thousandth part of a mile, the tortoise moves on a millionth part of a mile.' The millionth part of a mile leaves

the asunder about the fifteenth part of an inch, which names a sight and a feel; hence the tortoise is not yet overtaken. But the next step is a quibble. It affirms, that whilst Achilles passes over this millionth part of a mile, the tortoise moves on the hundred millionth part of a mile. This is a name without any corresponding existence in nature, hence the sophistry and the quibble. The last step is absurd, not from any defect of logick, but because the words become divested of signification.

> (Johnson, 1968 [1828]: 100)

Johnson was well aware that words idealize the Real; as he put it 'We should not confound verbal identities with the realities of nature' (1968 [1828]: 81).

Lewis Carroll told an Achilles and the Tortoise story of his own. What it illustrates, very amusingly, is that, in the case of a logical deduction (he uses a conditional as his example), it is impossible not to escape a vicious regress unless the two partners in dialogue begin with an agreement that is not enquired into, that is based on trust. Typically, Carroll sprinkles the story with sly puns (at the expense of Achilles, who fails to see what the Tortoise is demanding of him).

We have to be very careful with that word 'fictitious' which I used a moment ago, for we have to recall the fact I pointed out earlier that pure logic is something really played by logicians, just as a game of Hobbits and Orcs played by children is really going on. The paradoxes of Zeno when thought about by human beings are a real state of intention-matching systems in bodies that occur when they are put out of engagement with intention-matching in practice and yet still operated as if they were still in engagement. So 'fictitious' must not be taken to mean *unreal* in the sense of the problem not being a real problem for such systems, for such paradoxes do exist as a real oscillatory state of such systems when put into the condition described. Put in computer form we would see an endless oscillation between 0 and 1 that would never resolve itself – like the Terminator in *Terminator 3* who, dithering between 'Kill' and 'Abort', was held in vibrating inaction.

Compare what J. A. Bernadete says about these and similar paradoxes. He is talking of cutting a stick in half in half a minute, cutting one of the halves in two in a quarter of a minute, one of these quarters into an eighth in an eighth of a minute, and so on:

> How is our failure to be explained? There are many factors at work: our lack of adroitness, the bluntness of the knife, the splintering of the wood, etc. In a word, *sludge*. There is always sludge that frustrates our efforts to implement the ideal in practice...Although this principle of recalcitrance is familiar to us all, it has generally been believed to be merely contingent in nature, a brute fact that has no intelligible warrant. Is it perhaps otherwise?
>
> (Bernadete, 1964: 252–3)

We have seen now just what kind of intelligible warrant can be given. This intention-matching system, logic, cannot securely pin down the world mutually. It cannot even securely pin it down for the single agent, for he is riding from moment to moment on the assumption that the intentions he has are correct for the situation he is in, that the identities he projects are getting a perfect grip on whatever portions of the flux he is sorting into singularities, including himself. He can be tempted, of course, to turn that necessary *assumption* into a fixed belief, forgetting that the element of play is present. And to think that infinitesimally discrete portions of the continuum supposedly exist in their separateness in a way identical for all is *to forget just this*. To repeat, in such paradoxes we are pretending to have a common interest in something we have no way of rendering common.

Just as when our eyes focus on 'infinity' and we see a blur at the end of some apparently converging railway lines, so too all talk of infinity must move out of the range of what can be mutually fixed, even by this partial ironic overlap process that we take it to be. It can be treated as fixed only in the fictions of higher mathematics, as Barry Smith has convincingly argued (Smith, 1975: 91–101).

The Gordian knots of the self-reference problems can be cut in another way. Of the Paradox of the Cretan Liar and all similar paradoxes, we can say that they are attempts to apply logic as an intention-matching system at the same time as refusing to match intentions. If we take any statement as *prima facie* an attempt to match intentions with another person, for Epimenides the Cretan to say 'All Cretans are liars' is for him to imply by his very statement *per se* 'I am trying to match intentions with you on something' at the same time as making a particular statement which implies 'I am not trying to match intentions with you.' All outright liars are aiming at a mismatch of intentions with their interlocutors; this is what lying is.

Russell's Paradox of the Classes can now be unlocked with the same key. The paradox goes like this:

> Most classes of things are not members of themselves. For example, the class of all trees is not itself a tree; the class of all flags is not itself a flag. So we can call all those classes 'non-self-membered' classes. But some classes are members of themselves: for example, the class of all things are not trees is a member of itself, for it is not a tree; the class of all ideas is itself an idea. Let us call these 'self-membered' classes. Now ask to which of the two types, self-membered or non-self-membered, does the class of all non-self-membered classes belong? [You will find that if you say that it *is* a member of itself that immediately debars you from including it, whereas if you say that it is *not* a member of itself, it immediately becomes a member.]

We can follow out logical implications interminably as long as we do not apply the system to anything mutually. But in the Paradox of the Classes the intention-matching system *is* put into engagement, for we are making it apply to something mutually, namely, itself. The ambiguity that is endemic to all normal communication but which we can tolerate just because we can test out our interfusing perspectives on the Real intensifies into paradox as soon as the intention-matching system is turned upon itself, for, in using it, we are forced *to pretend our own pretence of intention-matching.*

For the best analogy of what is going on, see Tony Lumpkin's pretending that he is pretending in Oliver Goldsmith's *She Stoops to Conquer.* He and his mother, Mrs Hardcastle, have agreed to pretend that some jewels are stolen (in order to get his mother out of the awkwardness of yielding them up to her ward, Miss Neville, who is now demanding her rightful possession of them), and Tony, in pursuance of this deceit, is 'to bear witness that they are gone'. Tony, however, is in league with Miss Neville, and actually steals them himself to put them in Miss Neville's hands. His mother knows nothing of this, and, when she finds that they are in truth missing, she discovers that she cannot convince Tony that they are in fact gone – yet note his replies:

> MRS HARDCASTLE: I tell you, Tony, by all that's precious, the jewels are gone, and I shall be ruined forever.
>
> TONY: Sure I know they're gone, and I am to say so.
>
> MRS HARDCASTLE: My dearest Tony, but hear me, They're gone, I say.
>
> TONY: By the laws, Mamma, you make me for to laugh, ha, ha! I know who took them well enough, ha, ha, ha!
>
> MRS HARDCASTLE: Was there ever such a blockhead, that can't tell the difference between jest and earnest. I tell you I'm not in jest, booby!
>
> TONY: That's right, that's right: you must be in a bitter passion then nobody will suspect either of us. I'll bear witness that they are gone.

With pure logic, 'by the laws', we are pretending that we are matching intentions exactly, that we are in that impossible pure agreement. When we try to make it refer to itself, we are forcing it to pretend its own pretence of intention-matching as pure agreement, but, as we can learn from Tony Lumpkin, pretending that you are pretending comes out real. When he says 'I'll bear witness that they are gone', his mother thinks he is falling in with the pretence that they had earlier agreed on, that is, he is *lying*, but, as he and we know perfectly well, he is *telling the truth* for he can bear witness that they are gone because he took them himself!

In the Paradox of the Classes we are saying, at one and the same time, 'This is pure pretence' (on the level of our current agreement that it shall refer to nothing in the Real) and 'This is real' (for there is no doubt that the human brains applying the logical apparatus at that very moment are part of the Real – for they are *really* pretending). It can rightly be called an extraordinary pun in which the Second Clue arises from our own actions.

We can thus see how Russell's 'Theory of Types', which was a device to avoid the paradox, misses the explanation by doing something strictly at odds with the guiding principle of pure logic: he tried to escape the self-reference by introducing an *ad hoc* rule. His trick was as follows: he decided by fiat that a predicative expression (such as 'is a non-self-membered class') was a 'propositional function' that was unspecified until the *type* of logical subject it could be attached to was specified, and so he could conclude that such subjects could not include anything that was defined in terms of that predicative expression. This resulted in there being a hierarchy of 'types' of expression so that one lower down the hierarchy could not be sensibly used in conjunction with one higher. But this is to go inside the proposition and lay down rules about what should and should not be referred to, when referring in itself is an act foreign to pure logic. What he can now be seen to be doing is trying to legislate a real ambiguity away. The same can be said of more sophisticated endeavours to banish the paradox such as that derived from the work of Ernst Zermelo and Abraham Fraenkel, which also lays down an *ad hoc* rule in which an ascending hierarchy of sets is established (one which significantly regresses into the realms of the 'transfinite'; see Clark, 2002: 169). The clash of intention-matching is there in the paradox, and all that Russell and the others are doing is to remove the intention clash without realizing what they are doing. Anyone, like Russell, who 'gets into a bitter passion' about self-reference paradoxes 'can't tell the difference between jest and earnest'!

In Russell's Barber Paradox,

> A man of Seville is shaved by the Barber of Seville if and only if the man does not shave himself. Does the Barber of Seville shave himself?

It is plain that the implication of the first sentence, as a first sentence by a speaker that we have no reason to distrust, is that he is speaking a truth, that is, as a necessary though not sufficient condition of truth from a speaker, he is trying to match intentions with you, and so is not likely to be deliberately lying. However, the fact of his putting the question implies either

(1)   that he is the equivalent of a kindly examiner figure, one who knows that the question is fair, that is, he is conveying to the 'student' that there is a straightforward 'yes-or-no' answer to his question, and yet this very implication renders his first question a lie, for, if either answer were true, that first statement could not be truly uttered;

or

(2)   that he is genuinely ignorant of something, and yet the first statement clearly contains the implication that he is *not* ignorant of it.

In both cases the logic-system interlocks two utterances one of which is intention-matching and one of which is not. Take the first as intention-matching, and the second is not: take the second as intention-matching and the first is not.

Other paradoxes yield because it can be seen that the speaker's meaning changes from one part of the problem to another. Joseph Heller's 'Catch 22' is of this order:

> Orr would be crazy to fly more missions and sane if he didn't, but, if he was sane, he had to fly them. If he flew them, he was crazy and didn't have to; but, if he didn't want to, he was sane and had to.
> (Heller, 1985 [1961]: Ch. 5)

The speaker's meaning changes here because the intentional interpretations of 'crazy' and 'sane' keep switching between those of the rebel (the pilot Orr) and that of the authority (the officers placed in command). From the officers' point of view simple refusal, counting as 'sane', implies the ability to fly a mission, and being 'crazy' (in ways other than flying a mission) as a sufficient reason for excusing someone from the duty: Orr sees agreeing to fly a mission as falling under 'crazy' and therefore regards himself as rightfully excused if he does so agree. The riddle has Bateson's double-bind character, where the 'Master' is claiming to share intentions with the 'Slave', but, when the 'Slave' attempts to carry out the orders, he discovers that his own intentions are denied and that he is regarded as having disobeyed.

Mark Sainsbury suggests that paradox can be defined as an argument in which 'an apparently unacceptable conclusion' is 'derived by apparently acceptable reasoning from apparently acceptable premises' (Sainsbury, 1995: 1), but it is plain that to attribute it thus is to miss the underlying causes.

I would say that there are four kinds of paradox. One may conveniently draw in here F. P. Ramsey's distinction in his *Foundations of Mathematics* and blend it with the definitions. He divided the paradoxes that he considered into two types: the 'logical', that is, those that can be stated in logical symbolism (such as Russell's Paradox of the Classes), and 'semantic', those that involve 'some psychological term, such as meaning, naming or asserting'. Type (2) below corresponds to his 'logical' category, and Type (3) with his 'semantic' (Ramsey, 1954: 76–7):

(i)   Those, like Zeno's, that pretend to refer to real entities which, in fact, speaker and hearer could never succeed in even getting a partial overlap of reference, that is, they are pretending to regard as common and singular what they could never match intentions about.

(ii) Those that involve a logical system being illicitly used in reference to what is already a complete pretence of intention-matching, namely, itself; for example, Russell's Paradox of the Classes. We can see also its relation to Gödel's Theorem, which Quine has called a 'veridical paradox' (for Gödel see van Heijenoort, 1966; Quine, 1976, 17) for at an essential stage in his proof Gödel made use of one set of logical symbols (numbers) *to refer to* 14 primitive logical symbols, and the proof also depends on getting a statement about non-theoremhood in the very symbolism to which that statement refers.

(iii) Those that involve intention-matching conflicts like the Barber or the Liar, when to credit one of the utterer's meanings is to render the other a lie, and vice versa.

(iv) Those, like 'Catch 22', that contain a conflict between two speakers' meanings, whether those be of two persons, or whether, in comic or tragic cases, they be of the same person – Touchstone or Oedipus. Paradoxical pictures, such as Schuster's Fork (3 prongs or 2?) fall into this category and can be analysed like jokes (look for the Ambiguous Element).

So pure logic, except for the paradoxes it cannot escape, takes no risks. In being purely fictive it takes itself out of relation to the Real, except for its being embodied in real practices undertaken by human beings. It can be said to be the ghost of the Idealization of the Reciprocity of Standpoints, dead because it is no longer engaged with actual life. Feuerbach called it 'the outward forms of shared thought' (Feuerbach, 1903–11: Vol. II, 173). The subtleties of what are worked out from its axioms represent what would occur if actual human beings were indeed faced with *singular* entities at the corners of the triangle. What pure logicians and pure mathematicians are pursuing with their 'discoveries' is what such imaginary perfection would produce if extended without limit, a human construction of narcissistic fantasy as unrestrained as a child's fantasy about fairyland, a fantasy that still retains its own inner 'logic'. I heard today a girl of six (Lucy King) endlessly talking with a proper dramatic seriousness of a fairyland in which she lived: meeting a new girl on the playground, she quickly made friends, and then, when we had to leave, said to her, 'Do come round to see me at midnight when we fairies are busiest. You needn't worry – I'll send you home in a magic basket.'

One last kind of problem that has exercised logicians has concerned human decision in a situation where an entity is changing its criteria of identification. Two examples have taken centre stage here, and my metaphor is apt: one is known as 'Theseus's Ship' and the other the Sorites Paradox.

In Plutarch's *Lives* in the story of Theseus it is told that the thirty-oared galley that Theseus sailed in was preserved in Athens down to the time of Demetrius of Phalerum:

At intervals they removed the old timbers and replaced them with sound ones, so that the ship became a classic illustration for philosophers of the disputed question of growth and change, some of them arguing that it remained the same and others that it became a different vessel. (Plutarch, 1976: 28–9)

Thomas Hobbes rendered the problem more complicated by posing a further question. He asks us to imagine that the old timbers that had been removed were preserved and that later, when the whole of the original ship had been removed, these old timbers were put back together again; he then asks 'Which is the original ship – the one with all the timbers replaced or the one that has been reconstructed from the old timbers?' (Hobbes, *De Corpore*, II, xi, 7). The answer to the whole dilemma, in either version, amusingly, is given away in Plutarch, for there he says that philosophers were arguing about whether it remained the same or had become a different vessel. Have we not seen abundantly that the singularity of an entity is bestowed by two or more persons agreeing to idealize their differing selections from the Real? Therefore, the only way for the problem to be solved is for the persons concerned to reach an agreement. If they can't, even if both are quite willing to try and each is not aiming to deceive the other – too bad, for that often happens in life. So the problem dissolves into one of human choice. There was an actual example of this kind of problem; it occurred in a court case about the value of a vintage car. The would-be buyer maintained that an Italian 'OM' car supposedly dating from 1923 was nothing of the sort because so much of it had been replaced, and the seller maintained the opposite, that it was still worthy of the original identification. The judge in the case came down on the side of the seller on the ground that in the case of all vintage cars of established provenance, this process of substitution was a fully acknowledged practice and there was no precedent of its having ever been challenged. End of argument.

The other problem, the 'Sorites' (from Greek σωρος, 'soros', *a heap*), takes the case of a heap of sand from which one removes one grain and then another and so on. The question is then asked, 'When does the heap cease to be a heap?' The answer is as straightforward as the one above, namely, that human decision, *based on someone's motivational preferences*, comes into *play*, and that last word is significant. If someone has bought the heap to make mortar out of it, he will not accept two grains as a heap but a pile that looks sufficiently like in size to what he saw when he paid for it. For both these problems, there is no use attempting to answer them *within* logic for that is to try and perform a paradox, for logic is working on the assumption of a pure and unchallengeable agreement, and yet the problem is proposed as if there isn't one.

A story. It is said that, in Phrygia during a time of troubles, an oracle declared that the troubles would cease if they appointed the first man to approach the temple of Zeus as king. This was a certain Gordius, a peasant, riding in his wagon, and, in honour of the moment, he tied the wagon to the statue of the god with a complex knot and prophesied himself that 'whoever unloosed the wagon would conquer all Asia'. When Alexander visited Phrygia and was told of this, he struck through the knot with his sword. Did he logically fulfil Gordius's prophecy, and, if so, how?

6
Faith

> Man in truth is made of faith.
>   (*Chandogya Upanishad*, III, xiv, 4; Mascaró, 1975: 114)

> The reason was, there was nothing there but faith.
> Faith made the whole, yes all they could see or hear
> Or touch or think, and arched its break of day
> Within them and around them every way.
>   (Edwin Muir, 'Nothing There but Faith', ll. 1–4 Muir,
>   1960: 238–9)

> 'But there is no Religion?' reiterates the Professor. 'Fool! I tell thee,
> there is. Hast thou well considered all that lies in this immeasurable
> froth-ocean we name LITERATURE? Fragments of a genuine Church-
> *Homiletic* lie scattered there, which Time will assort: nay, fractions
> even of a *Liturgy* could I point out . . . But thou as yet standest in no
> Temple; joinest in no Psalm-worship; feelest well that, where there
> is no ministering Priest, the people perish? Be of comfort! Thou art
> not alone, if thou have faith.'
>   (Thomas Carlyle, *Sartor Resartus*, Bk. III, ch. vii, ll. 228–40, 246–8;
>   Carlyle, 2000 [1833–4]: 186)

1. Singularity, idealism and realism

It might seem odd to begin a chapter on faith both communal and religious
by immediately returning to the subject of pure logic, but it provides a
convenient point of entrance to the argument. We have seen that it is
essential for speakers to project a hypothetically perfect agreement on the
rules of language, both semantic and syntactical, in order for a sufficient
overlap of their differing references and understandings to be obtained so
that the hopeful updating of hearer by speaker can go through. Unless we
had this *partial* overlap, paradoxically achieved by the assumption, the

'taking-for-granted', of a *complete* one, no such updating could be performed. Recall that the updating can be qualitative or quantitative (for no guarantee of singularity is given by the process). When the correction has been taken up by the hearer, then the two in dialogue resume the supposed identity of their differing identification of the portion of the Real concerned. That word 'concerned', usually ignored as to its further implications, is a reminder that no knowledge is gained or transferred without the impulse of motivation to set it on its way.

As some philosophers have pointed out, the process of adjustment, even if it is of an external entity, nevertheless produces a change in the selves involved, in their understanding of their problem, and in the language they are using. The entry into language necessarily requires that one's perceptions are going to be changed, and thus one's motivations. As F. C. S. Schiller asserts, 'A successful judgement will affect…its maker, the situation, and the terms by which it is apprehended' (Schiller, 1929: 205). The ideal but not real superimposition of their perceptual choices from their sensory fields is maintained by a species of unconscious trust, induced by the fact of this needful performance. The fact that the current agreement may hide future possibilities of disagreement has to be fictively laid aside if the dynamic of the transformation in the statement is to work. To quote F. C. S. Schiller again: 'Identity is the postulation of the irrelevance of differences' (1929: 348), but neither can know what constitutes an irrelevance for the other particularly when the trick is to behave in the present as if there aren't any! Add to that the spurious feel of certainty that comes from our indeed making our 'own' selection from the Real, one that looks for all the world to be the same as everyone else's.

This is the mutual performance for the utterance of a normal statement. If there is a form of trust required, it behoves us to examine what kind of trust or faith this is or should be. But first consider what is happening to that trust when the two in dialogue enter the world of pure logic. In Chapter 5.7 (pp. 171–3), we saw that pure logic is the most fictive of our linguistic activities because its key rule is that we shall never apply it to the Real. I called it the 'ghost' of the intention-matching that we engage in when we do attempt to refer to the Real; the word is apt since there is no life in a logical proposition for, not only does it tell no one anything since they are taken to know already, but also it is entirely free of motivation, hence its 'purity'. It must not refer and it must not update: a look back at the paradoxes we discussed in that chapter will remind you what happens when we try to make it do either of those things.

Now what does refraining from referring actually imply? If it is so 'pure' that our bodily motivations have vanished together with the differences in our sensing and those in our perceiving, then, from one point of view, in doing pure logic we would become equivalent to two angels in eternity, in which all our words have been conceded long ago to be matched with all possible referents. This would mean that in one strange sense our faith had reached its zenith in the perfect harmony of our understandings. But, paradoxically, it would also mean that the actual nerve of faith had disappeared, for there would be no doubt against which we have to strive, no risk that our partner could misunderstand us or we her. We would not have to be in any degree courageous in trusting the other because of the fear that her understanding might contain something profoundly disturbing or distressing or fearful to us that she innocently did not happen to mention since the present context did not demand it. To the angels in that logical heaven no such doubts of unblameworthy but frightening difference could ever surface between them. And, most peculiarly for angels, they could never surprise each other by doing something especially kind that was not expected – that is, it was not in the promise in the view of one of them, but implied from the beginning for the other. And this is how we are acting – and I am using the word in its dramatic sense – when we do pure logic and pure mathematics. We are acting the absence of the risk that attends all human statements, risk of good as well as evil. So we have to admit that *it is really completely free of faith*. No wonder I called it a ghost of our intention-matching process, for all intention is as absent as in a dead body. In pretending a *pure* trust, we have banished all trace of a *real* one – because the bodies are as good as gone! In the study of natural language, as Horst Ruthrof reminds us, the body cannot be left out (Ruthrof, 2000: 6–21).

But there is a consequence here for our concept of the proper moral faith required in the use of ordinary language. Faith *cannot* be sure of what it hopes for. The picture on the front of the current anthology on faith and reason published by Oxford University Press is an appropriate one for it shows two swimmers, one in the act of diving from a diving-board into the sea and the other waiting to do so, observing the diver's leap with some trepidation. Kierkegaard did write of a 'leap of faith' (Kierkegaard, 1946: 200). In language we have seen in any case that there is no way in which two persons can come to a logically perfect understanding, since we only speak when there is a motivational problem. The theory of perception that underpins this theory shows that it is actually impossible to make our separate referents turn into one: the corners of the triangle remain forever fuzzy behind our imaginary mutual exactness. So to believe that a true faith is an unshakeable guarantee of what it hopes for is to distort the nature of faith. Peter Sztompka, the sociologist, gives as his core definition of trust, 'Trust is a bet about the future contingent actions of others', but this distorts the ethical demand, for we are betting that everything will turn out like the winning of a dice-throw: on the contrary, we should be as prepared for failure (Sztompka, 1999: 25). Sztompka should have followed out the implications of his own view of the relation of human bodies to the societies within which they have their being – or becoming, as he insists. He sees both as having a 'virtual' existence, which is as much as to say that both are imaginative projections upon the Real, and, to use the analogy of an acted drama again, have an ongoing reality within the Real (Sztompka, 1991: 93).

How many people saying 'I do' in the marriage contract believe that their interpretation of marriage is what will count above all others? J. L. Austin said that 'performative' utterances like 'I do' in which words are actions in themselves were to be judged by the 'felicity' of their outcome, that is, in this case, whether the promise was kept (Austin, 1975: 14). Compare here George Eliot's amusing account of a marriage ceremony that was certainly flawed according to Austin's tenets but yet worked felicitously. The parson, given to drink, had said to the woman 'Do you take this man to be your lawful wedded *wife?*' and to the man 'Do you take this woman to be your lawful wedded *husband?*' No one noticed the mistakes but the verger, and when later privately he expressed his Austinian doubt about the 'felicity' of the vows, the parson pooh-poohed his misgivings with the specious excuse that what mattered was the signing in the register – that 'was the glue' (Eliot, *Silas Marner*, Ch. VI). Austin's very use of the word 'felicity' – *happiness* – gives away the fact that it has to be left to the individual human beings to judge whether the happiness they expected has been achieved, whether it conforms to their desires and avoids their fears. Now if the two people making that contract are in love with each other, what is a loving person, A, to do if the beloved, B, turns out to understand the promise in what is a distressing and alarming way to A but not to B, who had expected to behave in that way from the beginning in 'all good faith', as we say?

This unavoidability of misconstruction applies as much to threats as to promises. Recall the scene in the Battle of Pelennor Fields in *The Lord of the Rings* where the Lord of the Nazgûl mocks Merry and Eowyn with the cry 'No living man may hinder me!', only to be killed by Eowyn's thrust between crown and mantle. This is an *echt* narrative moment: I am sure you can draw the five-fold diagram for yourself, starting with 'man' as the Ambiguous Element.

Indeed, there is nothing in that methodological *assumption* of agreement that rules out the emergence of cross-purposes that up to some moment had been entirely concealed *from both parties*. It is one thing to take for granted that everything will be plain and above board, and actually to believe it to be beyond adjustment. 'Sincerity' may be evidenced by all parties, but that does not rule out this risk. The persona in Davies's poem being guided through the fog by the Blind Man might have been innocently led into difficulties (say if the Blind Man was not aware that a hole in the pavement had been dug up by electricity men that afternoon).

This faith is thus paradoxical in its very nature, for what is ruled out is what is hoped for. Shelley expressed this thought memorably:

> To hope till Hope creates
> From its own wreck the thing it contemplates.
> (Percy Bysshe Shelley, *Prometheus Unbound*, Act IV)

which is as much as to say that the wreck of hope was what was contemplated, and yet that the sacrifice resulting brought with it and even constituted what unknowingly was hoped for. Or consider the wonderfully equivocal last two lines of Hardy's 'The Darkling Thrush':

> Some blessed Hope, whereof he knew
> And I was unaware.

which are open to our taking the thrush's ecstasy as justified but his 'knowing' as unjustified. In view of these strange consequences, the nature of our linguistic faith needs a closer scrutiny.

For what are we hoping for when we mime a perfect agreement in language? It cannot merely be, as the pragmatist might argue, some achievable and anticipated utility of the near-future, for there is virtually no end to the implications of purpose in our actions. One can see the pointlessness of the utilitarian analysis on Jeremy Bentham's 'felicific calculus', in which he tried to assess outcomes of happiness in terms of the 'intensity', 'duration', 'certainty or uncertainty', and 'propinquity or remoteness' of pleasures and pains (Bentham, 1961 [1789]: 36–7). Nor can it be some ultimate union of law and desire. We are into the problem Jacques Lacan has teased out from the incompatibility of 'Symbolic' law and 'Real' *jouissance*, that of a fantasmatic pursuit of a 'lost object', the remnant or surplus that would complete our 'lack', the dream goal that draws its power from the womb in which all our desires were identical with the law that gave them a magical synchronous satisfaction (Lacan, 1977: 184–6). Such a union has its nightmarish obverse, for were the Real of our *jouissance* to be identical with absolute law, the extreme of free desire would be mechanically determined. Slavoj Žižek has delineated for us the horrors of such a union in the images of Gothic literature (Žižek, 1991: 219–22). It can be seen in the fascination of the 'terminators' in the *Terminator* films, where motivation shows at its most terrifying when linked to unconditional certainty. The ironic humour that has welded Schwarzenegger's catch-phrase 'I'll be back' into public memory relies on a voice that combines an apparent polite acceptance of disappointment, that is, *a thwarting of will*, with *a relentless pursuit of it* – for, according to its inexorable programme, the Terminator returns driving a truck crashing through the police station door!

Belief in the precise dictionary meaning of words, in any logical 'correspondence' to the Real, is therefore nonsensical for there are no singularities to correspond with their projections of singularity, however much that fiction is essential to communication and even though we can have no doubt that our attempts at final reference do play over the Real. This theory does uphold realism, but it is a realism of the flux, the continuum, matter, *materia prima*, Plato's (and Kristeva's) χωρα, 'khora', Husserl's υλη, 'hyle' – a realism of the flow of becoming upon which we project our fictive singularities. Robert Kirk may want to mock the notion with his phrase 'cosmic porridge', but his metaphor – and his double assonance – have a wry appropriateness nevertheless (Kirk, 1999: 52).

Recall the outcome of the theory of perception in Chapter 3, that sensation is Real, and, quite beyond our voluntary control, changes in proportionate step with what it responds to in the external Real; and that it is empirically likely that it can exist in some unfortunately mutated or damaged brain entirely in the absence of a thinking mind, a thinking subject. To repeat: sensation is not of itself *subjective*. F. H. Bradley used to insist that the phenomenal had a real aspect – 'Everything phenomenal is somehow real' (Bradley, 1969 [1897]: 127). According to Bishop Berkeley, sensation can exist only in a *mind* (Berkeley, 1963 [1710]: 156–7), whereas, from what we know at present, it can exist in a brain without a mind. On the other hand, we only know our ambiguous perceptual selections, tentatively held in concert with others; furthermore, both those others and ourselves also remain so held as 'objective' selections in the process of endless, hopefully viable negotiation. Again Berkeley, in common with many a philosopher of today, cannot detach sensation from the notion of a thing or person: 'Everything that exists is particular', but that is systematically ambiguous, for, yes, the 'things' we pick out of the Real are 'particular' in our language and have to be for it to work, but they remain imagined convergences of differing selections from differing sensations for all that (Berkeley, 1963 [1710]: 223). The Real, Gadamer's 'infinity of the unsaid', always outruns our perceptions (Gadamer, 1975: 416). *'Existence without essence is mere appearance'* and *'Essence without existence is mere thought'*, as Feuerbach put it (Feuerbach, 1903–11: Vol. II, 278, his emphases); the former can be taken to mean that sensing without perception, without the fictive convergence of our separate choices from it, can provide no intersubjective knowledge, and the latter that, as we saw above in our look at pure logic, that without relation to what bodies sense, no thought can get a purchase on the Real. It is Kant's 'Thoughts without content are empty, intuitions without concepts are blind' all over again but given new scientific support (Kant, *Critique of Pure Reason*, A51, B75). To counter Berkeley: *esse percipi non est*, that is, 'perceiving is not being', and *sentire est esse*, that is, 'sensing is being', that is, a part of the Real (Berkeley, 1963 [1710]: 114). So no concept could capture existence, not even that of God, as the Ontological Proof of the Existence of God would have it.

What is strange about Bishop Berkeley is that he appears to commit himself consciously to the Idealization of the Reciprocity of Standpoints. When his puppet voice Philonous ('lover of knowledge') was challenged by the feeble opponent Hylas (one of the Argonauts led astray by beauty) about differences in sensory experiences from person to person (Hylas had brought up the difference between an ordinary view of something and its look through a microscope), Philonous replies:

> Strictly speaking, Hylas, we do not see the same object that we feel; neither is the same object perceived by the microscope, which was by the naked eye. But in case every variation was thought sufficient to constitute a new kind or individual, the endless number of confusion of names would render language impracticable. Therefore to avoid this as well as other inconveniences which are obvious upon a little thought, men combine together several ideas, apprehended by divers senses, or by the same sense at different times, or in different circumstances, but observed however to have some connexion in nature, either with respect to co-existence in succession; all which they refer to one name, and *consider as* one thing.
> (Berkeley, 1963 [1710]: 282–3, my emphasis)

The key words are 'consider as', for they are equivalent to 'take to be', 'treat *as if*'. So Berkeley believes that men are able to connect these various experiences into one abstract notion but without making the error that there exists 'one single, unchanged, unperceivable, real nature, marked by each name' – a view that sits well with Triangulation theory. Berkeley does not want to countenance *singularities* in a flux outside men's understandings, for he does not want to countenance the idea of an external flux at all. Nevertheless, he appears to be convinced that the 'connexion' of ideas is made by all men in the same way, for he sees that language could not proceed unless a measure of agreement upon names was acted upon. There is no exploration, of course, of the fact that the 'connexion' he speaks of is set in train by our motivations, or that men's motivations differ. It is tantalizing to see that, if he had seen the hypothetical nature of the agreement he took to be necessary to language, and that its necessity arose from the need to get a first provisional grip on the Real prior to an updating of understanding in the hearer, he would have stated the core of Triangulation theory. However, for him God superstitiously existed as the guarantor of our verbal agreements.

It is of course the flaw in all idealism that it reduces existence to thought. This is the result of treating the provisional agreement necessary for a statement to be made as if it were unconditional, turning a mutual agreement into an 'impersonal' truth. In Hegel's system, Idealism did try to take account of our endless negotiation about singularities, but Hegel thought of his process as inevitably advancing towards a perfect match of word and world in the 'Absolute'. His dialectic does indirectly take account of the triangular nature of our adjustment of each other's interpretations of the world, for a story or a joke could be said to proceed by means of a 'thesis' (the meaning that results from the 'strong wrong clue' of the initial intentional perspective) to an antithesis (the meaning that results from the 'faint right clue' of the second one), the 'synthesis' being the acceptance in the public language of the new meaning, itself to be the 'thesis' of a subsequent performance of the dialectic. As noted before, the word *aufhebung* that Hegel uses for the transformation combines the notions of a 'raising' of a concept to a new level with an 'annulment' of the original concept. What is wrong with this is the underlying belief in a necessary advance, coupled with another that its actual aim is the Absolute, when all that a statement can depend upon is our *hope* that the adjustment of knowledge is of benefit to all. His commitment is to the ultimate truth of the real being the rational and the rational being the real, even if only as some grand finality. Inevitably, then, Hegel's philosophy suffers from an inadequate notion of faith as he claims to know, not to hope, that such an impossible union awaits the course of thought (Hegel, 1966 [1807]).

Andrew Seth well knows the danger of turning the abstract notion of singularity into a given feature of one's ontology:

> The transcendental theory of knowledge, because it is an abstract inquiry, necessarily speaks of a single Self or logical subject; but this singularity is the singularity that belongs to every abstract notion, and decides nothing as the singularity or plurality of existing intelligences. We can have absolutely no right to transform this logical identity of type into a numerical identity of existence.
> (Seth, 1887: 29)

As he nicely puts it elsewhere, 'even an atom is more than a category' (1887: 124). Since not all of the Real is captured in any identification, any thing or person is like an iceberg, with an indefinite part of its being out of conceptual view (though with some not out of Real *sensory* view). The iceberg image applies just as much to the self, as Seth's remark indicates. One can fairly say that the individualism of modernity from the seventeenth century onwards has insidiously tempted us to divinize in it a 'uniqueness' that it does not possess. Our bodies and their sensations reach down into the ocean of the Real beyond our conceptualizing, and in any case that conceptualizing has to be done with the aid of others. Richard Rorty is thus in error when he claims that 'There is nothing there deep down inside us except what we have put there ourselves' (Rorty, 1982: xlii). The American poet e. e. cummings has a fitting epithet for us all – 'each-otherish'. Novalis's thought that we cannot be sure of anything without the other is echoed by Feuerbach:

> That which I alone perceive I doubt; only that which the other also perceives is certain.
> (Feuerbach, 1966 [1843]: 59)

The Poet and the Blind Man required the other in dialogue to assist them in the Real – though there is no banishing of risk. Keep in mind the fact that it is the power of the other to show the Real as invading the supposedly sacrosanct self that banishes the whole notion of solipsism as attending this theory. Here we have a motivation for St. Augustine's stress upon 'grace', for it is plain that we can take no moral decision without being within the order of language with the imperative upon us to take account of and transform its tradition. However, to rigidify that tradition in one's favoured view of it is to become an '*objectivist* relativist'.

Idealism about the Self and that about the Thing are equally untenable. Marx Wartofsky has seen this typified in two original statements:

> Descartes' *Cogito, ergo sum* and Berkeley's *Esse est percipi* express the same idealistic thesis, in the active and passive moods respectively. In the former, *thinking* is *being*; in the latter, *being thought* is *being*.
> (Wartofsky, 1977: 243)

Within the terms of the present theory it becomes clear that idealism is a form of superstition, in that it turns what is only a tool in the utterance of a statement, the core initial Idealization, into a given reality. This is to privilege the Symbolic over the Real. Furthermore, it is a narcissistic superstition because it favours a single interpretation as beyond intersubjective correction. There is narcissism still present whether, as someone near the core of a society's authority, one aligns oneself with the enacted law, or whether, as someone near the periphery of the application of a society's codes, one takes current rebellious desire as one's key motivation. Tyrant or anarch could equally take idealism as a guide. Truth is taken as blessed by the harmonious logical coherence of all thought. It is plain that there is no *impersonal* knowledge: the 'impersonality' is just a phantom raised by our faith in each other. Every fact is loaded with value, but, because we do not wish to suggest that our faith in each other could be questionable, a matter of risk, we hold to the 'objectivity' of fact, forgetting that 'fact' comes from the Latin *factum*, 'made'.

Edmund Husserl's phenomenology falls to this critique. Husserl cannot get away from his epistemology centring on a 'determinable x' that precedes the perception of it. He believes that it lies at the core of his 'noema', standing for the object itself stripped of its properties, so that, if I mistake in a shop a mannequin for a woman, there was *one* object I was relating to. The 'noema' is the sum-total of my conceptions of anything; if I walk up to a tree, all the different impressions I have had contribute to the concept of it. But to make a full reference to the object I have to perform a 'noesis' that relates the noema to the ὕλη, the 'hyletic data', the sensory experiences. All this might seem to work if we confine it to a single person, but Husserl does not see that we each make our own 'noesis' and what our individual 'noema' does with our own body's 'hyletic data' cannot wholly match that of others, and the test whether it passes muster or not for the time being depends on contingencies of judgements of satisfaction by all those involved as well as possible irruptions in the Real itself – and they may include, as we now know, a transformation in the singularity of 'the' object itself (for example, it wasn't one mannequin, it was a mother and a child – in his examination of such a mistake over a mannequin he never considers this possibility; Husserl 1973: 92). So there is no given *x* in the Real however much in dialogue with another we project a common noema in order that a statement can follow. If one considered the performance by two persons of the *fiction* that they have a noema in common, then one would be on the way to bending Husserl's analysis to the present theory. When he tried to reach 'the things themselves' by carrying out an 'epoché', a bracketing-off of our experience from reference to the world, we only reach the structure of the needful fiction of singularities, one which Husserl does not see as such. There are no 'things themselves', only a multiple over-lapping of each person's selections from what is *presumed* to be roughly the same portion of the Real. So Husserl, too, is superstitious in his retention of his deter-minable *x* as having some definite relation to a pre-existing singularity in the Real. Typically, like many another, he states the Idealization without seeing its implications since he cannot move to the intersubjective level: 'this is a horizon in the sense of a *presumption* of a constant empirical unity' (Husserl, 1973: 333, my emphasis). Even when in later work he did wrestle with the interrelation-ship of the sensory with the concept, allowing that experience could give us more detail than before, he cannot get away from that detail being characterized as 'new determinations of *the same thing*' (1973: 32). He was aware that the sensory could be experienced without being perceived: he cites the barking of a dog which breaks in upon our attention and we realize that we had been hearing it before without identifying it as barking. So this is a recognition of non-epistemic experience, a 'raw feel' as raw, a neutral sensory given free of interpretation (he called it a 'pre-predicative experience'), but he still held to our perceiving something that was '*one* and the *same*' (1973: 60–2).

But idealism is not alone in this superstitiousness. Realism of the Object variety, that sees the world as made of discrete, publicly recognizable entities, whether things or persons, is just as much to be criticized for this ethical flaw. Whereas idealism lauds the singularity of entities from the perspective of the observing mind, so realism does so from the aspect of the world as a complex of brute external facts. Truth becomes a matter of correspondence with given objectivities. This is to make each corner of the triangle into a predetermined *Ding-an-Sich*, the 'thus-and-so' of John McDowell and Michael Tye (McDowell, 1994; Tye, 1999). But those tags '*an-Sich*' and 'thus-and-so' betray the human element of choice, for they cannot be 'as such' or 'thus-and-so' *to no one*. To say that Direct Realism is a superstition is thus to carry an unexpected attack into the enemy camp with a weapon of its own. When direct realists were complimenting themselves on their level-headed, no-nonsense ontology, it emerges that to think with them of the world as made up of Austin's 'dry-goods', neat proprietary parcels of accessible commodities open to balance-sheet enumeration, a view that seems far from all irrationality, is to open oneself to the justifiable accusation of being lost in what certainly could be termed a solipsistic dream because of the narcissistic impulse behind it. A dangerous relativism lies behind this insistence on the 'objective', all the more insidious because it regards itself as secure in an *anti*-relativist stance.

So the conclusions are also radical. There are no singular objects or selves external to us, and no singular self internal to us (Giles, 1997), since they represent only constantly updated attempts at practical co-ordination of differing perspectives on the continuum through the useful myth of the discreteness of 'an entity'. This realism of the continuum is not a formal realism, because there is no correspondence to 'the facts'; nor is it anti-realism because it does allow one to consider the real of the continuum apart from the way it is represented in human judgement. This being so, *pace* Saul Kripke, there can be, as we saw earlier, no 'Causal Theory of Reference' (for that begins with a singular referent), no 'rigid designation' (for it is impossible, except in the useful hope, to designate any 'thing' rigidly), no real essences, no natural kinds, no 'baptizing', except within the mythico-religious play of pure reference that we have to perform ('baptize' is a metaphor that gives away its superstitiousness; Kripke, 1980). Objectivist philosophers are only telling us what to play, without knowing that we don't need to be told because we are already playing the language-game anyway as a testimony of our faith.

Both old-fashioned idealists and positivistic realists thus stand convicted of a lack of faith, of a blind wish to take what should only be the first move in the language-game for reliable evidence of truth and certainty. They can fitly be compared to members of idolatrous cults, in which the central tenets are beyond all correction, divinely guaranteed by an imagination out of control, driven by an inward fear of accepting the burden of a true faith, that is, one aware of its own risk. Their watchwords, particularly for the direct realists, may be 'reason' and 'common sense', but the realists are too blinkered to see that an open-eyed trust in the other is humanly prior to both of these. All they are doing is consecrating habit and familiarity to the danger of all who listen to them, and arrogating to themselves a precipitate and unstable assurance.

2.   What philosophers of religion have been saying

We have already seen that to take faith to be certainty lodges one in paradox. Have not theologians down the ages echoed the words to Christ of the father of the mad child, 'Lord, I believe: help Thou mine unbelief'? (Gospel of St Mark, IX, 24). So to lodge an absolutely secure belief in God upon God as an existing entity, or to see His existence guaranteed by the functioning of religious language, or to take the revelation of His word as a unshakeable guarantee of faith is to move into superstition.

A number of attempts have recently been made to trace a connection between religion and the theory of knowledge. Whatever epistemology philosophers or theologians rely upon is crucial to the course they will pursue. There are some who follow a Wittgensteinian approach, in which religious meaning, like any other language-game, is established by its use, for the use comes to embody and to legitimize the rules which govern it. In a comment on the co-operation that brought those rules into being, Wittgenstein noted that 'The word "agreement" and the word "rule" are *related* to one another, they are cousins' (Wittgenstein, 1967 [1953]: 86e, his emphasis). For the committed Wittgensteinian, once a rule has been agreed upon that is virtually the end of the matter: any deviations can henceforth be seen as 'queer', even meaningless, because the public nature of the agreement has guaranteed the correctness of the applicability of the rule. He does, however, allow that reform of the language is possible (1967 [1953]: 51e), yet gives no explanation of how this could come about, since a private understanding is regarded as suspicious, associated with the impossible 'private language' (1967 [1953]: 94e–96e). In the present theory, on the other hand, any agreement, however publicly secure, is always open to challenge from a private point of view upon that public language; otherwise, this would appear to block the evolution of concepts. This correction comes, not from a *private language*, but from a *private understanding of the public language*. Here, then, is an indication that the Wittgensteinian epistemology can be opened up to critique.

There are many theologians and philosophers of religion who take their bearings from Wittgenstein. William P. Alston, for example (1991, 1993), has a notion of sense perception based on a reliance upon the common 'doxastic practices', the general opinions and judgements, that have been established over time. They become 'innocent until proven guilty', deserving to be employed until we have good reasons for abandoning them (1991: 153). Alston does differ from Wittgenstein in refusing to accept an *a priori* justification for the reliability of sense perception on the ground that all such claims assume what they set out to prove, unable to escape what he calls 'epistemic circularity'; this is to rely on sense perception in the course of the argument to prove its reliability (1991: 120). He argues that one can avoid such circularity by appealing to the fact that we use our doxastic practices in successful prediction, whereby he supports the claim that our perceptual beliefs do fit the realities we perceive, that we are put into 'accurate cognitive contact' with actual things (1991: 137). Since actual perceptions find their own internal support in such practices, so can the perception of God be supported within the society of religious persons, namely, by mystical experiences of God, which then amount to 'direct perception' of Him. For Alston, therefore, since he believes in 'actual things', there is sufficient justification for regarding God as real. Since our cognition is capable of 'grasping the ways things are in themselves', this permits the knowledge of a 'supreme reality that really exists through which one can find ultimate fulfilment' (1995: 55–6).

Another, more ingenious defence of belief in God has come from the philosopher Alvin Plantinga. He rejects the notion upon which 'natural theology' is based, that in order to justify a belief in God we have to search for evidence of His existence. He points out that, although we have no grounded evidence for the existence of other minds, yet we regard their existence as 'properly basic', an unquestioned belief without which our lives could not proceed. In the same way, there are committed believers in God for whom such a belief is 'properly basic' in exactly the same way, and just as far beyond evidential proof as that of other minds. A belief in God as creator and source of all good does provide a genuine spiritual support for the adherents of religion, and it is arrogant to assume that evidence must be produced in this case but not in others equally without such mundane backing. He argues that to think that there is some kind of 'ethical' requirement in thought that we should always have some public evidence for our knowledge is a deceptive extension from other fields (such as science and law) into an area where it has no sound application (Plantinga, 1998).

Nonetheless, there are some philosophers of religion who are non-realists, seeing God as some kind of projection. They hold to a view of science as an activity that has successfully objectified nature to the point where natural theology has been rendered powerless to justify a belief in God. Don Cupitt, for example, sees modernity as having made the world finally disenchanted, so that nature can only be seen as morally and religiously neutral and devoid of all magic (1980: 17), a disenchantment that must be reversed, but without recourse to an objective god. It is now impossible to articulate a relation to a God through knowledge. The appeal to facts and evidence is mistaken; religious language is not descriptive but expressive, the authority of God to be found in that 'of religious categories in a person's life' (1980: 56). Cupitt still traces the reality of God to religion's established language-game, a sufficient grounding for such a notion and also for values such as self-transcendence and autonomy, but refuses to grant the notion of God real entityhood. There is an unconditional 'religious requirement' of a Kantian kind, an 'autonomous inner imperative that urges us to fulfill our highest destiny as spiritual self-conscious beings emerging from nature'. This is what 'the will of God' is (1980: 94–5).

Cupitt also says that our life is a 'story', an 'inner drama of our response to the eternal religious requirement' (1980: 166). Much of what he argues could seamlessly fit in with what is argued in this book, for he insists that 'fiction logically precedes factuality', and that our lives have the character of narratives in which there is a constant play of knowledge; he sees our conversation as 'an endless contest of narrative hypotheses' in which we 'long for a master story, a story that will stick and really make enduring sense of life' (Cupitt, 1991: 81, 69). His claim differs from mine, though, in seeing the whole of our being as made up of this exchange of signs, a network 'made up of messages flying back and forth', and even goes so far as to say that 'what is not a sign is not significant', that 'there is no thing outside language' (1991: 45, 135). While I would agree that there is no *thing* outside language, and that we do inhabit the world of signs and would not have what entityhood we have without it, I differ from him in believing that we do have direct access to what lies outside language, in that we *sense* it. He is wrong, therefore, in claiming that 'our world is not made up of Being any longer, but of symbols and conflicting arguments' (1993: 48), for this is to leave out that upon which all our symbols have to work, namely, the Real.

He sees faith as entirely non-rational, the acceptance of a moral imperative 'to pursue religious values', a matter of principles and not facts. An objective god is an illusory paternal authority: instead of seeking the certainties of 'the big Ego', rather, one is to encounter the Other in the activity of the language-game within which we are bound (1994: 103). Thus he also takes up a thoroughly Wittgensteinian position, believing that there is only 'the flux of language-formed events' (1994: 53). In his epistemology there is an endless series of interpretations of what the sensory fields present, while language, with its structure of interdependent differentiations, publicly determined, gives us 'no single point of entry and no exit' (1994: 54). As with Wittgenstein, there is the same reliance on the public language, the same refusal to allow a step outside that language, and the same admission that meanings can change, but without any explanation of how this last can come about.

Outside these Wittgensteinian views, however, natural theology still has some adherents. Richard Swinburne, for example (1996: 20), sees the world as consisting of objects with obvious properties governed by physical causal laws yet denies that within such a system human purpose can be given any explanation, since in his view a deeper notion of order and beauty forever evades attempts to reduce religious experience and free will to material causes. It is God that keeps the world in being and maintains the laws of nature: in particular, in a bold 'God-of-the-gaps' argument, Swinburne derides science, arguing that modern Darwinism egregiously fails to account for the emergence of sensory consciousness (1996: 83). An explanation of as common an experience as the sensing of blue, for instance, is missing, the reason for its absence being that it is a 'mental event' divorced from 'brain events' (1996: 71). This he takes as a sign that, even though there is a close connection between soul and body, they are distinct.

Realists and non-realists about the existence of God nevertheless share a common view of science, that it provides objective knowledge about nature. The realists are determined to keep faith and reason, *mythos* and *logos* apart in order that faith can ground itself outside the sphere of evidential knowledge; they point to a sense of transcendence that challenges the notion of our being limited to the natural order. The non-realists point to the fact that science has banished the evidence for an objective personal god, a creator of the universe and guarantor of the highest value, and that therefore the only way of retaining the virtues of religion is to accept with Feuerbach (1957 [1841]) that God is the expression of changing social and personal ideals that have sustained society and personality throughout history. Both still see an old enemy as still a threat, the atheistic positivist for whom science has exposed religion for the myth it was and who has jettisoned the whole idea of a god forever.

R. B. Braithwaite (1971) argues from an atheist position in which the concept of God is reduced to no more than 'a behavioural policy', and which presents religion as a story, but in the sense of an illusion, a simulation of reality, functioning primarily as a psychological support. In this both materialists and theologians have moved little from the position of someone like Ernst Cassirer who, fascinated by myth as he was, remained insistent upon disengaging 'mythical thinking' from 'scientific thinking' (1977 [1955]: Vol. II, 60–70). A related distinction, just as rigid, can be seen in analytical philosophy, where there is a strong determination to keep fact and fiction apart (see, for example, Searle, 1975, and Walton, 1978). There is a rooted fear that a dangerous scepticism lurks inside this attempt to blur fact and fiction, echoing Wittgenstein's dismissal of 'queer' deviations from the 'compulsiveness' of conventional rule (1967 [1953]: 86e). Science is thus left by both realists and non-realists as a sphere on its own, divorced from matters of faith. They both adhere to scientific truth being an impersonal matter far removed from anything to do with the imagination. Perhaps they make an exception for the fact that advances in science are the result of some scientist's imaginative leap of thought, but that leap takes us to the firm ground of objectivity.

From the point of view of Triangulation theory, this distinction proves false, for it has rejected the notion that 'singular' entities pre-exist the human, intersubjective construction of reference. It is the singularity that is an illusion, a methodological tool created by two agents mutually imagining a pure convergence, a tool that cannot be given up without the loss of the required partial superimposition of differing perspectives. Swinburne's notion of a world of given objects is only the needful mutual pretence of 'mundane reality', cast over the Real continuum as an ongoing and forever adjustable hypothesis. Our incessant corrections of each other and thus each other's selves reveal that we are not dealing with given objects and persons, but only with a recalcitrant Real.

It is worth repeating here what was shown in Chapter 3.6 (pp. 100–2) that the correction of objectification is a correction of the subject itself: with a shock the objectification of ourselves is shifted about upon existence. Blank non-epistemic existence shows through the cracks in the epistemic 'objectivity' of the self. Hence, even the slightest scrap of information proves the existence of the Real and cancels all possibility of solipsism. There is even the irony that we may accept a correction of concept that is actually maladaptive, not in our interest at all, but *it will still prove the existence of a real that lies beyond our current concepts*. It also proves the existence of our sensory fields, thus breaking through Berkeley's barrier. The singular objects we (fictively) *perceive* are only rough experimental guides to the Real that we (really) *sense*. Moreover, although we have no access to the sensory fields of those who corrected us, we *can be sure that they have sensory fields*. As we saw earlier, 'other minds' prove to be something with which we do have some contact, and also, finally, we can be sure that, although our concepts of our self and of other selves are only tentative, *we and they are players in the language-game*, which moves through time sustaining our mundane 'reality'. So no Cartesian demon arguments can apply, those that try to make us entertain the thought that some demon might be fooling us in the manner of *The Matrix*. Though that film was powerful in its providing a metaphor for those for whom a current ideology or fanatical belief has distorted their projection of the mundane world, it cannot work as an allegory of sceptical doubt against Triangulation theory.

One of Swinburne's proofs of the existence of the soul thus finds no support here, for it is not the case that the sensing of 'blue' is undoubtedly 'mental' (Swinburne, 1996: 80). Sensing is not subjective, but part of the Real, as we have abundantly seen. Whether it is a baby who has not learned the word 'blue' or a child who has, the experience remains a provision of the *knowledgeless* base of our sensing. It is only evidence which we have to learn to interpret. There can be no conscious learning, in either man or animal, no mind, unless the two modules in the system, the sensory one and the pleasure/pain one are working together with memory. Consciousness is the outcome of this process, with knowledge at once creating and serving desire. But with those two modules out of connection with each other and memory, no consciousness would be possible, no selfhood, even though the experiences could still be present, perhaps in the most vivid of states.

Thus we are making public agreements, setting up rules of language and logic, in order to enable us to make revisions of those agreements. Wittgenstein's remark that 'the word "agreement" and the word "rule" are cousins' thus has force. Every informative statement is based on the concealed *faith* of the Idealization of Reciprocity of Standpoints. All logic and all reason are maintained by presuppositions that we in a common faith project in order to achieve a rough-and-ready co-reference that enables us to move language onward to a novel reference. The 'Laws of Thought' are no more than a spelling out of what the Idealization demands, namely that every reference to 'A' shall be identical to every other ('A is A'), that no crossing of criterial boundaries will be allowed ('A cannot be both B and not-B'), and there can be no blurring of definitions (A is either B or not-B'). Why are these to be held to? – because our faith in each other's commitment to common reference to the ideal singularity we are projecting must not appear to be impugned. Logic owes all its grandeur to the empirical successes that are the result of the faith of human co-operation, but these successes of fit never provide the 'accurate cognitive contact with actual things' that Alston has claimed. The singularity of those things is an needful artifice created by our adherence to those 'laws'; their 'necessity' is an illusion that the very weakness of our faith and the strength of our narcissism tempt us to see as some metaphysical edict. It had been pointed out by Didier Coste that 'A is A' is strictly a paradox, for it asserts absolute identity across two entities that by virtue of their enumeration as two are different (Coste, 1989: 9).

Bishop Berkeley was thus right in one sense when he said that God guaranteed the perceiving of things. Since this faith in the word ('In the beginning was the Word and the Word was with God') has created all human beings ('Who made you?' – 'God made me'), all the history of human speech, nationhood and culture arises out of a common idealization, then we might say that a virtual god guarantees the consistency of all we see and all we are. There is not the secular on the one hand and the mythical on the other. The only pure *mythos* is the pure *logos*, that is, pure logic and pure mathematics, where the validities can never be challenged since they never refer to the world, the agreement there being at its purest, its most imaginary. In contradistinction, we must say that every identification we make 'impurely' *in the world*, every perception, depends upon faith. So Alvin Plantinga is denied his claim that a belief in God is 'properly basic', for he is confusing the properly basic place of faith in all our lives and in its support of the 'objective' world about us with the frankly superstitious claim that an objective god exists. When he tries to make such humdrum facts as 'I am sitting on a chair' as the building-blocks of our experience, or when he feels uplifted by the contemplation 'of a flower or the starry heavens' into the conviction that God is responsible for 'them', he is illicitly turning our rightful thankfulness and wonder at the singularities that our ancestors have epistemically made of the Real in the great continuing game of speaking humanity into a barren delusion (Plantinga, 1983: 80).

Here, with my tongue in my cheek, I could be said to have provided an *Epistemological* Proof of the Existence of God or the gods for any religion without claiming that He or She or They are objective – which is, paradoxically, a simultaneous proof of His or Her or Their existence and His or Her or Their non-existence. Ironically, it was done with the help of science, although that science is not that of the positivists. And He or She or They are creators in the sense that every objectification arises out of the game of faith, so everything we recognize, including ourselves, speaks of Him or Her or Them. So there is a sense in which we can deny Cupitt's claim that the world has become 'disenchanted' and join Plantinga in responding to its wonder, for it has never ceased to be a construct of our imaginations out of the distributions of the Real and therefore it remains as enchanted as any child or poet could desire. I would say that this is why one theologian has been tempted to say that there is to be found a divine 'incomprehensible mystery' in 'our (indefinitely extendible) comprehension of contingent particulars' (Lash, 1988: 236).

We must also reject Alston's claim that God is objective, for no entity ever is. 'He' is rather the game in progress through history. Our concepts are never 'innocent'. Not only is God not an object, but there is no such thing as a 'common object': we merely act as if there were. Yet Alston claims that in his realist view 'human cognition is capable of grasping the ways *things are in themselves*' and that we can get a conceptual understanding of 'the Real as it is in itself' (Alston, 1995: 55, my emphasis). Despite Kant or Husserl or Alston, there are no *Dinge-an-Sich*, because we cannot get the intersubjectivity out of that '*Sich*', as we saw above. As we have just seen, to believe in common objects absolutely is thus a form of superstition, arising from a narcissistic desire to avoid the risk of the game. Nor is there any 'epistemic circularity' in this argument since we do directly *sense* the Real, even if we do not *know* it.

What Euripedes put into the mouth of his Hecabe gets nearer to the state of the case: 'It is by *Law* that we believe the gods exist' (Euripedes, *Hecabe*, 1963 [425 BC]: 87). G. B. Kerferd comments on this passage thus: 'Euripedes is here prepared to explain the gods as owing their existence to human belief.' 'Law' (νομος, *nomos*), according to the Pre-Socratic philosopher Lycophron, 'becomes an agreement and guarantee of things that are just between citizens' (Kerferd, 1999: 170–1, 128). But that 'agreement' must be ready for poetic transformation. Brian Wicker has asked that theology 'accommodate both philosophical speech about God and poetic speech about him, and to bring them into a single unified theory' (Wicker, 1975: 87). Successful or not, this is what the present theory is attempting.

There is a further consequence which has relevance to theology. Consider what becomes of the free will–determinism issue if the Triangulation Argument goes through. It implies that a pure de*termi*nism is not describable by us, since there are no timeless singularities to match up to our ideal 'terms'. Any one of us can come up with a new criterion for the application of a term, and we can ask whence comes that adjustment? It arose by the projection of a new gestalt because of a new wish in the observer. So it is certainly free in the sense that it was not present in the language currently used to define the concept under discussion, and had its origin in the will of a particular 'individual' applying some 'public' concept in a novel, 'creative' way, acting 'divinely' upon the primeval 'chaos'. We next recall that any concept is a direction of will, and any speaker inducing an alteration of it in others is by that same token altering their selves. If the hearers come to accept that adjustment, that constitutes a concession to the speaker that they were before not fully in control of what they were doing: the speaker shows them that they were to a degree *determined* since they did not know what they were doing, and now, having heard the statement, are 'freer' than before in that their wills are better directed. But this is what happens *when any informative statement is made which produced an acknowledged success in action.* Hence, it is wrong to think of free will as something without a basis in the Real and equally wrong to think of our terms as producing a binding necessity. Necessity in language is only a product of the Idealization, and depends on faith as much as truth does. Since our words are never going to count the Real, never systematize it according to given singularities, any 'necessity' in the Real will always be beyond our measurement. I am no expert in quantum theory, but I would ask anyone who is to consider it in the light of Triangulation theory, for it may be that at the level such calculations are made, the ability to fix our fictive singularities on the Real breaks down and produces paradoxes. So it is not strange that we should link free will with the divine as well as the external order, for both are bound together in the language process.

Nor can God, therefore, be *believed* to be omniscient though we must *regard* Him *as if* He is. Our imaginative faith projects the impossible goal of a final match of word to world, which is logically equivalent to saying that 'God', our faith in each other, is – finally – omniscient, that is, He must have reached the state of those angels we spoke of earlier who can never be surprised at anything, good or bad. The paradox is acceptable, for that is only our common noble lie, which we henceforth will *all* know is valuable, and we retain it as the fiction we cannot do without in spite of the risks we run. Thus, since we all know, as we use it, that paradox is inevitable (just as children playing seriously do, well aware that a sandcastle is not a castle even as they 'march their whelk-shell soldiers in'), we shall not get ourselves into a logical panic worrying whether our 'omniscient God' knows what we are 'freely' going to do beforehand, or whether God could set Himself a problem he can't solve (for a demonstration of what tangles the logicians get into over this question and also that of the free will–determinism issue, see Yandell, 1999: 303–40; 2001: 237–60). So we can be reassured that God 'has a transcendence beyond the natural order' (Runzo, 1993: 169), without ever falling into the superstitious notion that He exists objectively; He exists only as part of the game we have to play and are playing, and that *has a Real aspect*, as any play has a Real aspect. However much we have faith *in each other*, we really know perfectly well that a risk remains and that our faith would not be faith unless that risk is taken into account.

To the question of what a proper faith is we now turn.

3.   Faith and superstition

The hidden mutual faith of language, nevertheless, needs a closer look. If this theory is correct, this 'naïve and unreflecting faith' as the psycholinguist Ragnar Rommetveit has called it (Rommetveit 1978: 31), has made all language, and therefore all that is human: communication apparently displays a need to trust other members of the group, but it remains questionable at what point it becomes describable as 'altruistic'. The performance requires this initial trust that enables sensory and intentional correction to go through, but it is a trust that is so second-nature that it is entered into without thought. This is no surprise since it is an evolved behaviour, and therefore at its basis is *not normative*. It is strange enough that we are imagining the perfection of the objective world together out of the brute real that confronts us, but that it is supported by a trust in the imaginative game is even stranger. The perfect objective world, as Josiah Royce said, is thus actually a transcendental structure, logically timeless, but remaining always contestable (Royce, 1976 [1899]: 73). To the surprise of some logicians, one can say that we actually live in a 'possible world', an 'objective reality' held tentatively in place by our mutually imagined projection on the brute evidence of the undoubted real. No wonder that it is believed that 'a spiritual…affinity' binds the social (Geertz 1996: 42).

So what kind of faith are we joining in if it cannot be absolute belief in the Object – or the Self – or any final 'Absolute'? If reason is but our make-believe in a perfect agreement, it may be that already one of us in the language-game can see where a new interpretation can break the apparent rational validity of the scheme. An individual that produces a correction in the language has been able, while within language, to take a step outside it. Cupitt is thus mistaken in saying that there is 'no entry and no exit' from it. The allegorical interpretation of the Cretan Liar paradox that we made before is working here: an informative statement always moves from English/Cretan[1] to English/Cretan[2]. Even in an everyday statement such as a mother saying to her daughter 'Dad is outside in the garden', 'Dad' did not mean at the end of the mother's statement what it meant for the daughter at the beginning. The perfect word-meaning never arrives: as was noted before from Gardiner, the living ox discussed by two French-speaking observers makes its own new, if infinitesimal, contribution to the word-meaning of *bœuf* (Gardiner, 1944: 109). There is only ever the 'rule-governed transgression' that is language, according to Ricœur (Ricœur, 1983: Vol. I, xi).

What then is Cupitt's 'autonomous inner imperative', his 'religious requirement'? Gregory, as we saw, maintains that all our perceptions are hypotheses (Gregory, 1993). So what kind of hypotheses are these that we have not been consciously aware of applying? Similarly, what kind of faith is it that we are all involved in without being ordinarily aware that we are? If we now see that reason and faith, far from being opposed and distinct, are intimately bound up with each other, then faith is something necessarily attendant on our every act and thought. In every moment of living we are acknowledging the vast history of the game that our species has played, and enjoying the successes that past players have achieved. Our very identities at the levels of family, culture, nation and world have been shaped by means of our participation in the faith of the game. There is no opting out of the rule which says that we must perform the Idealization of Reciprocity of Standpoints; we could not think or speak unless we did. This raises a curious question about the core of such a faith, for its core looks for all the world like one of Plato's 'Noble Lies'.

Sigmund Freud in *The Future of an Illusion*, is critical of Hans Vaihinger's view (1924: 313–27) that religion ought to be performed *as if* it were true:

> This line of argument is not far removed from the *Credo quia absurdum*. But I think the demand made by the 'As If' argument is one only a philosopher could put forward. A man whose thinking is not influenced by the artifices of philosophy will never be able to accept it; in such a

man's view, the admission that something is absurd or contrary to reason, leaves no more to be said. It cannot be expected of him that precisely in treating his most important interests he shall forego the guarantees he requires for all his ordinary activities. I am reminded of one of my children who was distinguished at an early age by a peculiarly marked matter-of-factness. When the children were being told a fairy-story and were listening to it with rapt attention, he would come up and ask: 'Is that a true story?' When he was told it was not, he would turn away with a look of disdain. We may expect that people will soon behave in the same way towards the fairy-tales of religion, in spite of the advocacy of the 'As If'.
   (Freud, 1985 [1927]: 210–11)

Illusion shimmers in this very passage. As a lover of literature and an interpreter of literary works Freud might have asked whether there was after all something in those fairy tales that caused the 'rapt attention'. It is a question his disciples among psychoanalysts, taking their lead from him, have indeed asked about fairy tales (Bettelheim, 1976). But in this passage he apparently *approves* of a child who thought that only objective experience was worthy of attention. This child's 'matter-of-factness' is attributable to exactly the same cause as the behaviour of the white man in Alabama who ran onto the stage to prevent Othello murdering Desdemona. Logical perfection of objectivity is a fiction. Freud's matter-of-fact child believes the part-fiction of commonsense objectivity to be wholly true, and mistakenly discounts the myth of the fairy tale, of which, in spite of its being 'absurd' and 'contrary to reason', there was certainly more to be said, as his father might have told him on better recollection of his own theories. One is reminded by this child of the Scotsman Charles Lamb amusingly introduced us to:

Above all, you must beware of in direct expressions before a Caledonian. Clap an extinguisher on your irony, if you are unhappily blest with a vein of it. I have a print of a graceful female after Leonardo da Vinci, which I was showing off to Mr. * * * * After he had examined it minutely, I ventured to ask him how he liked MY BEAUTY (a foolish name it goes by among my friends) – when he very gravely assured me, that 'he had considerable respect for my character and talents' (so he was pleased to say), 'but had not given himself thought about the degree of my personal pretensions.' The misconception staggered me, but did not seem much to disconcert him.
   (Lamb, 'Imperfect Sympathies')

There is another kind of child who falls into superstition of another kind, the one who, so seduced by the myth she is playing, is tempted into actually believing it; like the Scotsman, she literalizes it. There is the story of the father, a smoker, who was working busily at his desk. His little girl, aged four, came into his study and began to pester him to play with her. Snatching at the first thing that came into his line of sight, he picked up three spent matches from his ashtray, one of which was nearly wholly burned through, and said, 'Here you are! Go and play with *them*.' The little girl took them eagerly and went off, thankfully for him, into the next room. However, after ten minutes there came a loud shriek from the next room, followed by sobs. He rushed in to find his daughter gazing at the table on which lay the three matches. She was sobbing with fear, and cried out, 'Take the witch away, Daddy!'

The suggestion that religion might have something of the fictive about it has produced protests from a wide variety of authorities besides Freud: Edward Caird, attacking Comte – ' a worship of fictions, confessed as such, is impossible' (1885: 167); Cassirer – 'Without belief in the reality of its object, myth would lose its ground' (1944: 72); Edmund Leach – 'religious behaviour cannot be based upon an illusion' (Leach, 1968: 525); and Alasdair MacIntyre calls the attempt to employ a myth while not believing it 'doublethink' (MacIntyre, 1967: 437). Alston thinks that such an approach to God is 'crashingly implausible' (Alston, 1995: 56); Paul Badham – 'God cannot be truly loved if we believe him to be only a non-real concept of our own choosing' (Badham, 1993: 185); John Macquarrie – 'we may ask whether these religious ideas would not lose their value for life if once we had decided to use them as fictions' (Macquarrie, 1963: 82). Plato's Noble Lie is hardly noble if it is going to be a mere device of propaganda: on the other hand, if we are as matter-of-fact as the child, the advantages of religion for a community would seem to evaporate, a prospect that caused even Durkheim concern (1976 [1915]: 427–9); but even so, his 'religion cannot be an illusion' has an element of truth.

When you watch sensible children playing a game, say, of Hobbits and Orcs, there are two levels of action you can discern:

(i) *The level of the make-believe.* This is the level of the pretence, that at which there are real hobbits and orcs for the players. However serious the acting, though, the sensible kind of child will not slip into the superstition of the man in Alabama. Something real in him tempted him to take the play for real, but the child who knows how to play can handle such realities through the indirections of drama without believing these indirections themselves to be real (though the child who cannot play properly, like he who cries when he is 'taken prisoner', or the little girl with the burnt match, is unable to maintain a due detachment, which is something Freud should have been well placed to explain).

(ii) *The level of the reality.* This is the level of actual children performing a game; no one would say that because the hobbits and orcs are a fiction, the children playing are too. But there is something to add: there is a relation imaginatively established between the level of children as social beings, and the level of the play, the hobbits and orcs, the figures of authority and anarchy that they are playing. There is a partial, metaphorical reality in their make-believe which they are imaginatively exploring without ever believing the pretence wholly true.

By the same token religious myth exists on these two levels, and always has done. Religion cannot be illusion in Freud's sense – it is as real as the second level of the children's game, and in the same way there is an imaginative relation between the myth and the process of our social being. Caird's, Cassirer's and MacIntyre's rejection of religion as a conscious fiction might have an unforeseen consequence. It could imply that the lie is noble as long as the public at large are not aware of it, a view that matches Spinoza's, that mythology was invented for the masses (*Tractatus Theologico-Politicus*, Ch. 5); or, for a more up-to-date example, consider this from Roger Scruton:

> Like Plato, a conservative may have to propagate the 'Noble Lie'. He might in all conscience seek to propagate the ideology which sustains the social order whether or not there is a reality that corresponds to it. For even if there is no reality, the politician can in any case do no better than provide new myths for old.
>   (Scruton, 1980: 139–40)

Baudrillard has pointed out that when the Iconoclasts broke the idols (or the Taliban the Buddha statue), what they really could not stand was the thought that perhaps God was no more than an image (1988: 169). But Spinoza's and Scruton's cynical dictum is adhered to today by many in authority who know that, not only is the power of the myth still with us, but it is been fastidiously abandoned by the promulgators of rational wisdom. Equally benighted are those among the masses who take the myth literally, whether in would-be religious or openly fascist cults. What Vaihinger himself said, quoting Carl Forberg, is fitting medicine for such self-deceptions: 'it is not the (theoretical) belief that the kingdom of God is coming which constitutes religion; but the endeavour to make it come, even if we believe it will never come' (Vaihinger, 1924: 326). Erasmus in his *Praise of Folly* was not afraid of 'doublethink': 'To destroy the illusion is to ruin the whole play, for it is really the characterization and make-up which hold the audience's eye. Now what else is the life of man but a sort of play?' (1971 [1509]: 104). It is not Pascal's advice – 'Act as if you believe and belief will come by itself' – but 'Act as if you believe and go on knowing that you never will.'

But this is precisely what we are already doing in every statement that we make. Every statement is a 'noble lie', because we have to hold a fiction temporarily as a fact. Fortunately, we are all adept in accepting the alteration of that fictitious fact as the Story of the Statement proceeds. If Cassirer and the rest were correct with their rationalistic dismissals, no one could ever speak! For Cornelius Castoriadis, however, the imagination is inextricably involved in the institution of society, in which we are all performing what he calls an 'endless rectification of the code', and it is possible for 'every expression is essentially tropic', that is, based on a figurative transformation, one that 'turns' a meaning by changing the intentional perspective on it ('trope', as we saw earlier, is from the Greek τρεπειν (trepein), 'to turn'; Castoriadis, 1987: 351, 348). Craig Calhoun has pointed out that the force of the traditions of a nation lies not in the supposed objectivity of those tales but in the telling of them: 'What gives tradition (or culture) its force is not its antiquity but its immediacy and givenness' (Calhoun, 1997: 34). And in this theory that 'immediacy and givenness' arises from the act of playing itself. To shrink from playing is to do what Freud's son did.

If everyone were in the secret of the communal myth, it would be truly a noble lie. Faith has to extend itself in imagination. We need to stage again the dramatic power of myth and outdo its performances of the past, for many of them, though not all, were tainted with superstition. We must try to become masters of the tremendous illusion that really wraps us round. As the Chinese did in their religion we might call in professional actors to help us, for, by reminding us forcibly of the reality of its fictiveness, that would help us to act better. Certainly no one individual can do it on his or her own. Nor can one bring faith into the open by public fiat as Robespierre and Comte tried to do, for that would be the Ignoble Lie all over again. The conditions must be made auspicious for its growth in the community itself. If a child can play seriously, why not the 'masses'? The anthropologist reminds us that the savage is 'a good actor' (Marett, 1914: 45). There are plenty of savages among the masses at the moment who display a primordial expertise in the power of the mask and the masque. But it cannot be done in a society where too many try to make the fixity of given identities a central principle, and who follow cults based on narcissistic certainties, for this would weaken our recognition of the religion we have.

An appropriate illustration of the dramatic stance that is required of us is that performed by Hardy's persona in 'The Shadow on the Stone' (pp. 53–6), for he determinedly ignored the Second Clue that would have supposedly enforced the transformation. He knew full well his wife was not behind his back, but he did not turn round 'to prove' it. We know 'full well' that there is no objective 'divine father' or 'mother', but we have to behave as if there is for all that, for it is that very behaviour that actually has created – and is creating – the only God there can be.

Faith is not something we can choose to take up or fail to have. We could identify neither subjects nor objects were we not engaged in the faith that binds us all in the game of language. This puts a new light on St Augustine's dictum *Nisi credideritis, non intelligitis* ('Unless you believe, you shall not understand') (St. Augustine, *De libero arbitrio*, Bk. I, para. 4). What we have to try to do is to recognize that we have what we are taking advantage of. It would be a mistake, though, to think that the faith is simply that the outcome of any correction must ultimately be to our personal advantage, for our own story is no different from the stories we tell each other: it may be that some new insight from someone we trust, far from fulfilling our desires, goes markedly against them, or, to our humbling surprise, fulfils those desires further than we expected. The real both in persons and outside them may throw up completely unexpected challenges – or pleasent surprises – that make nonsense of the firmest of blind trust.

Many theologians cannot bring themselves to entertain the thought that the divine might be no more than human faith and its progress through history. They protest that to take the notion of the Creator of nature away from God is to rob Him of all his power, and they busy themselves in trying to recapture a place for him as the designer of the universe. This is a crass mistake. Their fear is that science has banished the notion of God as Creator of all that is. After all, there are atheists like Richard Dawkins who passionately believe that science has dismissed such a mythical notion and put it in 'Trash' where it has been 'emptied' beyond recovery. But science, as Michael Polanyi insists, is just as much dependent on faith as any other kind of knowledge: 'we must now recognize belief once more as the source of all knowledge' (Polanyi, 1962: 266). We saw before (p. 140) that Kuhn's 'paradigm' being replaced by the innovation matches the structure of the Statement and thus shares its faith. Myth is not 'incipient science' as some have tried to see it (Blanshard, 1974: 440): rather, science is invisible myth.

Nevertheless, if the common faith has been responsible for all the words and statements of language from man's first entrance into humanity – since it is language that makes him human – then every *thing* and every *self* has been created as a recognizable entity in the service of life out of the stubborn and non-human Real, and is still being maintained there bravely but not stubbornly by that same faith. That Real, recall, includes the sensory experiences which are not human in themselves; we have the Real uncomfortably right inside our brains, not merely in the rest of our bodies, but it is as well that it is since we owe it our life. No surprise then that from the first man's religion has, sometimes clumsily and sometimes beautifully, tried to acknowledge this debt to the faith of our ancestors. If you thought it quaint that the Romans had a god for everything, including every action – '*Deferenda* for fetching wood, *Commedenda* for chopping it up, and *Adolenda* for burning up the brushwood' (Cassirer, 1946: 42), then you ought to revise your view of them. The 'animism' that the Victorian anthropologist E. B. Tylor thought characteristic of primitive peoples, the investing of ordinary objects with personal 'spiritual' life, is hardly primitive in bearing witness to the human faith that selected fictive singularities all round them. His contemporary Max Müller was nearer to the truth in believing that the key to religion and myth lay in language, though he thought that the early peoples first gave personal names to objects, which led to the spiritualizing of them; hence, according to him, the survival of the gender in nouns; but he also made a significant pun, between the Latin *nomina*, 'names' and *numina* 'gods' (see Pals, 1996: 19).

This theory gives a proper scientific grounding to Berkeley's insight about God being responsible for all perceptions. In the Uitoto Indian myth of creation is the assertion 'In the beginning the Word gave the Father his origin' (Pals, 1996: 45). God is Log*os*, but not log*ic*. Look around you now – can you not feel a sense of awe at the fact that everything you 'recognize' you owe to the immense and marvellous labour of humanity in history, including everything you are able to be conscious of in yourself? Do not think that the primeval 'chaos' that existed before 'creation' has been banished, for you are *sensing* it now. That creation in language has arisen from a faith in endless development with every statement spoken by everyone, to which you cannot help making your own contribution. Nietzsche's 'Thingness is created by us' needs to be carefully read because of that treacherous first-person plural: the 'us' is not just ourselves at this present moment in time, but all those who have contributed to the great narrative of our language and whose contributions are still active (Nietzsche, 1968: 307). One needs the grandeur of Carlyle's powers of rhetoric to do it justice:

> If now an existing generation of men stand so woven together, not less indissolubly does generation with generation. Hast thou ever meditated on that word, Tradition: how we inherit not Life only, but all the garniture and form of life; and work, and speak, and even think and feel, as our Fathers and primeval grandfathers, from the beginning have given to us?…As palpable life-streams in that wondrous Individual, Mankind, among so many life-streams that are not palpable, flow-on those main-currents on what we call Opinion; as preserved in Institutions, Polities, Churches, above all in Books. Beautiful it is to understand and know that a thought did never yet die; that as thou, the originator thereof, hast gathered it and created it from the whole Past, so thou wilt transmit it to the whole future. It is thus that the heroic Heart, the seeing Eye of the first times, still feels and sees in us of the latest; that the Wise Man stands ever encompassed and spiritually embraced, by a cloud of witnesses and brothers; and there is a living, literal *Communion of Saints*, wide as the world itself, and the History of the World.
>
> (Carlyle, 2000 [1833–4]: 182)

So, if we learn from Carlyle, it is not only the creating God of language that has an active part in our everyday lives, having made us human and enabling us to go on with the great and challenging game of being human, but all the persons of the past have an immortality in what they have imaginatively contributed, which is also still as active, allowing them still to contribute. When someone dies, it is only that they cannot now participate in the later stages of the game with their immediate comment on how the singularities are to be transformed, but, since all their words and sight of their actions are still active in those that heard them or read them, their influence is still as real in the drama. As human beings *before we die*, the best of us is what we are contributing to the spiritual-fictive game, and that does not stop with our death. *Whether we are living or dead*, the game carries on for us with the kind of reality of the children's game has. A children's game, by its metaphors, never literally believed by the children, who, nevertheless, manage to cope in those metaphors with matters of which in their conscious minds they have no sure understanding, enables them to handle those matters at one remove. This is Freud's insight, the one he signally did not apply to his own son. If you are like the little girl child who cries because of the burnt-match witch, you will be making the same mistake as Carlyle if you think that the 'Communion of Saints' is 'literal', having some kind of ghost-presence about us. That would constitute a failure of your imagination, in being unable to recognize that what we together create in our game is a web of *fictions* that moves through time as *real* behaviour by us all, although what we are trying to attain retreats as we try to approach.

> Yet all experience is an arch wherethro'
> Gleams that untravelled world, whose margin fades
> For ever and for ever when I move.
> (Tennyson, 'Ulysses', ll. 19–21)

The real meaning of 'spiritual', since it applies to it what we are *imagining* together, cannot therefore be seen, heard or measured, but it is a part of the Real nevertheless, for the game is Real. This is our true immortality, and we are immortal in this sense *whether we are living or have died*. This is the true meaning, too, of the word 'transcendent' when it is applied to God. The continuing naming and perceiving of all things out of the Real chaos, and the part in it that we cannot help *playing* in creation of ever-fictive 'reality' – those are real enough. *Mythos* and *Logos* are not to be divided; as Jerome Bruner has argued, there is no such oppositional contrast (Bruner, 1960: 276). Edward Thomas has a perceptive poem on words which brings out their spiritual power, their ancestry, and their paradoxical nature – in that oxymoron 'Worn new':

> But though older far
> Than oldest yew, –
> As our hills are, old, –
> Worn new
> Again and again
> (Edward Thomas, 'Words', ll. 32–6)

The sociologist Max Weber, like many a late Victorian, was dismayed by the 'disenchantment' of the world. He considered that the rationalization and intellectualization of life had led to the enchantment of things retreating into 'the transcendental realm of mystic life or into the brotherliness of direct and personal human relations' (see Gerth and Mills, 1967: 155). Similarly, Matthew Arnold, in his 'Dover Beach' spoke of 'the sea of faith'

> Retreating to the breath
> Of the night-wind down the vast edges drear
> And naked shingles of the world.
> (Arnold, 'Dover Beach', ll. 26–8)

and he too saw the only hope in the confines of personal love; 'Ah, love, let us be true/To one another!' Surely, now, after a century in which social faith has been mangled from its proper nature by cowardly superstition of various kinds, we ought to set about re-enchanting our world with play, with stories, with myths, that we shall no longer take *literally*, but which we shall see as part of the *real* ongoing drama. The magic of animism is still with us, for we depend on it every day in our performance of the real fiction, as many children seem to be aware before the 'shades of the prisonhouse' have closed upon them. Morris Berman, who seeks for a 're-enchantment of the world', has rightly said that 'realities are articles of faith' (Berman, 1981: 217). The afflatus of mystical joy is thus still available to the grown-up, *materialist* make-believer for the make-believing is a real, communal, ongoing act. One of Wordsworth's greatest passages in which he expresses his nature-mysticism speaks of

> Therefore am I still
> A lover of the meadows and the woods
> And mountains, and of all that we behold
> Of this green earth; of all that mighty world
> Of eye and ear, – *both what they half-create*
> *And what perceive.*
> (William Wordsworth, 'Lines composed a few miles
> above Tintern Abbey', ll. 102–6, my emphasis)

The Creation out of Chaos goes on all the time, and we are the present creators out of that chaos, which is also present. The joy in that engagement, that 'half-creating' that is the faith of mutual naming, can enchant the non-human, non-divine Real, for every act of naming is an act of play. To express the last lines with a closer philosophical truth, one would have to say 'half-perceive and half-*receive*', since what we *perceive* we owe to our human ancestors and our own imaginative quest, and what we *receive*, our sensations, are real, out of our control in our own bodies as they move in proportion to the external

Real. Only in this way can we attain the oneness with the infinite that the mystics claim. If we say with Shelley that

> The One remains, the many change and pass;
> Heaven's light forever shines, Earth's shadows fly;
> Life, like a dome of many coloured glass
> Stains the white radiance of eternity
> Until Death tramples it to fragments.
>   (Percy Bysshe Shelley, *Adonais*, LII)

the 'white radiance', the transcendence of that Oneness is made by our imaginations, the iridescence of the Many by the refraction of the Real with that ideal, but, since it is a really imagined play which creates them both, Death cannot 'trample' this essence of our life 'to fragments'. Has not the 'spirit' of Shelley just done something in our present as you read him? Mystics do not attain to some objective 'infinite': they participate in the ecstatic hope of our real play. Though it is superstitious to believe with Richard Swinburne that 'God is an object' (Swinburne, cited by Messer, 1993: 51), yet our imaginations, that create the 'timeless', move in time. No wonder Paul Tillich said 'The question of the existence of God can neither be asked nor answered' (Tillich, 1951: 236) for Enlightenment rationality is bemused by imagination's ambiguities.

Reigniting the enchantment through our accepting that it is play that we are playing – and that 'we' embraces all humanity past as well as present, a thought which is the source of much of the awe that one can feel in seeing a tree as Blake wanted us to see it – brings what 'God' did in the past back into living recognition. This is a real thing that our ancestors have done and are still doing. Then, being able to see again 'God' in every object as the mystics did, and children in their fun do, we shall also see why God can 'never be named', why he is a *deus absconditus*, the *via negativa*, the *huperousios*, the 'beyond-substance' of Dionysios the Areopagite (Happold, 1963: 190–6). 'He' is the faith by which all language is possible, and so is not to be placed within it. Here lines from the *Kena Upanishad*, one of the Hindu holy scriptures, are apposite:

> What cannot be spoken with words, but that whereby words are spoken…
> What cannot be thought with mind, but that whereby mind can think
> What cannot be seen with the eye, but that whereby the eye can see.
>   (Mascaró, 1975: 51)

This is the faith that has made words and the thinking selves that become possible within language, but 'He' also cannot exist outside that faith; to talk of 'Him' as a person is only a metaphor. As regards the last refrain about the 'eye', if we interpret that 'seeing' as *perceiving*, the paradox makes rational sense, for we could not share our perceptual discoveries unless we entered the faith. God is Kant's *focus imaginarius*, the ideal of a supreme being as 'a regulative principle of reason' (*Critique of Pure Reason*, A619, B647), a non-existent guide for real people inside a real game. It explains how God can be both in history and be 'transcendent', how He can be both 'absolute' and 'immanent' in man, how He can be both 'personal' and 'socially constructed' – and how we must aspire to His heaven knowing full well that there is no such place.

Cupitt describes such a view as we are recommending here as 'expressivist' as against 'realist':

> [Expressivists] say that the sense in which mathematical objects exist is given in the way mathematicians talk about numbers, and the same in which physical objects like chairs exist is given in the way we talk about physical objects. Similarly, the sense in which God is real is given in the language and practice of religion.
>
> (Cupitt, 1980: 57)

The parallel he draws needs qualifying. (1) In pure mathematics numbers are a pure fiction without reference to the world, which is what happens when we take faith as absolute certainty – or commit ourselves to superstition, for that ensures the failure of our reference to the Real. (2) Objects are the mutual selections that we make from the continuum and *treat as if* they were singular, the fictively perfect superimposition of our differing 'referents'. (3) God is the fiction that hopefully keeps our referents, and, hence our fears and desires, in harmony – while we are to accept that such pure harmony is unobtainable. Here the (2) is the faith that accepts risk; (3) is the necessary but imaginary focus of that faith beyond that risk; and (1) is the kind of play that mutually and consciously rules out all risk and thus guarantees that knowledge will run into ignorance.

The theologian Rudolf Bultmann wanted 'to demythologize' the stories of Christianity to get back to the true revelation, the κηρυγμα (*kerygma*), 'proclamation', that lay behind the distortions of myth (Bultmann, 1958: 84). This was a mistaken attempt to arrive at certainty, all the more mistaken in its abandonment of the myth as play. The egregious fault is to take the myth literally and so give it up on supposedly rational grounds: what is required is that we realize that we are already inside the myth of language and our duty is to carry its poetry with a child's seriousness up into our lives. This is the 'religious requirement' that Cupitt is in search of. Those who think it 'too whimsical, too paradoxical' to play the 'As If' thus, as Cupitt describes their view, are bound within it already and are paradoxical themselves in not admitting to it (Cupitt, 1980: 100, xii). The hysteria of the child fearful of the burnt-match witch could await them. Bultmann was, nevertheless, correct in a conclusion he drew about the 'reality' of God. He believed that we could not speak about God without at the same time speaking about ourselves, and he sums up this view with a remark which fits unproblematically into the present argument: 'Not what God is in Himself, but how he acts with men, is the mystery in which faith is interested' (Bultmann, 1958: 43). Any prayer to Him is therefore addressed to no one, but, if it confesses its impossibility and accepts its dramatic significance alone, it will have worth.

Taking the objective world literally and not metaphorically is to fall into what I call the 'pseudo-faith'. This is to engage in the inescapable act of trust that every statement demands but rigidly believe that the agreement with the other does point to a certain and all-satisfying future in which the other will always see that agreement as we understand it. For this is what it is to take *singular* objects and persons for real. We are projecting a 'common' world of mundane 'reality' by this act of trust, a world which does not actually exist in the way we must treat it. What we are selecting those 'singularities' from is real enough, but those guides to action that are our 'shared' concepts are no more than guesses that have worked out so far. The 'man of common sense' is thus blindly superstitious, even as he compliments himself on his level-headedness and avoidance of all things 'fanciful'. As we saw in the preceding section, both idealism and direct realism are superstitious at base.

What is too disturbing for many to confront is the fact that the agreement we have with the other, however much we *take it for granted*, is never without the risk of coming apart unexpectedly, since we only *took* it *for* granted – more disturbingly, not because the other has deliberately deceived us, but possibly because he or she happened to understand the agreement differently and neither of us knew about that difference, because the earlier context never brought it to light. Triangulation theory shows us that no final convergence of understanding is in fact possible: there is no certainty, even for the carrying out of some utilitarian act tomorrow, and definitely not for the achievement of some absolute final bliss. Yet strangely, the assumption of perfect singular reference has that implication, which is blatantly paradoxical, since it seems to turn mere 'assumption' into a wholly impossible conviction. What is wrong with Kant's theory of ethics is that it begins with the Idealization of Reciprocity, claiming that we have to act so that our rule can be universalized to all: what he should have added is that we also have to wait to see how the other takes it, for we might have to make some painful alterations to it!

What, then, are the motivations of such literalizing of the 'objective' world? What induces people to remain in the state of pseudo-faith?

(1) We have the mistaken idea that objectivity entails existence, when all it shows is that, yes, it is *chosen* from existence, but each person is choosing differently at the very moment that they have to pretend that they have chosen the same portion as everyone else. How insidiously easy, then, is it to move from the employment of what is only one half of a linguistic method (for the other half of the statement subverts the

'agreement') to the conviction that all is as we each currently conceptualize it. There, it seems, in all its bland facticity, is the 'single' thing or self before us – who could doubt 'its' existence?

(2) It is deeply disconcerting to think the other does not understand what one is saying at the very moment that an act of trust is being performed. It looks like suspicion of the other, though in actuality it is an acknowledgement of their genuine difference from oneself. Austin thought performatives were confined to promises like 'I do' in the wedding service, but all statements have this performative aspect for all are promises that a 'common' understanding will remain 'true'. How ideal, then, is the promise, when the convergence of motive cannot be guaranteed even with 'the best will in the world'? And what do you say when someone does morally *more* than the 'sincere' words 'stated'? Are you going to call that an argument for scepticism too?

(3) It is consoling to our narcissism and our fear to believe that the agreement reached will be exactly as we have ourselves understood it. It hides the ever-present threat of the Real's contingencies, both in the world of things, in the other, and in our own self. The French philosopher Emmanuel Levinas has been notable in drawing attention to the ineradicable difference of the other from the self; the other cannot be compassed in the 'samenesses' of language, as the novelty of the future continually reveals (Levinas, 1994: 42–8). This approach is therefore much in sympathy with the conclusion reached by Richard Kearney, that an awareness of our 'narrative' selves cannot now be escaped and we must abandon any notion of a unique essence perduring through time. As he says, we are ourselves 'stitched from the fabric' of the stories around us (Kearney, 2002: 150–4). What must be added is that we are involved in the telling and that brings risk as well as happiness. Maurice Blanchot warned of the 'violence' of language: 'something is there that is beyond reach' (Blanchot, 1993: 212). Derrida acknowledges the danger: 'Faith is needed where perception is lacking' (Derrida, 1999: 80).

(4) The language-game, as we saw above (pp. 179–80), has in entirely hypothetical view the impossible perfect union of desire and law, and, for the narcissist, that union is taken to be a real promise, that life does in reality hold out the full satisfaction of 'one's' desire as conceived of in the present, the oneness of that stale self being guaranteed as unchangeable by the misconstruction of what the trust of language involves.

(5) It is reassuring and flattering to think that one's own understanding is blessed by a 'public' one, which is again the equivalent of being convinced that that our desire and the law are at one. The agreement with our partner in dialogue we naturally and rightly take as part of the whole venture of language by all who speak it, and we equally correctly have an underlying awareness that we are contributing, even in the smallest degree, to the great human task of trying to match words to the world.

So again it appears tempting to move from what is actually only experiment to conviction.

(6) Many people, for all sorts of personal reasons, are unable to remain in a state of doubt. Like the child who cries when he is 'taken prisoner' in the game of Hobbits and Orcs, a person troubled by the constant challenges of living an 'identity' gets lost in a fearful obsession with certainty. Such persons cannot play the language-game, finding the movement from interpretation to interpretation shakes their too rigid sense of self. It is often said, mistakenly, that neurotics are 'insecure': on the contrary, they are *too secure*, since 'identity' is no more a given than any other singularity – it is 'in play' in both senses of that phrase, 'loose' and 'make-believe', and play implies risk.

(7) The engagement in language, which is the very thing that makes us human, and is so immediate to our identity, invests everything we feel, think or do. It is, nevertheless, perhaps because of that very intimacy, of all things the most elusive and most puzzling. It is as if the eye should try to see itself without a mirror. It is no surprise, therefore, that it is frightening to enquire into the status of its future-regarding nature, into the risks in world and self that it hides even as it endeavours to deal with them.

(8) And, since religion is a make-believe in real actual progress, and its performance therefore really involves paradoxical behaviours, the rationalist mind can only wince away in distaste from such 'illogical' requirements. Acting is altogether suspect from the viewpoint of the puritan logician, since it raises questions about reliance upon singular identity. He sees something devilish about the sceptical dissenter who puts forward such aesthetic nonsense.

The acceptance of risk, therefore, characterizes a proper faith: the affectation of absolute certainty, superstition. It is the superstitious who are being inconsistent, for, since we 'only talk about the problematic', in just engaging in talk they are admitting to the risk (F. C. S. Schiller, 1929: 88).

This is why this way of viewing God cannot be shaken by 'the problem of evil'. The Archbishop of Canterbury confessed in January 2005 that faith might be disturbed by the magnitude of the Indian Ocean tsunami disaster: but those who view faith in the light of this theory were already prepared and their faith is by no means shaken. The accusation of pessimism thus passes this kind of faith by, because, whatever the Real may attack us with, the hope is not impugned for it took account of denial. Faith is perhaps best seen as a kind of Keatsian 'negative capability', which he defined as

> That is when a man is capable of being in uncertainties, mysteries, doubts, without any irritable reaching after fact and reason.
>
> (John Keats, letter to Benjamin Robert Haydon, December 1818)

Superstition, on the other hand, is determined upon to be convinced, and, ironically, often on the scantiest of evidence. A due examination of evidence, after all, might disturb that conviction, which is held in place by the fears outlined above. It is clearly superstitious, then, even to regard it as a problem that 'evil' is in 'God's world'. There is no Devil just as there is no God, but, if the superstitious imagine a devil or devils, that imagining will take its place in the Real game and produce Real evils. Those poor women in the seventeenth century who were *treated as if* they were witches by King James really were burned alive. It is disturbing, not only to find that satanic cults are finding more adherents (and that crimes are being committed under their influence), but that the churches still believe in exorcism. Although the Church of England treats the 'demons' officially as 'inner demons' and not as objective ones going about seeking whom they may devour, in Italy the Roman Catholic Church has just opened a college for the study of Satanism and is performing 300 exorcisms a year. They are being just as superstitious as the Satanists themselves.

One must not underrate those fears of the fictive explanation, because, when the outcome of this argument is squarely faced, the conclusions are not encouraging. Indeed, when once I explained the argument to a sociologist, Dick Pels, who gave it a not unsympathetic hearing, he remarked laconically, 'You have a hard sell.' Why should it be so?

If no act of trust between two persons can rule out the fact that each may innocently misunderstand the other, and that is what Triangulation theory appears to prove, then the full consequences do point to some dire possibilities. What happens in the future when the two who have pledged their 'sincere' trust in each other discover that the new circumstances bring it about that they are now harshly at odds in intention when they expected to be in harmony?

The happiest outcome is that some compromise can be arrived at in which each one yields up something that they desired or accepts something that they feared. Take the second 'happy' ending that Dickens wrote to *Great Expectations* at the insistence of Bulwer Lytton: one can hardly say that the marriage would be made without compromise on both sides, without a thoroughgoing reinterpretation of what Pip's former idolizing of his Courtly Lover, the inaccessible 'star' Estella, entailed.

The next possibility is that one of them makes a sacrifice alone, perhaps seeing the situation as comic at their expense. They can laugh themselves into a new identity in spite of the distress involved, and share in the new interpretation even though it runs counter to their wishes. Think of the denouement of many a comic drama in which the character who has been shown to be a fool in some respect is cajoled into accepting his disillusionment or disappointment. Take the last scene of Sheridan's *The Rivals*: one of the characters, Sir Lucius O'Trigger, is deprived of what he sought, namely, the hand of the beautiful Lydia, and yet the playwright presents him as saying, and to others, like Mrs Malaprop, who have been similarly thwarted,

Come, now, I hope there is no dissatisfied person, but what is content; for, as I have been disappointed myself, it will be very hard if I have not the satisfaction of seeing other people succeed better.
(Richard Brinsley Sheridan, *The Rivals*, Act V, scene iii)

This is how Donald E. Polkinghorne sees the comic plot:

In the comedy plot, the story begins with a regressive narrative in which life events are problematic and move the character away for happiness, but then a progressive moment develops in which happiness is restored.
(Polkinghorne, 1988: 168)

But not all fools after being exposed and frustrated can content themselves with the sight of the happiness of others. We saw earlier that Malvolio, aptly named, is not at all 'content' with his predicament (p. 65), nor is he as socially benevolent as Sir Lucius. On discovering how he has been rendered ridiculous, and being unable to forget the mockery he was subjected to when imprisoned as a madman, he declares, 'I'll be revenged on the whole pack of you!' and rushes out in rage. Olivia's note of sympathy softens the tone, but one is not wholly convinced that the duke's request to his attendants will succeed:

OLIVIA: He hath been most notoriously abused.
DUKE OF ILLYRIA: Pursue him, and entreat him to a peace.
(William Shakespeare, *Twelfth Night*, V, I, ll. 378–9)

We who joined in the laughter are left somewhat uneasy. The same is true of Molière's Alceste in *Le Misanthrope*. Alceste, although all misunderstandings are now out in the open, will not accept the comic correction, even at the price of losing his beloved:

ALCESTE: Trahi de toutes parts, accablé d'injustices,
Je vais sortir d'un gouffre ou triomphent les vices.

[Betrayed on every hand, weighed down with wrongs,
I must flee from the abyss where vices dwell in triumph.]
(Molière, *Le misanthrope*, V, vi, ll. 135–6)

The last possibility is the most daunting one, that of the tragic outcome. There is nothing to rule out the possibility of the two who have pledged their trust in each other finding themselves so much at odds that the sacrifice demanded of both involves extreme suffering resulting from neither being able to alter the newly discovered intentions which were unconsciously implicit in their earlier commitment. Human beings are not computers; the extent to which they can be reprogrammed has a limit. The circumstance may be such that there is no way to avoid suffering on both sides, because the intentions go deep down into their Real nature. I used the familiar Iceberg metaphor earlier for the depths of intention in the Self, and the aspect of the connotation I thought apt was that the hidden element passes out of conscious recognition. It is, after all, a corner of the triangle and therefore fuzzy to us; all the same, it remains real. One cannot brainwash people into agreement, for that Real element of difference is at the basis of their life. It is what the interaction of their personal history and the particular nature of their bodies has produced.

The concept of original sin, although regarded wholly from the point of view of the idealized rigidity of language, Lacan's 'Symbolic Order', was an indirect admission by the early church fathers that no individual can match the idealization, for the idealization of its very nature has no singular existence. What they could not admit to was that there is a possibility that on some occasions it cannot be clear whose interpretation is to be privileged, that the 'original sin' could be said to be just as much on the side of the other, perhaps on the side of the holy Superego. It only sidesteps the problem to assume that the 'public' interpretation takes precedence, for there is no ruling out the chance that just one person's interpretation, differing from the customary one would actually prove to be better in the long run for the majority, a truth Sextus Empiricus was concerned to stress:

> Truth is a rare thing, and on this account it is possible for one man to be wiser than the majority.
> (Sextus Empiricus, 1955: Vol. I, 179)

The awkward conclusion is that in a tragic case the only resolution, apart from actual physical conflict, is to ask for *a rivalry in sacrifice* from the parties concerned. This is far from being a compromise, since it might involve the death of one or both of the persons concerned. This is what tragedy is, as tragic stories make all too clear. The rival Intentional Perspectives upon the Ambiguous Element cannot settle to a favoured gestalt as in the Joke, or, hopefully, as we have just seen, in any comic situation.

Take Oedipus in Sophocles' play. One cannot remove the dilemma by trying to regard the *husband's* love for Jocasta as of no import and privilege the *king's* concern to discover the criminal responsible for the plague – or vice versa (Figure 59). Both perspectives go down deep into the Real in Oedipus – where, then, is Oedipus's 'original sin'? A husband's love for his wife is at the basis of the family, and the family structure is that upon which the state is built: a king's duty to pursue and right to punish the incestuous and murderous wrongdoer is also at the core of the state. What the play does not flinch from is confronting the intractable dilemma. One cannot fall back on the soothing self-deception that God's harmony will compensate for – or

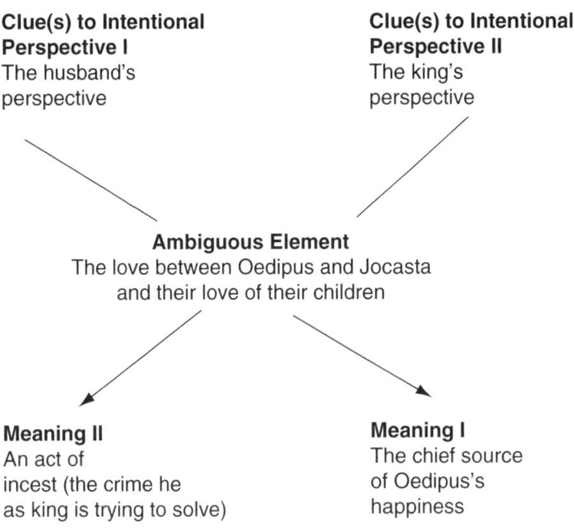

Figure 59

indeed has already – all such terrible catastrophes in eternity. Thomas Hardy confronted such dilemmas and counselled us to do the same:

> If a way to the Better there be, it exacts a full look at the Worst.
>   (Hardy, 'In Tenebris II', l. 14)

Some may try to protest that to admit to such an unnerving analysis of tragedy opens the door to anyone committing a crime to use it to excuse their fault. Even now we have sophisticated criminals consciously using their abused childhoods as a covering excuse. It was the burden of the song 'Gee, Officer Krupke!' in *West Side Story* (Bernstein, 1994: 389–420). What has to be said in answer is that we should still try in all cases to discover if possible what it is in the Real that has produced the deviation from the supposed norm. This is not to adopt the motto of *Tout comprendre, c'est tout pardonner*, for behind that complacent epigram is the belief that a complete knowledge is achievable, which is ruled out by the theory. It does certainly lead us to view crime in a more understanding light, and incline us to the policy of rehabilitation for crime rather than vengeful punishment. It clearly prevents us from demonizing evil as a thing-in-itself, although we might try to get an indirect hold upon the occurrences we call 'evil' by consciously playing out a myth of a devil. This is what the Rangda religious theatre in Bali is doing. This is a place to say how horrifying those legal practices are that allow relations of murder victims to witness the executions of those convicted of the murder with the excuse that those relations 'want closure'.

Closure would be better achieved by joining in a ritual play about murder in the manner of the Greeks, or, at least, by going to see Aeschylus's *Agamemnon* or *The Eumenides*. Imagine a performance of *King Lear* in which members of the audience replaced each other in the parts as the play went on – to experience at one remove what it is like to be a Goneril or a Gloucester; it would be a new kind of *Lehrstück* ('learning play') in the Brechtian manner. Revenge, it can now be seen, is a form of superstition, for it works on the false assumption that some kind of moral balance can be restored, when the only restoration possible is forgiveness on one side with *or without* penitence on the other. This is what a Levinasian acknowledgement of the 'alterity' of the other implies. However, what the present theory also implies is that, if all of us are 'each-otherish', it is no use anyone protesting a lack of responsibility for playing in the language-game when, to begin with, it is that which has bestowed the sense of self in the first place, and, secondly, some social responsibility for the conditions in which the murder became possible cannot wholly be shuffled off. We ought not, for example, to protest that 'innocent victims' have been the target of terrorists. Someone can be the innocent victim of a tsunami (if no one could be blamed for not setting up warning systems) but not of a 9/11 disaster. Though the trail of responsibility may be veiled and tortuous to trace, yet those who died in the World Trade Towers and the Madrid and London bombings were not without some historical link to the causes of rage in the Middle East.

So with personal calamity of this tragic kind not impossible for any one of us, it is not to be wondered at that people seek consolation in superstition, for one thing superstition always promises is the certainty of an order in the universe providing some form of personal guarantee, even though its mode may be to divinize the demonic, or see it, as the Manichaeans did, as containing struggle between evil forces and good, or imagine that one can side with fate by indulging in such practices as astrology or by observing neurotic disciplines. It is still the error of the child who cannot play properly. I recall a common complaint often shouted out to a transgressor of the code when childhood games were in progress: 'We're not playing – you won't be dead!' How many people in a state of grief cannot emerge from it precisely because the effect upon them of their loss leads them to refuse to accept the death? It is like saying, 'I'm not playing – I won't let her be dead!' Sadly, it also prevents them seeing what immortality actually consists in, the continuing part their 'loved ones' are still playing in the human drama.

The psychologist Jerome Bruner is one who is prepared to see our situation as essentially dramatic:

> When we enter human life, it is as if we walk on stage into a play whose
> enactment is already in progress – a play whose somewhat open plot

determines what parts we may play and toward what denouements we may be heading.
(Bruner, 1990, 34)

His use of the word 'open' is a reminder that the script and the role are not fixed. The play may 'already be in progress', but we are not absolved from taking a part which can alter how that script is to be written and how that role is to be played in future. A body entering the Symbolic Order is not like clay passive in the hands of a potter: we are engaged in how the play is to go whether we like it or not. The superstitious are those who want to fix the role in one way. Unlike Freud's child playing 'Fort-Da' they cannot move from 'Da' to 'Fort' repeatedly as life demands of us, even though they are doing this with every statement they speak or hear. The same emphasis appears in another form in the anthropologist Victor Turner's insistence that in our lives from moment to moment we are all crossing thresholds, that 'liminality', a moving from concept to concept, characterizes all our thought. This is how he believed non-civilized peoples performed their myths and rituals, that is, with an awareness of their dual nature. All the gods who are fools and tricksters – Hermes, Loki, Wakdjunkago, Eshu-Elegba – inhabit this threshold region (Turner, 1974: 580).

What is ironic is that in superstition we see the dramatic and poetic impulse deformed in the service of fanaticism. Renata Salecl has spoken of the 'violent poetry' of the fascist (Salecl, 1968: 158). One of the reasons that we have not been able to see the value of the myth in our life is the fact that it was so prostituted by the Nazis. *Hitler has given myth a bad name.* He blackened further the possibilities of enchantment in the game that had already been rubbished by the rationalistic puritans of the Enlightenment. But he patently was not like the child who can play seriously without losing the detachment of disbelief.

The hope inside language thus needs a careful analysis. It cannot be a conviction, only a faith, that

Sin is behovely, but all shall be well, and all shall be well, and all manner of thing shall be well.
(Juliana of Norwich, *Revelations of Divine Love*, ch. xxvii)

Language does operate on the *hypothesis* that 'all manner of thing shall be well', that is, that all entities in the universe shall find a rational place in the divine scheme, one that shall be 'well' for the desires of everyone, that the Word is with God, but that is only the indispensable phantom of agreement that we need to start a statement and with which we conclude it after the transformation. Juliana of Norwich, one can see, could not help acknowledging the paradox, in that initial 'Sin is behovely'. Kant would have said that we must not turn our 'regulative principle of reason' that creates a god into a *constitutive* one (*Critique of Pure Reason*, A620, B648). The hope can also not be for some utilitarian target closer in time than eternity, for that is only tentative, since it cannot ignore the essential transformations that we as hearers are to have presented to us in statements as we proceed in language. Therefore, the strange commitment has to be to the speakers around us themselves as fellow-players, all knowing full well that there is no common hope in the Real. F. C. S. Schiller has a neat summary of what faith must be:

> It seems preferable to define it as the mental attitude which, for the purposes of action, is willing to take upon trust valuable and desirable beliefs *before* they have been proved 'true'.
> (Schiller, 1912: 357)

As a result, the faith has to be a form of *love*, for only love can face the prospect of the possibility of a rivalry in sacrifice. Christianity is often mocked for the tenet that one must 'love one's enemy', but, since those we love are others, with Real alterity within them, they are already our enemies. It is worth mentioning that Christianity is far from being the only religion to place compassion as one of the highest virtues: Lao Tzu praises the 'virtue of non-contention' (Lao Tzu, 1963: 130). Only the superstitious believe that those they 'love' will never do anything hateful to them.

If *troth is prior to truth*, as this argument appears to show, then it is equally the case that *love is prior to troth*. In every word we speak, then, there should be an awareness that in the language-game the promise may be of death, and how we behave to the other will become a vital element in our moral being. This is surely the meaning given to the phrase applied to holy ones in the past, who, 'died every day they lived', as Malcolm's mother is said to have done in *Macbeth* (Shakespeare, *Macbeth*, VI, ii, 111). Cupitt has also foregrounded this thought, that the sense of impending death is what gives life its enchantment: 'the unity of living and dying . . . is eternal life' (Cupitt, 1995: 4). A short poem of A. E. Housman's is evocative here:

> I did not lose my heart in summer's even,
> When roses to the moonrise burst apart:
> When plumes were under heel and lead was flying,
> In blood and smoke and flame I lost my heart.
>
> I lost it to a soldier and a foeman,
> A chap that did not kill me, but he tried;
> That took the sabre straight and took it striking,
> And laughed and kissed his hand to me and died.

That the foeman laughed at the tragic instant shows himself far in advance of Malvolio and Alceste. He was accepting his loss in the game with the proper courage. It was the obverse of that child accused with 'I'm not playing – you won't be dead!', for he was prepared to be really dead in the game, and showed his love of his enemy in doing so. That moment he turned into a story by occupying a new intentional perspective on the incident and the two participants, his last act a Second Clue. Notice that his act was not one of a martyr's self-abnegation, sacrifice seen as some kind of masochistic idolatry before the Superego. He did not betray the Real in himself, for he took the blow as he was striking himself. As Lacan would put it, he did not 'give up on his Desire' (Lacan, 1992: ch. 20).

It is not easy for everyone to play as serious children do. Those for whom any acting is a threat to identity often cannot cope. Clifford Geertz noted that in the Rangda religious dramas in Bali, some actors of Rangda, a mythical witch, sometimes ran amok and 'held whole villages in terror' (Geertz, 1975: 115). On the other hand, many people turn to it naturally, as Marett said. Most children start with the knack for doing it, for it is play. What has to be stressed is that we are already doing it as we *speak*, and therefore have already committed ourselves to threats to our identity.

So we have to participate in a mutual hope, but, even as we project together the *Promised* Land, we have to remember the impossibility of pure mutual promise. Our mutual hopes only converge in the imagination of them, and that is what we must play. Hence the *Credo quia impossibile*, 'I believe because it is impossible', of Tertullian in the fifth chapter of his *De Carne Christi*. This is why the Incarnation is such a powerful myth, because it expresses the impossibility of the Real in the body ever matching the Symbolic Order of language, while to be human requires, to use Cupitt's verb, bodies (the Flesh) to embed themselves in the idealization of language (the Word) in order to be selves at all. That the central image of the incarnated Christ should be a crucifixion, the tragic acceptance of a *criminal* identification, explains another aspect of its power. It is not that 'the Word was made flesh and dwelt amongst us' once only (St Luke, I, 14): each of us has to accept our own incarnation, that flawed identification between Real and Symbolic, every day. We, like that other criminal, Oedipus, are Lacanian 'split subjects', endlessly seeking to complete our 'lack', but what Lacan did not bring out is that we need with others to imagine that completion *without ever believing it possible*. To put the choice of *Aut fides, aut ratio*, 'Either faith or reason', is thus one that falls to the Fallacy of Many Questions (the usual example of this fallacy is 'Have you stopped beating your wife?'), for they are not separate, as reason depends upon faith. Truth depends upon troth – and troth upon love.

The Cross also has an adventitious relevance to the diagram we have used to analyse the Story and the structure of the Statement (Figure 60). It seems appropriate in a work that has kept a place for the suffering body and all the sensuous imagery within which it lives that the link between the Cross and our recurring diagram should be presented to the reader's eye – for we all have eyes to see. I am sure that you can by now set it up for yourself, the comedy and tragedy of life. Turn the diagram through 45 degrees. Won't we obviously and metaphorically be tempted to see ourselves where Lakoff and Johnson put all suffering, disvalue, pain and frustration? – at the base of the Cross, in our *lowly* plight (Lakoff and Johnson, 1980: 22–4) looking up to the God *on high*, and won't there strike across other equally noble desires and fears which are just as immediate to us and which will not be denied, so that God will appear to be elsewhere, not in that dimension of height at all?

We all take ourselves to have the same initial lowly position in that our highest hope, our *common* faith, has the same transcendent end, the *Summum Bonum*. Consider the traditional names for it: the Kingdom of Heaven (which brings out the union of Law and Desire, Symbolic and Real), Eden (in which the labour of all action will cease and joy come unsought for), Eternity (timeless existence, thus without risk either from shame in the past or fear for the future), Abode of the Blessed (where all in common can be good for ever and recognize each other as that without any painful disagreements

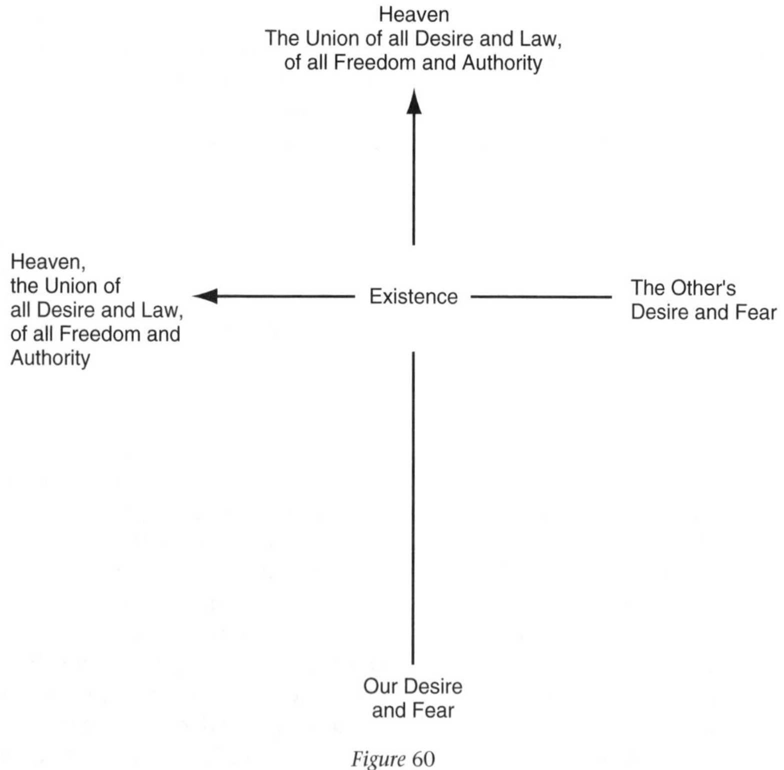

Figure 60

about what constitutes the Good), paradise (where the Good, the True and the Beautiful are united in Keatsian fashion without paradox). The reader can no doubt provide more. The great irony is that we *have to* imagine that we are all at the same place in the same lowly position with that gloriously universal end in view in order to talk – and thus be human – at all. That is where the Idealization must put us. What is unexpected, unless you accept that the common position is a necessary fiction, is that suddenly you shall find, in the very next statement that you hear, that the Final End was not as you conceived it; it is where you never thought it would be. You can then see yourself if you like over on the right with another heaven in view with the rest of mankind still holding to a mistaken hope, or, equally well metaphorically, you can see the Other in that position with his or her heaven at variance with yours. And where shall we place God? Well, Christianity gave His answer. Not Browning's 'God's in His heaven –/all's right with the world' (for that is a charming and helpful evocation of the fictive idealization), but *God on the Cross with us*, suffering the paradoxical incarnation we all painfully share, in which the Good, the True and the Beautiful never coalesce, even as we *must* have faith in them together. What immediately comes to my mind are the third movements of Sibelius's Fourth Symphony and Vaughan Williams's Fifth Symphony, both of which express ravishing 'immortal longings' which are *denied*. 'Our sweetest songs are those that tell of saddest thought' (Shelley, Ode to a Nightingale', 86).

With the Incarnation thus being so powerful a metaphor it is unsurprising that it should have had a central place in Christian ritual, in the Communion, which is both an acceptance of the god into us all as well as a reminder of the crucified Christ ('Do this in remembrance of me'). What is significant for our argument is that the symbolism of the bread and wine standing for God's body and blood in that *sacrifice* is turned into the occult conviction of transubstantiation. It is both tragic and comic that theologians should have worried so long over the 'reality' of God's 'body' and 'blood' in the bread and wine, when all that was really happening was the dramatic performance of a useful metaphor for our 'incarnation' with 'God'. They were turning a valuable fiction into a narcissistic reality – a much greater, self-deceiving, fiction.

This first interpretation of the Cross, however, could be replaced by another which is more general still. Symbols have multiple interpretations. Keep the desire from the *Summum Bonum* as represented by the arrow pointing upwards, but see it as the fictive union of all our desires that the idealization of reciprocity projects, that is, the Symbolic: then the arrow across is the Real, whether in ourselves or in the other or in its brute character outside human beings, in the tsunamis of the world. The Real, as has been argued in the Triangulation Argument, is there within our bodies and their brains just as much as in the non-human world elsewhere. The paradox is that we would not have our identities without our bodies; we would not have all the sensory and motivational experience that is the basis of our lives without those basically *non-symbolic* portions of the Real. So we are bound in paradox, for covertly the *Summum Bonum* is the place where body and soul will be reunited, according to the Christian myth of the Last Day, and paradisal *physical* joy will attend us – but that is the *jouissance* of the *Real*, the very thing that is subverting our 'hopes'. Yet we must hope for that *future* impossibility, knowing it impossible. Our constant concern in every *present* moment of our lives is thus the engagement in the great Story, in the endlessly failing and succeeding attempt to bring Symbolic and Real, Word and World, together, fraught as it is with both splendours and miseries.

It is ironic that this theory, which has a scientific basis (though its view of science is not a positivistic one; Wright, 1992c), is able to show how a paradoxical, hence, absurd stance, one plainly 'irrational', can be given a rational explanation. It has shown how the notions of faith, God (or gods), immortality and myth are not without a grounding and a value in human activity, and that therefore it is a mistake to believe that they can be wholly abandoned, especially when what they represent is still active within us. Science itself is certainly not outside this theory, for it is just as much based upon trust, however much it disguises the idealization of reciprocity with terms like 'impersonal truth' and 'objective fact'. One can cite Helmholtz, one of the nineteenth century's greatest scientists:

> Trust in lawlikeness is thus at the same time trust in the comprehensibility of the appearance of nature. While: should we presuppose that this comprehension will come to completion, that we shall be able to set forth something ultimate and finally unalterable as *the cause* of the observed alterations, then we shall call the regulative principle of our thought which impels us to this the *law of causality*. We can say that it expresses a trust in the complete *comprehensibility* of the world.
>
> (Helmholtz, 1977: 142)

That 'trust in complete comprehensibility' is no other than the idealization, the mutual paradoxical *hope* that an 'ultimate' agreement will be reached *when no such attainment is possible*. This is the – irrational – 'regulative principle' that we are bound to use.

It is to be expected, since we are dealing with absurdity, that a comic aspect of the failure of the superstitious perfect hope has often been brought to notice. A prime example is the third book of Rabelais' *Gargantua and Pantagruel* which recounts Panurge's attempts to get advice on how to find a suitable wife. The trouble is that he has a particular criterion for a wife, among many such 'ifs and buts', that he wishes to be certain of before taking the plunge. This key criterion is that, before he marries her, he wants to be *absolutely sure* that she will not make a cuckold of him. He consults a Virgilian oracle, a dream, a sibyl, a deaf-and-dumb monk, a poet, an astrologer, and the bells of Varennes – which say to him 'All will be well with you, well, very well' except when he gets near to them, when they say 'Don't marry, don't marry, don't, don't, don't, don't, don't. You'll soon be sorry, be sorry, a cuckold you'll be.' A theologian advises him to marry 'to escape the fires of concupiscence', adding that he won't be a cuckold 'if it please God'. This condition fills Panurge with hopping frustration, and he protests that he will not be able to attend God's 'privy council' to argue his case. A philosopher he meets with called 'Wordspinner' is even less use as his replies to Panurge's questions are all riddling, exactly in the same manner as Leigh Hunt's 'B' (p. 1) or Orlick's to Pip (p. 11), both of whom refused to engage in the Idealization with their partner in dialogue:

> PANURGE: Let's put the case that I'm married.
> WORDSPINNER: Where shall we put it?

A wife who makes a cuckold of you is *unfaithful* all right, but your faith in her at the moment of marriage cannot be based on certainty, no more than any other kind of faith. The risk is there; nor can you pretend that, having entered into a relationship with another, you can absolve yourself from some responsibility for what they do. Panurge was wanting not to have anything to do with that responsibility, as if one could be in a relationship and consider oneself hermetically sealed from all degree of influence upon the other. Incidentally, Rabelais was not just making an idle joke when he sent Panurge off to consult with a whole range of dealers in *superstition*. For another amusing example of the same kind, where someone tries to have the benefit of trust without the risk, see the Confidence Man's dialogue with the Barber on the subject of buying something on credit in Herman Melville's *The Confidence Man* (Melville, *The Confidence Man*, Ch. XLII).

Feuerbach repeatedly drew attention to the fact that you cannot objectify yourself without the other, so it is equally true that the other cannot objectify herself without you (Feuerbach, 1903–11: Vol. II, 17). In any case, love cannot make conditions; John Caputo puts it well:

> But to offer hospitality to the 'wholly other' is to expose yourself to a 'surprise', to being overtaken by what you did not see coming, to get more than you bargained for, since hospitality is not supposed to be a bargain, but a gift.... Conditional hospitality is as incoherent as conditional love, as loving someone but only up to a point, after which we lose interest.
> (Caputo, 2001: 162)

His metaphor of Bargain is interesting, for words have often been compared to money as was noted before (Chapter 4.4; see Cupitt, 2000: 82–3). The 'ground' of the metaphor contains curious similarities: the persons exchanging money at a commercial transaction are superficially idealizing the value of the money as the *same*, but the buyer and the seller nevertheless have a *different* estimate of the value of what it is being exchanged for, and that is common to the utterance of a statement, for speaker and hearer cannot share exactly the same understanding of it although they affect to; there is the performance of trust, and on many occasions it is real in the case where both wish to benefit both. Furthermore, the carrying out of that bargain *changes the value of the money*, for we all know that the value of our currencies change every moment according to what is being bought and sold with them. So our words, promises, laws and rules are subject to the same changes of value, and we can be as much 'surprised' by what either of them may come to mean. It is part of the game that makes us and that we make.

The field of human concern that will be our last exploration is that of the related one of nationalism and patriotism, the question of the social and political applications of the Idealization of the Reciprocity of Standpoints. The same question presents itself: what is the type of faith to be that underpins them?

4.   Nationalism and patriotism

The two dominant positions on patriotism and nationalism that have structured debate over the past two decades have been the Modernist case and that of the 'Primordialists' and 'Ethno-symbolists'.

For the Modernist, nationhood is the product of an invented ideology, one that has been developed to serve the needs of growing industrial states that required a literate and technically competent population, an organization bureaucratically centralized, and an economic and military power which could be readily expanded and deployed inside and outside its borders. 'Invented' is here used in a disparaging sense, as of Plato's 'noble lie', a modern myth to replace the apparent failure of the old religious bonds to provide the desired solidarity. The case in its many varieties is a historically causal one, the outcome of the rationalizing of the needs of emergent capitalist states in a world where ease of communication produced increasingly rapid and more extensive control.

For the Primordialist and the Ethno-symbolist, on the other hand, the nation has deeper origins, psychological, sociobiological or anthropological. They point to the ethnic group the members of which have a sense of a common history, culture and often territory. The truth of that history is likely to be to some extent fictitious but it nevertheless provides the core of group loyalties. The emotional links originally based on kinship ties become extended to the wider group. It is these cultural givens that the later developments on which the Modernists concentrate have made use of, but which pre-existed those developments. Much is made of the ceremonies, rituals, symbols and myths which, far from being parts of a 'noble lie' promulgated by an elite or a powerful class, form real constituents of the individual identities of the group's members. These symbolic acts reflect the need of the national group to achieve, maintain and protect its political independence.

There are central issues here which require philosophical exploration but which neither side has fully examined. They revolve around the relation of the individual to society, identity to collectivity, and particularly around perception, language and the theory of knowledge itself. This has been recognized: national forms of life, according to Avishai Margalit, are 'parasitic upon human beings' basic need to express themselves' (Margalit, 1997: 84). Political scientists have held themselves away from such enquiry, perhaps because it savours of the crossing of disciplinary boundaries. How often in current discussions one notices a distaste for any search for general theories of nation, ethnicity, nationality or nationalism. From Anthony Smith's warnings that, because of the complexity of the empirical issues, there is no possibility of supporting sweeping generalizations in this field (A. Smith, 1994: 392) to Ernest Gellner's assertion that there cannot be a general explanation of nationalism, only particular answers (Gellner, 1997: 95), there have been numerous such shyings away from abstraction. These are understandable caveats if one confines the scope to historical nationalism as such, but one cannot rule out the possibility that a philosophical investigation might contribute towards the comprehension of what is happening at present both academically in the world of theory and politically in the world at large. One recent philosophical study (Gilbert, 1998) limits itself to undermining the arguments of a wide variety of nationalist projects, which it does with exceptional clarity and thoroughness, but, in spite of raising key issues, not only eschews commitment to a general theory, but also openly refrains from recommending anything positive. In the academic debate it is recognized that major philosophical dilemmas lie beneath such a topic as the individual and society, so there is a disinclination to pursue them in the discourse. They are 'conundrums' the consideration of which is best left aside. Nevertheless, this absence leaves unmistakable deformations and lacunae in the texts that allow positions to be maintained that are not philosophically secure.

Yet political philosophers of the past have not scrupled to start out with arguments founded on a theory of human nature. Hobbes, notably, began with the 'motion of bodies', building up to a materialist theory of human motivation (Hobbes 1962 [1651]), Montesquieu with 'the attraction of pleasure' (Montesquieu 1989 [1748]: Vol. I, i). One can, indeed, argue that no one can engage in social and political science without some underlying assumptions about the human organism, its collective behaviour, its sensory experiences and its powers of knowing, even if those assumptions are only implicit. So it is not a straying over the disciplinary boundary of social theory if one places an argument about patriotism and nationalism in a book that explores the universality of narrative structures in our life, that sees imagination at the core of human communication. If Triangulation theory is correct, advance in the theory of patriotism and nationalism has been impeded precisely because epistemological questions have been neglected.

It is not uncommon in the literature on nationalism to find indirect acknowledgements of the 'as if'. Here is an example from Roger Scruton, writing on the family tie, that he correctly sees as an analogy for the national one:

> a transcendent bond that exists, *as it were*, 'objectively' outside the sphere of individual choice.
> (Scruton 1980: 33, my emphasis)

Note here the indirect cancellation of *absolute* faith and an acknowledgement of the 'as if' in that almost unnoticed phrase, 'as it were', and also in the inverted commas that he could not help putting around 'objectively'. But Scruton wants the faith to be a given tie. We have seen that communication displays a need to trust other members of the group, and the last section has shown that it is questionable whether at the level of everyday talk we are aware of how it is to be rendered as 'altruistic'. We asked how something *evolved* could be regarded as be *normative*? The performance requires this initial trust that enables sensory and intentional correction to go through, but it is a trust that is so second-nature that it is entered into without thought. To enter language at all we have had to engage in it whether we realized it or not and, in addition, by virtue of that entering blindly to accept the vast historical tradition that sustains it. There are, because there have to be, percepts and concepts shared by all who can understand each other, together with judgements all would make and rules of judgement which all subscribe to. If understanding is to be possible, there must be, in Strawson's phrase, 'a massive central core of human thinking which has no history' (Hollis, 1982: 75), except that to say that 'it has no history' unfortunately gives away a superstitious move, for the timelessness of something that has a historical base is, nevertheless (openly accepting the paradox), to be *imagined*, not believed in. Peter Strawson and Martin Hollis, like David Wiggins, are exhorting us, quite correctly, to maintain the common projection that most of our acts of referring pick out secure singularities. They are making the same mistake as many others, however, in not seeing the *necessary* mutual faith that is part of our method for getting a partial coinciding of our separate perspectives. Hollis's own words gave this away, for he said that all '*subscribe to*' the 'rules of judgement', which points to the human *choice* involved in their establishment. We have to see our reference to 'things' and 'persons' as 'having no history'; otherwise we could never get our differing views of the real into some sort of common harness. This is what the sharing of understanding, to which Hollis is indirectly bearing witness, really is, an effect of our social hope.

Which is why we hear so many of them, like the philosophers quoted before, uttering the exhortation, that we must *presuppose, assume* that there are objects before us, but they, like those philosophers, use 'presuppose' and 'assume' with the meaning of *unquestioningly believe*. Take Donald Davidson as an example: 'We can't even take a step towards interpretation without knowing or assuming a great deal about a speaker's beliefs' (Davidson, 1984: 196). Notice that he uses *knowing* as equivalent to *assuming*, which is the blatant error. Now how do we interpret this? Of course, we agree – yes, we have to behave *as if* we coincide in belief with our interlocutor, for we should not be able to move into even partial co-ordination unless we proceeded on this *assumption*, this hypothesis. Davidson is therefore right to insist upon the 'Principle of Charity', that we should take most of what the other says as true, but he is wrong in thinking that this provides some kind of guarantee that our agreements are somehow equivalent. To be *charitable*, after all, is to lay aside a difference that might be of moment to oneself. Our agreements are plausibly equivalent: that is, as far as our happiness goes, we have not discovered any major mismatches, but that does not mean that the personalized semantics in our own bodies could ever equate ideally to anyone else's. We have only viable, provisional constructions that by their very nature can never logically merge with those of the other.

I think it is right to bring in an *argumentum ad hominem* here. Why is it that these philosophers want to take the Idealization of Reciprocity for real? Is it disturbing to them to accept that the real is full of shocks? That human language, human science has only provisionally mapped its changing landscape? What induces this attempt to become authoritarian about the successful objectifications they are currently making? How insidiously easy it is to move from the practical performance of perfect co-reference to superstitiously believing in it, for the temptation to believe in one's absolute safety is very reassuring. But this turns a needful play – in two senses, *game* and *freedom of movement* – into bigotry. And some of those philosophers have the face to claim that such a healthy scepticism that can acknowledge the real as brute existence is subjective, idealist, and, worse, relativist, opening ethics and politics to the threat of anarchy.

The key point about faith made in the last section was that, even though we in all trust might take for granted that nothing the other understands but has not made mutually salient could be to one's own disadvantage, our social partner may in all innocence be understanding something that may either be of great danger to us or of far greater advantage than we anticipated. In addressing this problem, we brought out the central issue of faith and risk, and showed that it is by a paradoxical acceptance of that risk that faith can become an ethical one. Such a definition as the following by Adam Seligman admits the fact:

> Trust…is not only a means of negotiating risk, it implies risk (by definition, it is a means of negotiating that which is unknown).
>
> (Seligman, 1997: 63)

But I would add that it is also a means of negotiating the known, for that remains within time's arbitrary ambit of decision.

The theory presents the members of the group as being ignorant of the 'hypothetical' nature of their co-operative action. This ignorance would not matter very much if communication were guaranteed always to provide an improvement that benefited everyone equally, but, being an *evolutionary* development, it can do no such thing. The performance, successful as it has been in speeding up the rate of adaptation in the human species, does not operate to produce some kind of inevitable moral progress in which everyone is equally advantaged: if the performance is working basically at a tacit level, one cannot gauge moral worth by it. At this primitive stage the communication is hardly doing more than earlier evolutionary patterns ensured, that is, no more than a coping with the local contingencies of some evolutionary niche, and there is no security, no normativity, in that. One is faced with a human group that is behaving in communicative ways that depend on an apparent coinciding of differing referents that apes the character of what we might call a genuine human trust. Desire and fear, indeed, a wide range of emotion will be tied into that behaviour, but there will be no morality. After all, liars are unconsciously aware that there is a blind faith to undermine, even though they, as the story of the Chinese peasant showed, remain just as blind about the supposed security of even what they say.

It looks as if group solidarity is 'brute' in a double sense, a chance, natural, animal happening, and that any individual's private calculation is just as 'brute' in exactly the same way. The conclusion is bleak but morally inescapable, but the mechanical 'trust' ironically points to the only ethical possibility: it has produced the chance of an impossible process of an endless pursuit of justice and happiness that can only be maintained by a publicly conscious, mutual act of play. Morality only enters into the equation when a subject begins to get a glimmer of what is going on, when the *tacit automatic trust* begins to turn into an *active postulate of faith that does not believe in its own objective*. This is the way in which a mythification of thought, despite Terry Eagleton's fears, can have a moral foundation; he thinks that 'it demeans the people' if they are exposed to the manipulations of ideological myth (Eagleton, 1991: 12).

The postulate of faith cannot be a perfect agreement that will inevitably lead to justice and happiness for both individual and group: as we have seen, it is a postulate that never expects the perfection it postulates to be finally realized. This is not what the evolved 'trust' aims at, if it could be said to aim at anything. But this is, as we have seen, just how language works: the fact that evidence never turns into pure information is what determined the co-ordination process in the first place. One way of saying it is that we have to behave as if evidence will turn into information, while knowing perfectly well that it never can. The meaningless evidence of the senses can never provide propositional information: a footprint a detective uses as a clue is not a *statement* of truth. If a proposition is the dynamic game of transformation that two have to play, nothing in the Real can be playing it. It would be like saying that the Real is telling us a story. Of course, people often use the Story as a metaphor about clues – Holmes could say to Watson, 'Now, Watson, what story is this footprint telling us?', but it would be Holmes who was telling the story, not some shapes in the soil nor the equally meaningless Real sensings in the heads of Holmes and Watson that were structurally isomorphic to certain regions of energy and mass outside them.

It has been argued that, although we pick up the social rules that guide our community in the very shaping of our individuality, we cannot act as moral beings until we become 'self-reflective', until there is a 'personal resonance' which is not merely a 'self-fulfilment', but a 'situated freedom' (Taylor, 1989: 510, 515). Such an oxymoron as 'situated freedom' seems to have an explanation under the present hypothesis. When in the statements of language we accept a correction from another subject, we hopefully acknowledge that before the correction we had to a degree been 'determined', since our willed actions concealed a self-defeating misunderstanding of a concept, of a 'term'. When we are ourselves the corrector, we seem to have discovered a new authority and a new freedom simultaneously. In both positions in a communication, Speaker or Hearer, we have to hold to the 'tradition' of language in order to effect its transformation, that is, to use the linguist's terms again, to play at being changelessly synchronic in order to be dynamically diachronic. The result, however, cannot be safely brought philosophically within the ambit of either the received authoritarian wisdom or the rebellious challenge to that 'wisdom'.

In discussing comedy and tragedy in the last section we brought out the darker side of the case, for the practical success of that 'authority' and 'freedom' is not entailed. A subject, deeply socialized to the point that its motivations have made a self closely linked by faith and loyalty to the patterns of behaviour in its society, can discover a new interpretation already implicit in its behaviour which contradicts its other most strongly held commitments. If some reconciliation can be made, the outcome would have a comic character, the sufferer being able to laugh at his own 'self-deception'. If not, it would be a *tragic* situation, the self torn inwardly by rival interpretations of itself, neither of which yield to adjustment, which, indeed, may point to outcomes in action utterly incompatible with each other. Othello is a good example of someone committed to the nation of Venice to the point where his identification with it becomes so extreme that he takes the threat of his wife's adultery as a moment in which he must adhere with like extremity to the courtly honour code of his time, taken to be definitive of a *Venetian* gentleman's identity. He did not even become fully self-aware of the cause of his predicament, only finally of the effects of the ambiguity that divided him. All his experience was subject to a doubled categorization. Here is a further proof of the knowledge-less condition of bodily experience, for only such experience could accept *two apparently equally valuable but opposing categorizations at the same time*. In the extreme cases of tragedy no resolution is possible: one would have to brainwash the person to erase the rival intentions. The risk is greater than we would like to admit.

Such unhappy identification can take other forms. Identities under threat endeavour to turn the faith of performance into a superstitious certainty, which turns their group into a guarantor of security, beyond the mutual correction that the faith exists to allow. The authority of received knowledge is transformed into an authoritarian conviction, driven by a motivation that is permitted a rabid satisfaction. It shores itself up by intensifying the epistemic boundaries of the group, ethnic and territorial, sustaining the comfort of a safe identity through oppressing those outside the national and cultural boundaries (Žižek, 1989: 175–8).

One may find here the explanation of the difference between liberal and illiberal nationalisms (Kymlicka, 1997: 63). It is therefore in part correct with the Modernists in the nationalism debate to fear the 'invention' turning into superstitious illusion (Miller, 1995: 32) but mistaken to think on that count that non-superstitious mythical imagining is not a part of all community. The evolutionary advantage of the performance of perfect agreement is to allow correction of that agreement; this calls for nations that are able sometimes to experience shame as definitive of their identity (Anderson, 1999). Too often two groups appear: those who are so psychologically over-secure they must take the myths, rituals and ceremonies as if they were representative of a final truth; and those in power who are cynically prepared to capitalize upon this pathological excess. The fascist treats the logical timelessness of the faith as if it were real, so that it becomes a narcotic at once stimulating and stupefying: but, as Ronald Jacobs and Philip Smith have argued, *there is no narrative in extreme nationalism* since it eschews irony in self-reflection both at personal and national level (Jacobs and Smith, 1997: 68–9; see also Connolly, 1992: 141). Thinking of Yeats's words,

> The best lack all conviction, while the worst
> Are full of passionate intensity
> (W. B. Yeats. 'The Second Coming', ll. 7–8; Yeats, 1952: 211)

what is to be said is that, ironically, we must lack 'conviction' and replace it with faith, for it is rather the worst who are full of pathological conviction, hence, their 'passionate intensity'. Mention must be made of the Stalinist distortion, in which neither the cynical elite nor the cowed populace believe the myth, but both go through the motions of its *non*-corrigible performance (Žižek, 1989: 197).

If in the nationalism discussion we are 'not to underestimate the importance of aesthetic considerations' (A. Smith 1991: 162), the way to engage
with symbolic acts is to perform them with all the seriousness of children
who know how to play well, that is, with a grave concentration that at no
point falls into belief and which thus facilitates the transformation. This is
how a subject must cope with the 'duality of structure' that Anthony
Giddens says ties the social agent to the social structure of which he or she
is member (Giddens, 1977: 121); here we see it as a narrative structure.

What was said earlier about Pascal's recommendation as regards religion is
worth repeating in this political context: he said that it would be wise to
perform the pious rites and ceremonies in the hope that religious belief
would come (Pascal, 1947 [1670]: 65–9): what this theory recommends, you
will recall, is that we perform the rites and ceremonies, both national and
religious, while remaining perfectly aware that belief will *never* come. That
this is not the Stalinist double-deception is shown by the fact that the
purpose of the performance is not to rigidify the myth or overawe the populace
but to facilitate its adaptive change through all being aware that they are
playing. It echoes the poet Alice Meynell's conviction that true religion was
nothing but 'the Way' and never 'the Goal' (Meynell, 1923: 64). The 'brute'
quality of both 'individual' and 'group' can only be escaped through the
entrance into the moral play, with the open-eyed awareness by everyone that
nothing 'natural', bodily or social, can either warrant or produce the longed-for
ideal. At the moment both religious and patriotic rites are performed with a
kind of embarrassed awkwardness, as if the performers are saying 'We do
patriotically believe, but this flummery is so *passé*' (in England the word
'flummery' has become the word of choice to describe any public ritual that
employs any aesthetic means, such as barristers' and judges' wigs). The
feebleness of the performance gives an abiding impression that the participants
do not in fact believe what they are doing, hence the growth of cynicism,
the decline of church attendance. But to be human is to be as a little child –
when playing. We do need grand ceremonies – and 'grand narratives' – in
which *we do not believe* and yet we must play openly with enthusiasm.
Music, art, drama must take on a public role, and money must be spent on
obtaining the best aesthetic results.

If all are to be in the secret of the Noble Lie as a lie, then there must be
occasions when we are 'off-stage', when the myths and rituals can be
subjected to criticism, to satire, to 'offensive' attack. None of this should disturb
the seriousness of the play on 'on-stage' occasions. Children can step in and
out of play without a hitch. We need a Saturnalia, not merely as a relief
from the demands of the Symbolic Order, for in that form it too easily in
the past became part of a ruling ideology, an Ignoble Lie in Plato's fashion
that allowed a letting-off of steam, but as a moment for a detached consideration, aimed at a hopeful improvement. Hence, those who protest that attacks
on religious belief are automatically 'blasphemy', are grossly superstitious,

unable to play seriously. Of course, those who use a religious identification in someone else as a means whereby in racist fashion to shore up their identity are as guilty of superstition.

We should all be ready to play, and a start can be made in the schools, for what they signally lack is the aesthetic support for the myths that we need to revive. How can you expect that children will take up a British identity if we do not play it together? How much less disaffection and delinquency among the young would there be if the Story gave them a grounding for their identity that frankly confessed its risk? The fact that so many feel embarrassed is a very bad symptom of the inability to play in the way that they did when they were younger. What children do naturally, that is, pretend without believing, just needs to be kept up. Our schools will not then seem like Wordsworthian prisonhouses. It is no use the Conservative Party thinking that patriotism will be encouraged by a little history teaching about Nelson: if children took part in a play about him (one that brought out his moral struggles), then the result might be different. But none of the political parties at the moment could see him as one who acted a 'leading male part'. Let school 'uniforms' become costumes, fine ones, that meant something symbolically, and let the teachers wear some too, to indicate that respect is due to them that is *not* conferred by the costume, but by their place in the drama of society. For children today, such articles as trainers consciously symbolize the false values of commerce. Do not imagine for a moment that adults being 'sensible' enough to despise specific symbolic public signs is harmless and has no effect on the young, who unconsciously clamour for symbol: the vacuum is soon filled up with superstitious nonsense. I often think that teachers lost a little something of their awe and their powers of discipline when, under late-Enlightenment pressure, academic gowns were officially considered 'old-fashioned' and 'authoritarian'.

Attitudes to Santa Claus are revealing in this respect. Most children are well aware by the time they are five or six that Santa Claus is a performance, but they go along with it, as do many parents. Its symbolic significance renders 'him' too morally valuable to abandon. The belief in 'him' is actively performed by parents and children who *both* know it is a healthy act of theatre. Those who actually do try to go on deceiving their children are like those in religion and nationhood who must still hold on to their superstitious aspects instead of realizing their valuable ones, and they are thus likely to turn their children into cynics. Just as the sensible among us do not want to give up Santa Claus while we know he is just a pretence because we know that pretence makes a real contribution to what Christmas symbolizes, so too 'God' and the 'Nation' cannot be given up, because they represent real aspects of our social and moral life. At the moment there are many young people who are cynical about both precisely because they have detected the element of superstition within many who profess religion and patriotism, and no doubt a considerable number who are caught up into cults religious and political by the false reassurance of such superstition.

The national faith is thus not *historically primordial* but *epistemologically immediate*. There has always been an 'invention' and thus one cannot reject it on the ground that there is always a reaching back into the ethnic past (Hutchinson, 1994: 26). What has caused confusion in the nationalism debate is the fact that the present faith makes use of the past identity of the group. Of course, we 'feel as if they [the imagined histories] had always existed' (Billig, 1995: 25), but this is hardly surprising since the mutual performance accords *logical timelessness* to the meaning of all words by which we refer to any 'entities', which includes ourselves, our group and its homeland. Nations are groups of people 'who *share stories* about the world' (S. Clark, 1996: 68, my emphasis). Since the mutual game of the nation does itself have a history and a traditional territorial place, how easy it is to enhance that *past* 'rootedness' (to the point of its being a 'golden age') with the actuality of the *present* transcendent faith, and equally with its future utopian projections. However, Herder was right to say myths are not delusions, and, anticipating Piaget, that language was matter of assimilation and reappraisal, out of which conflict strengthened collectivities (Herder, 1969: 27, 23). Is not a true patriotism a social commitment that allows for Ferdinand Schiller's 'clashes of postulates', that confronts the possibility of serious discord with those one loves?

One can also see why Hobbes, Locke and Rousseau were led to propound theories of a 'social contract', for the faith has been there from the beginning of human speech, existing as an essential for selves to come into being – they did not precede it. One can here concede to the conservative view that society is not a temporary contract: it is an inescapable, evolved structure of co-operation, but it does not of itself bless either (for the right wing) public solidarity, or (for the left) private insight. Progress is not to be ensured with either nostrum: a pure authority is not with authorities or tyrants, nor a pure freedom with revolutionaries or criminals. One can see why Hobbes' view of the human individual is so grossly distorted, for he sees the individual as rigidly separate and unique, his selfhood carefully shored up with and by his property. A genuine faith is one that accepts the inevitability of risk to the 'each-otherish' self. The only way to deal with the salutary shocks and unequivocal terrors of contingency of the Real is to be brave enough to accept that, since, narrative that has made you   by those who knew how to exist in a story – you too must face the risk of comedy and tragedy. Should this theory turn out to be right, it would be better if we all knew it especially when we do face each other in conflict.

So, if it should be the case that a tacit form of 'faith' is the basis of human speech, sociation and identity, this still provides no certain deliverance for either group or individual. If there is no pure truth, there is no pure deceit: knowledge remains a co-operative venture with no unchangeable national or personal identity to be relied upon. Nevertheless, it would be wise to enact the faith knowingly, that is, in all dramatic seriousness project the perfect coincidence of our wills and world while remaining ready for the shocks from the real in ourselves, in the other, and in nature at large. This drama is myth as 'a lived reality' in Victor Turner's view, wherein we 'grow through anti-structure and conserve through structure' (Turner, 1974: 298), another indirect specification of what the Statement is. From the point of view of this theory, ideology is an essential part of community. The existing 'structure', 'tradition', the synchrony, does have a real aspect just as a theatrical play has a real aspect, but our adhering to the tradition remains as that of involved *actors* joined in the postulation of an ever-receding point of hope. The maintenance of tradition that Hans-Georg Gadamer has insisted upon (Gadamer, 1975: 245) expresses the need to uphold the 'naïve and unreflecting' faith, as Rommetveit described it, but Gadamer also claimed that 'an element of rule-free genius [is] always at work' (Gadamer, 1975: 166) – even though you will see from the point of view of this theory that that word 'genius' is overly optimistic. At least, with this stance we will be withheld from attributing occult 'evil' to those whose inward fears have made them literalize into consciousness either, on the right, the 'authority' of the imagined convergence or, on the left, the 'freedom' of the bodily drive. If the faith is not to be in any finality, the social solidarity it produces will then be permeable, not only between members of the same nation but across nations, as Mazzini wished (1907 [1858]), and the solidarity of the identity of each ego within those nations will be just as permeable. In this way the fear that Martha Nussbaum has that patriotism can only turn into nationalism can be shown to be unjustified (Nussbaum, 1996). As Frantz Fanon says, 'National consciousness, which is not nationalism, is the only thing that will give us an international dimension' (Fanon, 1967: 199)

Therefore, there is support here for the Ethno-symbolist, for, in spite of Max Weber's pessimism regarding a 'disenchanted' objective world, by the present argument the objective world has never ceased to be 'enchanted', the reason being that it is by mutual acts of imagination that we maintain it. As has just been noted, we live in an only 'possible world' constructed out of a dangerous Real. Myths, with their own narratives, have performed what we are performing. The arts – drama, music, dance, painting, sculpture, architecture – have all enacted the transformations at the centre of knowing. Of course, it may be right in the wake of Plato for the modernist Ernest Gellner to suspect the 'inventions' of those who have cynically manipulated the myth from Numa Pompilius onwards, but utterly misguided to dismiss it as something *of itself* suspicious and superfluous. We need 'grand narratives', grand only when we take them as narratives. Classical modernists have no conception of nations as logically timeless in the social performance; hence, it is easy for them to mock at the idea of nations invented as existing before time. But the only 'noble lie' is to be one in *which all are in on the secret*, not as a lie to be encouraged for selfish reasons by a cynically non-believing elite in order to keep the superstitious plebeians in their place as Plato, Spinoza and Scruton recommend. It implies that we should therefore retain symbolic foci of our social groupings as long as we take them only as real in so far as the communal dramatic projection of them is itself a real and needful act. To put it another way, it is vital that we act together on the *supposition* of a utopian hope without ever believing it achievable. Ideology and utopia thus both have an essential part *to play* in our human life.

To give one particular example. It is, in my view, absolutely vital that a nation have a symbolic focus, a monarch or a *non*-executive president. It will be as with God, a *focus imaginarius*, but it must be distinct from the executive power, which is only concerned with achievable matters within a short time-frame, matters of current utility, one might say. But since, according to this argument, the *focus imaginarius* should have an unreal, 'eternal' point of aspiration, it must *simultaneously* and *paradoxically* represent the hope of unity that never can be achieved. This fictive, mythical status will attract to it the aura of the true faith that accepts risk. What is detrimental in such an arrangement is that loyalty to it will turn superstitious. The monarch will be seen as actually possessing a godlike position, and the state will have begun its decline, as when Octavius Caesar effectively put an end to the Roman Republic by declaring himself the divine Augustus. The 'divine right' of the monarch will be unconsciously hypostatized instead of being knowingly hypothesized. That a 'divination' in Britain of our present queen is performed by some is indicated by the little true story that a Member of Parliament was rebuked by a court official for referring to the Queen at a formal occasion as 'the leading lady'. But this is precisely how we, as serious players, should see her in order to give her a proper loyalty. Nor should we see it as unpatriotic, when we are off-stage, to see her satirized, for she is only the player of the role – there is no doubt that the monarchy as a role could be improved (for example, by divesting it of its gross wealth) and that the current player might on occasions receive advice on how to play it. To believe that the aura of dignity about her is real *outside the play we are playing* is to fall into superstition. So, a word of advice to Australia: if your next vote for a republic is successful, do not make the gross error of having an *executive* president; and one to France, Russia, the USA, and all the Asian, African and South American republics, provide yourself with one as soon as possible. Take Spain, Germany, Eire, Sweden, Denmark, and Norway as good models in this regard. The *focus imaginarius* has a real part to play. When a Russian non-executive president can actually find satirical attacks on him on prime-time television as funny as many of the audience do, then Russia will have become a real democracy. When Sikhs and Christians in Britain can see plays with 'blasphemous' scenes in them without regarding them as 'offensive' attacks on their identity, then Britain too will be a real democracy.

So the scope of Triangulation theory is very wide. Should the implications be as we have seen, we have clarifications of the nature of perception, know-ledge, language and its figures, narrative (embracing comedy and tragedy), the relation of structure and agency in social theory, patriotism and religion. The reaction of one philosopher, Peter Hare, on taking this in was 'It can't be that simple.' It was at that moment that I gained some confidence in the theory, for it brought home to me precisely why it has escaped notice so long: if, in order to obtain a rough co-reference, we have to behave as if we already have a perfect one, to bring to everyone's notice this hidden ploy is deeply disturbing, since it implies a risk in everything we have identified and so looks like the most extreme scepticism. On the contrary, what it points to is the need for the faith that accepts risk.

The foregoing has been an explanation of the cause of the solidarity that the Primordialist attests to, indeed, solidarity of any kind, on the left as well as the right. The 'story' here began with a scientific possibility. Its conclusion has been reached through finding that, if that possibility were the case, what was implied, as part of the scope of the theory, was that the structure of narrative would be therefore built into both the theory of the nation and that of the person. It relies on the epistemological nature of play, which in turn is based on the fundamental distinction between knowledge-less sensory experience and the motivated perceptual system that sustains all learning. In finding a kind of involuntary mutual 'hypothesis' as the method produced through the evolution of both mind and communication, the recommendation has been to bring this into the open, to make the 'lie' noble by *everyone* knowingly telling it.

The step from the evolved to the normative was that of turning the unthought reliance on the blind faith into a deliberate performance of it as an open but unrealizable postulate, as Royce insisted, that is, all members of the group aware of its being based on a faith without a final goal, a faith, as Meynell put it, purely in 'the Way'. It also matches Kierkegaard's move from the 'ethical' to the 'religious' (see Slavoj Žižek on this move, 1999: 211–12, 321–2). This public decision to enact a hypothesis, literally to perform a myth with the aim of continually narrating it differently, requires both courage and dramatic imagination. It is the only way to keep law and freedom together, by acknowledging that they will never converge. It is neither a complacent reiteration of what has already been elicited from the real nor an impatient dismissal of past tradition, for both of those condemn themselves to be lost in a pure pretence.

This view is not a new one, evidenced by the large number of supporting voices from the past that have been quoted, and yet it may come to your ears as strangely radical. Why is it that no one else wants to say it? That impression of strangeness is itself a clue to the fact that, because faith is at the core of our sociation and our selfhood, our very humanness, the argument has been discountenanced and even ignored because it seems to challenge faith. So superstition has been the very cause of its being overlooked: the fear is too great, as in the case of the boy in Freud's account who was dismissive of fairy tales. The fact that we are involved in a huge make-believe about timeless singularities is rejected as weird, counter-intuitive, even treacherous, but I am putting it to you that those reactions are fearful, timid, cowardly, like the timidity of those who cannot act on the stage because of a supposed threat to their self-hood. It is a response that indicates a failure of true faith. Besides, you already engage in the play every time you utter or understand a statement. So that boy should not be your model, but the child who can play seriously without getting lost in it.

> 'And a little child shall lead them.'
> (Isaiah, xi. 6)

The two prejudices I have mentioned several times, the fear of relativism and that of the fictive, are very powerful, since they reflect the complacency of all of us in the face of the consoling 'reality' of things and persons. Theodor Adorno acknowledged the link between the two prejudices at the same time as getting close to Schutz and Rommetveit's 'Idealization of Reciprocity of Standpoints':

> The un-naïve thinker knows how far he remains from the object of his thinking, and yet *he must always talk as if he had it entirely*. This brings us to the point of *clowning*.
> (Adorno, 1973: 14, my emphasis)

The over-earnest rationalist has already rejected this idea of performing religion and nationhood: to quote one of them, Baron d'Holbach, an actual Enlightenment philosopher:

> A vigilant, virtuous, enlightened and just government which seeks the public good *in good faith*, has no need of fables, or lies for governing reasonable subjects.
> (d'Holbach, 1966: vol. I, 347, my emphasis)

But he is already doing what he rejects, for, through the very act of making a statement, in mutually projecting the certainty of our knowledge of all things and persons, he is already performing that trust-without-a-final-reward, that myth-without-its-ground. This philosophy is not so radical as it may appear to be. In addition, any who are tempted to say with Plato that the 'common people' could never swallow such aesthetic subtleties, are not only forgetting the readiness of the common people to join in play and ritual, but also are falling into the convenient elitist error of believing that the truth lies with the 'educated', the 'cultured' and the existing 'authorities' (an insidiously misleading metonym). If language is essentially a corrective system, anyone has the right to offer his or her correction for consideration. This (democratic) theory allows for authoritative adjustments of the truth from anybody, any *body*. This makes an insistence upon identity cards a gross act of *distrust in the people*. I noted earlier that what goes on in parliaments is paradoxical, for there they are altering laws – strictly an illegal act. Anyone who rejects this theory must ask for parliament to be closed down on the ground of the paradoxical behaviour that appears to make up most of its activities.

One immediate practical consequence for Britain of adopting the philosophy here would be for England to give up the superstitious fear that prevents it from yielding its central place in the 'United Kingdom'. England should withdraw to a parliament of its own for all domestic issues (as Scotland has already done), and Wales should be given equal place. There could still be a federal parliament for non-domestic issues, and that could be held alternately in Edinburgh, Cardiff and London in order to emphasize the fact that England was no longer some kind of shrunken imperial leader of British nations. The 'United Kingdom' as at present constituted is still a run-down version of the British Empire. Such an act of humility on the part of England – an admission of the *equality* of the nations of Britain – would no doubt aid greatly in the settling of the Northern Ireland problem. It would also solve at one stroke the problem of the 'West Lothian' question, the anomaly of Scottish MPs' voting on specifically English issues, and also have the advantage of sidestepping John Prescott's hopeless policy of trying to make regions of England work separately *without any power* (the electorate of the north-east voted sensibly in 2004 when they rejected his toothless proposals). The Labour Party clearly does not understand what a proper patriotism is since, fearful of losing the votes of the superstitious readers of *The Sun*, it is still amazingly and blindly following the old imperialistic dream. It is not without significance that, when considering reform of the honours system, New Labour could not bring itself to give up the 'Order of the *British Empire*'.

What Slavoj Žižek has called 'the obscene superego' is at work in both extreme left and right (Žižek, 1991: 141–53), a release of *jouissance* that gives itself a risk-free objective law to countenance its destructive libidinous acts. Those who commanded the massacres in Cambodia, Bosnia, Rwanda, East Timor and Darfur, and, too, the football hooligan, the nail-bomber who chooses Pakistanis, blacks and homosexuals as his victims, the vigilante who hurls bricks through the windows of the paedophile (and the windows of the paediatrician), the extreme nationalist in Northern Ireland who jeers and throws missiles at four-year-old Catholics, the 'Real IRA' Omagh bombers, the Hindu who demolishes the mosque, the Taliban Muslims who ordered the destruction of the Buddha statues, the Palestinian suicide-bomber, the Israeli Jew who calls for the ethnic cleansing of all 'Zion' in the name of 'security', the anti-Semite, the anti-abortionist who assassinates doctors who perform abortions, the haters of asylum-seekers and gypsy travellers – are all *superstitious*. They are fearful of the risk of identity. These fundamentalists are *too secure*, blinded by their *jouissance*. The great error has been superstition all along and we have not seen it. In a letter to *The Times* recently on the subject of students taking amulets, soft toys and astrological trinkets into examinations, the writer recounted how, forty years before, her headmistress, having found a pupil doing just that, had called all examinees into the whole-school assembly in order to give them an admonitory sermon on superstition. It is a tiny but significant clue that few headteachers today, if any, would dream of doing such a thing – the worse for us.

We have to act the myth, not allow it to act upon us. Those who have tried to banish the myth, cannot succeed; the old-rationalist endeavour to suppress or ignore it only produces corrupt forms like fascism because the poetic nature of our living will not go away. Provide the vulnerable children in our schools with no myth to act and you find them not merely with amulets, but with Mohican haircuts, tattoos, and rings through their noses, encouraged by commercial media that are quick to capitalize on superstition, so that they become all the more ready to be animal-rights terrorists at one end of the political spectrum or members of the BNP at the other. The myth, whether patriotic commitment or religious belief, must be entered into openly, aware of its curative fictive nature. There is no getting away from symbolism: the Prime Minister may wear what appears to be a ordinary suit but yet he sits at the front in parliament – why *at the front*? And recall the Labour government's fuss over the wearing by groups of youths of baseball caps and anoraks with hoods; it is keenly ironic that haters of 'flummery' should nevertheless find a challenging use of symbol to confer identity highly significant. The same inconsistency showed up at the same time in the proposal by the Home Office minister Hazel Blears that youths on community service should wear bright orange 'uniforms' in order to shame them.

Evidence is not *information*, the *existent* is not the *objective*: knowledge is merely our hopeful projection upon the existent, our current assessment of the evidence as indicating what we should do in the future and have done in the past with the external world, with others and with our 'selves'. The solution is to import the aesthetic into the ethical, which, besides providing a protection against paralysing the narrative of human life, enables and demands a full recognition of the place of tragedy and comedy, a common courageous acceptance of the risk of play. This is what a true faith in a nation and the identities within it has always been and still is, and, if we work in the spirit of Mazzini, we could then carry that performance to the level of the comity of nations.

A child of five would understand this. Send somebody to fetch a child of five.

(Groucho Marx)

References

Abbott, H. Porter (2002) *The Cambridge Introduction to Narrative*. Cambridge: Cambridge University Press.

Adair, Gilbert (1984) *Alice through the Needle's Eye*. London: Macmillan.

Adorno, Theodor W. (1973) *Negative Dialectics*. Trans. E. B. Ashton. New York: Continuum.

Aesop (1971 [6th century BC]) *Fables of Aesop*. Trans. S. A. Handford. Harmondsworth: Penguin Books.

Ahlberg, Janet and Allan Ahlberg (1982) *The Ha Ha Bonk Book*. Harmondsworth: Puffin Books.

Aitchison, Jean (1996) *The Seeds of Speech: Language Origin and Evolution*. Cambridge: Cambridge University Press.

Allix, Louis (2004) *Perception et réalité: essai sur la nature du visible*. Paris: CNRS Éditions.

Alroy, Daniel (1995) 'Inner Light'. *Synthèse*, 104: 147–60.

Alston, William P. (1991) *Perceiving God: the Epistemology of Religious Experience*. Ithaca and London: Cornell University Press.

Alston, William P. (1993) *The Reliability of Sense Perception*. Ithaca and London: Cornell University Press.

Alston, William P. (1995) 'Realism and the Christian Faith', *International Journal for the Philosophy of Religion*, 38: 1–3, 37–60.

Anderson, Benedict (1999) 'Indonesian Nationalism Today and in the Future'. *New Left Review* 235: 3–17.

Archer, Margaret (1995) *Realist Social Theory: the Morphogenetic Approach*. Cambridge: Cambridge University Press.

Attardo, Salvatore (1994) *Linguistic Theories of Humor*. Berlin and New York: Mouton de Gruyter.

Austen, Jane (1960 [1816]) *Emma*. London: Oxford University Press.

Austin, J. L. (1975) *How to Do Things with Words*. Ed. J. O. Urmson and M. Sbisà. Oxford: Clarendon Press.

Austin, J. L. (1976 [1962]) *Sense and Sensibilia*. Ed. G. J. Warnock. Oxford: Oxford University Press.

Badham Paul (1993) 'The Religious Necessity of Realism', in Joseph Runzo (ed.), *Is God Real?* Basingstoke: Macmillan, pp. 183–92.

Bailey, J. O. (1970) *The Poetry of Thomas Hardy: a Handbook and Commentary*. Chapel Hill, North Carolina: University of North Carolina Press.

Bal, Mieke (1985) *Narratology*. Toronto and London: Toronto University Press.

Barthes, Roland (1977) *Image-Music-Text*. Trans. Stephen Heath. London: Fontana/Collins.

Bates, Catherine (1999) *Play in a Godless World*. London: Open Gate Press.

Bateson, Gregory (1978) *Steps to an Ecology of Mind*. London: Paladin.

Baudrillard, Jean (1988) 'Simulacra and Simulations', in Mark Poster (ed.), *Jean Baudrillard: Selected Writings*. Cambridge and Palo Alto: Polity Press and Stanford University Press.

Bentham, Jeremy (1961 [1789]) *An Introduction to the Principles of Morals and Legislation*, in *The Utilitarians*. Garden City, New York: Dolphin Books, pp. 1–398.

Benveniste, Émile (1939) 'Nature de signe linguistique', *Acta Linguistica*, 1: 23–9.

Benveniste, Émile (1971) *Problems in General Linguistics*. Trans. Mary Elizabeth Meek. Coral Gables, Florida: University of Miami Press.

Ben Ze'ev, Aaron (1989) 'Explaining the Subject–Object Relation in Perception', *Social Research*, 56: 511–14.

Berkeley, George (1963 [1710]) *A Treatise concerning the Principles of Human Knowledge*, in *A New Theory of Vision and Other Writings*. London: Dent, pp. 87–195.

Berman, Morris (1981) *The Reenchantment of the World*. Ithaca and London: Cornell University Press.

Bernadete, J. A. (1964) *Infinity: an Essay in Metaphysics*. Oxford: Clarendon Press.

Bernstein, Leonard (1994) *West Side Story*. New York and London: Jalni Publications, Inc. and Boosey and Hawkes.

Bettelheim, Bruno (1976) *The Uses of Enchantment: the Meaning and Importance of Fairy Tales*. New York: Alfred A. Knopf.

Bhaskar, Roy (1978) *A Realist Theory of Science*. Sussex: Harvester.

Billig, Michael (1995) *Banal Nationalism*. London: Sage Publications.

Bineham, Jeffrey L. (1990) 'The Cartesian Anxiety in Epistemic Rhetoric: an Assessment of the Literature', *Philosophy and Rhetoric*, 23/1: 43–62.

Bitzer, Lloyd F. (1971) 'The Rhetorical Situation', in Richard L. Johannesen (ed.), *Contemporary Theories of Rhetoric: Selected Readings*. New York: Harper and Row, pp. 381–93.

Bitzer, Lloyd F. (1980) 'Bitzer on Tompkins (and Patton)', *Quarterly Journal of Speech*, 66: 90–3.

Blackburn, Simon (1984) *Spreading the Word: Groundings in the Philosophy of Language*. Oxford: Clarendon Press.

Blanchot, Maurice (1993) *The Infinite Conversation*. Trans. S. Hanson. Minneapolis: University of Minnesota Press.

Blanshard, Brand (1974) *Reason and Belief*. London: George Allen & Unwin.

Boring, E. G. (1942) *Sensation and Perception in the History of Experimental Psychology*. New York: Appleton-Century-Crofts.

Bradley, F. H. (1969 [1897]) *Appearance and Reality: a Metaphysical Essay*. London and Oxford: Oxford University Press.

Braithwaite, R. B. (1971) 'An Empiricist's View of the Nature of Religious Belief', in Basil Mitchell (ed.), *The Philosophy of Religion*. Oxford: Oxford University Press, pp. 72–91.

Brakel, J. van (1992), 'Natural Kinds and Manifest Forms of Life', paper presented at the Congress of the Schweizerische Gesellschaft für Logik und Philosophie der Wissenschaften, May.

Brandom, Robert B. (1994) *Making it Explicit: Reasoning, Representing, and Discursive Commitment*. Cambridge, Mass.: Harvard University Press.

Breuilly, John (1996) 'Approaches to Nationalism', in Gopal Balakrishnan (ed.), *Mapping the Nation*. London: Verso, pp. 146–74.

Brewer, Bill (1999) *Perception and Reason*. Oxford: Clarendon Press.

Brooks, Peter (1984) *Reading for the Plot: Design and Intention in Narrative*. Oxford: Clarendon Press.

Brown, Richard H. (1983) 'Theories of Rhetoric and the Rhetorics of Theory: Toward a Political Phenomenology of Sociological Truth', *Social Research*, 50/1: 126–57.

Brown, Richard H. (1987) *Society as Text: Essays on Rhetoric, Reason and Reality*. Chicago and London: University of Chicago Press, 1987.

Brummett, Barry (1976): 'Some Implications of "Process" or "Intersubjectivity": Postmodern Rhetoric', *Philosophy and Rhetoric*, 9/1: 21–51.

Brummett, Barry (1982) 'On to Rhetorical Relativism', *Quarterly Journal of Speech*, 68: 425–37.

Bruner, Jerome (1960) 'Myth and Identity', in Henry A. Murray (ed.), *Myth and Mythmaking*. New York: George Braziller.

Bruner, Jerome (1990) *Acts of Meaning*. Cambridge, Mass.: Harvard University Press.

Bultmann, Rudolf (1958) *Jesus Christ and Mythology*. New York: Charles Scribner's Sons.

Burke, Kenneth (1957) 'Antony on Behalf of the Play', in *The Philosophy of Literary Form: Studies in Symbolic Action*. New York: Vintage Books.

Burke, Kenneth (1962) *A Grammar of Motives*, and *A Rhetoric of Motives*. Cleveland and New York: Meridian Books.

Butler, Joseph (1970 [1726]) 'Preface', in T. A. Roberts (ed.), *Butler's Fifteen Sermons Preached at the Rolls Chapel; and A Dissertation of the Nature of Virtue*. London: SPCK, pp. 2–16.

Caird, Edward (1885) *The Social Philosophy and Religion of Comte*. Glasgow: James Maclehose and Sons.

Calhoun, Craig (1997) *Nationalism*. Buckingham: Open University Press.

Campbell, John (2002) *Reference and Consciousness*. Oxford: Clarendon Press.

Caputo, John D. (2001) 'Messianic Postmodernism', in D. Z. Phillips and Timothy Tessin (eds), *Philosophy of Religion in the Twenty-First Century*. Basingstoke: Palgrave Macmillan, pp. 153–66.

Carlyle, Thomas (2000 [1833–4]) *Sartor Resartus*. Ed. Rodger L. Tarr and Mark Engel. Berkeley: University of California Press.

Carroll, Lewis (Dodgson, Charles) (1940 [1889]) 'What the Tortoise Said to Achilles', in *The Complete Works of Lewis Carroll*. London: Nonesuch Press, pp. 1104–8.

Case, Thomas (1888) *Physical Realism, being an Analytical Philosophy from the Physical Objects of Science to the Physical Data of Sense*. London: Longmans Green.

Cassirer, Ernst (1944) *An Essay on Man: an Introduction to the Philosophy of Human Culture*. New Haven and London: Yale University Press.

Cassirer, Ernst (1946) *Language and Myth*. New York: Dover Publications.

Cassirer, Ernst (1977 [1955]) *The Philosophy of Symbolic Forms: Vol. 2, Mythical Thought*. New Haven and London: Yale University Press.

Castoriadis, Cornelius (1987) *The Imaginary Constitution of Society*. Cambridge: Polity Press.

Cherwitz, Richard A. and Croasmun, Earl (1982) 'Beyond Rhetorical Relativism'. *Quarterly Journal of Speech*, 68/1: 1–16.

Cherwitz, Richard A. and Hikins, James W. (1986) *Communication and Knowledge: an Investigation in Rhetorical Epistemology*. Columbia, South Carolina: University of South Carolina Press.

Cherwitz, Richard A. and Hikins, James W. (2000) 'Climbing the Academic Ladder', *Quarterly Journal of Speech*, 86/4: 375–85.

Chisholm, Roderick (1954) 'Sellars' "Critical Realism" ', *Philosophy and Phenomenological Research*, 15/1: 33–47.

Cicourel, Aaron V. (1971) 'The Acquisition of Social Structure', in Jack D. Douglas (ed.), *Understanding Everyday Life*. London: Routledge & Kegan Paul.

Clark, Romane (1982) 'Sensibility and Understanding', *The Monist*, 65: 350–64.

Clark, Michael (2002) *Paradoxes from A to Z*. London and New York: Routledge.

Clark, Stephen R. L. (1996) 'Nations and Empires', *European Journal of Philosophy* 4: 63–80.

Cohan, Steven and Shires, Linda M. (1988) *Telling Stories: a Theoretical Analysis of Narrative Fiction*. New York and London: Routledge.

Collingwood, R. G. (1982 [1939]) *An Autobiography*. Oxford: Clarendon Press.

Collingwood, R. G. (2002 [1940]) *An Essay on Metaphysics*. Ed. Rex Martin. Oxford: Clarendon Press.

Connolly, William E. (1992) 'The Irony of Interpretation', in Daniel W. Conway and John E. Seery (eds), *The Politics of Irony: Essays in Self-Betrayal*. New York: St. Martin's Press, pp. 119–50.

Cornford, Frances (1954) *Collected Poems*, London: Cresset Press.

Coste, Didier (1989) *Narrative as Communication*. Minneapolis: University of Minnesota Press.

Croce, Benedetto (1909) *Logica come scienza del concetto puro*. Bari: G. Laterza & Figli.

Cupitt, Don (1980) *Taking Leave of God*. London: SCM Press.

Cupitt, Don (1985) *Only Human*. SCM Press.

Cupitt, Don (1991) *What is a Story?* London: SCM Press.

Cupitt, Don (1993) 'Anti-Realist Faith', in Joseph Runzo (ed.), *Is God Real?* Basingstoke: Macmillan, pp. 45–55.

Cupitt, Don (1994) *After All: Religion without Alienation*. London: SCM Press.

Cupitt, Don (1995) *Solar Ethics*. London: SCM Press.

Cupitt, Don (2000) *Philosophy's Own Religion*. London: SCM Press.

Danby, J. F. (1949) *Shakespeare's Doctrine of Nature: a Study of* King Lear. London: Faber and Faber.

Dascal, Marcelo and Gross, Alan G. (1999) 'The Marriage of Pragmatics and Rhetoric'. *Philosophy and Rhetoric*, 32.2: 107–30.

Davidson, Donald (1978) 'What Metaphors Mean', in S. Sacks (ed.), *On Metaphor*. Chicago: University of Chicago Press.

Davidson, Donald (1984) 'On the Very Idea of a Conceptual Scheme', in *Enquiries into Truth and Interpretation*. Oxford: Oxford University Press, pp. 183–98.

Davidson, Donald (1986) 'A Nice Derangement of Epitaphs', in Ernest LePore (ed.), *Truth and Interpretation: Perspectives on the Philosophy of Donald Davidson*. Oxford: Blackwell, pp. 433–46.

Davidson, Donald (1989) 'The Myth of the Subjective', in Robert Krautz (ed.), *Relativism, Interpretation and Confrontation*. Notre Dame, Indiana: Notre Dame University Press, pp. 159–72.

Davidson, Donald (1991)'Three Varieties of Knowledge', in A. Phillips Griffiths (ed.), *A. J. Ayer: Memorial Essays*. Cambridge: Cambridge University Press, pp. 153–66.

Davies, Paul (2005) 'Emergence: the Sum of the Parts', *New Scientist*, 185/2489: 34–7.

Davies, W. H. (1951) *The Collected Poems of W. H. Davies*. London: Jonathan Cape.

Dennett, Daniel C. (1992) *Consciousness Explained*. London: Allen Lane, The Penguin Press.

Derrida, Jacques (1973) *Speech and Phenomena and Other Essays on Husserl's Theory of Signs*. Trans. David Allison and Newton Garver. Evanston, Illinois: Northwestern University Press.

Derrida, Jacques (1976) *Of Grammatology*. Trans. Gayatri Chakravorty Spivak. Baltimore. Maryland: Johns Hopkins University Press.

Derrida, Jacques (1991) 'Différance', in *A Derrida Reader: Between the Blinds*. Ed. Peggy Kamuf. New York and London: Harvester-Wheatsheaf, pp. 59–70.

Derrida, Jacques (1999) 'Hospitality, Justice, Responsibility', in Richard Kearney and Mark Dooley (eds), *Questioning Ethics*. London: Routledge, pp. 65–83.

Dewey, John (1896) 'The Reflex Arc Concept in Psychology', *Psychological Review*, 3: 357–70.

Dilthey, Wilhelm (1913–67) *Gesammelte Schriften. 7* vols. Gottingen.

Dreyfus, Hubert L. (2002) 'Samuel Todes's Account of Non-conceptual Perceptual Knowledge and its Relation to Thought', *Ratio*, 15/4: 392–409.

Durkheim, Émile (1976 [1915]) *The Elementary Forms of the Religious Life*. London: George Allen & Unwin.

Eagleton, Terry (1991) *Ideology: an Introduction*. London: Verso.

Edelman, Gerald M. (1989) *The Remembered Present: a Biological Theory of Consciousness*. New York: Basic Books.

Edelman, Gerald M. (1992) *Bright Air, Brilliant Fire*. London: Allen Lane, Penguin Press.

Edelman, Gerald M. and Tononi, Giulio (2000) *Consciousness: How Matter Becomes Imagination*. London: Allen Lane.

Empiricus, Sextus (1955) *Outlines of Pyrrhonism*. 4 vols. Trans and ed. R. J. Bury. London: Heinemann.

Erasmus, Desiderius (1971 [1509]) *Praise of Folly*. Trans. Betty Radice. Harmondsworth: Penguin Books.

Euripedes (1963 [425 BC]) *Hecabe*, in *Euripedes: Medea and Other Plays*. Trans. Philip Vellacott. Harmondsworth: Penguin Books.

Evans, Gareth (1982) *The Varieties of Reference*. Oxford: Clarendon Press.

Evans-Pritchard, E. E. (1965) *Theories of Primitive Religion*. Oxford: Oxford University Press.

Ewing, A. C. (1930) 'Direct Knowledge and Perception', *Mind*, 38/154: 137–53.

Fanon, Frantz (1967) *The Wretched of the Earth*. Harmondsworth: Penguin Books.

Feinberg, Joel (1964) 'Action and Responsibility', in Max Black (ed.), *Philosophy in America*. London: George Allen & Unwin, pp. 134–60.

Ferguson, Rosalind (1975) *The Penguin Rhyming Dictionary*. Harmondsworth: Viking.

Feuerbach, Ludwig (1903–11) *Gesammelte Werke*, 12 vols. Ed. W. Bolin and F. Jodl. Frankfurt-am Main: Fromman Verlag.

Feuerbach, Ludwig (1957 [1841]) *The Essence of Christianity*. Trans. George Eliot. New York and London: Harper and Row.

Feuerbach, Ludwig (1966 [1843]) *Principles of the Philosophy of the Future*. Trans. Manfred H. Vogel. Indianapolis: Bobbs-Merrill.

Fingarette, Herbert (2000) *Self-Deception*. Berkeley, California: University of California Press.

Fish, Stanley (1981) 'Why No One's Afraid of Wolfgang Iser', *Diacritics* (March): 2–28.

Fisher, Walter R. (1987) *Human Communication: Toward a Philosophy of Reason, Value and Action*. Columbia, South Carolina: University of South Carolina Press.

Freud, Sigmund (1985 [1927]) *The Future of an Illusion*, in *Civilization, Society and Religion: Group Psychology, Civilization and its Discontents, and Other Works*. Ed. Albert Dickson. Harmondsworth: Penguin Books, pp. 179–241.

Frost, Robert (1951) *Complete Poems of Robert Frost*. London: Jonathan Cape.

Fukuda, Shigeo and Inagaki, Sinichi (1988) *Game-Pictures of the Edo Period*. Tokyo: Shoseki.

Furth, Hans G. (1987) *Knowledge as Desire: an Essay on Freud and Piaget*. New York and Guildford: Columbia University Press.

Gadamer, Hans-Georg (1975) *Truth and Method*. London: Sheed and Ward.

Gardiner, Sir Alan (1932) *The Theory of Speech and Language*. Oxford: Clarendon Press.

Gardiner, Sir Alan (1944): 'De Saussure's Analysis of the *"signe linguistique"* ', *Acta Linguistica*, 4: 696–719.

Geertz, Clifford (1975) *The Interpretation of Cultures*. London: Hutchinson.

Geertz, Clifford (1996) 'Primordial Ties', in John Hutchinson and Anthony D. Smith (eds), *Ethnicity*. Oxford: Oxford University Press, 1996, pp. 4–5.

Gellner, Ernest (1997) *Nationalism*. London: Weidenfeld and Nicolson.

Gerth, H. W. and Mills, C. Wright (1967) *From Max Weber: Essays in Sociology*. London: Routledge & Kegan Paul.

Gibson, James J. (1968) *The Senses Considered as Perceptual Systems*. London: Allen & Unwin.

Gibson, James J. (1971): 'The Information Available in Pictures', *Leonardo*, 4/2: 27–35.

Gibson, James J. (1977) 'The Theory of Affordances', in Robert Shaw and John Bransford (eds), *Perceiving, Acting, and Knowing: Toward an Ecological Psychology*. Hillsdale, New Jersey: Lawrence Erlbaum Associates, pp. 67–82.

Giddens, Anthony (1977) *New Rules of Sociological Method*. London: Hutchinson.

Gilbert, Paul (1998) *The Philosophy of Nationalism*. Boulder, Colorado: Westview Press.

Giles, James (1997) *No Self to be Found: the Search for Personal Identity*. Lanham, New York and Oxford: University Press of America.

Glasersfeld, Ernst von (1984) 'An Introduction to Radical Constructivism', in Paul Watzlawick (ed.), *The Invented Reality*, New York: W. W. Norton, pp. 17–40.

Glasersfeld, Ernst von (1986) 'Steps in the Construction of "Others" and "Reality" ', in Robert Trapp (ed.), *Power, Autonomy, Utopia*. Norwel, Massachusetts: Plenum, pp. 107–16.

Glasersfeld, Ernst von (1989) 'Facts and the Self from a Constructivist Point of View'. *Poetics*, 18: 435–48.

Gombrich, Ernst H. (1969) 'The Evidence of Images', in Charles S. Singleton (ed.), *Interpretation, Theory and Practice*. Baltimore: Johns Hopkins University Press, pp. 35–104.

Gombrich, Ernst H. (1973) 'Illusion in Art', in Richard. L. Gregory and Ernst H. Gombrich (eds), *Illusion in Nature and Art*. London: Duckworth, pp. 193–243.

Gombrich, Ernst H. (1977) *Art and Illusion: a Study in the Psychology of Pictorial Representation*. London: Phaidon.

Gombrich, Ernst H. (1982) *The Image and the Eye: Further Studies in the Psychology of Pictorial Representation*. London: Phaidon.

Grassi, Ernesto (1980) *Rhetoric as Philosophy: the Humanist Tradition*. University Park and London: Pennsylvania State University Press.

Grayling, A. C. (1985) *The Refutation of Scepticism*. London: Duckworth.

Gregg, Richard B. (1984) *Symbolic Inducement and Knowing: a Study in the Foundations of Rhetoric*. Columbia, South Carolina: University of South Carolina Press.

Gregory, R. L. (1993): 'Hypothesis and Illusion: Explorations in Perception and Science', in Edmond Wright (ed.), *New Representationalisms: Essays in the Philosophy of Perception*. Aldershot: Avebury, pp. 205–31.

Grice, H. P. (1967) 'Meaning', in P. F. Strawson (ed.), *Philosophical Logic*. Oxford: Oxford University Press, pp. 39–48.

Grice, H. P. (1975) 'Logic and Conversation', in Donald Davidson and Gilbert Harman (eds), *Logic and Grammar*. Encino, California: Dickenson Pub. Co., pp. 64–75.

Griffiths, Paul (2001) 'The Limits of Narrative Theology', in Keith E. Yandell (ed.), *Faith and Narrative*. Oxford and New York: Oxford University Press, pp. 217–36.

Groos, Karl (1898) *The Play of Animals*. New York: D. Appleton & Co.

Gross, Alan R. (2000) 'Rhetoric as Technique and a Mode of Truth: Reflections on Chaim Perelman', *Philosophy and Rhetoric*, 33/4: 319–35.

Haas, Robert (1994) *The Essential Haiku: Versions of Basho, Buson, and Issa*. Hopewell, New Jersey: Ecco Press.

Habermas, Jürgen (1982) 'A Reply to my Critics', in John B. Thompson and David Held (eds), *Habermas: Critical Debates*. London: Macmillan, pp. 219–83.

Habermas, Jürgen (1984) *The Theory of Communicative Action, Vol. I: Reason and the Rationalization of Society*. Trans. Thomas McCarthy. London: Heinemann.

Hacker, P. M. S. (1987) *Appearance and Reality: a Philosophical Investigation into Perception and Perceptual Qualities*. Oxford: Blackwell.

Hacking, Ian (1999) *The Social Construction of What?* Cambridge, Mass.: Harvard University Press.

Hamlyn, D. W. (1971) 'Epistemology and Conceptual Development', in Theodore Mischel (ed.), *Cognitive Development and Epistemology*. New York: Academic Press, pp. 3–24.

Happold, F. C. (1963) *Mysticism: a Study and an Anthology*. Harmondsworth: Penguin Books.

Harding, Gregory (1991) 'Color and the Mind-Body Problem', *Review of Metaphysics*, 45: 289–307

Harman, Gilbert (1990) 'The Intrinsic Quality of Experience', in J. Tomberlin (ed.), *Philosophical Perspectives 4: Action Theory and the Philosophy of Mind*. Atascadero, California: Ridgeview Pub. Co., pp. 31–52.

Harnad, Stevan (1987) 'Category Induction and Representation,' in Stevan Harnad (ed.), *Categorical Perception: the Groundwork of Cognition*. Cambridge: Cambridge University Press, pp. 535–65.

Hart, H. L. A. (1961) *The Concept of Law*. Oxford: Clarendon Press.

Hegel, G. W. F. (1966 [1807]) *The Phenomenology of Spirit*, in *Hegel: Texts and Commentary*. Trans. and ed. Walter Kaufmann. Garden City, New York: Anchor Books.

Heil, John (1993) *Perception and Cognition*. Berkeley, California: University of California Press.

Heijenoort, J. van (1966) 'Gödel's Theorem', in *The Encyclopedia of Philosophy, Vol. III*. Ed. Paul Edwards. New York and London: Collier Macmillan, pp. 348–57.

Heller, Joseph (1985 [1961]) *Catch 22*. London: Black Swan.

Heller, Mark (1990) *The Ontology of Physical Objects*. Cambridge: Cambridge University Press.

Helmholtz, Hermann von (1901) *Popular Lectures on Scientific Subjects: First Series*. London: Longmans Green & Co.

Helmholtz, Hermann von (1977) *Epistemological Writings*. Ed. Robert S. Cohen and Yehuda Elkana. Dordrecht: D. Reidel Pub. Co.

Herbert, George (1971 [1634]) *Selected Poems of George Herbert*. Ed. Gareth Reeves. London: Heinemann.

Herbert, Thomas Walter (1970) 'Rhyme', in Joseph T. Shipley (ed.), *Dictionary of World Literary Terms*. London: George Allen & Unwin, pp. 274–8.

Herder, Johann Gottfried (1969) *J. G. Herder on Social and Political Culture*. Trans. and ed. F. M. Barnard. Cambridge: Cambridge University Press.

Hermelin, Beate (1976) 'Coding and the Sense Modalities', in Lorna Wing (ed.), *Early Childhood Autism: Clinical, Educational and Social Aspects*. Oxford: Pergamon Press, pp. 135–68.

Hikins, James W. and Zagacki, Kenneth S. (1988) 'Rhetoric, Philosophy and Objectivism: an Attenuation of the Claims of the Rhetoric of Inquiry', *Quarterly Journal of Speech*, 74/2: 201–88.

Hikins, James W. and Zagacki, Kenneth S. (1993) 'Rhetoric, Objectivism, and the Doctrine of Tolerance', in Ian Angus and Lenore Langsdorf (eds), *The Critical Turn: Rhetoric and Philosophy in Postmodern Discourse*. Carbondale, Illinois: South Illinois University Press, pp. 100–25.

Hirst, R. J. (1966) *The Problems of Perception*. London: George Allen & Unwin.

Hobbes, Thomas (1839 [1655]) *Elements of Philosophy, The First Section: Concerning Body*. Trans. Sir William Molesworth. London: John Bohn.

Hobbes, Thomas (1962 [1651]) *Leviathan*. Ed. John Plamenatz. London: Collins.

Hoffman, Joshua and Rosenkrantz, Gary S. (1997) *Substance: Its Nature and Existence*. London and New York: Routledge.

Holbach, Paul H. T., Baron d' (1966) *The System of Nature: or, Laws of the Moral and Physical World*, 2 vols. Trans. H. D. Robinson. New York: B. Franklin.

Hollis, Martin (1982) 'The Social Destruction of Reality', in Martin Hollis and Steven Lukes (eds), *Rationality and Relativism*. Oxford: Blackwell, pp. 67–86.

Hooker, Clifford (1995) *Reason, Regulation and Realism: Toward a Regulatory Systems Theory of Evolutionary Epistemology*. Albany, New York: State University of New York Press.

Horibuchi, Seiji and Inoue, Yuki (eds) *Stereogram*. London: Boxtree.

Humboldt, Wilhelm von (1971 [1836]) *Linguistic Variability and Intellectual Development*. Trans. Georg C. Buck and Frithjof A. Raven. Philadelphia: University of Pennsylvania Press.

Hunt, Leigh (1929) 'Wit Made Easy, or a Hint to Word-Catchers', in *Essays (Selected)*. London: Dent, pp. 317–20.

Husserl, Edmund (1973) *Experience and Judgment*. London: Routledge & Kegan Paul.

Hutchinson, John (1994) *Modern Nationalism*. London: Fontana Press.

Jacobs, Ronald N. and Smith, Philip (1997) 'Romance, Irony and Solidarity', *Sociological Theory*, 15: 60–80.

Jakobson, Roman (1987) *Language in Literature*. Ed. Krystyna Pomorska and Stephen Rudy. Cambridge, Mass.: Harvard University Press.

James, William (1977) *The Writings of William James: a Comprehensive Edition*. Ed. John J. McDermott. Chicago: University of Chicago Press.

Johnson, Alexander Bryan (1968 [1828]) *A Treatise on Language*. Ed. David Rynin. New York: Dover Publications.

Johnstone, Christopher Lyle (2001) 'Enthymeme', in Thomas O. Sloane (ed.), *Encyclopedia of Rhetoric*. Oxford and New York: Oxford University Press, pp. 247–50.

Johnstone, Henry W. (1959) *Philosophy and Argument*. University Park, Pennsylvania: Pennsylvania State University Press.

Jubien, Michael (1993) *Ontology, Modality and the Fallacy of Reference*. Cambridge: Cambridge University Press.

Julesz, Bela (1960) 'Binocular Depth Perception of Computer-generated Patterns', *J. Bell Telephone Co.*, 39, 1125.

Karcevskij, Sergei (1964) 'Du Dualisme Asymétrique du Signe Linguistique', in Josej Vachek (ed.), *A Prague School Reader*. Bloomington, Indiana: Indiana University Press, pp. 81–7.

Kearney, Richard (2002) *On Stories*. London and New York: Routledge.

Kearney, Richard (2003) *Strangers, Gods and Monsters*. London and New York: Routledge.

Keats, John (1947 [1820]) *Poems*. Ed. Gerald Bullett. London: J. M. Dent.

Kerferd, G. B. (1999) *The Sophistic Movement*. Cambridge: Cambridge University Press.

Kharms, Daniil (1971) 'An Optical Illusion', from *Mini-Stories*, in *Russia's Lost Literature of the Absurd: a Literary Discovery. Selected Works of Daniil Kharms and Alexander Vvedensky*. Trans. and ed. George Gibian. New York: W. W. Norton & Co. Inc., p. 68.

Kierkegaard, Søren (1946) *A Kierkegaard Anthology*. Ed. Robert Bretall. Princeton, New Jersey: Princeton University Press.

Kirk, Robert (1999) *Relativism and Reality: a Contemporary Introduction*. London and New York: Routledge.

Kripke, Saul A. (1980) *Naming and Necessity*. Oxford: Blackwell.

Kripke, Saul A. (1982) *Wittgenstein on Rules and Private Language*. Oxford: Basil Blackwell.

Kuhn, Thomas S. (1970) *The Structure of Scientific Revolutions*. Chicago: University of Chicago Press.

Kymlicka, Will (1997) 'The Sources of Nationalism: Commentary on Taylor', in Robert McKim and Jeff McMahan (eds), *The Morality of Nationalism*. New York and Oxford: Oxford University Press, pp. 56–65.

Lacan, Jacques (1977) *The Four Fundamental Concepts of Psycho-Analysis*. Trans. Alan Sheridan. Ed. Jacques-Alain Miller. London: Hogarth Press and the Institute of Psycho-Analysis.

Lacan, Jacques (1992) *The Ethics of Psychoanalysis, 1959–1960. The Seminar of Jacques Lacan, Book VII*. Ed. Jacques-Alain Miller. Trans. Dennis Porter. London and New York: Routledge.

Lakoff, George and Johnson, Mark (1980) *Metaphors We Live By*. Chicago: Chicago University Press.

Lao Tzu (1963) *Tao Te Ching*. Trans. D. C. Lau. Harmondsworh: Penguin Books.

Lash, Nicholas (1988) *Easter in Ordinary: Reflections on Human Experience and the Knowledge of God*. London: SCM Press.

Leach, Edmund (1968) 'Ritual', in *International Encyclopedia of the Social Sciences*, ed. D. L. Stils, New York and London: Free Press and Macmillan, pp. 520–6.

Leeper, R. W. (1935) 'A Study of a Neglected Portion of the Field of Learning: the Development of Sensory Organization', *Journal of Genetic Psychology*, 46: 41–75.

Leff, Michael C. (1999) 'The Habitation of Rhetoric', in John Louis Lucaites, Celeste Michelle Condit and Sally Caudill (eds), *Contemporary Rhetorical Theory: a Reader*. New York and London: Guilford Press, pp. 65–78.

Lemon, Lee T. and Reis, Marion (eds) (1965) *Russian Formalist Criticism: Four Essays*. Lincoln, Nebraska: Nebraska University Press.

Leonard, Harry S. (1967) *Principles of Reasoning: an Introduction to Logic, Methodology and the Theory of Signs*. New York: Dover Publications.

Levinas, Emmanuel (1994) *The Levinas Reader*. Ed. Seán Hand. Oxford: Blackwell.

Lévi-Strauss, Claude (1968) 'The Structural Study of Myth', in Thomas A. Sebeok (ed.), *Myth: a Symposium*. Bloomington and London: Indiana University Press, pp. 81–106.

Lewes, George Henry (1874) *Problems of Life and Mind*, 2 vols. London: Trübner & Co.

Lewis, C. I. (1929 [1916]) *Mind and the World-Order: Outline of a Theory of Knowledge*. New York: Charles Scribner's Sons.

Lewis, David K. (1969) *Convention*. Cambridge, Mass.: Harvard University Press.

Lotze, Hermann (1884) *Metaphysic in Three Books: Ontology, Cosmology, and Psychology*. Oxford: Clarendon Press.

Lowe, E. J. (1996) *Subjects of Experience*. Cambridge: Cambridge University Press.

Lynch, Michael P. (2001) *Truth in Context: an Essay on Pluralism and Objectivity*. Cambridge, Mass.: MIT Press.

Lyotard, François (1984) *The Postmodern Condition*. Trans. G. Bennington and B. Massumi. Manchester: Manchester University Press.

MacIntyre, Alasdair (1967) 'Myth', in Paul Edwards (ed.), *The Encyclopedia of Philosophy, Vol. 5*. New York: Collier-Macmillan, pp. 432–7.

MacIntyre, Alasdair. (1981) *After Virtue: a Study in Moral Theory*. London: Duckworth.

Macquarrie, John (1963) *Twentieth-Century Religious Thought: the Frontiers of Philosophy and Theology, 1900–1960*. London: SCM Press.

Malebranche, Nicholas (1980 [1674–5]) *The Search after Truth*. Trans. Thomas M. Lennon and Paul J. Olscamp. Columbus, Ohio: Ohio State University Press.

Marett, R. R. (1914) *The Threshold of Religion*. London: Methuen.

Margalit, Avishai (1997) 'The Moral Psychology of Nationalism', in Robert McKim and Jeff McMahan (eds), *The Morality of Nationalism*. New York and Oxford: Oxford University Press, pp. 74–87.

Marr, David (1982) *Vision*. San Francisco: W. H. Freeman.

Martin, Graham Dunstan (1981) *The Architecture of Experience*. Edinburgh: Edinburgh University Press.

Martin, Wallace (1986) *Recent Theories of Narrative*. Ithaca and London: Cornell University Press.

Mascaró, Juan (1975) *The Upanishads*. Harmondsworth: Penguin Books.

Matilal, Bimal Krishna (1986) *Perception: an Essay on Classical Indian Theories of Knowledge*. Oxford: Clarendon Press.

Matson, Floyd W. (1964) *The Broken Image*. Garden City, New York: Anchor Books.

Maturana, Humbert R. and Varela, Francisco J. (1980) *Autopoesis and Cognition: the Realization of the Living*. Dordrecht: D. Reidel.

Maund, J. B. (1975) 'The Representative Theory of Perception', *Canadian Journal of Philosophy*, 5: 41–55.

Maund, J. B. (1993) 'Representation, Pictures and Resemblance', in Edmond Wright (ed.), *New Representationalisms: Essays in the Philosophy of Perception*. Aldershot: Avebury Press, pp. 45–69.

Maund, Barry (1995) *Colours: Their Nature and Representation*. Cambridge: Cambridge University Press.

Mauthner, Fritz (1923 [1901–2]). *Beiträge zu einer Kritik der Sprache*. Leipzig: Meiner.

Mazzini, Giuseppi (1907 [1858]) *The Duties of Man and Other Essays*. London: Dent.

McDowell, John (1985) 'Values and Secondary Qualities', in Ted Honderich (ed.), *Morality and Objectivity: A Tribute to J. L. Mackie*. London: Routledge & Kegan Paul, pp. 110–29.

McDowell, John (1994) *Mind and World*. Cambridge, Mass.: Harvard University Press.

McGrath, Alister E. (2004) *The Science of God*. London: T. & T. Clark International.

Mead, George Herbert (1910) 'Social Consciousness and the Consciousness of Meaning', *Psychological Bulletin*, 7: 397–405.

Merleau-Ponty, Maurice (1970) *Phenomenology of Perception*. Trans. Colin Smith. London: Routledge & Kegan Paul.

Messer, R. (1993) *Does God's Existence Need Proof?* Oxford: Clarendon Press.

Meynell, Alice (1923) *The Poems of Alice Meynell*. London: Burns, Oates and Washbourne.

Miller, David (1995) *On Nationality*. Oxford: Clarendon Press.

Miller, Jonathan (1988) 'Jokes and Joking: a Serious Laughing Matter', in John Durant and Jonathan Miller (eds), *Laughing Matters: a Serious Look at Humour*. Harlow: Longman, pp. 5–16.

Montesquieu, Charles Louis de Secondat, Baron de (1989 [1748]) *The Spirit of the Laws*. Trans. and ed. Anne M. Cohler, Basie Carolyn Miller and Harold Samuel Stone. Cambridge: Cambridge University Press.

Morgan, Conwy Lloyd (1923) *Emergent Evolution*. London: Williams and Norgate.

Muir, Edwin (1960) 'Nothing there but faith', in *Collected Poems 1921–1958*. London: Faber and Faber, pp. 238–9.

Muir, Frank and Norden, Denis (1976) *The My Word! Stories*. London: Methuen.

Nietzsche, Friedrich (1968) *The Will to Power*. New York: Vintage Books.

Novalis (Friedrich von Hardenberg) (1837) *Schriften, Vol. II*. Stuttgart.

Nussbaum, Martha (1996) 'Patriotism and Cosmopolitanism', in Martha Nussbaum, *For Love of Country: Debating the Limits of Patriotism*. Boston: Beacon Press, pp. 2–17.

O'Hear, Anthony (1985) *What Philosophy Is: an Introduction to Contemporary Philosophy*. Harmondsworth: Penguin Books.

Opie, Iona and Peter (1959) *The Lore and Language of Schoolchildren*. Oxford: Clarendon Press.

Oxfam (1978) *The Crack-a-Joke-Book*. Harmondsworth: Penguin Books.

Palmer, Leonard (1972) *Descriptive and Comparative Linguistics*. London: Faber

Palmer, Stephen E (1999) 'Color, Consciousness and the Isomorphism Constraint', *Behavioural and Brain Sciences*, 22: 935–44.

Pals, Daniel L. (1996) *Seven Theories of Religion*. New York and Oxford: Oxford University Press.

Pascal, Blaise (1947 [1670]) *Pensées*. Trans. W. F. Trotter. London: Dent.

Peters, Ted (1978) 'Metaphor and the Horizon of the Unsaid', *Philosophy and Phenomenological Research*, 37: 355–69.

Piaget, Jean (1955) *The Child's Construction of Reality*. London: Routledge & Kegan Paul.

Piaget, Jean (1969) *The Mechanics of Perception*. London: Routledge & Kegan Paul.

Piaget, Jean (1970) *Genetic Epistemology*. New York and London: Columbia University Press.

Pichon, Édouard (1940–1), 'Sur le signe linguistique', *Acta Linguistica*, 2: 51–2.

Pitcher, George (1971) *A Theory of Perception*. Princeton, New Jersey: Princeton University Press.

Plantinga, Alvin (1974) *The Nature of Necessity*. Oxford: Oxford University Press.

Plantinga, Alvin (1983) 'Reason and Belief in God', in Alvin Plantinga and Nicholas Wolterstorff (eds), *Faith and Rationality: Reason and Belief in God*. Notre Dame, Indiana: Notre Dame University Press, pp. 16–93.

Plantinga, Alvin (1998) *Warranted Christian Belief*. Oxford: Oxford University Press.

Plutarch (1976) *The Rise and Fall of Athens*. Trans. Ian Scott-Kilvert. Harmondsworth: Penguin Books.

Polanyi, Michael (1962) *Personal Knowledge: Towards a Post-Critical Philosophy*. London: Routledge.

Polanyi, Michael (1969) *Knowing and Being*. Chicago: Chicago University Press.

Polkinghorne, Donald (1988) *Narrative Knowing in the Human Sciences*. Albany, New York: State University of New York Press.

Price, Hubert H. (1961) *Perception*. London: Methuen.

Propp, Vladimir (1979) *Morphology of the Folk-Tale*. Trans. Laurence Scott. Revised and ed. Louis A. Wagner. Austin and London: Texas University Press.

Putnam, Hilary (1975) *Reason, Truth and History*. Cambridge: Cambridge University Press.

Putnam, Hilary (1982) *Realism and Reason: Philosophical Papers, Vol. III*. Cambridge: Cambridge University Press, pp. 229–47.

Putnam, Hilary (1993) 'Reason without Absolutes', *International Journal of Philosophical Studies*, 1: 179–92.

Quine, Willard Van Orman (1960) *Word and Object*. Cambridge, Mass.: MIT Press.

Quine, Willard Van Orman (1971) 'The Inscrutability of Reference', in D. D. Steinberg and L. J. Jakobovitz (eds), *Semantics*. Cambridge: Cambridge University Press, pp. 142–54.

Quine, Willard Van Orman (1976) *The Ways of Paradox and Other Essays*. Cambridge, Mass.: Harvard University Press.

Quine, Willard Van Orman (1987) 'Epistemology Naturalized', in Hilary Kornbluth (ed.), *Naturalized Epistemology*. Cambridge, Mass.: MIT Press.

Quintillian (2001 [95]) *The Orator's Education*. Trans. and ed. Donald A Russell. Cambridge, Mass.: Harvard University Press (Loeb Classical Library).

Ramachandran, V. S. (1998) *Phantoms in the Brain: Human Nature and the Architecture of the Mind*. London: Fourth Estate (see also under Smythies).

Ramsey, Frank P. (1954) *The Foundations of Mathematics and Other Logical Essays*. Ed. R. B. Braithwaite. London: Routledge & Kegan Paul.

Raskin, Victor (1985) *Semantic Mechanisms of Humor*. Dordrecht: D. Reidel.

Renan, Ernest (1931 [1882]) 'What is a Nation?', in A. Zimmern (ed.), *Modern Political Doctrines*. London: Oxford University Press.

Richards, I. A. (1936) *The Philosophy of Rhetoric*. Oxford: Oxford University Press.

Richardson, Justin (1959) 'The Oocuck', in J. M. Cohen (ed.), *Yet More Comic and Curious Verse*. Harmondsworth: Penguin Books, p. 88.

Richmond, Frank M. (1936) *School Yarns and Howlers*. London: Universal Publications.

Ricoeur, Paul. (1974) *The Conflict of Interpretations*. Evanston, Illinois: Northwestern University Press.

Ricoeur, Paul. (1978) *The Rule of Metaphor: Multidisciplinary Studies of the Creation of Meaning*. Trans. Robert Czerny with Kathleen Mclaughlin and John Costello. London: Routledge & Kegan Paul.

Ricoeur, Paul (1981) *Hermeneutics and the Human Sciences: Essays on Language, Action and Interpretation*. Trans. and ed. John B. Thompson. Cambridge: Cambridge University Press.

Ricoeur, Paul (1983) *Time and Narrative*, 3 vols. Chicago: Chicago University Press.

Rimmon-Kenan, Shlomith (1983) *Narrative Fiction: Contemporary Poetics*. London and New York: Methuen.

Rommetveit, Ragnar (1974) *On Message Structure: a Framework for the Study of Language and Communication*. London: John Wiley & Sons.

Rommetveit, Ragnar (1978) 'On Negative Rationalism in Scholarly Studies of Verbal Communication and Dynamic Residuals in the Construction of Human Intersubjectivity', in Michael Brenner, P. Marsh and Marilyn Brenner (eds), *The Social Contexts of Method*. London: Croom Helm, pp. 16–32.

Rorty, Richard (1980) *Philosophy and the Mirror of Nature*. Oxford: Blackwell.

Rorty, Richard (1982) *The Consequences of Pragmatism*. Minneapolis: University of Minnesota Press.

Royce, Josiah (1958 [1885]) *The Religious Aspect of Philosophy: a Critique of the Bases of Conduct and Faith*. New York: Harper.

Royce, Josiah (1976 [1899]) *The World and the Individual, First and Second Series*. Gloucester, Mass.: Peter Smith.

Runzo, Joseph (1993) 'Realism, Non-Realism and Atheism: Why Believe in an Objectively Real God?', in Joseph Runzo (ed.), *Is God Real?* Basingstoke: Macmillan, pp. 151–75.

Russell, Bertrand (1923) 'On Vagueness', *Australasian Journal of Psychology and Philosophy*, 1: 84–92 (read before the Jowett Society, Oxford).

Russell, James (1978) *The Acquisition of Knowledge*. London: Macmillan.

Ruthrof, Horst (2000) *The Body in Language*. London: Cassell.

Ryle, Gilbert (1966) *The Concept of Mind*. Harmondsworth: Penguin Books.

Sacks, Oliver (1986) *A Leg to Stand On*. London: Picador.

Sainsbury, R. Mark (1995) *Paradoxes*. Cambridge: Cambridge University Press.

Salecl, Renata (1968) 'See No Evil, Speak No Evil: Hate Speech and Human Rights', in Joan Gopjec (ed.), *Radical Evil*. London and New York: Verso, pp. 150–68.

Saussure, Ferdinand de (1977) *Course in General Linguistics*. Trans. Wade Baskin. London: Fontana/Collins.

Schafer, Roy (1980) 'Narration in the Psychoanalytic Dialogue', *Critical Inquiry*, 7(1): 29–53.

Schiappa, Edward, Gross, Alan R., McKerrow, Raymie E. and Scott, Robert L. (2002) 'Rhetorical Studies as Reduction or Redescription?', *Quarterly Journal of Speech*, 88/1: 112–20.

Schiffer, Stephen R. (1972) *Meaning*. Oxford: Oxford University Press.

Schiller, F. C. S. (1902) 'Axioms as Postulates', in Henry Sturt (ed.), *Personal Idealism*. London: Macmillan, pp. 47–133.

Schiller, F. C. S. (1912) *Studies in Humanism*, London: Macmillan.

Schiller, F. C. S. (1929) *Logic for Use: an Introduction to the Voluntarist Theory of Knowledge*. London: G. Bell & Sons.

Schiller, Johann Christoph Friedrich von (1967 [1795]) *On the Aesthetic Education of Man*. Trans. and ed. Elizabeth M. Wilkinson and L. A. Willoughby. Oxford: Clarendon Press.

Schopenhauer, Arthur (1969 [1818]) *The Word as Will and Representation*, 2 vols. Trans. E. F. J. Payne. New York: Dover Publications.

Schrag, Calvin. O. (1969) *Experience and Being: Prolegomena to a Future Ontology*. Evanston, Illinois: Northwestern University Press.

Schrag, Calvin. O. (1980) *Radical Reflection and the Origin of the Human Sciences*. West Lafayette, Indiana: Purdue University Press.

Schrag, Calvin. O. (1986) *Communicative Praxis and the Space of Subjectivity*. Bloomington, Indiana: Indiana Uniuversity Press.

Schrag, Calvin O. (1997) *The Self after Postmodernity*. New Haven and London: Yale University Press.

Schutz, Alfred (1962) *Collected Papers, Vol. I: the Problem of Social Reality*. The Hague: Martinus Nijhoff.

Scott, Robert L. (1967) 'On Viewing Rhetoric as Epistemic', *Central States Speech Journal*, 18: 9–16.

Scott, Robert L. (1993) 'Dialectical Tensions of Speaking and Silence', *Quarterly Journal of Speech*, 79 (1): 1–18.

Scruton, Roger (1980) *The Meaning of Conservatism*. London; Macmillan.

Searle, John (1975) 'The Logical Status of Fictional Discourse', *New Literary History*, 6(2): 319–32.

Searle, John (1999) *Mind, Language and Society: Philosophy in the Real World*. London: Weidenfeld and Nicolson.

Sedgwick, G. G. (1967) *Of Irony: Especially in Drama*. Toronto: University of Toronto Press.

Seligman, Adam B. (1997) *The Problem of Trust*. Princeton, New Jersey: Princeton University Press.

Sellars, Roy Wood (1919) 'The Epistemology of Evolutionary Naturalism', *Mind* 28 (112): 407–26.

Sellars, Roy Wood (1922) *Evolutionary Naturalism*. Chicago and London: Open Court Publishing Company.

Sellars, Roy Wood (1932) *The Philosophy of Physical Realism*. London: Macmillan.

Sellars, Roy Wood (1965) 'The Aim of Critical Realism', in R. J. Hirst (ed.), *Perception and the Physical World*. New York: Macmillan, pp. 235–44.

Sellars, Roy Wood (1969 [1916]) *Critical Realism: a Study of the Nature and Conditions of Knowledge*. New York: Russell and Russell.

Sellars, Roy Wood (1970) *The Principles, Perspectives and Problems of Philosophy*. New York: Pageant Press International.

Sellars, Wilfrid (1956) 'Empiricism and the Philosophy of Mind', in Herbert Feigl and Michael Scriven (eds), *Foundations of Science and the Concepts of Psychology and Psychoanalysis. Vol. I*. Minneapolis: Minnesota University Press, pp. 253–329.

Sellars, Wilfrid (1981) The Carus Lectures I, "The Lever of Archimedes"; II, "Naturalism and Process"; "Is Consciousness Physical?", *The Monist*, 64 (1): 3–90.

Seth, Andrew (1887) *Hegelianism and Personality*. Edinburgh and London: William Blackwood.

Shannon, C. E. and Weaver, W. (1949) *The Mathematical Theory of Communication*. Urbana, Illinois: University of Illinois Press.

Shklovsky, Viktor (1965) 'Art as Technique', in Lee T. Lemon, and Marion Reis (eds), *Russian Formalist Criticism: Four Essays*. Lincoln, Nebraska: Nebraska University Press, pp. 3–57.

Shopen, Tim (1974) 'Some Contributions from Grammar to the Theory of Style', *College English*, 35: 775–98.

Sidgwick, Alfred (1934) 'Verbalistic Tendencies', *Mind*, 43: 409–23.

Skinner, B. F. (1957) *Verbal Behavior*. New York: Appleton-Century-Crofts.

Smith, A. D. (2002) *The Problem of Perception*. Cambridge, Mass. and London: Harvard University Press.

Smith, Anthony (1991) *National Identity*. London: Penguin Books.

Smith, Anthony (1994) 'The Problem of National Identity: Ancient, Mediaeval and Modern', *Ethnic and Racial Studies*, 17: 375–99.

Smith, Barry (1975) 'The Ontogenesis of Mathematical Objects', *Journal of the British Society for Phenomenology*, 6: 91–101.

Smith, David Woodruff (1989) *The Circle of Acquaintance: Perception, Consciousness and Empathy*. Dordrecht: Kluwer Academic Publishers.

Smythies, J. R. and Ramachandran, V. S. (1997) 'An Empirical Refutation of the Direct Realist Theory of Perception', *Inquiry*, 40: 437–8.

Sosa, Ernest (1987) 'Subjects Among Other Things', in James E. Tomberlin (ed.), *Philosophical Perspectives, I: Metaphysics, 1987*. Atascadero, California: Ridgeview, pp. 155–87.

Spinoza, Baruch (1958 [1670]) *The Political Works*. Ed. A. G. Wernham. Oxford: Clarendon Press.

Sprat, Thomas (1922 [1667]) 'A Simple and an Ornate Style', in Henry Craik (ed.), *English Prose Selections, Vol. III, Seventeenth Century*, pp. 270–1.

Spurgeon, Caroline. F. E. (1935) *Shakespeare's Imagery and What It Tells Us*. Cambridge: Cambridge University Press.

Steiner, George (1998) *After Babel: Aspects of Language and Translation*. Oxford and New York: Oxford University Press.

Strawson, P. F. (1949) 'Truth', *Analysis*, 9/6: 83–97.

Strawson, P. F. (1959) *Individuals: an Essay in Descriptive Metaphysics*. London: Methuen.

Stroud, Barry (1984) *The Significance of Philosophical Scepticism*. Oxford: Clarendon Press.

Suls, Jerry (1983) 'Cognitive Processes in Humor Appreciation', in P. E. McGhee and J. H. Goldstein (eds), *Handbook of Humor Research, Vol. I: Basic Issues*. New York: Springer Verlag.

Swinburne, Richard (1996) *Is There a God?* Oxford: Oxford University Press.

Szabados, Béla (1974) 'Self-Deception', *Canadian Journal of* Philosophy, 4: 51–68.

Sztompka, Piotr (1991) *Society in Action: the Theory of Social Becoming*. Chicago: University of Chicago Press.

Sztompka, Piotr (1999) *Trust: a Sociological Theory*. Cambridge: Cambridge University Press.

Tarski, Alfred (1983) 'The Concept of Truth in Formalized Languages', in J. H. Woodger (ed.), *Logic, Semantics and Metamathematics*. Indianapolis, Indiana: Hackett.

Taylor, Charles (1971) 'Interpretation and the Sciences of Man', *Review of Metaphysics*, 25: 3–51.

Taylor, Charles (1989) *Sources of the Self: the Making of Modern Identity*. Cambridge: Cambridge University Press.

Tillich, Paul (1951) *Systematic Theology*, Vol. I. Chicago: Chicago University Press.

Todes, Samuel (2001) *Body and Mind*. Cambridge, Mass.: MIT Press.

Todorov, Tsvetan (1977) *The Poetics of Prose*. Trans. Richard Howard. Oxford: Oxford University Press.

Travis, Charles (2004) 'The Silence of the Senses', *Mind*, 113.

Turner, Victor (1974) *Dramas, Fields and Metaphors: Symbolic Action and Human Society*. Ithaca and London: Cornell University Press.

Tye, Michael (1992) *The Imagery Debate*. Cambridge, Mass.: MIT Press.

Tye, Michael (1999) *Ten Problems of Consciousness: a Representational Theory of the Phenomenal Mind*. Cambridge, Mass.: MIT Press.

Tye, Michael (2000) *Consciousness, Color and Content*. Cambridge, Mass.: MIT Press.

Unger, Peter (1988) 'Conscious Beings in a Gradual World', in Theodore E. Uehling and Howard K. Wettstein (eds), *Midwest Studies in Philosophy, XII*. Minneapolis and Oxford: University of Minnesota Press, pp. 287–333.

Vaihinger, Hans (1924) *The Philosophy of 'As If'*. London: Kegan Paul, Trench, Trübner and Co.

Van Inwagen, Peter (1990) *Material Beings*. Ithaca and London: Cornell University Press.

Vico, Giambattista (1970) *The New Science of Giambattista Vico*. Trans. Thomas Goddard Bergin and Max Harold Fisch. Ithaca and London: Cornell University Press.

Vološinov, V. N. (1973) *Marxism and the Philosophy of Language*. Trans. Ladislav Metejka and I. R. Titunik. New York: Seminar Press.

Wade, Nicholas (ed.) *Brewster and Wheatstone on Vision*. London and New York: Academic Press.

Walton, Kendall L. (1973) 'Pictures and Make-Believe', *Philosophical Review*, 32: 283–319.

Walton, Kendall L. (1978) 'How Remote are Fictional Worlds from the Real World?', *Journal of Aesthetics and Art Criticism*, 37 (1): 11–23.

Warren, Richard M. and Warren, Roslyn P. (1968) *Helmholtz on Perception: Its Physiology and Development*. New York: John Wiley.

Wartofsky, Marx W. (1977) *Feuerbach*. Cambridge: Cambridge University Press.

Weiskrantz, Lawrence (1999) *Consciousness Lost and Found: a Neurological Explanation*. Oxford: Oxford University Press.

Wheeler, Post (1984) *Tales from the Japanese Storytellers*. Ed. Harold G. Henderson. Rutland, Vermont and Tokyo: Charles E. Tuttle.

White, Hayden (1981) 'The Value of Narrativity in the Representation of Reality', *Critical Inquiry*, 7 (1): 5–27.

Wicker, Brian (1975) *The Story-Shaped World*. London: Athlone Press.

Wiggins, David (1986) 'On Singling Out an Object Determinately', in Philip Pettit and John McDowell (eds), *Subject, Thought and Context*. Oxford, Clarendon Press, pp. 169–80.

Wilcox, Stephen and Katz, Stuart (1984) 'Can Indirect Realism be Demonstrated in the Psychological Laboratory?', *Philosophy of the Social Sciences*, 14: 149–57.

Willeford, William (1969) *The Fool and his Sceptre*. London: Arnold.

Williams, Bernard (2002) *Truth and Truthfulness: an Essay in Genealogy*. Princeton and London: Princeton University Press.

Wilson, John Cook. (1926) *Statement and Inference*, 2 vols. Oxford: Oxford University Press.

Winnicott, Donald W. (1965) *The Maturational Processes and Facilitating Environment: Studies in the Theory of Emotional Development*. London: Hogarth Press and the Institute of Psycho-Analysis.

Wittgenstein, Ludwig (1967 [1953]) *Philosophical Investigations*. Trans. G. E. M. Anscombe. Oxford: Basil Blackwell.

Wolterstorff, Nicholas (1983) 'Can Belief in God be Rational?', in Alvin Plantinga and Nicholas Wolterstorff (eds), *Faith and Rationality: Reason and Belief in God*. Notre Dame and London: University of Notre Dame Press, pp. 135–86.

Woodfield, Richard (1996) 'Introduction: Mapping the Ground', in Richard Woodfield (ed.), *Gombrich on Art and Psychology*. Manchester and New York: Manchester University Press, pp. 1–26.

Wright, Edmond (1976) 'Arbitrariness and Motivation: a New Theory', *Foundations of Language*, 14: 505–23.

Wright, Edmond (1977) 'Words and Intentions', *Philosophy*, 52: 45–62.

Wright, Edmond (1978) 'Sociology and the Irony Model', *Sociology*, 12, 523–43.

Wright, Edmond (1979) 'Logic as an Intention-Matching System: a Solution to the Paradoxes', *Journal of the British Society for Phenomenology*, 10 (3): 164–71.
Wright, Edmond (1981) 'Yet More on Non-Epistemic Seeing', *Mind*, 90: 586–91.
Wright, Edmond (1982) 'Derrida, Searle, Contexts, Games, Riddles', *New Literary History*, 13: 463–77.
Wright, Edmond (1983) 'Inspecting Images', *Philosophy*, 58: 51–72.
Wright, Edmond (1985) 'A Defence of Sellars', *Philosophy and Phenomenological Research*, 46 (1): 73–90.
Wright, Edmond (1986a) 'Dialectical Perception: a Synthesis of Lenin and Bogdanov', *Radical Philosophy*, 43: 16.
Wright, Edmond (1986b) 'Wilcox and Katz on Indirect Realism', *Philosophy and the Social Sciences*, 6 (1): 107–13.
Wright, Edmond (1990) 'New Representationalism', *Journal for the Theory of Social Behaviour*, 20: 65–92.
Wright, Edmond (1992a) 'The Entity Fallacy in Epistemology', *Philosophy*, 67: 33–50.
Wright, Edmond (1992b) ' "The Neglected Technique of the Witticism": a Philosophical Inquiry', *Newsletter of The Freudian Field*, 6 (1–2): 76–92.
Wright, Edmond (1992c) 'Gestalt-switching: Hanson, Aronson and Harré', *Philosophy of Science*, 59 (3): 480–6.
Wright, Edmond (1992d) 'The Original of E. G. Boring's "Young/Mother-in-law" Drawing and its Relation to the Pattern of a Joke', *Perception*, 21: 273–5.
Wright, Edmond (ed.) (1993a) *New Representationalisms: Essays in the Philosophy of Perception*. Aldershot: Ashgate.
Wright, Edmond (1993b) 'More Qualia Trouble for Functionalism: J. R. Smythies' TV-Hood Analogy', *Synthèse*, 97 (3): 1–18.
Wright, Edmond (1996) 'What it Isn't Like', *American Philosophical Quarterly*, 23 (1): 23–42.
Wright, Edmond (1999) 'The Game of Reference', in Matjaz Potrč (ed.), *Connectionism and the Philosophy of Psychology. Acta Analytica*, 22: 179–96.
Wright, Edmond (2000) 'The Joke, the "As If", and the Statement', in Michael Levine (ed.), *The Analytic Freud*. London and New York: Routledge, pp. 294–311.
Wright, Edmond (2001) 'Faith and the Real', *Paragraph*, 24 (2): 5–22.
Wright, Edmond (2005) 'Perceiving Socially and Morally: the Question of Triangulation', *Philosophy*, 80 (311): 53–75.
Wright, Elizabeth (1999) *Speaking Desires Can be Dangerous: the Poetics of the Unconscious*. Cambridge: Polity Press.
Yandell, Keith E. (1999) *Philosophy of Religion: a Contemporary Introduction*. London and New York: Routledge.
Yandell, Keith E. (2001) 'Narrative Ethics and Normative Objectivity', in Keith E. Yandell (ed.), *Faith and Narrative*. Oxford and New York: Oxford University Press, pp. 237–60.
Yeats, William Butler (1952) *The Collected Poems of W. B. Yeats*. London: Macmillan.
Žižek, Slavoj (1989) *The Sublime Object of Ideology*. London: Verso.
Žižek, Slavoj (1991) *For They Know Not What They Do: Enjoyment as a Political Factor*. London and New York: Verso.
Žižek, Slavoj (1999) *The Ticklish Subject: the Absent Centre of Political Ontology*. London and New York: Verso.

Index